Grow old along with me
the best is yet to be

Other anthologies from Sandra Haldeman Martz

When I Am an Old Woman I Shall Wear Purple

*If I Had a Hammer:
Women's Work in Poetry, Fiction, and Photographs*

*The Tie That Binds: A Collection of Writings about
Fathers & Daughters / Mothers & Sons*

If I Had My Life to Live Over I Would Pick More Daisies

I Am Becoming the Woman I've Wanted

Threads of Experience
With Fabric-and-Thread Images by Deidre Scherer

Grow old along with me the best is yet to be

Edited by
Sandra Haldeman Martz

Papier-Mache Press
Watsonville, CA

Copyright © 1996 by Papier-Mache Press. Printed in the United States of America. All rights reserved including the right to reproduce this book or portions thereof in any form. For information contact Papier-Mache Press, 135 Aviation Way, #14, Watsonville, CA 95076.

First Edition

05 04 03 02 01 00 99 98 97 96   10 9 8 7 6 5 4 3 2

ISBN: 0-918949-86-6 Softcover
ISBN: 0-918949-87-4 Hardcover

Editorial Support by Shirley Coe

Copyediting by Candace Atkins

Cover art "Counterpoint" © 1995, fabric and thread by Deidre Scherer

Cover design by Cynthia Heier

Interior design by Leslie Austin

Text composition by Erin Lebacqz and Leslie Austin

Proofreading by Erin Lebacqz

Editor photograph by Thomas Burke

Manufactured by Malloy Lithographing, Inc.

Library of Congress Cataloging-in-Publication Data
    Grow old along with me—the best is yet to be / edited by Sandra Haldeman Martz.
        p. cm.
      ISBN 0-918949-87-4 (hardcover: acid-free paper). — ISBN 0-918949-86-6 (softcover: acid-free paper)
      1. Aged, Writings of the, American. 2. Old age—United States—Literary collections. 3. Aged—United States—Literary collections.
I. Martz, Sandra.
PS508.A44G76 1996
810.8'09285—dc20   95-52135
                                                      CIP

For Dan

Contents

xi   Editor's Preface

1   Manon Reassures Her Lover
Martha Elizabeth

2   Letting Go
Allison Joseph

4   Deeper, Wider, Finer
Peter Cooley

6   In the Autumn
William Borden

12   Nearing Menopause, I Run into Elvis at Shoprite
Barbara Crooker

13   The Man Who Loved the Woman Who Loved Elvis
Terry Amrhein Tappouni

15   To the Husband Who Stands at the Sink
Cortney Davis

16   At the Reunion
Mark DeFoe

17   Illusions
Michael S. Glaser

19   Reflections in Green Glass
Davi Walders

21   Bountiful Harvest
Sally Whitney

29   Fathers Playing Sons
Robert L. Harrison

32 Hands
    Michael Andrews

35 Aerodynamic Integrity
    Rose Hamilton-Gottlieb

44 Nothing's Been the Same Since John Wayne Died
    William Greenway

47 Dance Class
    Ann Cooper

49 Getting Older
    Jane Aaron Vander Wal

50 Bonuses
    Dori Appel

51 Queen of Cards and Powders
    William Ratner

62 She Stands in the Cold Water
    James Lowell McPherson

63 Then and Now
    Phyllis King

65 For an Anniversary
    Gailmarie Pahmeier

66 What Remains
    Amy L. Uyematsu

67 The Widow and the Gigolo
    Marion Zola

68 A Woman Like That
    Peter Meinke

76 Papier-Mache
    Mary Elizabeth Parker

82 Spring Cleaning
    Sharon H. Nelson

84 Harvest
    Shirley Vogler Meister

85 Spring without Burpee Seeds
Jean Blackmon

88 Sam, At Sixty
Pat Schneider

89 The Gathering
Lois Tschetter Hjelmstad

90 Investing
Savina Roxas

93 Rema
Sara Sanderson

95 Pebbles and Crumbs
Ric Masten

98 Instructions for Ashes
Ellen Kort

99 What Faith Is
Lisa Vice

108 What Do Old Women Talk About?
Eunice Holtz

112 Retrospective Eye
Katherine Govier

119 The Well
Christopher Woods

120 Retired
Daniel Green

121 Emmaline
Willa Holmes

127 A Free Man
Judith Bell

136 Meditation for Twilight
Albert Huffstickler

137 Washing Helen's Hair
Anne C. Barnhill

142 The Fallout Fantasy
John Laue

144 Laundry
Grace Butcher

147 The Chance of Snow
Kathryn Etters Lovatt

157 Widow
Eleanor Van Houten

158 Choices
Nancy Robertson

160 Flying Time
Elisavietta Ritchie

163 Can Opener
Dianna Henning

165 The World of Dolores Velásquez
Eliud Martínez

170 Wisdom Women
CB Follett

172 Prayers for My Aging
Arupa Chiarini

173 Romance in the Old Folks' Home
Michael Waters

176 Her Game
Floyd Skloot

177 Drying Apricots
Maggi Ann Grace

180 Dance
Lynne Burgess

185 Front Porch Partners
Elizabeth Crawford

Editor's Preface

My professional interest in the subject of aging began in the early 1980s when as a new editor and publisher I compiled *When I Am an Old Woman I Shall Wear Purple*, an anthology of poetry, prose, and photographs exploring women and aging. Both the book and the process of creating it changed my life in ways I could not have envisioned: defining my life's work, redefining my attitudes about growing older, and connecting Papier-Mache Press with readers and writers around the world.

While editing *Grow Old Along with Me—The Best Is Yet to Be*, I reflected on how this anthology differs from its predecessor. The answer is found, I feel, in both the social changes that have occurred in the last ten years and in the changed perspectives of the writers. Much of the material in *When I Am an Old Woman I Shall Wear Purple* was written in the early eighties. About half of the writers in the collection were in their mid-forties or younger, women my age. They painted tender word pictures of mothers and grandmothers and older women friends. They, and I, viewed aging earnestly, poignantly, tenderly—and with a certain distance.

Today my generation is firmly entrenched in middle age, marching stalwartly ahead of the baby boomers. Two-thirds of the women writers whose work was selected for *Grow Old Along with Me* are over fifty; one-third are over sixty. This is *our* story now: our age spots, our menopause, our arthritic bones.

Our expectations about growing older have shifted dramatically in the last decade, influenced by the prospect of longer life spans, increased awareness of health and fitness, more positive media images of older women, and the changed perceptions of women's roles in a world that grew out of the social movements of the sixties and seventies. We expect to be taken more seriously—by politicians, by the medical community, by our religious leaders, by our families. But we also demand the freedom to take life less seriously—to be unconventional, to flaunt our grey hair and wrinkles, to be age proud. It's an exciting time to be an older woman.

Compiling *Grow Old Along with Me* also provided the opportunity to look at another perspective on aging: how men feel about growing older. Over the last several years an increasing number of men have attended anthology readings around the country. Their level of interest in the issues discussed and their enthusiasm about participating in this type of emotionally evocative exploration of aging prompted me to broaden the scope to include both men and women.

For most of my editorial life, my work has focused on women writers and women's issues. I wasn't sure what kind of material to expect from male writers. Any assumptions I had, however, were challenged by my commitment to keep an open ear, an open heart.

In the end the differences between what men and women had to say about aging were minor. The men in the stories and poems seemed a little more likely to define themselves through their work, to be more reflective about the mark they felt they had (or had not) made on the world, or to be more anxious about retirement and what they would do with their lives afterward. But these issues also surfaced for some of the women. The women in the stories and poems generally seemed better prepared for their old age, more excited about new beginnings as family structures shifted. Yet there were also men on the brink of new adventures and experiencing new personal insights. Particularly satisfying were the writers who spoke from the other side's point of view—men writing about women and women writing about men—the result, perhaps, of writers who are really caring listeners.

Common threads ran throughout the material: the need to be loved, the importance of family connections, an acceptance of the aging process. There were observable differences when the writings were grouped by age of the characters in the stories. Self-assessment, both physical and psychological, was most likely to emerge in the stories and poems depicting people in their fifties and early sixties. Those in their late sixties and seventies often focused on letting go, retirement, loss of life partners. The very old were especially eloquent when celebrating life's simplicity.

It is hard to find the right words to describe the photographs. Beautiful. Courageous. Tender. Vigorous. Joyful. They stand alone as visual poems. They complement and illuminate the text. The work would not be the same without them.

As with the previous anthologies, only a very small percentage of the total submissions could appear in this collection (eighty poems, stories, and photographs drawn from more than 7,000 pieces submitted from across the U.S. and Canada). However, all of the material helped to inform and shape the finished work. Reflecting the hopes, fears, joys, and sorrows of a community of writers, I feel certain that the authors also speak for the larger community of women and men, old and young, who are transforming the terrain of old age. Their words leave me challenged and eager to greet the future. I invite you, dear reader, to "Grow old along with me—the best is yet to be."

—Sandra Haldeman Martz

Grow old along with me!
The best is yet to be,
The last of life, for which the first was made:
Our times are in His hand
Who saith 'A whole I planned,
Youth shows but half; trust God: see all nor be afraid!'

—Robert Browning
"Rabbi Ben Ezra"

Photo by Marianne Gontarz

Manon Reassures Her Lover
Martha Elizabeth

When I cannot sleep, I stroke you,
and like a napping cat that purrs
and stretches when touched, you linger
with pleasure on the edge of waking,
curling far into slumber. You know
that I am watching, you are safe.
Your skin is soft, smells fresh.

I love how your face is sculpted,
the drapes and furrows, how your cheek
laps over your forearm as you sleep.
I love how your skin moves under my hand,
the way it sags on the muscle and bone,
as the skin of a ripe peach
slips loose almost without the knife.

I have no hunger for young flesh,
unripe, firm but tasteless by comparison.
You are still at the very peak
of ripeness, sweet, with the tang
that quenches thirst. I would like
to take a gentle bite from your shoulder,
golden in the faint light from the window.

Letting Go
Allison Joseph

I wear no bra, abandon
hooks and closures,
let my body drift
into its own idea
of adulthood, my skin
less firm, scars
and stretch marks
showing me how far
I've come, telling me
I'm no longer young,
that this body will
record all I do on
its ledger: every callus,
every spidery vein,
every bit of pleasure.
Now, I can touch knees
no longer smooth
or enticing, feel arms
that have held too many
boxes of books,
shrug shoulders
that stoop a little now,
closer to the ground,
to life. I don't bother
to guess where this body's
going, to predict its
passions or motions,
preferring its surprises—

arms reaching farther
than I thought they could,
legs walking me into towns
I don't know. Wiser,
saner, my body goes
where it wants, knowledge
of sinew and cell all
it needs to know,
all it wants to tell.

Deeper, Wider, Finer
Peter Cooley

Each dawn for the man a new face
swims up in his shaving mirror.
The eyes stare back, in charge of everything:
the jawbone, the nose, each year more like his father,
both twisted a little to the left, cubistic,
rearranged by a seventh grade football accident.
It is all here: the new day glazed
in stubble he will scrape like an engraver
burning the plate with fine lines of his razor
while he creates himself—as while he slept,
after sex the night before or during his rush
into the woman or late today at his desk—
so too the sculptor will be at work on him,
pulling the lines at the sides of his eyes wider,
deepening the crevices on both sides of his nose,
crossing the brow with cross-stitching of its trade,
preparing the corpse handsomely, masterfully,
for his rightful position among contemporaries.

Photo by Teresa Tamura

In the Autumn
William Borden

In the autumn of the year, in the autumn of his life, he waded into the dry, brown leaves as if he were walking into the sea. He marched knee-deep, the leaves spraying and flying—a dusty splashing, like hopes crumbling. He inhaled the dust of his life.

The afternoon was cloudy, and the air was chill. The park was empty. As he climbed the hill, leaves crawled up his socks and pecked at his legs. Leaves flew up to grab at his jacket and trousers, and he remembered walking through the field beside his house when he was eight and the tall grass exploding with grasshoppers. They landed on his pants, on his shirt, clinging to him in desperation, like refugees from a war zone. He ran, flailing at them.

His grandfather would hold a grasshopper between his thumb and forefinger and touch his other forefinger to the grasshopper's mouth. A drop of brown liquid would appear on his fingertip. "Tobacco juice," his grandfather would say. The boy believed him.

His grandfather knew magic. It was a magical spell, a verse from the Bible, and it stopped bleeding. He remembered the time his grandfather was sitting under the tree in the front yard, smoking his pipe, and he, the boy, ran out to tell him that his brother had cut his hand.

Grandpa nodded. He kept on sitting and puffing on the scarred, blackened pipe as if nothing in the world had changed. It was a secret spell, repeated silently in the mind. Within minutes the bleeding stopped, and the boy went out to tell his grandfather, so his grandfather could stop saying the spell and go back to whatever it was he went back to in his mind.

When the boy was a teenager and his grandfather was in the nursing home, nothing seemed to be going on in his grandfather's head. He visited his grandfather regularly at first, and the old man seemed glad to see him. His grandfather's thin, weak hand reached up from the bed to grasp the boy's hand. The old man smiled, and his eyes teared a little.

The nursing home smelled like all nursing homes. He didn't know what the odor came from—urine, medicine, age, sadness, the embrace of death—maybe all combined. Autumn has a smell. It's the scent of dead leaves crackling underfoot, crumbling, collapsing into dust, as corpses finally do.

After a few months, his grandfather's eyes, filmed by a membrane of moisture, seemed not to recognize him. When the boy went to the bed where his grandfather was supposed to be and looked at the frail figure there between the railings of the bed—all the beds had railings, like cribs—it was not the man who had pinched tobacco juice from grasshoppers' mouths. Yet the boy recognized something.

When his grandfather died, it was ascribed to old age. How could old age be a killer? As easily as, say, middle age—a disease he could imagine never recovering from. He could picture himself keeling over, at eighty, from the effects of middle age. Old age attacked the joints and spilled brown spots over the skin; it sunk cheeks, dimmed eyes, dropped teeth. But middle age—middle age attacked the mind, the soul, the way one thought about things. It was insidious, as sneaky as water rising silently in the basement when no one's looking.

None of his middle-aged friends had died yet. They and he were more subject to breaks and strains—those little deaths of autumn. Four winters ago he had slipped on the ice and broken his leg. His wife had tripped on the stairs and broken her arm; she had a plastic elbow now. There were among his friends broken ribs, migraines, bad teeth, and almost universal lower back pain.

There were books that told of people dying and then returning—visions of light, cataclysms of ecstasy, bliss down to their toes—and, when they returned, they were no longer afraid of death; yet they relished life even more. He wasn't sure he wanted to come that close. Besides, it wasn't death exactly that he was grappling with; it was the idea of death.

Of autumn.

He reached the top of the hill. Leaves were strangely absent on the other side of the hill. Then he saw, at the bottom of the hill, a great heap of dried leaves. Children had gathered them into one magnificent pile, so they could leap into it.

He was a practical, skeptical, scientific man. Yet he was open-minded. Years ago, like his students, he had read Castañeda. The Indian sorcerer had advised Castañeda to keep death over his left shoulder. Or was it the right? And was that different from death breathing down your neck?

Take each breath as if it's your last—some mystical tradition, he couldn't recall which, advised that. Or did they say to breathe as if it were one's first breath? He took a deep breath. That was my last breath, he said to himself.

That was depressing.

He imagined his next breath was his first.

Millions of breaths to look forward to. Autumn to look forward to. He kept breathing, gasping his life, in and out. It made him dizzy, light-headed. Was he having a mystical experience?

No, he was hyperventilating.

Still, how many mystical infusions had he rejected because he had explained them away?

On the other hand, from all his reading, it seemed that you could not mistake a true mystical experience. The real thing, it was clear, grabbed you by the nape of the neck and shook you until you believed it.

Was he too old now for a mystical experience? They tended to hit in the mid-thirties. Jesus died at thirty-three. Dante was thirty-five when he got lost in the dark wood. Gopi Krishna was thirty-five when his kundalini popped up his spine and blew his mind into another dimension. During *his* thirty-fifth year—nine years had passed since then—he had waited, with anticipation, for the universe to smack *him* into cosmic consciousness.

It never happened.

He wasn't altogether sorry. The thing was scary, really. Turned you upside down. Made you a vegetarian.

It would have brought a lot of problems, and he didn't need more problems.

Of course, a mystical experience in the autumn of one's life was not impossible—no more than winning the powerball or escaping prostate trouble or falling in love was impossible. They just weren't likely.

In the past, whenever he had fallen in love, it had gotten him in trouble. There was the student, the hippie girl who wore combat boots and no bra, ten—was it twelve?—years ago. There was the Flemish woman, raven-haired and a practitioner of homeopathy, he met on his sabbatical in Europe. There was the new woman in the department, a deconstructionist who liked to be tied up, a mere two years ago. Trouble, every one of them. Complications. Discoveries. Jealousies. Scenes. Tears.

Affairs were simply too much trouble. Like the garden—an annual labor, a seasonal duty: you rent the rototiller; you plant, water, weed; you suffer the ravages of gophers, rabbits, hail; and at the end you have a zucchini the size of a cannon. Affairs were like that. A lot of work, and then, at harvest time, there's more than you can handle. Rapture turns against you. Everything's out of control.

Everything seemed to wash over him—marriage, affairs, children, tenure, committees, classes, tax returns—an ocean of time and events he was drowning in.

He took a deep breath and wondered if it was a first breath or a last. Or if he should even be breathing while he was drowning.

The Sufis talked about the "mother breath"—seven beats for the inhalation, hold for one, seven beats for the exhalation, hold for one, and repeat.

He tried it.

He wondered how fast he was supposed to count.

There was always something they didn't tell you.

Maybe he would become a Sufi. He wasn't sure where he should go. Turkey, maybe, but the political situation there was unstable. He was always wanting to go somewhere and become something after reading a book. After reading the first

Castañeda book, he had gotten out a map of Mexico and wondered if he could find Don Juan and become his apprentice. He was going to spend a year in a Zen monastery. He wanted to study dolphins with John Lilly. He tried to change the oil in his car after reading *Zen and the Art of Motorcycle Maintenance*.

So it wasn't that he never tried to put his reading into practice. It was that things never worked out. Sitting cross-legged, trying *zazen* on his own, made his knees hurt; he limped for a week. He watched *Lila and Yoga*—or whatever it was called—on the educational channel, but one of the *asanas* had triggered his lower back pain, and for weeks afterward he had popped muscle relaxants. And, of course, driving to Mexico was absurd. No one knew if Don Juan even existed; besides, he had his classes to teach, and he couldn't afford it, anyway, what with the girls' dancing lessons, his teenage son's car insurance, and his wife's tuition for graduate school in psychology.

He looked down at the huge pile of leaves. The sun had set. The park was still deserted, except for him and the squirrels. The Sufis, he remembered, spun. He crossed his arms over his chest, as the dervishes did, and he turned counterclockwise, as they did.

He had read a story once about the Sufis who were praying and chanting and spinning in a certain mosque in a village somewhere in the world; after they had prayed and chanted and spun for a long time, the room seemed ready to explode. Universal enlightenment seemed at hand. But then the sheik brought the dancing and chanting to a lower pitch, slowed it down, brought everyone back to earth. A visitor, disturbed, heartbroken, disappointed, asked the sheik, Why?—Why stop, when they were almost *there*? Because, the sheik answered, not everyone in the mosque was ready for enlightenment. And if you're not ready, enlightenment can destroy you. We wait, even the most advanced, until everyone is ready. Then, together, we will become one with the universe.

Spinning faster, he felt as if a thin wire were humming up

and down his spine. He was losing himself in the spinning. He knew nothing, thought nothing, was nothing.

The wire broke. Dizziness picked him up by the heels and threw him down the hill.

He was rolling. He was in the leaves, covered, buried, drowning. He was laughing, picking the leaves out of his mouth.

He stood up, dizzy still. He didn't try to brush the leaves off. He couldn't find his cap. He ran unsteadily up the hill, turned, stood a moment—he could barely see the mound of leaves in the gathering darkness—then flung himself onto the earth and rolled, rolled, rolled—into the leaves again, the dry leaves crackling like little firecrackers, like sparks of electricity, like a loud rush of language from another dimension.

Over and over he ran up the hill, he rolled down, he swam in the ocean of leaves—he lost his shoe—he didn't care—he lost his keys—he didn't care—he was losing his mind—good—until, finally, exhausted, breathless, sightless in the dark, he lay spread-eagled on the now flattened and scattered leaves. He couldn't have told who he was. He was lost. He was a goner. He was as crazy as a loon and he didn't care. His heels drummed the ground. He barked like a coyote. He howled like a wolf. He loosed his Tarzan yell, dormant these thirty years.

He walked—hobbled, actually, because he never found his shoe—the six blocks to his home. Leaves covered him like a costume, a motley, like the Sufis and other fools wore. He climbed his front steps. He could see into his living room, see his family watching television. He smelled like leaves. He reeked of autumn. It was in his hair and in his socks and under his collar. But he liked feeling that dusty, scratchy residue. He opened the door. He entered his house. He was grinning. He was breathing the mother breath. One-two-three-four-five-six-seven-hold-seven-six-five-four-three-two-one-hold—repeat.

They were grinning back at him.

Repeat.

Nearing Menopause, I Run into Elvis at Shoprite
Barbara Crooker

near the peanut butter. He calls me ma'am, like the sweet
southern mother's boy he was. This is the young Elvis,
slim-hipped, dressed in leather, black hair swirled
like a duck's backside. I'm in the middle of my life,
the start of the body's cruel betrayals, the skin beginning
to break in lines and creases, the thickening midline.
I feel my temperature rising, as a hot flash washes over,
the thermostat broken down. The first time I heard Elvis
on the radio, I was poised between girlhood and what comes next.
My parents were appalled, in the Eisenhower fifties, by rock
and roll and all it stood for, let me only buy one record,
"Love Me Tender," and I did.
I have on a tight Orlon sweater, circle skirt,
eight layers of rolled-up net petticoats, all bound
together by a woven straw cinch belt. Now I've come
full circle, hate the music my daughter loves, Nine
Inch Nails, Smashing Pumpkins, Crash Test Dummies.
Elvis looks embarrassed for me. His soft full lips
are like moon pies, his eyelids half-mast, pulled
down bedroom shades. He mumbles, "Treat me nice."
Now, poised between menopause and what comes next, the last
dance, I find myself in tears by the toilet paper rolls,
hearing "Unchained Melody" on the sound system. "That's all
right now, Mama," Elvis says, "Any way you do is fine." The bass
line thumps and grinds, the honky-tonk piano moves like an ivory
river, full of swampy delta blues. And Elvis's voice wails above
it all, the purr and growl, the snarl and twang, above the chains
of flesh and time.

The Man Who Loved the Woman Who Loved Elvis
Terry Amrhein Tappouni

Buck Wallis wore his pompadour
high and glistening black,
a perfect downy ducktail
nestling against his neck.
Summers he sweltered down
in Florida, his imitation
leather jacket sticking
to him like plastic wrap
on pudding, knowing all
the time it wasn't enough.

The woman he loved still
slept with a velvet Elvis
on the wall above the foot
of her bed, slept on her back
so whenever her eyes opened
they would light on him,
his plush face aglow with
light from the hall, ripe
plum lips slightly open,
tugged up on one side.
People stared, slid contempt-
filled looks at the twenty-eight-
year-old man with the woman
who was turning fifty, even though

they said she looked good
for her age. The way he smiled
at her annoyed them in ways
they didn't understand. Men pulled
back their shoulders, felt
the yearning of their women.

What he knew was simple.
When "Love Me Tender" spilled
from the record player, and she
took him to her bed,
he was The King.

To the Husband Who Stands at the Sink, Intent on Shaving
Cortney Davis

There is a woman in your shower,
her body visible through the green
canopy of steam. She isn't as young
as she used to be, but you've said
you hardly notice. Now her dark hair
cleaves to her neck like leaves
and beads of water decorate her skin,
slide opal and diamond bracelets down
the blood flush raised by heat.
Everyday she walks or lifts weights,
praising the way thighs tighten,
how muscles rise and divide her back
into twin slices of fruit—sweet,
succulent, firm against the lip.
Now she admires the long arm she raises
to direct the spray against her breasts;
have you looked away from the mirror
to watch? In case you have, she turns,
giving you freely her profile, this map
of the body complete with betrayals
slightly hidden behind the wavering glass.
One hand ringed in gold
slowly approaches the faucet. Languid,
wide-awake, she prepares to emerge
like a water bird slipping from water
into air, feathers slicked, stripped clean
of anger and sorrow, not yet of expectation.

At the Reunion
Mark DeFoe

Blundering from our own lifeboats, we clench
flesh thought lost, backslap and hug, flash snapshots
of kids, those blessed torments of love, parade
the new wife with the tight thighs. Giddy with
survivor bravado, we puff our jobs,
kite our incomes, balloon our travel plans,
add wings to the old hacienda.

We search out the one who understood us then,
lock secret fingers, sway in the spell
of golden oldies. Smoky dreams slow dance
through the crowd like a tipsy magician,
vanishing bald spot and crows-feet.

Ah, we croon old tunes, losing not one word,
each moment grand cliché, but completely ours,
the sexiest, classiest class of all.

We toast the shades who have passed, touch glasses
and believe. Around us are those who knew
us when. In their eyes we meet the boy
who dropped the pass that lost The Game,
the girl almost runner-up for May Queen.

And yet a gleam of sweetness there, that allows
again the tender seed of self that was.
Let the band play on, corny as they are.
Take my hand. For this last dance we have returned.

Illusions
Michael S. Glaser

With age, with reluctance,
I lose my illusions,

look back on those sweet desires
I imagined as prize,

as though I knew
what I was being drawn into.

Only late am I learning
what attention must be paid

and how help comes
not to blaze a path of light

but to sustain our faltering steps,
to see us through the night.

Photo by Robert Ullman

Reflections in Green Glass
Davi Walders

For C., J., and all brave women who love.

Too early to be fashionable, two women perch
on stools eating *ensalata,* our faces reflected
in the glass above the bar, our backs a partition
between Catalan, coffee, and laughter. It is dusk
in Barcelona. Waiters balancing *tapas* high
in smoky air tell us what we already know.

We are out of sync, but we have taken a stand
to sit at the bar because of our feet,
our stomachs, and our desires. We will not eat
again at midnight to lie bedded in our bloat,
staring into darkness, deprived of dreams
by dinner and aging bodies that will not adjust.

We lean, tired, looking into milky green glass.
Longer than Liceu's curtain, it shimmers like rain
on old copper, encircling Picadillos on the *passeig.*
Beveled shelves, triangles of herb brandy, Chartreuse
and necks of rioja bottles frame our silhouettes.
We are women beyond the blur of crowded tables.

Two women, dining too early, happy to be out
of the rain, damp feet warming on zinc, we talk
of friends at fifty who buy answering machines,
wait for calls, keep money hidden in drawers, open
separate accounts, begin and end careers, take lovers,
let them go, reweave, unravel, gather and lose,
tighten and loosen their hold on children, thighs,
lies, and fears. Reflections dancing in green glass,
out of sync, out of touch, out of the rain,
out of laughter, out of love for women walking
in the world—we raise our *vino blanco*, saluting,
drinking in the Spanish dusk, laughing at fifty.

Bountiful Harvest
Sally Whitney

Heat from the sun is warm against my neck as I bend over John's okra plants, looking for the fuzzy green spears that are the peak size, moments before they become large and tough. "Can't let 'em get too old," John says to me, as he has every summer of the twenty-five years we've been married. I shove my straw hat back on my head and glare at him, although he can't see me because he is tying up tomato plants that last night's rain pushed away from their stakes. The garden is John's comfort zone, the patch where when his hands are busy his tongue often loosens. So I follow him into the dirt and heat and bugs sometimes, to talk.

Today I want to talk about his birthday. In two weeks he'll be fifty years old, a milestone I consider worthy of celebration, but every time I mention it, he makes a joke and talks about something else. "So what do you want to do for your birthday?" I ask. I twist an okra stem until the pod falls into my basket.

"Can it," he says and throws a tomato at me. His curly hair with flecks of white in the curves is pressed under his stained leather cap, reminding me of an old-fashioned paperboy in a Norman Rockwell print. By reflex, my hand shoots out and stops the red pulp from splattering against the side of the house. I grimace at his pun. What I really want to do is give him a surprise party, but I'm afraid he'll be angry, or at least unhappy, if I do. I can't tell for sure how he feels.

"How about going out for dinner? Or maybe a few friends over?"

"Don't make a big deal." His head is back down in the tomatoes, and I am staring at his derriere, still as slim and sexy as ever in his soft denim jeans. I sigh and pull off an okra that is hardly as big as my thumb.

The next day my sister comes by to return a book she borrowed. Her name is Alicia, and she is a compulsive dropper inner. "Any decision on the birthday bash?" she asks. She knows my dilemma and is unsympathetic. Her husband Martin loves parties and is only forty-five, anyway.

"Not an inkling." I throw my Pledge-soaked dustrag on the table and wipe my hands on my jeans.

"I'm telling you, Judy, just do it. He'll love it." Alicia goes to my refrigerator, takes out two Diet Cokes, and hands one to me. "Sit down and let me tell you about men." This is my younger sister who thinks she knows more about the opposite sex than I do. Grateful for any excuse to stop cleaning, however, I sit. "Where is John now?" Alicia asks.

"At the grocery store getting something for dinner."

"Is he cooking again?"

"I thought you were going to tell me about men."

"He wants you to think he doesn't want to be fussed over, but he does."

"I'm not sure." I remember his face at his last birthday.

He smiled as our daughters, home from college, gave him a candle-covered cake, but it wasn't a real smile. A real smile brightens his pale eyes and sparkles in the corners of his face. This smile said, "I'm glad you want to make me happy and I'll try to make you think you did."

"Then what does he want?"

"I think he wants to pretend he's not getting older."

"Kind of hard to deny, isn't it?" Alicia sips her Coke and curls her legs under her on the couch. The air conditioner hums in the window, but I am still warm from dusting. I hold my Coke can against my cheek.

"Why is it that somewhere in life, getting older becomes bad?" I hope Alicia doesn't think I'm being trite. If she does, she doesn't show it. "I can remember when I thought twelve must be the most wonderful age in the world. And then I wanted to be sixteen so I could drive, and twenty-one so I could drink, and even thirty was nice because I figured by that time, I was truly an adult."

Alicia turns and stretches her legs in front of her. She

looks more interested. "How about forty? Did you really want to be forty?"

I think back to that time in my life. "Yeah. I did. I spent my thirties staying up with babies and chasing after little kids. By forty, my life settled down. I had more time to think about me."

"But you don't want to be fifty any more than John does."

She is looking directly at me now, her face an expression of challenge she has used on me since she was five. I don't feel challenged.

"They say at fifty you earn the name 'wise old woman.' I think I'll like that."

Alicia laughs, steadying her Coke can with both hands. "That's what I'll call you, Judy," she says between laughs, "wise old woman. My wise old sister. Sort of like an owl."

"Who's like an owl?" John appears at the kitchen door, his arms wrapped around bulging sacks of groceries. He is wearing a white T-shirt with illustrations of endangered species front and back. A polar bear protrudes slightly over his belt.

Alicia composes herself and points her finger at me. "Your wife," she says. "Hadn't you noticed?"

"Stays up all night and sleeps all day." John grins in my direction.

"Get out of here, both of you," I say.

"I do have to go." Alicia stands and carries her Coke can to the kitchen. "Thanks for the book and remember what I said about the other thing." Her words trail her as she passes through again on her way out the front door.

"What other thing?" John sets the sacks on the kitchen counter, pulls out a box of cereal, and puts it on the top shelf next to the rice, raisins, peanut butter. Always the same order. Once I tried to put tea bags between the rice and raisins. John was grumpy all day.

He is looking at me now, one eyebrow cocked like a question mark. I put my arms around his waist and lay my head against his chest. He smells like bananas and Brute. "She's talking about your birthday," I say. "We want to do something big."

"I'm big enough already." John chuckles and gently pushes me away. There is no mirth in his laugh. "Besides, it's not a big deal."

"I think it is." Suddenly, I'm tired of dancing around the issue. "I think when a person achieves fifty years of life, that's something to be proud of, an accomplishment."

John folds a paper bag methodically, smoothing each crease between his fingers. His cheeks droop. "That's the problem, Judy," he says. "I don't have the accomplishment I wanted." He is quiet for a few minutes, and I wait. When he is ready, he goes on. "I've worked for the same company for twenty years. I've been an engineer, a technical specialist, a department manager, and a division manager. I thought by the time I was fifty, I'd be a vice president. It's a goal I set for myself, and I failed." He shrugs and goes back to folding the bag.

I have raised two daughters, cared for my mother when she was sick, and reached out to lots of friends in need, but I don't remember ever experiencing the pain of compassion that I feel now. I go to him again, and this time he doesn't push me away.

In the darkness that night, I stare at the ceiling and listen to John's rough breathing beside me. His in-and-out rhythm of air matches the tug-of-war in my mind. As he slips into deeper sleep, I know what I will do.

"Come help me," I say to Alicia on the phone the next morning. "I need your creative flair."

"No long guest list?" she asks when I tell her my plan.

"No long guest list." I'm sure.

The morning of John's birthday is cool with low-hanging clouds. I give him a Shoebox card at breakfast so he leaves for work with at least a hint of a smile. At 10:00 A.M. I cross my fingers and hope that the roses I ordered are delivered to his office on time.

After work, I hurry home to make sure everything is ready by the time John gets home. Alicia arrives at 4:30, Martin shows up at 5:00, and by 5:30 we are set. We turn off the lights, close the shades, and, giggling like children, hide behind the living room furniture. Very slowly, the door knob begins to turn.

I hold my breath to stop my giggling and watch the wedge of light pour through the widening crack of the door. As John steps across the threshold, I throw the switch controlling the outlet to which Alicia and I have painstakingly wired every light in the room as well as our ancient slide projector.

"Surprise!" we yell. The lights form a halo for the life-size image of John projected against the rear living room wall.

"Happy birthday to you," we sing at the top of our lungs while we clasp hands and dance in a ring around John, who looks dazed.

"Right this way," I say, and lead John to the dining room, where we have taken down the Andrew Wyeth prints that usually hang there and replaced them with blown-up pictures of John—John with our daughters when they were little, John hanging our fragile Christmas star, John with his dad and brothers at Thanksgiving.

"What is this?" John asks, but there's no anger in his voice. I seat him at the head of the dining room table and hold his hand while Alicia and Martin begin a slow procession from the kitchen carrying a two feet-by-four feet sheet cake slathered in lemon icing. They place it on the table in front of John, and he stares at it a full minute before he says, "Those aren't candles."

Stuck in the mounds of icing are an array of figurines, objects, and small photographs, each with a tag attached. John lifts a porcelain cocker spaniel out of a yellow drift and reads his card aloud, "This is for the time you pulled Corky out of the river and saved his life." John nods and licks the icing from the pooch's feet.

"Look at this one." Alicia grabs a red sedan and thrusts it at John.

"This is for the time you cosigned Alicia's car loan when we all thought she couldn't keep a job more than six months." John laughs and Alicia kisses his cheek.

The phone rings as John reaches for a plastic suitcase. I answer it and hand it to John. He pauses, then says, "Yeah, I have the cake right here. Which one? OK." He lifts a blue book labeled "Chemistry" out of the icing, studies the card, and smiles. "You could have passed it by yourself." He talks a while longer, then hands me the phone. "It was Deborah," he says. I nod, knowing our other daughter will call soon.

"I don't understand all this," John says, his eyebrows curving.

"We're celebrating who you are," I explain, "the person you've become in fifty years." Alicia, Martin, and I join John at the table now, cheering as he lifts each item, licks the icing from its base, and sets it in a row next to the cake. The row grows long, an army of testaments ready to do battle for John. John is smiling, not a pretend smile to make us feel good, but a real smile that spreads from his hairline to his chin.

"Oh, come on, Judy. This is too much," he says as he pulls a long green okra from the icing.

"That stands for the magnificent gardens you produce year after year." I pat his arm as he examines the pod.

"But it's too tough to eat," John says.

"It's not here to be dinner," I say. "It's here because it's big like your heart."

Photo by Marianne Gontarz

Photo by Teresa Tamura

Fathers Playing Sons
Robert L. Harrison

Challenged by youth, we played that day
like reflections in the mirror.
Old skills come back, but muscles don't
as our limbs defy our minds.

This game we played like pros of old
staring down at endless motion,
bringing in our belts a notch while
mentally melting our excess weight.

Ninety feet was still the same
but our glasses made it longer,
and our fastest was not as swift
compared to their sneaker dust.

But wisdom, I thought, was on our side
as I made a brilliant bunt,
only to have the ball die of age
and scar my back forever.

And I pitched like slo-mo Ryan
wheezing only a little, as my best
went straight down the pike
only to fly back into uncharted skies.

We tied the score between youth and age
and stopped only because of darkness.
We celebrated with good grace but knew
the future would catch us napping.

For they had keen eyes and miracle legs
and a knack for coming back,
but we ancient ones will never quit
for fathers must always beat their sons.

Photo by Bayla Winters

Hands
Michael Andrews

This year my hands turned old.

I can see the grief in them—
the scars, of course, stand out
skin flayed by knives and glass and bites
and the blisters big as half dollars
ripped from the calluses by the high bar
and the shovels and axes and hammers
shaping the earth,
but the earth always wins.

I can see the wars in them
Vietnam and Iran and Nicaragua and Bangladesh.
I can see the years of poverty
the inability to get published.
I can see Flo's cancer
and my blackouts
and all the creditors
and promises lost.

I can see the victories in them
small
and mixed with little scars.

The nails have turned to ridges,
each one a plowed field
waiting for a harvest that will never come.
They were never strong, but my hands are.
They are big and they are kind.
I guess they could be described as capable hands.

They have made so many things.
I used them to shape wood and books
to sculpture a poem and print a picture.
They have done their share of plumbing
and automobile mechanics, electrical wiring
and, yes, squeezing triggers.

They are coarse hands, but they are gentle.
They are magic for cat's ears
and dog's rumps and tickling children.
They are healers too.
They can rub the pain away
the fear
and the tears.

They can make love.

I saw them change early in the spring.
I thought it was darkroom chemicals,
the gasoline and the lacquer thinner.
I saw the skin go leather
textured and knobby
with rivers of wrinkles and lines
and five years of hard living.
I rubbed them with enough grease to pack an axle.
Not a single hand cream worked as advertised.
I changed detergents.
Nothing helped.

Driving into L.A. on the Harbor Freeway
my hands were caught in that fierce
morning sun
and they were old.
These days
when they have nothing to do
they are hiding in my pockets
or laying in the shade.

Still,
they are big and clumsy and friendly.

The kind of hands that brush tears away.

Aerodynamic Integrity
Rose Hamilton-Gottlieb

I meet my two friends, Mag and Addie, at Bill's Bike Shop. Addie climbs onto a flimsy-looking contraption and uses the kickstand for balance. She looks at home there. Her bones are as delicate as the fingers of chrome that hold the bicycle together, and her hair curves over her cheeks like silver crescent moons.

"Racing bikes. That's what you need for a ride like that." The salesman is a college jock type with a blond crewcut.

"It's not a race." Mag eyes the bicycles with mistrust.

Addie has challenged us to ride across her native state of Iowa on an annual odyssey sponsored by the Des Moines Register. A native of Southern California who's never seen any reason to land anywhere east of the Rockies, I don't seriously think we will do this. But my thighs could use a little trimming. And I'm ready for something.

The salesman doesn't even look at Mag, who leans toward me and whispers, "See what I mean, Sally? He doesn't even see me."

At our last book club meeting, Mag said, "What I fear most is becoming like the old lady..."

"Elderly woman," I corrected.

"The elderly woman you almost run down in the supermarket before you realize she's there. You know, the one the waiter never asks if everything is OK?" We were discussing Germaine Greer's *The Change* since we're all experiencing menopause in one form or another, and truth to tell, have been experiencing it all our lives in the sometimes whispered, sometimes ridiculed, always feared, idea of it.

"Don't be paranoid," I say now, but Crew Cut relates only to Addie, who nobody ignores. He wheels out a metallic red space-age contraption and pats the narrow seat. "You want something light. Slim tires. Low handlebars. Something with aerodynamic integrity."

"With what?" I ask.

Addie climbs on and curves herself over the handlebars. "See how the wind will flow over my head?"

"Isn't that a boy's bike?" I look for my childhood bicycle, one with a frame designed to protect a young girl's virginity, embarrassed to admit that the last bike I rode required the rider to pedal backward in order to stop.

Mag peers through tortoise shell-framed glasses at the complicated system of wires looped over the handlebars. "Are all those gears necessary?"

"You need gears. Lots of them."

Twenty-one gears in all. We start at my house and pedal down the bike lane. Our maiden voyage, Mag calls it, but it's not clear sailing. We teeter dangerously on the skinny tires, off-balance, weaving over the line, not sure of the gears. My hair creeps from under the helmet into my eyes, but I'm afraid to let go of the handlebars long enough to push it back.

My hair was another germaine topic at our last book club meeting. I was complaining to Mag that my hairdresser had tried to sell me on a tint. "It's this in-between stage I hate," I lied. "Actually, I look forward to being a...a...a..." I couldn't think of a word to replace *brunette* on my driver's license.

"Greyhead?" Mag asked dryly.

"Seriously, don't you think I'll look good in grey? I mean with my summer coloring?" Trying to warm to the idea, I added, "Maybe I'll hurry things along by covering what's left of the brown."

"To dye or not to dye. That is the question." Mag ran her hand through her pageboy, once silky chestnut, now streaked with coarse silver.

Addie slammed her hand down onto the table and said, "I challenge you." Since Addie's own hair had turned a stunning shade of pewter in her early thirties, she was understandably bored with the conversation. And, since Addie's challenges are hard to ignore, here we are.

"Watch it, Sally," Addie shouts, too late. I clip her back

fender. With my back curved into a widow's hump and my hands at the level of my knees like some missing link, I can't see more than a foot beyond the front tire, and every time I raise my head to enjoy the smogless January sky, I swerve out of control.

Back home, I untangle myself from the instrument of torture. My neck is stiff, my wrists ache, my back hurts, and the narrow seat may have done permanent damage to parts I hope I'm not through using yet. I chuck off the helmet and glimpse in the window, hair matted with sweat. "If this is supposed to make me feel young, it's not working."

"You need a haircut," Addie says.

"No, I need new friends."

Mag careens into the driveway, falls off, then limps to where I've collapsed on the front step. "That was very nice, Addie," she says, ever the diplomat and mediator, "but Sally and I need different bikes."

Back at the bike shop, Crew Cut says, "You need a hybrid, a cross between a mountain bike and a street bike. Stay with the lighter frame but get touring-style handlebars. Keep the smooth tread but get wider tires for balance."

"And a bigger seat," I put in. He ignores me.

"Of course you'll lose up to four miles an hour." He shakes his head.

"It's not a race," Mag says firmly.

Addie trades in hers too, then insists we buy biking pants, the fashion crime of the century, in my opinion. I'm sold, finally, by the padding in the seat, but we resist the sales pitch on skin-tight jerseys and opt for thigh-length T-shirts.

"I'll design a logo," Mag volunteers.

I knew Mag couldn't be trusted. Her logo is a picture of Baba Yaga on her broomstick. Obese, greasy haired, snaggletoothed. (Last summer we read *Women Who Run with the Wolves*.) And beneath this slimy old hag, the words, "The Three Crones." In-your-face-we're-old-so-what.

Mag, who's into goddess stories and myths and Jungian psychology, responded to Addie's challenge with, "You know, this might fulfill a need we read about; that is, the lack of ritual in our culture to mark the transition period between youth and old age. Like a rite of passage into a golden age filled with possibilities and adventure."

"In Iowa?" I asked.

Addie, who knows when to encourage Mag, said, "Oh there's lots of ritual. True believers dip their back wheels in the Missouri at the beginning of the week and their front wheels in the Mississippi at the end."

"Perfect." Mag clapped her hands. "It's rife with symbolism."

All that talk about water reminded me that my bladder is in need of repair—my last shred of argument. "What about bathrooms?"

"Ever hear of cornfields?" Addie quipped, then quickly added, "From what I hear, the Porta-Potti concession cleans up at the ride."

We each order two of Mag's T-shirts, but I wear mine fraudulently, secretly ashamed of getting old.

After six months of Addie's relentless training, we ride fifty miles in one day. Addie says with the group energy supplied by ten thousand bikers, we'll easily do the required sixty- to eighty-mile days.

I get a haircut.

"My, look at all that grey on the floor," my hairdresser comments tactlessly.

I look down at the last of my former brunette status.

"How about a little tint? I had a cancellation."

I'm tempted. "How long will it take?"

"About an hour. Make that two hours if you add a cellophane treatment to lock in the color."

I check my watch. I still have twenty-five miles to ride before it gets dark, and in spite of my old hair, my muscles yearn for action.

"Next time," I say.

For Addie and Mag and me, the ride starts a day early, at the mosquito-infested junction of the Rock and Big Sioux Rivers, which forms the border between Iowa and South Dakota.

We have pedaled the fifteen miles from our motel in Sioux Center to dip our back tires in this tributary of the Missouri. I was for not doing this part and saying we did, but Mag insists we need all the ritual we can get.

We dip our tires and pedal back through the deepening twilight. I feel the strength in my legs and in my lungs and in our friendship. "Thanks for making me do this. I could go across the whole state tonight."

Addie lifts her arms and embraces the evening. "A piece of cake."

We meet a few other purists, including two young men who pass us on the way back, balancing a bucket of river water between them. "What on earth?" Mag asks.

"It's for our buddies. We drew the short straws; they get to drink beer."

"That's cheating," Addie calls out, but they've left us behind, the full bucket perfectly balanced between their racing bikes.

At the motel, we wash our clothes, put on our one change, which we will sleep in tonight and ride in tomorrow, and take in performances by the Senior Citizen Kitchen Band, a local ventriloquist, and the country comedy team of "Ezra and Lubas." We play "cow bingo" and observe a hay-bale stacking contest at the fairgrounds and watch this town of five thousand swell to a colorful tent city. Most of the bikers are young, with every muscle and curve ensheathed in spandex.

At Sunday's opening ceremony, the mayor's speech includes the weather report: "Sunshine, with highs in the seventies. Wind five to ten miles an hour in the northeast. That means a gentle tailwind. I checked the topography maps," he says, "and the good news is that it's 749 feet downhill from here to Burlington. The bad news is that it's 495 miles."

"Anyone for a head start?" Mag says.

We leave before the National Anthem and set out into the Iowa dawn, three abreast, cornfields on both sides of the two-lane highway, which has been closed to traffic. Our destination is Spencer, sixty-one miles, a paltry distance for veteran bikers such as we.

We travel light with one clean set of clothes, a plastic raincoat, a toothbrush, and hormone replacement pills. Mag is on my left, Addie on my right. A few other early birds whiz past, but most of the bikers are waiting for the town fathers to dump a huge tub of river water across the starting line. Addie says it's to accommodate those without the integrity to do the real thing, and Mag says it's typically American fast-food ritual.

For the moment, we share the morning with only a red-winged blackbird, scolding us on the wing. "Look," I say, "a native Iowan wants to race," and I surge forward after the bird, feeling about ten years old. In my mirror, I see Mag and Addie laugh. "See you in Spencer," I call out. "Last one there buys the beer."

I pedal on alone, so engrossed in the morning I hardly notice a roar in the distance. I slow to let Mag and Addie catch up. From behind comes a young male voice, "On your left." Startled, I move to the right, only to hear another voice, this time female, "On your right." I glimpse creamy skin beneath wraparound sunglasses as she passes, so close I smell her bubblegum.

"Stay in your lane," she snaps, "or you'll cause an accident."

I open my mouth to tell her to get rid of the gum before she chokes on it, but am checked by another "On your left," followed by an "On your right." And another and another. I stare at the concrete ahead, not daring to even glance at the passing scenery lest I veer in either direction and get hit. I clench the handlebars, check my mirror for Addie and Mag, but they are gone. I almost collide with a man with a tattoo on his arm and more hair on his legs than I have on my head. "Sorry," I apologize, but he's out of earshot and another biker moves into his place, shows me the back of his T-shirt: "If you can't run with the big dogs, stay on the porch." I try to slow down, but I'm trapped in a fast-moving river of chrome and rubber and spandex-covered flesh. I fight panic. I've lost my friends.

The day stays cool, but my palms are slippery with sweat and anxiety threatens to choke off my breath. My legs itch from at least thirty mosquito bites. I struggle to keep up, but feel like a tangle of driftwood in swift water.

"Speed up, you old crone, or get out of the fast lane." Damn T-shirt.

"How?" I gasp, but the owner of the voice is already gone. I long, not for the slow lane, but to get off altogether. This was a mistake. I am too cautious. Too slow. Too old. Yet I pedal on as the hours go by.

Foolishly, I begin to cry. I look at my odometer. I have gone twenty-five miles and I'm tired. Every muscle hurts, not from pedaling, but from tension. I see myself swept along in terror until my heart gives out. I see my bicycle drop and unsuspecting bikers pile up in a chain reaction, not seeing me until it's too late. Like the old lady with the shopping cart.

I'm thirsty. Others tip water bottles at full speed, but I know my balance isn't good enough. The sun is straight up now, and humidity settles like dew on my already sweat-soaked body. I have to go to the bathroom.

"Rumbles!" A shout from up ahead. Bikers veer to the left and to the right, exposing a speed bump made of strips of concrete. Afraid to leave my lane, I bounce over it at full speed. My neck creaks, my teeth shake, my bladder leaks. I hear laughter and it makes me mad enough to demand, "On your left." It works, and I'm one lane over. Five more "On your lefts" and I pull off onto the shoulder.

I look at the flawless youth straining toward the next town, and the next, eyes on the pavement, shoulders hunched, bodies conforming perfectly to the laws of aerodynamics to maximize energy, save time, create speed, get there first to see who can drink the most beer. No thank you. I toss my bicycle in the ditch, grab the water bottle, and make for the cornfield.

I wade through head-high green leaves until I'm a million miles from the ride. I guzzle water. I pee. I drink and pee at the same time. Finished at last, I discover my knees are locked into a squatting position. An ugly grasshopper leaps at me, convinces me I can stand. I find a spot where the corn is thin and I lie down on the fragrant earth to sleep. Or die. I don't care which.

I awake looking up at the crones on Mag and Addie's T-shirts.

"We saw your bike," Mag says. "Are you OK?"

I'm about to resign when Addie says, "Wow, did you take off. We thought you'd be in Spencer by now. How's it feel to be a jock?"

"You mean joke."

"How long were you asleep?" Mag asks.

I look at my watch. "About an hour. You two just get here?"

"We just happened to see your bike. I thought we were going to stick together," Mag said, resentful now that it's obvious I haven't had a stroke.

I struggle to my feet and lead the way out of the cornfield, try to control my disappointment that my bike hasn't been stolen. "Look, I don't know if I can ride any more," I start to say, but Addie is still shaking her head in disbelief. "Do you realize how far ahead of us you were?"

I think. I was an hour ahead of them. I check my watch and odometer. I have ridden thirty miles in a little over two hours, on a treadmill my aging heart was not designed to endure. Yet it had endured. I realize something else. "I'm starved."

"Come on," Mag says, "I just saw a Sweet Corn for Sale Two Miles Ahead sign."

I get on my bike and follow, shaky and clinging to the rough shoulder of the road.

"On your left, honey." A grey ponytail beneath a scarlet helmet, thighs of pure cellulite, a wrinkled face turned blissfully to the eastern horizon. She moves around me and in her place is a young man with a beard on an ancient touring bike with a sign, Gears Are for Wimps. A couple ride tandem, pulling a homemade cart with a sleeping child. Fifties music hits me like a shot of adrenaline as a teenager passes, a boom box on wheels in tow.

A pothole yawns before me, and I steel myself to change lanes. Palms sweating, I cry out, "On your right," and miraculously, a place opens up for me. "Thank you," I say to an elderly man on a recumbent bike who drifts by with his face turned upward to billowy clouds.

"You're quite welcome, young lady," he replies. Apparently,

here at the end of the line, there's room for amenities.

A group of six comes along, dressed in black-and-white spotted jerseys with little rubber horns attached to their helmets. Cows. They laugh and call out to one another. A pink rubber swan behind a biker's seat. A kite attached to a fishing pole attached to handlebars. No one seems to care when they get to Spencer or if they get there at all. It's just like that annual spoof on the Tournament of Roses, the Doodah Parade. Everyone is having fun. I'm having fun. There's a conspicuous absence of spandex, and I wonder where all these people were last night. Why didn't I see them then?

I look at Mag on my left and Addie on my right. "A piece of cake," Addie says, just before they both swerve to avoid a speed bump. On purpose, I bounce over it and call out a warning to those who come after, "Ruuuummbbllesss." I hear my fragmented voice, like an old sheep baaing, and I laugh. Is that my laugh, that cackle floating over the cornfields, or is it some ancient Baba Yaga riding on my back?

Once again I have left Mag and Addie behind, and I stop to let them catch up. I pull off my helmet to feel the breeze on my scalp, and in the mirror I catch sight of my silver hair. Above my blue eyes and summer skin, it looks good. I notice a turn in the road up ahead and I see thousands of bicycles curving with it, winding over the tender land, the sun flashing on beautiful chrome and metallic color. I move back into that Doodah Parade, and head downhill to the mighty Mississippi, a gentle wind at my back.

Nothing's Been the Same Since John Wayne Died
William Greenway

My world isn't hers, skin
like mocha coffee she climbs
into each morning, air pouring
through her throat clear
as creek water, no line where
brown legs slide into
silk shorts. She's my student
but I'm in class now, aerobics,
flunking in a room of convex
mirrors and dumbbells, though
she's patient, pities me, the
sounds I make for air. It's
hopeless as a dancing bear, Disney
hippo in a tutu, a friend's
father. She wants to pop
candy in my mouth when I do
something right. To her, cigarettes
smell like burning celery, liquor
is shellac, her heart has a slow
beat and sticks to it, she can bench press
me. I sort of pity *her*, daughter
I never had, how far she has
to go, how dirty and heavy.
But she's perfect now, and even
her hard music gets under my
fat, sets my frog legs jumping
in jeans stores.
She's working hard to get me young,
I'm aging her fast, and three times
a week we keep meeting here.

Photo by Marianne Gontarz

Photo by Roger Pfingston

Dance Class
Ann Cooper

Mothers and grandmothers,
we coax our morning muscles
and contort our arthritic toes,
cavorting to throbbing rhythms.
Never mind the beanpole teacher,
younger than our daughters,
who shouts steps and encouragement
and knows she'll never be that old.

Humor is our sustaining virtue.
No pain, no gain, we laugh,
tight thighs are the prize,
grateful we can undertake
routine maintenance for our
sagging, high-mileage bodies.

Inside we are graceful, slim,
and young—recollecting jeté,
plié, and grand battement;
floating in gossamer gowns
across Swan Lake landscapes.
Glimpses in the mirrored wall
show us our lissome body myths.
We are immune to absurdity.

Small boys pass the windows,
grinning. We clown for them—
parody bad backs, pull faces,

confirm their preconceptions
with proof of weird and agéd.
We are witches and doubt not
that stiff, wrinkled, and old
beats the sole alternative.

Getting Older
Jane Aaron Vander Wal

no longer will I try to impersonate youth
cancel my facial with the surgeon's blade
let the wind and sun erode
aging tissue fascinates me

no longer a brittle walking bush am I
my hair shall grow long straight and grey
catching insects for its food
scorning the hairdresser's chemistry

exercise class memories fade fast
into the toes of discarded running shoes
I shall move only when sunlight sucks me out of my chair
anointing my walks
and causing me to bend down over short flowers

Bonuses
Dori Appel

The monthly service charge
has vanished like magic
from my bank statement.
It's because I'm fifty-five,
and it's only the beginning!
In five more years the food co-op
will discount all my groceries,
and in another five I'll qualify for
social security, bargain movies,
vacations at special rates.
Airlines will reduce their fares,
then call my name for early boarding,
the drugstore will fill prescriptions
minus ten per cent, and eventually
the newspaper will send
a deferential young reporter
to take down my advice on life.
Finally, when I am as dry and light
as a dragonfly's wing
and no longer satisfied with
mere discounts and reductions,
I'll slip out quietly,
absolutely free.

Queen of Cards and Powders
William Ratner

It is Sunday, and Saspi is waiting for a man. She has been waiting for two weeks. He works across the street at night as a greeter at Carmelita's L.A. Salsa Club and Dinner House. He is Armenian, but the waiters and parking attendants call him the Cubano because of his pencil mustache, his neatly tailored linen suits, and the fact that he speaks a rapid Spanish like a Cuban. The Cubano sleeps during the afternoons and wakes at dusk to prepare for work as the greeter. But on Sundays he rises early. He stops at Saspi's store to buy cigarettes, and he walks alone to St. Mary's Armenian Apostolic Church.

Saspi sits behind her counter at the International European Delicatessen on Vermont Avenue, surrounded by the fragrance of crushed mint and the sumac, paprika, and sesame on the Armenian pizza and *tahin* bread she can no longer eat. She has just turned sixty, and Dr. Sarkis tells her that fat is her enemy.

It was exactly two Sundays ago that the Cubano caught hold of Saspi's wrist as she handed him his cigarettes. She stared at his thin, umber face, his eyes shaded by thick brows. He smelled of lime and honey. With callused fingers and the elegance of an older man he stroked her palm, white as eggshell. They stood like this for some time, drifting between softened breaths. Then the Cubano withdrew his hand, and saying nothing, he left.

Saspi dresses by her mirror and thinks of the firm cut of his jaw. She wants to place her hands there. She dreams of being with the Cubano, lying with him in straw, in sunlight.

She hopes that her friend Maria Theresa will not ask again if the Cubano has come for his cigarettes. She has decorated this poor man with so many lies. This morning in the store she tells Saspi, "He screamed out your name in his apartment last night. I swear to la Virgin. It woke me. He was up there pacing like a wolf. He broke a glass too, probably a blood ritual to win you. He worships you, Saspi. I saw him take a picture of you with his Instamatic. Don't let him down. Ah, to hell with him, don't let me down. I've put a lot of hope into this, girl. I have a friend from the botanica I'm going to bring over. She can help get you the Cubano."

Soon Saspi will walk the half mile to St. Mary's in hopes of seeing him. This makes her want to eat. She eyes the tins of baklava and raisin cookies and sips her coffee. Coffee has become her pleasure. She has rearranged the shelves so that the Plexiglas bins of coffee beans are closer to her, and she can reach in and stir them with her fingers and smell the sooty black Turk Kahva she imports to make the little cups of Armenian coffee for her customers—old men who claim her coffee gives them renewed sexual prowess, immigrants who crowd around the cash register and discuss the Armenian earthquake, churchgoers who boast about their grandsons and drop coins into the plastic donation box on the counter for the children of Armenia and Karabagh.

Dr. Sarkis walks through the door. His suit coat is always buttoned even on the hottest days, and he carries his backgammon board—a tiny attaché case covered in scuffed tawny leather with burnished hinges. He opens it and fingers the round wooden game pieces as if touching a lover.

"You seem disappointed, Saspi. Were you expecting someone else? You're dressed like you're going to a wedding."

"I'm closing up soon. I'm going to church."

The doctor feigns a shocked expression. "Did an archangel come to you in your sleep? What about your customers?"

"They can get coffee over at McDonald's."

"The Sunday brunch at church is fatty, Saspi."

"I'm not going there to eat."

"Why are you going?"

Saspi glances at the avenue. Mist is burning off under the midmorning August sun. Rusted white security gates are stretched across the front of Carmelita's. She is weary of Dr.

Sarkis. He proposed marriage to her over a year ago and only a month after his wife died. Saspi suspects the woman probably expired from all the cleaning, polishing, and laundering he required of her.

"I'm going to hear my sister sing in the choir, Doctor."

"Nahreen's been singing in that choir forever."

"So she's had time to get good; I should hear her sing."

Saspi steps behind the deli case and busies herself preparing the doctor's cup of coffee.

"Be sure not to stir it, Saspi; you'll disturb the sediment."

She removes the stainless steel *cezve* from the flame and pours the sugary black liquid into his cup. When Saspi was a child her mother told her that the best weapon against a lecture from a man is silence, not the silence of obeisance but simply to ignore him in the hope that his need to commandeer the ship, as she put it, might subside. Passing sixty means that Saspi will probably have to endure even more lectures about blood sugar, fat-to-muscle ratio, the chastity of older women.

Saspi's husband, Seto, has been dead for nineteen years, yet the memory of his lectures is as fresh as the headache that has begun to fill her brow. Seto gave advice until the day he died of prostate cancer at age fifty-one. In a small double room at Queen of Angels Hospital, with plastic tubes taped to his nose, liquids dripping into bruised punctures, he declared, "The store must be free of clutter, or the business will evaporate like tea in the desert."

Seto was like a Chinese fortune cookie; open him up and there was always a message inside. Saspi wished one of his tubes contained a sleeping potion, a strong one.

"No one thinks for themselves anymore," he continued. "Armenians born over here are too influenced by their women. Our son is eight years old now. You will have to teach him some discipline. It's always been lacking in your family's blood."

A long silence followed. Just as she thought he had fallen asleep he muttered, "Sex for a widow is unthinkable." With that Seto fell silent one final time and died.

Outside St. Mary's Armenian Apostolic Church teenagers are gathered around tables buying and selling CDs and cassettes of Armenian music. In the parking lot men are talking in the shade of the Chinese elm. She does not expect to find the Cubano here. He holds himself apart from others. Whenever he comes to the store he is quiet and alone. Saspi's friend Maria Theresa who lives in his building says she has never seen the Cubano bring anyone home to his apartment.

Saspi climbs the granite steps of the church and enters the sanctuary where her footsteps are muted by thick burgundy carpet. Slow, cheerless chords of the pipe organ mask whispers of the congregants. The stained glass windows are like illustrations from a children's Sunday school text, possessing none of the majesty of the cavernous stone cathedrals of Constantinople and Yerevan where her mother took her and Nahreen as children, where light fell to the stone floors from massive windows ignited by rosettes of cobalt, amethyst, and sun.

The church organist sits under the high scalloped ceiling with his back to the mass, pressing the yellowed keys, tapping the wooden foot pedals with his worn oxford shoes. The drone of the organ, a doleful underpinning to her older sister's voice in the choir, brings Saspi a winnowed calm. Nahreen's singing has always sounded like faded aristocracy, a zephyr blowing through heavy silks, the voice of a warrior, perfect in pitch and cadence. Electricity should be shut off when Nahreen sings.

An old woman stares at Saspi. Is it so obvious that she has come in search of a lover? What right has this old one to stare like this? If Saspi encounters the Cubano here, what will she say to this quiet man? She feels like an awkward girl, too dressed up for the occasion. She looks at her patent leather pumps and wonders how many women have broken an ankle looking for a man.

Saspi watches Father Magarian, hooded in velour and dark purple, drift past the altar rail. Does he feel something for the women in the congregation who seem to adore him? When he works in the rose garden behind St. Mary's, does he sweat like other men? Or is his smell always like that of the church, of bread and sugar, of dust and children? Unlike the younger priests, he does not trim his beard; it protrudes past his robe, somber and virile. She imagines the feel of it against her cheek and wonders how many of the other women think of him in this way. A younger priest sings the mass and swirls the incense burner back and forth on its brass chain, teasing the air with smoke.

Nahreen has told Saspi about the women who go to priests—unhappy wives of crippled soldiers, young girls just beginning to menstruate, widows, and whores. Behind heavy oak doors, the priests' chambers smell of sour wines and wells.

When she was seven years old, Saspi said to old Father Sarkissian, "Draw us the devil, Father." The priest led her to her mother in the quiet of an early mass. He lifted her mother's scarf, and whispered something. Saspi reached for her hand, but her mother pulled it away and closed her eyes in prayer.

For the first time in years, Saspi is comforted by burning the thin, white candle for her mother. She remembers dreaming of a house where she and her mother trailed their hands along walls and cornices of spice, and dipped their hands together into barrels of powdered nutmeg and rubbed it into each other's hair—to save their dreams, her mother said. Saspi misses her mother's hickory-colored hair, the lemony sweat on her skin. She misses her sense of order, the way she arranged the bottles and bags of seasonings by size and shape on the shelves and in the neatly papered cupboards.

When her mother spoke she pronounced her words slowly and with care as if a prelude to prayer. She dressed like a gypsy in a long purple skirt of regal wool showing the roundness of her hips, and in a yellow sleeveless blouse like a furious sun. She glowed against the hills. Saspi would clasp her mother's arms and stroke the warm skin, trying to cover it so men would not stare so often.

"Men always lie about their fathers," she told Saspi. "They invent battles they never fought. They'll tell you they rode with thousands of Balkan guerrilla fighters and harassed the Turks."

Saspi wonders if the Cubano was ever a hero. Had he defended their people? Had he ever killed? He was not yet born when Armenian blood of millions soaked into the sand at the feet of the Turks.

For years after her mother died Saspi rubbed nutmeg into her skin and hair at night. When she was a girl it protected her from her father and the harsh way he scrubbed her face with a mildewed woolen rag, against the emptiness of his prayers he whispered by her bed. He addressed God the way he did the accounting for the store, with no thought of perfection or grace, but with a petty tidiness like a forest animal that blindly washes its food in infected water but is satisfied that it is water nonetheless. Her father lived his life with a slate and a rag. Her mother languished in a dream of a house of nutmeg.

The mass has ended. Worshippers drift down a carpeted stairway toward the basement for the weekly Sunday brunch. Saspi doubts that the Cubano is here at all. She feels absurd in this place of immigrants' christenings and funerals.

Crumpled up in the mail slot of the store is a note from her friend Maria Theresa, an invitation for Saspi to come to her apartment tonight. She has invited the woman from the botanica, and promises that she will produce a revelation. Saspi would like that. Instead of trudging upstairs to her own apartment as she does every evening, tonight she will go to Maria Theresa's for a revelation.

She gathers a package of cracker bread, a can of Greek olives, a large piece of feta cheese, and a bag of pistachios. Saspi's husband disapproved of women who drank or smoked. To avoid fights and recriminations, Saspi simply didn't do either while he lived. But tonight she takes a bottle of Polish vodka from the liquor shelf and a pack of filtered cigarettes from behind the counter. It is a hot night and she carries no sweater.

Across the street, limousines and expensive automobiles are pulling up in front of Carmelita's. Bright yellow spotlights make the nightclub glamorous and alluring. She does not see the Cubano. Saspi walks past women dressed in silks, crepe, and chiffon billowing out from their young bodies. The perfumes remind her of nighttime crowds when she was a little girl, carnivals, the scent of jasmine and lilac, confections, and smoke. The glamour of the street disappears as she enters the Hollymount Apartment Hotel and climbs the ratty carpeted stairs. The place smells of lard and cooked peppers.

At the end of the hall, Maria Theresa stands in her doorway wearing slippers and a silk dressing gown embroidered in swans on a Chinese landscape. The apartment looks dark, as though she is not expecting anyone. From inside comes the smell of burning coffee and sage. The furnishings are a few brown plastic laminate tables with matching chairs, bulbous brass-colored lamps, and drab tufted love seats. Saspi empties the groceries onto the tiled kitchen counter.

"I've brought some things for your baby," she says.

Maria Theresa picks up the bottle of vodka and smiles at Saspi. "This is not for the baby."

A pounding comes from the apartment above. "All the time that *vieja* up there is making tortillas!" Maria Theresa shouts at the ceiling, "You're not in Zacatecas anymore, lady. Why don't you buy them at the Pioneer Market like everybody else?"

As Maria Theresa takes three glasses down from the cupboard, a tall, dark-skinned Hispanic woman emerges from the bedroom. She wears the white pants and jacket of a health practitioner. Her left eye appears to wander.

"Saspi, this is my friend, Reina." Maria Theresa places her hand respectfully on the woman's shoulder, guiding her close to Saspi. "Reina has a shop on Sunset, Saspi, *Olo Ochun Botanica*. She gives advice."

Reina reminds Saspi of Romanian gypsies who passed through her village when she was a child. Her grandmother said that gypsies left severed hands underneath childrens' beds and warned that she should never look down there or the lonely hands would leap up and throttle her.

As Reina moves she makes the apartment walls darken. She clasps Saspi's hand and speaks in a deep alto voice, "Your friend Maria Theresa is concerned for you. She says you are fixing to love someone and need help with that." Reina does not move her eyes. One seems to look deep into Saspi, and the other stares somewhere else.

Maria Theresa fills the glasses with vodka, and the three women drink. *"Que sabrosa, que rica,* Saspi. My boyfriends never drink anything this good." Maria Theresa scrunches up her face and shudders as the liquor flows down her throat.

She sniffs the perfume on Saspi's wrist and smiles. "It's time for the Cubano, Saspi. Are you in love with him?"

Saspi feels her face turn warm.

Maria Theresa giggles, "He's as handsome as any TV game-show host, Saspi. He looks like Cantinflas, the movie star."

Saspi leans forward in her chair. "He dresses like a dance instructor. And his mustache looks as if it's made of enamel paint."

"When you are close to him, what happens?" Maria Theresa's face is flushed and beautiful.

To Saspi this is a wonderful new game. "When he comes in the store I want to pull his stubby little ears."

"Take him, Saspi, make him your sweetheart."

"Before he keels over and dies, eh?"

Reina startles Saspi as she suddenly leans forward and puts a match to a small twist of verbena. It is the hour of revelation. She extinguishes the flame with her fingers, letting the fragrant herb smolder in the ashtray. Reina has brought her skills and tangents in a floral cloth bag. She centers a translucent human-shaped candle on the glass coffee table and rings it with small envelopes of powders and a dozen postcards—images of God, saints, Jesus Christ, visions of purgatory and hell. A clear cellophane bag contains a tiny horseshoe magnet, iron filings, sequins, a seed pod, and a drawing of an Aztec soldier atop a horse with the Virgin of Guadalupe perched upon the horn of his saddle. There is a card with photographs of women in bathing suits and sheer peignoirs. Reina places this card in front of Saspi.

She slices open an envelope labeled *Polvo Especial* and taps out into a saucer a powder like a drug the color of talc. "This is *Ven a Mi.*" Reina speaks slowly and without expression. "It will give you good results in love between a man and a woman. Rub it on your neck and chest after you bathe. It calls love to you."

Reina draws her fingertips across the cards as if prompting thoughts or chemistry. She raises the candle up toward the ceiling light. A second, thinner body appears within it, an echo of rose. "When you are drawing a lover closer, you must make a mixture of sugar and honey and pour it over the top of the candle so it dribbles down the sides. A sweetness of love will attract him to you. Put your name four times down the center, at either side of it, and around the head. You burn it three times a day and pray. It represents humankind."

Saspi stares at the candle. The shape of breasts and a penis have appeared upon it. Reina fingers a card of a female figure clothed in pink. "This is la Virgin de la Carridad. You know Santaria? People pray to la Virgin in Cuba. They like her in Cuba. Goddess of Compassion."

"Where do you come from?" asks Saspi.

"I am from the old Managua before it was destroyed in the Christmas Eve earthquake and will never be again."

Reina stares fixedly at Saspi and begins running her hands very quickly over the table, pausing momentarily to point out details in the cards. "My ladies here," she says tapping the cards, "they possess things."

Saspi sees the image of a white jackass grazing in moss, a toad partly obscured by granite, a white owl perched in the crotch of a hill, a dog held aloft by bat wings, its face a Chinese war mask. Eve has loosed the apple. Bosomless nymphs bury their faces in her hair. They are rose dust. A serpent yearns to be her garment. Its jaw grazes her breast.

"My ladies ride serpents like they are lawn toys," Reina declares. "Nobody lies to them."

An etched figure in a high-waisted, caramel-colored gown attends the long chalky corpse of an old woman laid out on a bier of stone and touches her arm. The walls are blood and velvet. A figure is bent over a garden of lilies of the valley. She counts the blossoms among the folds of her dress.

Reina places two more cards in front of Saspi—a photograph of two lovers holding flowers and regarding each other from windows in separate houses, and a drawing of a man and woman chained together by the sea. "They are husband and wife. She is his tormentor. Her lover is splayed out on a rock nearby. His arms hide his face."

Saspi picks up the card. "My husband is dead twenty years and probably still feels tormented."

"The lover in the card is your Cubano," Maria Theresa says, glancing out the window. "He is on duty tonight, look quickly."

On the sidewalk below, the tiny figure of the Cubano ushers people briskly to and fro, helping women on with their wraps, offering his arm, opening car doors.

Maria Theresa pulls Saspi toward the window. "He's walking across the street. He's heading for your place."

The Cubano saunters casually across the broad avenue and peers into the black windows of Saspi's store and tries the locked gate.

Maria Theresa clutches Saspi's hand. "He's come for you, Saspi."

"He's just looking for cigarettes." Saspi's voice sounds tremulous and hesitant.

"No, no. It is working, honey. He's like the little remote-controlled race car I gave my nephew. Just move the joystick and it goes where you want it to."

Across the street the store is shuttered and dark. The Cubano appears to be waiting quietly by Saspi's door. He doesn't lean against the flagstone facade or light a cigarette. He simply stands there, attentive, alert, waiting. He is the picture of Saspi's desires.

"Go," Maria Theresa says urgently.

Saspi walks to the door. "I'm going to meet him." She is surprised at her own words. She wonders if this is another faithless gesture. She watches Reina gather up her cards, gently laying one atop the other. She imagines placing vestments upon Reina's shoulders, long floral gowns, resplendent and rich.

Reina, queen of cards and powders, expounder of the saints.

Saspi opens the apartment door. For a moment she studies Maria Theresa, the Mayan curve to her cheek, the stories in her eyes, dark as alleys. Saspi wonders if she has been lied to all her life. Maybe everyone lives like this.

She crosses the street toward the store, blinded for a moment by the spotlights at Carmelita's. She stares into the violet shadows and feels a warm Santa Ana wind on her face. The sky is a fine net of gauze streaked with black. The trees are healthy and thick with wide yellow blossoms, the yellow of old country weddings. This is a night free of memory.

She Stands in the Cold Water
James Lowell McPherson

She stands in the cold water, facing
south toward an invisible island.
In the Sunday morning quiet
the redwing blackbirds
shuffle nervously in a thicket
behind the beach. The loon
makes no sound at all in its
purposeful passage.

For sixty years and more
she has tested the waters
this way. Soon she will take
the plunge. Intrepid swimmer.
For her there is never
backing out. Never. She will dive
into the salt waves and there will be
friendliness and fellowship and
sisterhood, and a spot of
solitude.

Her landlocked husband, a creature of air
and dirt, leans against a boulder
and watches her. His silence
goes with her, and with the loon.
He guards towel, glasses, sandals.
His heart flutters in the thicket.
He rests quietly at the margin
of the liquid world, waiting.
When she rises, rebaptized,
from the sea, she will find
a harbor here.

Then and Now
Phyllis King

In the beginning
he was light in my arms.
Even in the act of love
I was afraid he would float away.
Only the sharp brush of our pubic bones
made me sure he would stay.
Now heavier with age
we sink into each other.
Comfort of flesh and warm clasp
assure us of permanence.

Sometimes I think
he hates the balding head,
the Santa Claus beard,
the comfortable waist,
that mask the fragile
and elusive spirit
that still floats
lightly in my arms.

Photo by Katie Utter

For an Anniversary
Gailmarie Pahmeier

"Still willingly I rage with you..."
        —*A. Wilbur Stevens*

Love, if I leave our life before you,
take this, my kitchen, as legacy.
Take the cayenne, the andouille,
the boudin, the hard, hard bread.
Serve fresh vegetables steamed
with vinegar, peppers to suck
from their stems, orange spice tea.
Make sure there is ice, chicory coffee.
Give everyone, including children, cloth napkins.
After dinner there should be music,
roll up the rugs and dance.

Love, if I leave our life before you,
imagine me in the arms of a boy
whose pickup truck carries his dreams.
I'll be eating apples, leaving lipstick on cans,
listening to rain-delayed games on the radio.
Love, whatever passes, I promise—
in our old age we will not want.
Here, come here. Taste this.

What Remains
Amy L. Uyematsu

    Older now, the woman is
        guarding the passageway—
              after children have left
      her room, she dances
        watches herself move
           hips and hair
  to this slow saxophoned phrase

retracing the steps
      only lighter now, the blue
curl of melodies she
      can finally call her own—
keeping time
    to the noiseless
        breath, keeping time
   to the jazzman.

The Widow and the Gigolo
Marion Zola

Here we sit dearest, both of us mad,
my love is dead and you're holding my hand.
Who would guess from that devoted gaze—
who but I , the willing victim, knows
the studied artifice that keeps it there?
It's all right, you know, to pose this way for
one another: the young but jaded seeker
after deeper, fuller wines who, in spite
of the arrangement, finds her quite delightful.
I, the mundane widow who, forsaking
pride for pleasure, believes his tenderness.

Last night, when I'd drunk too much and ordered
the band to play on, you echoed my shouts
as if it were the thing to do—clever you.
How long could it have taken to acquire
the art of petty conversation? Speaking
of food and who is here and what is chic
bores me dear. But never mind. Later when
it's dark and those wretched bells keep ringing
I won't cross the Piazza de San Marco alone,
and you, without a better place to go,
may accompany me home.

A Woman Like That
Peter Meinke

His legs throbbed every morning when he got up and stumbled to the bathroom. Rotten to get old, he thought. No good'll come of it. He looked in the mirror at his grizzled face. It's also rotten to be young, he remembered, and tried to think of when he had been happiest. My damn nose is growing longer! Could that be possible?

Daniel Daniels was sixty-eight and had been a moderately successful man, much loved by everyone, as moderately successful people tend to be. For forty years he ran a prosperous florist's shop in Bridgeport, before selling the business two years ago and joining the retirees in St. Petersburg. He had hoped the sea air would take the pains out of his hands and legs.

He was probably happiest in his thirties. He had loved his wife, his two good kids and, briefly, a mistress—Nancy Miller—who was his best friend. There was never talk of divorce, so their affair, though secret, had been a pleasant and companionable exception to the terror and guilt that usually accompany such activities. In fact, the four of them got along perfectly until the Millers moved away. And that had been that. The only real trouble with Daniel's wife, Linda, was her high-pitched voice, which grated on his nerves more and more as the years wore on.

There must have been other troubles, too, but at this point, ten years after her death, Daniel couldn't remember what they were; he remembered instead how pretty she was, how she would skip like a six-year-old when she was happy, how one martini would make her giggly and coquettish.

He had been lonely after she died, and his move to St. Petersburg had been taken partially to throw off this loneliness. He could have stayed with his children, who were married and well enough off, but they had their own concerns and he sensed he wasn't one of their major ones.

Now, for the first time in years, Daniel felt some of that old excitement coming back, and he shaved with care. He was going fishing with Julia Dodson! At least his hands were still steady, not like some of those poor old duffers he'd met sitting on the benches downtown where he went every day for his exercise. He'd walk up and down the pier, sometimes feeding the waddling pelicans, and then he'd play shuffleboard at the Mirror Lake Park in the afternoon.

That was where he had met Julia. Daniel, tall and lean, was naturally coordinated, a notable first baseman with the Bridgeport Bombers (forty years ago! Who the hell was president then?) and, within a month of his arrival in St. Petersburg, had become a respected shuffleboard player. Julia Dodson was one of the regular group of people who came to watch the men play.

Julia was from New Haven; they'd practically been neighbors! She had lived in St. Petersburg for three years, but her heart remained up North. Although she was sixty-two (she said), she looked younger. Her hair was white, piled on top of her head when it was hot, but her skin was still young—energy bloomed through her face and exploded out of her dark eyes. She was small and trim and always managed to look cool, especially among the overweight, red-faced, perspiring dowagers who frequented the park.

Widowed for eight years, Julia had been unable, on her small pension, to keep her lovely house in New Haven, and had come to St. Petersburg because of the gentler climate, which indeed she enjoyed. But the humid summers, the increasing numbers of tourists, and her tiny furnished flat oppressed her.

It wasn't long before Daniel saw her apartment, little more than an efficiency, some distance from the water, but not all that far from Daniel's more spacious quarters in a dignified old hotel. To his surprise, it was tasteless and common. Julia dressed stylishly in a muted, understated way, but her flat was loud, almost garish. The pictures and ornaments could have been won at a country fair, and she served him a cordon bleu meal on green plastic plates.

"You see why I hate it so," she said. "I've always been a house person. This is what the place was like when I found it, and I can't really bring myself to do anything with it; anything decent is so expensive. I'm in here as little as possible."

After that, they always met at his place. They spent long evenings together; sometimes they went out dancing at the casino in Gulfport. They enjoyed that, but it was vaguely depressing, too—just the old folks, doing the old dances: the waltz, the fox-trot, the tango. It seemed unnatural somehow, like premature burial. The young people were elsewhere, at the disco maybe, or the roller rink.

During the day she would walk around the lake with him, and watch him at his afternoon shuffleboard game. They went fishing a few times off the pier, and he would gallantly bait her hook and unhook the fish, usually flipping it to a pelican. They could see the fish jumping in its gullet—now *that's* premature burial, he thought. One day she caught a large striped sheepshead; he cleaned and filleted it, and she cooked it ceremoniously in his kitchen—candlelight and white wine, brandy and coffee.

Daniel had never been a particularly sensual man, but he was still virile and the lovely young girls walking along the pier would sometimes surprise him by bringing tears to his eyes. Why tears, idiot? Because the girls were no longer for him, he supposed; because they never even saw him. And because they would get old, too, sooner than they thought.

Prostitutes sometimes hung around outside the bars near the pier, but Daniel was afraid to approach them. Suppose they were diseased, suppose he accosted a plainclothes policewoman? He fantasized the headlines: "Old Geezer Arrested." "Disgusting Display by Senior Citizen." "Seamy Seaside Sex." So he had remained celibate.

But on this evening of the candlelit dinner—he had shaved so carefully!—Julia had stayed overnight. She seemed a little tipsy, and maybe he was, too. They had danced to radio music, and he kissed her. They were standing by the open bedroom door. She looked at him a long time, smiling.

"Daniel Daniels," she said. "What a funny funny name name." She smiled some more. "After all," she said, "we're not children."

The next morning, looking at her, he thought his heart would crack open. She looked so fragile, so small and vulnerable. How lucky he was, at his age! But when she awoke, he only joked.

"This is obscene," he told her. "I'm sixty-eight years old. I'm liable to have a heart attack."

Julia laughed. "Grow old along with me, the best is yet to be." She leaned back on the pillow and rolled her eyes. "And besides, old goats like you don't have heart attacks."

"What happens to us?"

"Old goats like you disappear into the woods or mountains and are never seen again, except from a distance, where you seem to be dancing or doing something illegal with some creature or other."

"I think I'll do something illegal with you right now."

"Oh, I hope so!"

So their affair had begun. They were just like kids; for six months they had been inseparable. They had discussed marriage, they discussed "living in sin." Daniel asked her to move in with him, but she wouldn't. She had an *idée fixe:* she wanted to live in a real house again, like real people.

He was uneasy with this idea, but in some ways the timing was right. Her flat was unsuitable, certainly, and his hotel had fallen on difficult times. There were strong rumors that it was going to be remodeled into an office building, and Daniel and the other residents would have to move—a very discouraging prospect.

But to take on a house! It wasn't the money—Daniel was by no means tightfisted, though this would severely deplete his savings; rather it was the work involved. He didn't want to maintain a house, put washers in leaky taps, clean out the gutters, mow the lawn. Hotel living was easy—all those little jobs are done for you.

Julia, however, had made up her mind, and her enthusiasm was catching. "Just the two of us, with our own property again! A garden and privacy, and a place to be proud of."

She took the lead, and followed the ads, and contacted the owners and real estate agents. They looked at dozens of places, but nothing appealed to her.

One day she came to his room, shining with excitement. "I've seen the perfect house," she said. "The owners are away but the real estate woman has given me the key. We can go and see it this morning."

They drove there in Daniel's car. Julia had no car; in fact, she seemed to have almost no worldly goods whatsoever.

And the house *was* lovely. It stood in a winding, tree-lined street on the outskirts of town. There were azaleas and camellias and jasmine in the front garden, which was cottage-scale and manageable, instead of the usual sprawling lawn. Inside, Daniel could see why it appealed to her. It was furnished with rocking-chairs, deep soft sofas, old desks, bookshelves; exactly what he knew she wanted. He had to admit that the house was just like her, right down to the furnishings.

But there were many drawbacks. It was in bad condition and needed a lot of work. It was more than he wanted to spend. It was a long way from the nearest supermarket, and the public transportation was unreliable—which was all right with Daniel, because he had a car and enjoyed a morning jaunt to the shops. But how could Julia get around? They'd need another car.

None of this disturbed Julia. "It's perfect for us!" And she swept him up with her until he agreed: It *would* be wonderful. He made an offer on Wednesday, the sale being somewhat complicated by the absentee owner, named Haworth, but before too many days passed all the papers were signed, all the checks handed over (with a faster beating heart), and the keys given to Daniel.

Julia had stayed away, perhaps out of delicacy, from these financial transactions. And she had so much to do: some shopping, some packing, final arrangements with her apartment.

Daniel was to pick her up the next day; they would begin moving in, and then next week (or next month—whenever they felt truly ready) they would be married.

He couldn't sleep all night: he was already feeling like a newlywed. He noticed his aches and pains had seemed to gradually disappear since he had known her. He got up early and bought a huge bouquet of white chrysanthemums (her favorite) from one of the corner flower girls—giving the puzzled teenager a five-dollar tip and a moony grin—and walked to Julia's apartment complex. Her place was on the third floor. He hiked up and rang the bell.

There was no answer. She always was a late sleeper, but today was a special day; Daniel found himself a little irritated. Then he thought, "This is the first time I've felt irritated in six months. Not bad. I used to live with irritation, an oyster with his pearl."

He strolled down to the pier, the chrysanthemums held high in his hand like an Olympic torch of love, and smiled idiotically at everyone who came by.

At lunch time he went back again, but she still didn't answer. This is getting ridiculous, he thought. He walked over to the Sandpiper, where they often met for lunch, then drove out to the house. *Their house.* He went in and opened some of the windows; they were casement windows and not all of them worked. He phoned her apartment: nothing. Daniel was beginning to worry. He didn't like surprises.

Finally, he drove back to her apartment and waited. When she hadn't returned by six o'clock, he went downstairs to the caretaker's room, but he was also out. In desperation, Daniel climbed back upstairs and knocked on the door of the apartment next to Julia's. A plump, middle-aged woman opened the door.

"I'm sorry to trouble you, but I'm looking for Mrs. Dodson."

"You must have the wrong apartment. I'm Mary Buxton." She fluttered curling false eyelashes at him.

"Yes, of course," said Daniel. "What I mean is, I thought you might have seen her today."

"I don't know any Mrs. Dodson." She put her hand on the

doorknob.

"She lives next door. I thought perhaps you'd know her."

"Oh, no, Sally Williams lives there, but she isn't there either. She's away a lot." Flutter, flutter. Daniel resisted an urge to shake the curlers out of her hair.

"Julia Dodson. She's a small lady with long, white hair, usually done up like this." He made vague gestures over his head, forgetting he was still clutching the chrysanthemums.

Mary Buxton smiled. "Oh, you must mean Julie Haworth. She stays here sometimes when Sally is away. Keeps an eye on things, you know. I've had coffee with her and Sally."

"Haworth?" He remembered the name. "Julia Dodson doesn't live here?" His brain was beginning to spin.

"No, Julie *Haworth*—it must be the same person, a very pretty little lady, she lives in a house somewhere but she hates it. All she wants to do is move to New England somewhere, but nobody will buy her house and she has no money. She really hates St. Petersburg. I don't know why she came in the first place. I like it here, myself, even though..."

Daniel's voice was shaking. "Do you know where she lives?"

"No. Somewhere on the edge of town, out in the boonies. Lots of trees, she said. Have you seen it? Why did you think her name was Dodson?"

But Daniel had already turned away. He ran outside, limped down the street, and turned blindly toward the pier, sitting down on one of the benches there, still holding the chrysanthemums.

After a while, tears ran down his face, but he was surprised to find that he was smiling, too. Dammit! She sold me her own goddamn house! What a woman!

Various plans whirled through his head: Go after her, bring her back; go to the police; go after her, wring her sweet neck. Put the house on the market, burn it down. Keep it as a souvenir. A young girl jogged by, her feet hardly touching the ground.

He had been a fool, certainly. Still, his heart went out to her. He understood her perfectly. Someone had said the hardest thing to understand about life is that we can understand it so well. The audacity of it! The bravery! If he ever found another woman, which was unlikely, Daniel wanted a woman like that.

    He sat there as evening rolled in over the bay, the bright sailboats fading in the dark. Pelicans edged toward him, looking for handouts. He tossed the chrysanthemums over the railing. In the black water they began floating away from the pier, like sea anemones heading home.

Papier-Mache
Mary Elizabeth Parker

Ellen rose awkwardly from kneeling before her bedroom chest and caught a glimpse of herself in the closet mirror: She looked like a ship's survivor grabbing at flotsam. Her face was smudged, her hair was unpinned. A flimsy carton of six harmonicas, district issue from 1963, was clutched in one hand, and clutched in the other was a Christmas apron handsewn for her by someone's mother.

An Amy's mother, she thought she remembered. The apron was pristine, still folded in tissue paper. She tied it around her waist. The white organza scratched and pricked her nose with must. She ran her palm down the appliquéd holly on the pocket, honoring Amy's mother's gift thirty years too late.

But she had to work steadily and try not to think, just move methodically from chest to bureau to closet to clean everything out. Jill would be here soon to start removing furniture, and Jill wanted anything else gone.

"Just keep the essentials, stuff you can't live without," she had said, and Ellen wondered if her daughter had any idea what that meant. Jill herself owned a nearly bare apartment, a motorcycle, a closetful of purple shifts, and a daughter, Augusta, three, as black-haired and sturdy as herself. Jill would make short work of this room, six trash bags and done, Ellen knew. Which was why she had refused to let Jill help.

Her own hands were moving more and more slowly in their task, as recesses of closets and drawers continued to yield shy loot: scribbled drawings and crayoned Valentine's cards, penciled scores of holiday songs she'd written for students to sing. She pored through the pile and found her favorite. "I wish I were one of Columbus's men, sailing over the blue," she sang tinnily to the room, "I wish those days could come back again, sailing over the blue." It sounded thin with no child's voice joining in. She'd teach it to Augusta, then, when they were all living in Jill's house; there had to be some way to fit in there.

Snow was still trailing down outside, and she scooted herself over to the window to rest her forehead for a moment against the icy panes. She wiped her perspiring face with the fancy apron.

There was so much here, it seemed as if she had kept everything: broken pairs of scissors, nubs of chalk, a district commendation from 1978, warnings not to requisition too much paste, stacks of spelling papers, stubby black pencils. She sat squarely in the middle and ran her hands over all this sea of objects, as if to raise from them some kind of Braille, a meaning. Finally, she took one harmonica from the package of six, for Augusta, and raised her hand over the trash bag to dump the rest.

Then she stopped for a moment. She didn't want to pare down further. She'd felt just fine living with all these objects, like acorns tucked into the niches of her apartment, still fat with possibility. Even though Arthur had been gone five years, she had not been too lonely, with her teaching. And although his hospital bills had eaten a large chunk of savings, she had managed all right since retiring last year.

But mother and daughter living together, she would never have dreamed that in her worst nightmares. Still, there was no help for it: Her certificates of deposit were failing as interest rates dropped further, and Jill had no money either—just too much expensive space after the divorce. Ex-husband, Tory, career army, was posted in a desert somewhere. She, Ellen, was being shunted in to take his place.

Ellen groaned at the thought of the bedroom in Jill's apartment, the ceiling—that had once been a modest white—sloppily painted with stars like a captured cosmos. Where on those electric-blue walls could her lace samplers make any kind of statement? How could she drape her cream-and-melon afghan over Jill's leather couch which was smudged with fingerprints? She imagined her bath set, blue cabbage roses on white, grimed by Augusta's hands in Jill's red bathroom with its gunmetal tub.

Then, in a shoe box stuffed with milk money receipts, Ellen

found the directions for making a pig. Like the papier-mache pig which had stood on her desk for twenty-three years, with her name looped around it in lavender script: Mrs. Lyles. Students had shanghaied it often, tucking it under their skinny arms and hauling it around the room, then perching it on top of the history corner, so that George Washington wore a pig on his head.

Ellen sat back on her haunches, forgetting that this was not a position she could rise from gracefully anymore. She reached for the phone on the bedside table and called Jill.

"I hope you're ready," Jill said, before Ellen could even get a word out. "I've got the van from Gerry, but I have to bring it back tonight. It's not going to be easy hauling stuff through this snow."

There was a random, scraping background noise as Jill spoke, and Ellen could see her daughter knifing crumbs out from a crack in the tabletop, or using a matchstick to poke mud from her boot soles. She had never in Jill's life seen her sit still.

"I'll help you move as much as I can when you get here," Ellen said, "but it's got to be later. There's something I forgot to do. Give me two hours," she said, and hung up.

Dipping and laving until the strips came out shining, she prepared newspaper strips in a bowl of thin paste. It was a dreaming motion, as smooth and deliberate as the snow arcing past the kitchen window. Then, aware of each dip of her too-pale, fleshy wrists, she laid the strips the length of the kitchen table. She had already fashioned a wire frame, with scraps gleaned from the utility cupboard.

Now, she held the wire head lightly and laid the first strips of papier-mache over it. It had been a long time since she'd worked like this. The menagerie of animals she'd formed for her first students—lamb, ostrich, alligator, pig—were all probably smashed to powder somewhere. As she built up this new pig's head, eye sockets and jowls and protrusion for a snout, her hands remembered the first pig she had designed years ago.

It had been feminine, round, painted pale pink and then etched with blue violets. She'd had a rough job to keep one of the boys from squeezing it, loving it too hard, when it was brought into class. Jill was like that boy, almost. Even now as an adult, Jill had clumsy boy's hands. Hands that checked the riggings for new bungee jumpers, then her own rigging before she flung herself out on the sky. What if Jill died that way, a demonstration leap, and she, Ellen, was the one left to raise Augusta? But she didn't want to think of that now. Make this pig, she told herself, just do it. She was building up the fat body now, the old rhythm fully alert in her hands.

She wrapped the last gummy strip around the belly of the pig. The pig was pale and wet, still newsprint black-and-white. Ellen's palms rested lightly on the pig head, as if it were a child's skull. Then she heard Jill drive up below, the tires of the van backing and scraping.

Jill burst into the kitchen and Ellen watched her appraise the piles of things still unsorted, unpacked. "I can't believe it, Elly," Jill said. "What is this? You were supposed to get this stuff out of here."

Ellen didn't answer. Although she was by now used to the familiar "Elly," it was still not the way she thought a mother should be addressed.

Without glancing at the pig, Jill marched through the still-cluttered apartment, her high-heeled boots pocking the floor with icy mud, a pacifier bobbing in her mouth. Jill was trying to quit smoking, and pacifiers were stylish, very de rigueur in California, she had said.

Augusta came behind Jill, swaggering too, even though her small, fat legs were still encased in snow pants. Copying her mother, Augusta stuffed paper scraps into trash bags. Then she swung around to Ellen for approval, her eyes shining. Her hands grabbed at a knickknack shelf for support and a cut-glass dragonfly slid off the shelf and broke. Shy now, Augusta brought the dragonfly to Ellen, poking the leg into the broken-off place to try to make it fit.

Then Augusta's eye was caught by the pig. She climbed

onto a kitchen chair and wrapped her arms around the pig. "I like it, Grandma Elly," she said. "It can be my puppy."

Ellen felt another presence at her side. Jill was standing there, no longer stomping around and stuffing things in boxes. "That's not a puppy, Gussie, hon," Jill said. "That's a Violetta Pig. Pretty soon, it'll have violets all over—little blue flowers." Jill was wearing a half-smile that worked oddly around the pacifier in her mouth.

Ellen stared. Yes, she had named the pig Violetta. But how had Jill remembered that? Even at that age, Jill was too busy falling out of trees, being the boy that Arthur never had. Now Jill was chucking this pig under the chin, as if the pig could enjoy it. She said, "If you'd made me one of these when I was a kid, I wouldn't have ruined it, you know. I tried to make a cat once on my own, but I couldn't get the tail to stay on." Ellen tried to imagine Jill's hands shaping a fragile length of wire. She looked at her large, forceful daughter, and at Augusta, who would probably be as forceful. Then she gently moved Augusta's thumb, which was pressing down against the pig's still-not-cemented ear, and looked around the kitchen for a clean cloth to drape the pig. There were three remaining boxes to be filled, and the pig could balance in one. It was still snowing, but if they went down the steps carefully, maybe nothing would break.

Photo by Teresa Tamura

Spring Cleaning
Sharon H. Nelson

The skeletons we keep in the closet
come out from time to time to clank their bones.
These are the ghosts we've settled with,
reminders of old wounds, lessons learned, tucked away,
out of sight, out of mind.

We push them back amongst the jumble,
try to keep them pressed down under
the out-of-season blankets,
equipment of sports we no longer practice,
the pile of too-good-for-the-rag-bag clothes we thought
we'd wash and iron and take along
to the church bazaar or crisis centre.
But we seldom get to it, to that final job
of tidying the bottom of the bottommost cupboard.

Some of us are organized, efficient.
The skates and football helmets our children outgrew
were traded in or up or out years ago.
We are frugal; *waste not, want not.*

Our minds are full of these old adages
we learned to keep in store,
along with strange, no longer useful bits:
great-grandmother's tissue-wrapped muff,
granny's rusting fruitcake tins,
annually inspected and ruefully rewrapped,
repacked, replaced, a set of things
our childhood fancies linger in.

Past and future coalesce
in objects worn but not worn out,
the lines and things we learned to keep,
in the keeping of which we learned to acquiesce.

Perhaps it's wool, or bolts of cloth, or the family silver.
There's always something in there,
something with some weight to it,
something at the backs of cupboards,
to hold down the visions we cannot afford to see,
that we overlook most purposefully.

We are creatures intent on survival,
single-minded, focused. Our mothers told us:
what you don't know can't hurt you.
Our mothers were liars, liars all.

They had cupboards too, and never told
what they kept there. Instead, exemplary, they taught
good housekeeping; amidst the neat and clean, they allowed
that every woman needs her special drawer
for hat pins, bits of string, and souvenirs
and a single cupboard for long-term storage,
a place to hide what won't fit in.

At the backs of our mothers'
messiest cupboards
our lives begin.

Harvest
Shirley Vogler Meister

With gusto, she plunged her hands
into pumpkin pulp, pulling
and scooping until the innards
and seeds slipped loose, and juice
ran down her arms in yellow trickles:
she didn't know she was purging pain.

Watching his wife, he finally felt
the scraping and cutting—the wounds
of the flesh—as if they were his own;
three decades of floods and droughts
on the grounds of marriage come
to harvest in a Hoosier heart
distracted by family pressures.

Newly-made bread and apple butter,
hay barns warmed by cattle breath,
farmwork under a waning sun,
tall purple phlox fading into fall,
pumpkin pies cooling on Halloween—
keen sensations blend into panic
and urgency, like the need to secure
the livestock before a blizzard hits.

Too late, too *tired*. Emotions sleep
like fallow fields, yearning for new
springs, new dreams: winter follows
autumn, and the pungent pumpkin
is frozen in plastic, waiting.

Spring without Burpee Seeds
Jean Blackmon

Every spring I take stock.

I look around my village to see what we might have lost since this time last year. The feed store still sells baby chicks. Someone plowed the fields at the north end again, and buds are swelling on the apple trees.

At my store, the Frontier Mart, we still sell asparagus gathered from along the irrigation ditch, and children still buy jacks, jump ropes, and kites. But near the door between the Popsicle freezer and the fifty-pound dog food, the garden seeds are gone.

Last year I received a letter from Mr. Burpee saying we hadn't sold enough to warrant his sending more. I miss getting the big parcel where tab A slid into slot B, and all that cardboard folded magically into a display of snapdragons and four-o'clocks, zucchini, carrots, and lima beans.

No sooner would I assemble the display than old men in coveralls would come to read the seed packets, to talk about sunlight, soil, and water requirements, to count the days until maturity. They fingered the envelopes like kids at the candy counter, then carried their selections away like packets of promise.

Three of my seed customers were Ramon and Julio Tenorio and Walter Ackerson. Maybe a storekeeper shouldn't play favorites, but in nineteen years of business, Ramon, Julio, and Walter are at the top of my list.

They grew corn and cabbage and raised pigs. Ramon and Julio were brothers from one of the old families. On spring mornings Julio and his horse, Smokey, plowed the field at the corner of Tenorio and Corrales Roads. Walter was a cowboy who had come down from Colorado in the 1940s. He's the only eighty-two-year-old I've known who rode his horse every day.

Ramon and Walter were best friends who traveled together. When Walter's car wouldn't start, they rode to my store on a tractor with Ramon in the driver's seat and Walter standing alongside. They bought Jimmy Dean sausage, single-edge razor blades, and shaving cream in a cup with a bristle brush. Heading home, the old tractor crept along the two-lane road at fifteen miles per hour, and cars moved into the left lane to pass. Traffic was light then, tractors commonplace.

On Friday nights when I saw Ramon and Walter's tractor parked at the Territorial House, I'd stop and find them in the bar. Ramon talked about family and farming; Walter told about his days as a cowboy on the Black Ranch. Around eleven I'd say, "Time for me to go. You guys behave."

Ramon looked offended. "I *always* behave," he said. "I work hard and when I go to church, I keep my eyes off the young girls."

Walter snorted and mumbled something about blowing smoke.

Julio, Ramon, and Walter haven't been in the store for a long time now. We didn't mark their last visit or say good-bye. One day we just realized they hadn't come in.

I'm told Julio and Ramon died more than a year ago, and Walter's gone now, too. I think of them whenever I think of spring and farming and Burpee seeds. It makes me look around to see what is missing. Then I memorize what we have left in case it turns up missing next year. What I'm trying to say is, if I'd known it was my last Burpee seed display, I would have paid more attention.

Photo by Eliud Martínez

Sam, At Sixty
Pat Schneider

He opens the front door with the force of a minor hurricane, the great bulk of him led by his belly, which is held in only metaphorically by wide, red suspenders. His face is bushy with beard; he feels like a warm version of the north wind, all blow, hair going white, beard wild with curl. His cap is blue with a protruding bill and white letters proclaiming, Friends Don't Let Friends Drive Fords.

"Hell-*o?*" he yells, the last syllable lifting, a question. Under the red suspenders, an orange tomcat grimaces on his T-shirt above the words, Gimme Coffee, Nobody Gets Hurt.

He brings what I have lost: Ozark country humor, sausage and milk gravy, biscuits, cornbread, lightning bugs at dusk, a million grasshoppers at noon.

He has left his truck's motor running, parked as far onto my lawn as the oak tree will allow. "Had a delivery in North Adams," he says, planting a wet, mustached kiss on my mouth. "Got any coffee?"

It's a busy day. I have plans. But I would make a pot of coffee for my brother if the world were coming to an end. Because the world we knew together *is* coming to an end, and he's the only one who remembers the day I roller-skated too fast down the hill, how I fell—how he picked me up and called me by my childhood name.

The Gathering
Lois Tschetter Hjelmstad

We sit around a table
in an unfamiliar restaurant—
my brother, my sister, and I
our mates smiling at us
from across the table
our parents (who are eighty-six)
completing the circle

The tinkle of ice in other glasses
the murmur of other conversations
are background to our communion

It has taken a long time
to come to this place
    past the early rivalry
    past the fierce competition
    past the wary friendliness
    past the hurts, both small and large

But somehow
we finally
cut to the chase

We lucked out—
it wasn't too late

I revel in the peaceful knowledge
I sigh for the lost years
I weep for the short tomorrow

Investing
Savina Roxas

I sit, pencil in hand, sorting out different publications on investing for good future returns. Under current holdings in my file, I'll put, "The Mathematics of Investing," and under technical analysis, "Baron's Financial Table."

Regulations, handbooks, and directories I'll put on the bookshelf. The next publication, "How to Draw Up Your Own Will," I won't file or put on the shelf. Better look at it right away. Need a well-documented will for the end of the best-is-yet-to-come years. Don't want the children to have any hassles about it when I'm gone.

If I call Swanson & Phillips, Esq. to draw up the will, it will cost $150 an hour, even just to talk on the phone. I'll take a stab at it myself. I'm sure that's why my brother-in-law is sending me all this stuff. Wants me to be a self-sufficient widow.

Actually, my sole beneficiary should be St. Anthony's Church. Hardly ever see the children. Too busy with their own lives, I suppose. Nothing I say or do brings them around very often.

Since Ed died two years ago, my life revolves around the church: Monday, Christian Women's Club; Tuesday, Bible Study; Wednesday, Tutor a Child in the School Program; Friday, Bridge Club; Saturday, Bingo; and of course, Mass on Sunday.

Then Ed's brother, in addition to all the other financial publications, gave me a subscription to the *Wall Street Journal*. He said, "This'll keep you out of the mischief of buying high and selling low." No doubt, referring to the Pittsburgh Brewing stock I bought at ten and unloaded at fifty cents on the dollar.

It takes great diplomacy to keep from letting him know that I just can't face the daily rundown of facts and figures on investing that appears in the *Journal*. So I'm giving it to my next-door neighbor, Bill, who has time and an interest in that sort of thing. All I ask of him is that he keep me updated on certain stock information to keep me solvent.

That's how I came to develop some interest in my aloof neighbors. In all the years they've lived next door, we've done no more than wave to each other. Lately, I've noticed that Elsie is turning into a grim-faced old lady. Hardly even waves now.

When Bill retired, I thought this might make a difference, make him and his wife friendlier. It didn't. Never see their children or friends coming and going from their house any more. But I do see Elsie going and coming from her daily walk. Often wish I had the get-up-and-go to do the same, just to keep my mind off what I should do to get my children to visit more often. Calling and inviting them doesn't work, too much other stuff on their calendars.

An article in the morning newspaper starts my thinking. Before long, I arrive at a plan that just may jolt my daughter out of her lackadaisical attitude toward me. On Saturday morning, she has the machine take care of the phone calls while she does the laundry. I leave a message about her future. Next, I call the *Daily News,* tell them to have a reporter at the Williamsburg Parkway Bridge at one o'clock for an interesting story. Then I drive up to the bank.

Although the phone rings off the hook several times after I get back home, I do not answer it. At twelve-thirty, I leave the house, the sun bright, the air as clear as it used to be in my East Hampton days. I nestle the shoe box under my arm for the two-mile walk to the Parkway Bridge along a road lined with Norwegian maples. The tall, broad-leafed trees shade the walk nicely. Along the way, a Good Humor truck slows down next to me. I wave him on. Don't need the empty calories, delicious as they may be. I start humming "Rock of Ages."

I arrive at the bridge and start across over the highway. In the distance, from behind me, I hear a woman's breathless voice call out, "Mother, Mother. Don't do it." It's my daughter's voice. I knew she'd come.

Ignoring her, I hurry to the middle of the bridge. Above the noise of the traffic below, I shout, "Why not? Until you invest more time in me, I'll keep throwing it away."

I spew the contents of the shoe box down on the parkway below. Hundred dollar bills fly up, around, and down. Cars stop, a crowd gathers. Some of the bills land at my daughter's feet. The *Daily News* reporter takes pictures and picks up some of the bills, and we talk.

The next morning the *Daily News* carries the story about a woman teaching her daughter how to invest her time. My son now calls me occasionally to take me to brunch after Sunday Mass. And, weather permitting, my daughter joins me for a walk to the Parkway Bridge.

Rema
Sara Sanderson

Busy knitting the seasons,
she changes colors often.
Yarn flying, Grandmother crochets love,
    tying in treasures;
        miles of vibrant tapestry
finery feathered and furred,
jeweled with pine pitch,
dried moss,
emerald lake.
Seashore foam she flings into spirit,
swirled in her white-pine hair.
On wet sand,
in wolf prints,
she marks the way.

Photo by Katie Utter

Pebbles and Crumbs
Ric Masten

last summer
whenever possible
my visiting granddaughter Cara
would worm her tiny hand into mine
and like Hansel and Gretel
we'd strike out from the house
up the "barking dog" trail
to the "creaky swings"—
don't you love the labels
little children put on things?—
and after a few "sky flying"
"watch me Grandpa" rides
it was on to the "sneaky table"
where hidden in the shade
beneath a giant live oak tree
we would split
the forbidden can of Coke I brought
    "damn it Dad her teeth will rot!"

rested and refreshed
we then ascend the "slidey steep"
to check the water level
in the "water keep"
to lift the lid and take a peek
then down the trail in single file we go
through the "witchy woods"
all the way to Arizona
which is what
my spouse has dubbed the shack
she uses as her dream shop and studio

Grandma it seems
also has a knack for naming things
   "if anyone calls
   tell them I'm in Arizona"

next stop—
the family memorial garden
where we solemnly commune with the trees
Kim and Emil have become
chanting softly as we pass
   "from ashes to ashes
   to flowering plum"

then wending our way
along a stretch of "dusty dirt"
we search for yesterday's footprints
covering them with today's
"backward walking" sometimes
   "to fool our enemies
   and friends"

and always during the final leg
of this backyard expedition
my companion lags behind—
little Miss Slowpoke
gathering specimens—
repeating after me the name
of every trailside shrub and tree
"eucalyptus—sticky monkey
lilac—sage—madrone"
and "don't touch that it's poison oak"
then suddenly—"we're home!"

last summer
Cara and I collected
and polished these moments
scattering them along the path
like pebbles
to be used in the distant future
the way a whiff of cigar smoke
brings my grandfather back
to poke about in the garden
with his walking stick
the way
my grandmother's face magically appears
at the taste of peppermint
her watchful presence close at hand
whenever I shake sand
from something that has been to the beach

I know
that on some faraway tomorrow
a sip of cola on a hot day
a pinch of sage
the creaking sound a rope swing makes—
these things with Cara's help
will bring me back to life again

and thankful as I am
for such life-extending crumbs
sadly I also know
that the cigar smoke and peppermint trick
can only be done by me—
in a couple of generations
it all becomes
a banquet for the crows

Instructions for Ashes
Ellen Kort

I will trust you to give away my turtle drum
rain stick   the redwood burl just beginning
to root   Return the borrowed books   old letters
hold me between thumb and forefinger   Drop
my ashes   dark as burnt paper   among chicory

alyssum   wild mint   Let me fall like sunlight
on irises unfolding purple wings   drop
blueward into sea   one salt crystal
the shell's secret core   Feed me

to summer trout   Let the hounds carry me home
through green gape of morning   a burdock
hooked tight   riding the fine mesh of fur
muscle and bone   falling in farmyards
rising up in the cow's small brown hills

crusted and dry   poked by a child's bare foot
Let me be welcome in folded leaves   cherry pit
appleseed   rose-colored moon inside the grape
If there is to be a eulogy   let it be

in the cloud of dust rising from hooves
a scar in some poet's hand   let it be
in riverbeds covered with snow   in the small talk
of birds   clam-colored light of early evening
Let it be one last milkweed pod   spitting seeds

What Faith Is
Lisa Vice

On Tuesday morning, my cat, Tommy, woke up, blinked his eyes in his slow deliberate way, but could not get down off the bed where he always sleeps, curled at my feet. When I lifted him to the floor, he stumbled lopsidedly like a drunk before he fell to his side, panting.

"It could be a brain tumor," the vet said, looking over my shoulder, as if he were addressing a ghost. "We see that sometimes in the old ones." Tommy lay in a heap on the table, crying pitifully, a terrified look in his eyes. With my hands on his thick orange fur, I felt him tremble and shake. I wanted to take him home, where I could press my face to his fur and talk to him properly. But the vet was saying something about tests, a chance of saving him, so I agreed to leave him overnight.

The next morning, the vet called to say he'd lost the cat. At first I took him literally, as if Tommy had gotten out of his cage, slipped out the door, and was on my doorstep right now, waiting for me to let him in.

"We can have him cremated," he was saying. Then I understood.

Every Wednesday, I have lunch with Doreen at the Monarch. Over egg salad sandwiches and iced tea, I tell her about the cat.

"From one day to the next, gone. Just like that." I have the sensation I am watching myself from a great distance. The sun is bright, shining directly into my face through the half-open slats of the blinds and I am glad for this. It gives me an excuse to squint and rub my eyes.

"Jean," Doreen says. "You can get another cat."

"I don't want another cat. I want Tommy. He wasn't just any cat."

"Maybe he was your child," Doreen says. "In a past life." Since Doreen went to that psychic fair at the community college, she's been talking this way, convinced she remembers sixteen of her past lives.

"Maybe," I say. Not that I agree, I just don't know what to say. Then I tell her something she wants to hear. "I have an interview."

Doreen's whole face lights up like a three-way bulb being flicked on, and the skin around her eyes crinkles into hundreds of folds. She squeezes my hand. I haven't worked in years, but I've been looking for a job since that day Doreen dropped by and found me in my pj's at three o'clock in the afternoon. She ran around pulling up the shades, saying, "You have to get a job or something. You need structure in your life."

So every morning I take a shower, comb my hair, then sit with the *Herald* folded open on my lap, circling possibilities: Front Desk Clerk. Bakery Sales. Receptionist. Cook.

"What's it for?" Doreen asks. My last interview was for an office worker-chimney sweep. I could see myself answering phones, swiveling in my chair to do some filing, then rushing off with a top hat on, climbing ladders, perched on a roof. Even though we both knew I was much too old to do such a thing, the young man who interviewed me had been very kind.

"A part-time innkeeper. Some kind of fancy bed and breakfast. But maybe I should cancel. I've got to do something with the cat."

"Do?" Doreen says. "Do? What are you talking about?"

"They said they'd cremate him. But I was reading in the paper how when they cremate your pet and give you a Baggy of ashes, it could be anybody's ashes. A Great Dane or a poodle or a Siamese. They just shove them all in together like it doesn't matter."

"What's all the fuss? The body's just a shell." Making comments like this is part of Doreen's psychic awakening. "It's like a chrysalis we crawl out of when our time comes." She waves up toward the ceiling where paper monarch butterflies dangle, decorating the restaurant.

Every year around this time, after traveling thousands of

miles, the monarch butterflies make their way across the bay to rest in the pine and eucalyptus groves of our town. They fly slowly between the houses, exhausted from their journey. When I first moved here, I thought they would arrive in droves, the sky would darken, the air would fill with the sound of thousands of powdery wings fluttering by. But the butterflies actually drift along, alone or in pairs, buoyed by the autumn breeze.

"You and Nila were like husband and wife, Tommy's parents," Doreen is saying, dabbing at her lips with her napkin.

I choke a little on my tea. My heart thumps so loudly I'm sure Doreen can hear it. "Then you know?" I almost blurt, thinking maybe she really is psychic after all. "Did you always know?" I want to ask.

When Nila was alive, I used to tell her people loved us, they wouldn't turn their backs on us if they knew the truth. But she never wanted to risk it. "I'm not ashamed," she insisted. "I just like having our secret from the world."

"Of course you were roommates this time around." Doreen sucks the last of her tea through her straw. "But you acted just like an old married couple. Who knows? Maybe you were a king and queen on the Ivory Coast. Or an ordinary frumpy couple in Queen Victoria's England. A married couple, I'm sure of it. I wonder how I knew you then?"

My car is out front and after Doreen leaves, I get in it and drive toward Lighthouse Avenue. I took a special course for older drivers a few months ago. Not so much for the better insurance rates, but because I was having trouble. I'd make it to a stop sign, then not know what to do. I couldn't remember where I was headed or who had the right of way. Once I pulled in front of a police car, and he asked to see my license. Now I look ahead, watching for pedestrians, careful of the cars backing out of parking spaces in front of the bank and bookstore. Always ready to yield to the drivers inching forward from the blind intersections.

When I get home, I tell myself that Tommy is not going to rush to the window to greet me. But still as I unlock the door,

I expect him to be there, rolling at my feet, offering his furry white belly. I look in the yellow pages and find the only pet cemetery is in Watsonville. I wonder what it involves to have a cat buried there. I wonder if there are headstones shaped like the pets buried under them. I can't imagine making the call. What would I say first? I sit on the sofa and stare at the ads on the page: Thor's Termite Control. Fleabusters. The Golden Dolphin Pet Shop. I read every word like it really matters to me.

I can hear the tick of the secondhand on my watch. I have another hour before my interview and my clothes are ready, so I lie back on the sofa. I keep thinking I see Tommy out of the corner of my eye, heading toward me. I have to restrain myself from calling out to him. Tommy would always come to me when I lay down. And when I wept he would creep slowly up my body until he rested on my chest, just under my chin.

"Tell me about yourself, while I read over your application," the owner of the inn says. I feel he has already dismissed me. I stare at my hands in my lap, the speech I prepared already fading. All I can think of is how I'm old enough to be his mother. I can hear Doreen in the back of my mind, urging me on, so I smile and speak as best I can.

"We do everything for our guests except polish their shoes," he tells me at one point. "Would you have trouble carrying a tray with champagne and an ice bucket up the stairs? There are a lot of stairs." Most of his questions begin with, "How would you rate yourself on a scale of one to ten, ten being the highest...?" Anything with numbers makes me panic but I take a deep breath. When he asks about my ability to make decisions, I announce in a loud voice, "Definitely a ten."

What must I have been thinking? Just trying to choose between spearmint gum or peppermint can leave me standing at the candy counter at Sprouse long enough for a line to form. But I have nothing to lose.

When I am leaving, a young woman wearing a thin white cotton blouse rushes up the stone steps, her sandals scraping the walk. I have an urge to wrap my arms around her. I am that hungry to touch. To be touched. I think of Nila murmuring into my hair, kissing my neck, her hands moving down my body, familiar as music. Would I really never feel this again? The thought takes my breath away. I lean against the stone wall watching the waves crash on the shore. A huge clipper ship, all the sails unfurled, glides like a mirage toward the harbor.

On the way home, I stop at the vet's. I'm still not sure what I'm going to do with Tommy. He is wrapped in a black garbage bag stuffed into the beige plastic cat carrier. It is unusually light as the boy hands it to me. Tommy was Nila's cat first, but I loved him too. I wonder what Nila would do now. I wonder what she would think if she could see me with a dead cat beside me on the front seat?

"Maybe I should have a Jewish funeral," Nila announced one night. She was driving us home from an Indian restaurant. I remember how it felt to sit in the dark car, to drive past the houses all lit up. I have no idea what prompted the discussion. Lord knows we were both old enough to be making such plans. But we'd never discussed it before. "I hate the idea of a stranger messing with my body after I'm dead," Nila said.

By the time we pulled up in front of the house, we'd both decided on cremation. It was fast, easy, and cheap. "Unless you buy a fancy urn," Nila said. I have often wondered if Nila had had a premonition. Like Doreen did when she dreamt of buildings crumbling the night before the Loma Prieta quake destroyed downtown Santa Cruz. Had she had a premonition? Or had she known all along and only pretended to be healthy? Pretended to be heading toward the future with me by her side?

When I get home, I take the cat out of his box. His body feels like an overripe tomato. I want to open the bag, but not right now. What I do is clear out the bottom of the refrigerator and put him inside. It's such a strange thing to do it actually cheers me up a little, and I take out a beer to help me think. Out the window three wild parrots fly by, their feathers bright green against the blue sky. They scream raucously, as if to tease the neighbor's parrot who screams back from the safety of its cage hanging beside the backdoor. I read somewhere that parrots outlive their owners. I wonder if this is how these three ended up swooping around town, resting on phone wires, calling from trees.

Nila had just celebrated her seventieth birthday. Seventy might seem old to some people, but it all depends on where you stand in relation to it. It seems young to me. But that's because I'm fifty-nine. Old? Ninety's old. But seventy? Nila was active right up to the end, riding her bike on the trails, hiking up Snively Ridge ahead of me.

When we first fell in love, Nila worried that if anyone found out what our relationship really was, she would lose her job. She was a children's librarian, after all. Imagine the scandal, she would say. So we let people think what they wanted all those years, never setting them straight. But when Nila died, nobody knew how to comfort me. They were surprised by the extent of my grief. "The money will be a big help," everybody said when they learned I was her beneficiary. "You can do whatever you want." As if this was what mattered. But it's not money I want. I want Nila. I want to wrap my arms around her soft waist and pull her close. I want to come home and find her on the sofa reading a book and lean over to kiss her. I want to walk down Pico Avenue, our shoulders brushing, our legs in rhythm, as we make our way to the sea.

The next morning, I am sure I feel a warm place by my feet where Tommy always lay. I imagine I hear the murmur of his purr. I get up quickly and go out to the kitchen. Even though there is the black plastic bag at the bottom of the refrigerator, I still reach for the can of cat food. Before I realize what I am doing, I have already filled his bowl. It sits on the counter while I sip my coffee. Outside the wind rattles the eucalyptus leaves. The sky seems to be clearing, the thick fog dispersing like wisps of smoke blowing out to sea.

I take the bag out of the refrigerator and untie the knot, pulling it open to look inside. And there he is. The familiar orange coat, the dark markings I loved to trace. I feel as if I'm unwrapping a fragile gift. There's my good boy. My Tommy, curled at the bottom as if asleep.

"Tommy," I say and pet the cold fur convinced if anyone saw me now they would never understand. They would think it morbid or even perverse. There is probably a law against it, but let them arrest me if they must. I've decided to bury Tommy out back. I put on my sneakers, get the shovel, and begin to dig in the far corner of the lot where Nila used to plant squash. The yard, always Nila's domain, is overgrown, a tangle of oxalis and marguerites choking the lavender and thyme. But the morning glories still climb up to the top of the porch like they have from the first year we bought the house and Nila planted them, fastening a trellis to the railing before the plants had more than two leaves.

"This is what faith is," she had laughed. It surprised us both when the flowers came back, year after year, planting themselves from the thick seed pods that fell to the ground, the vines reaching to the top of the steps, the bright purple blossoms cascading like a waterfall.

As I dig, I have this picture in my mind, as clearly as if I'm watching it projected on a screen. There is Nila in her nightgown, so small, her face deathly pale. I am beside her wishing she would say something, wishing she would open her eyes, give my hand an answering squeeze. One morning she sat up in bed, coughed, and her hand filled with blood. In a week her skin was as translucent as rice paper.

How I wish Nila were with me now, sitting in the red chair, watching me scoop the dark soil into a pile. I pry out a large stone and continue digging, moving rhythmically, as if to the steps of a dance, until the hole is deep enough so that years later, when someone else lives in our house, they won't unearth the bones.

There's a box under the house, just the right size. But first I wrap Tommy in his favorite blanket. Doreen has told me how in one of her past lives she was Egyptian. She was entombed with all her favorite possessions for her journey to the other side. I think of this now as I put in a fur mouse and a crocheted ball, along with a handful of treats, heart-shaped nuggets Tommy loved so much he would stand on his hind legs for one. I fit the box into the hole and scatter soil onto it. The soil makes a thumping sound, then it's just soil on soil, and I pack it down, push it down tight, not wanting the raccoons to come nosing around.

Dust to dust. The words of the funeral come back to me. It's not an end but a beginning. The voices singing "Holy, holy, holy." I remember how Nila and I used to stand in that church, Sunday after Sunday, year after year, side by side, never touching, afraid of offending someone. But in private we had wrapped our arms around each other.

My body is unused to the work I have done. My back aches and my fingernails are crusted and black, but I feel good as I sit on the back steps. I pray, as I have so many times, that Nila will forgive me. She died believing we were the only ones who knew. But the nurse at the hospital had understood. This I am sure of. She never thought for a moment that we were sisters or roommates. She always pulled the curtain to give us privacy and never came around it without stopping first to say a few words to the Italian lady who lay complaining in the other bed. She spoke loudly, as if warning us she was on her way.

When Nila died, I crawled onto the bed, pulling her into my arms. The nurse left me this way for a long time, even wheeled Mrs. Manetti down to the solarium where the TV blared. When she came back, she put her hands on my shoulders. She was a big woman who stood tall in her white pantsuit. She patted my back, murmuring, "I know. I know."

Then she brought towels and a washbasin of steaming water and left me alone. She'd understood, without saying anything, without asking, the way nurses understand the need for mothers of newborns to unwrap the swaddled babies and check every inch. I washed the familiar fingers, the scar on Nila's left palm where she'd cut herself on a broken glass, reaching into the dishpan. The bit of stone embedded in her knee that her mother had said would eventually work its way out. But skin had grown over it instead. I ran the warm cloth across the knobs of her spine, the smooth bones of her ribs, around the mole on her left shoulder and up the back of her neck, my hands sweeping her thick white hair aside. I washed her feet. Monkey feet I called them, and Nila would laugh and use her toes to turn on the radio, to pick pens up off the floor. I washed her, her skin as soft as crepe, and remembered the first time we kissed. How it had felt like coming home.

On the other side of the fence, my neighbor begins to rake his yard. His parrot, excited to have company, reaches its beak through the cage for a kiss. "What kind of bird are you?" the man asks. "What kind of bird are you?"

"I'm a lucky dog. Lucky dog," the parrot squawks. "Where's the cat? Here kitty kitty." Then it does an imitation of a police siren and begins its litany again.

I sit on the steps and think to myself: I loved a woman. And I am glad for this. I try not to regret all the times I never touched her in public. Not even when we were so old it didn't matter. Two old women hand in hand, what's the big deal?

Down in the weeds I see something move. It's a monarch butterfly struggling to fly. I think maybe it's injured and I should try to help, but as I watch, it spreads its wings. They are bright as stained glass, soft as velvet. I watch it lift itself up with great effort, and then I see, clutched in its tiny legs, another butterfly, its wings folded like hands in prayer, hanging beneath as they glide up over the fence.

Doreen would say it is a sign and I suppose it is, but I don't want to think about what it means. Instead I think how in a few minutes I will go inside and sit on the sofa with the newspaper. I will circle all the ads for jobs I will not get. I will not be a baby-sitter. Will not earn four hundred dollars a month delivering newspapers in my spare time. Will never fix anyone's car or drive a school bus. The idea of this makes me feel light-headed, almost giddy, as I head inside.

What do old women talk about if they don't talk about aches and pains and ill health?
Eunice Holtz

They talk about sunsets and the schedules of the moon
    about chickadees and goldfinches at the feeder and they
    check their bird books to identify the female rose-breasted
    grosbeak, and they name one female cardinal "Emily" because
    it's the most beautiful name Edna can think of.

They talk about the changing view from the second floor,
    north window
    about the profusion of impatiens growing outside the door
    about the Deerfield girl's basketball team, win or lose it's
    for fun and teamwork.

They talk about the delightful flavor of the vegetable medley
    served the night before
    about the lack of Queen Anne's lace growing this year
    about the garter snake's comings and goings from under the
    foundation of the garage.

They talk about the long life of a pet tarantula and they sit
    and watch in amazement as it sheds its skin again.

And they talk about volunteering at schools and for
    Habitat for Humanity.

And they remind each other to stop and listen to the wind in
    the tall pines across the road.

They talk about words—words for crossword puzzles and Scrabble and they always keep a dictionary handy to check on meanings.

They share Bible verses that fit current situations.

They share photos of parties and grandchildren and places they've been and they share student notes from recent Elderhostels.

They talk about potted plants and Edna teaches us to watch for the most amazing star within a star, within yet another star of her blooming hoya.

They talk about the positive, and when war and suffering need to be mentioned they remind each other to trust in God's power, still.

They talk about the delight of the changing seasons and they race to tell each other, on certain white winter mornings, to look quickly at the newly frosted world.

They talk of nieces and nephews and of the loving attention they've received from them.

They talk of their children and thank God for their capabilities and thank God for the richness the children bring.

They are quick to report the first sounds of the first spring peepers
    and they find it worth talking about when they hear
    the strange calls of the great horned owl as the young one
    begs food from its mother.

What do old women talk about? When they care about nature and
    all things bright and beautiful, they never run out of
    things to talk about.

But after saying all that, I must say, most of all they share
    a love of silence.

They know it's in silence they can hear best and learn most.

Photo by Teresa Tamura

Retrospective Eye
Katherine Govier

Christopher "Tyke" Ditchburn tiptoed past a piano draped with a Spanish shawl, between stacks of books and prints, and over the spare handwoven rug, intending to switch on the lamp. Seated in the darkness in a mission-style chair was Miss Ditchburn herself. So he thought of her today, as Miss Ditchburn. Erect, she stared fixedly into the winter garden. Her hair was thick and white, short as a man's; her neck was lined and thin, her hands lay motionless in her lap.

"Tyke?" The voice was deep and dry. "I know you're there. No use trying to surprise me."

He reached the lamp and pulled the thin chain. A cone of amber light fell over her lap. The shade was made of tiny gold beads of glass from the island of Murani, in the shallow basin of seawater off Venice. He knew its story as well as he knew his own. The house, the garden, her few treasures: he had come to think of them as his own.

She was nearly blind now, the great photographer. Old age had done that. Her sharpness, however, was undiminished. Impatience, selfishness, hauteur, stronger than ever. That she had agreed to work with him on the retrospective was something of a minor miracle. How Tyke had got lucky, when Professors Sullivan and Moore had been refused—though they were responsible, in part, for her current high standing—he did not know. Of course she was his mother, but that had never counted for much.

"I guess my timing is right," Tyke had said over the telephone grimly. "She keeps promising to die." And the curator had frozen in the midst of her victory leap in her Bloor Street apartment, to stand dismayed: Does Corinne Ditchburn's son hate her? More important, now that she's agreed, she can't go and die on us. Not on the Royal Ontario Museum of Art.

"I wasn't trying to sneak up." He trod more noisily on the

hardwood and put out a hand. The old woman, hard and forbidding and determined, even the line of her arm as it reached for him, seemed to scour him with her unclouded grey eyes. Yet he never knew if she really saw him.

So he's it, Cory thought. At the end of my life, my son the cod has come to record my confession. Why does he look like a cod? Or is he a flounder? I ate one, alive, in Yokohama; it was impaled on spikes at either end and the sides were sliced. So tender with green mustard. She smiled inadvertently. At least I can hardly see him. I'll keep my eyes on the light in the garden, watch how the day lengthens into spring.
"So you're it."
"I'm it," said Tyke. "No, actually you're it. I'm merely the means."

If I could stomach that, I can stomach anything. Now all I have to stomach is myself, since I've decided to do this thing. I said no for a long time. I said no whenever I thought they were interested in me because of Albert Bloom, whenever they said "pupil of..." I said no because I was not a war photographer. I said no. But look. Vanity wins out in the end. Vanity and the need to—

She sought for the words to justify herself to herself. Words were not her medium. Not justify. Not explain. *See.* The need to see it all, one more time.
"Where do we begin?"
"There will have to be a brief biography."
"Whatever for?" snapped Cory. "This is about my work. I didn't agree for you to exhibit my life, only my work."
"We'll leave that then," he said.

He pulled the cords which lowered the blinds, Levolor blinds which could be left down, the angle adjusted by twirling a plastic wand, but which she insisted on yanking up to the very top of the windows. Before she could complain he went on.
"The photographs have arrived from Del Zotto, Barr," he said. "I've got them all in boxes here. We'll have a look through." He drew out a pair of soft white cotton gloves, and pulled them

over his hands.

She had never liked this reverence. Loose, the gloves made his hands cartoony, the hands of a Mickey Mouse. Or sinister, like the hands of a surgeon, someone who performed an autopsy, thought Cory. Forensic surgeon.

He cleared the pine table, long, made of one piece of wood, which had been his grandmother Eliza Ditchburn's pride. With his softly gloved white hands, he opened the first of the large black-latched boxes. Carefully, he lifted the white cardboard folder and put it on the table. He opened it. The thin veiling paper lay over the print.

"I've sorted all the prints and all the negatives starting with the thirties. But I'd like you to look at them, just to be sure they're what we think they are. Can you see, in this light?"

It depended on her mood. She was like the deaf man who won't answer when spoken to but hears a whisper across the room.

"I haven't looked at those in forty years."

Delicate fingered, he slid the large exhibition prints toward her. "Here's what it says," he said, reading.

Fig. 1.
Corinne Ditchburn
Epiphany Fire in Chelsea,
London 1937.
Gelatin silver. 34 x 23 cm.

"It's mounted. Must have been shown before, in New York."

Cory put her long, tendon-striped forearms on the table. Under the light, her face pulled up close to its surface, she scanned the photograph, side to side, up and down. As if she were herself a beam of light, searching, as if she could sense what lay on the paper by exposing her face to it.

Oh, my. That fire. How I loved it. All fires. On the island, burning garbage in old oil drums. Bonfires on the rocks, the orange flames feasting on inky air. When the fire was hot enough, the rocks beneath would crack, making a sound like gunshots.

Perhaps I am an incendiary. Didn't I thrive on explosions? Beginning with the lightning that flung its brilliant web across the Northern Ontario sky, and the small wait, that silence, the intake of breath between light and sound. Praying time: how far away is it? One mile, two miles, three miles, then great bear's growl of thunder.

When I discovered the camera, it was that little explosion that captivated me. An explosion of light on an emulsion of silver bromide, a chemical bath. The shutter went, the black surface of paper was exposed for its split second to the glare of day. And an image bloomed in the blackness.

At first, the landscape was not damaged by these explosions: it still stood. It had been borrowed from, it had been reproduced. I owned the small explosion, I set it, I saw by it. For that fraction of a second when the flash went off, I was blinded, lost. Life stopped. I did not blow anything up. I had merely created. Afterward, there it was: the same landscape, unaltered, except as it would alter normally, the sun having moved a little along its path, the bicycle having rolled out of view, the wind having bent the tree.

It was only later that my camera exploded everything I pointed it at.

Before I ever went to war, I dreamed of explosions. At the munitions plant, those cordite straws that went through my hands, which I cut, and selected, and bundled would, when packed into a shell or a bomb, not stop, but propel the world. I thought of it that way, as a reaction of gases and solids, as a wave, pushing outward, turning darkness into light.

I loved the acrid smell of the cordite, and I loved the men and women who labored over it, the welders who went down into the tanks to mend the breaks in the cast iron. When they lit their torches it was an invitation to disaster. We blessed our foreheads with nitroglycerin every day we didn't work, to keep up our exposure. If we didn't, the headaches came. Crumbled cordite was shed all over the plant; we wore it like stardust.

We never thought we were making death. Not until the night the TNT shed exploded, and in the darkness I searched the runoff ditch for bodies. And when I found one—my first war casualty in Nobel, Ontario—my first instinct was to raise the camera, to capture him. Take him prisoner.

When I went to war, the camera protected me. I wore it like a shield in the face of overwhelming danger. If I was not immune, then I was especially charged, with a task, a name. I was there, Kilroy, my name scrawled on the wall. Corinne Ditchburn pressed this shutter. Despite massed armies, razed cities, fleeing millions, I stopped time for that split second.

Tracer bullets make a white arc on the black sky, as if a razor has sliced the dome and let in a hairline of heaven. When bombs hit, it's so bright that your eyes go black. When you open them, seconds or maybe years later, you only see white—smoke, dust, rubble, refractions. Sound travels more slowly, ricocheting from stone walls and mountainsides, being buried here, echoing there, arriving at last disconnected from its origin. So, blind, deaf, you crouch in the low-ceilinged world below explosions. Some new world is being born overhead, licked with fire, swaddled in smoke and thunder. You are a creature of mud and ooze, a worm. You lie awaiting death, expecting it, even hoping for it, wanting something quick, manageable, a respite. More terrifying is to know that you will not die, that when the darkness seeps off, the smoke has blown past, and the world you knew is gone, you will pick up your dead, and begin again.

Cory came awake in the dark of Toronto winter's early evening; she'd slept through tea time. Her pelvis had been rocked by some spasm, some recollection. Passion, that old dog that barked at her door now only in dreams. Nagging her: had it been a misspent life, after all? Perhaps she ought to have been, as Albert suggested, an anatomist of the senses. "You should be making love for a living," he told her once. And later, when she refused him: "I can't understand why you've given it up."

The sun had come through the January clouds that afternoon, exposing one by one the naked limbs of the birch, the lilac, the flowering crab. Sudden beauty was the best kind, sudden and brief, split second. It ambushed the barricades and twisted the heart. The sun often came through at the end of the day in London, too. That was its final joke, after you'd dashed in sloppy buckets of rain all day, from awning to awning, dodging the points of umbrellas.

"London's like that," Albert would say. "The end of things is best here. The end of summer, the end of the year. The end of each life. Don't you agree?"

"Don't you go getting valedictory on me," she'd said.

She leaned over the pine tool chest that her grandfather had made. He was a fair carpenter, it was always said of the man, who worked on the ships at Parry Sound in winter, caught rheumatoid arthritis and died at forty-four. Once the box had been filled with handmade planes, but she'd given those away, to Tyke. Now it held boxes of photographs, shots which she hadn't published, hadn't shown to Del Zotto, Barr, hadn't even shown to Tyke.

She was looking for a picture of Tyke on the rocks in front of the Ojibway, taken the day she came home from Europe. She dragged the book to where she could see. Perhaps this was it. But what she recalled—her son's shy joy, his little torso bursting with heart, his chin up so that his face became a dish of pure sun—was now only light and shadow.

"Don't you think it's interesting, what life has done to me?" she challenged Tyke, only yesterday, wasn't it?

"*Interesting?* Not the word I'd use, Mother. See how you distance yourself? Even from your own tragedy?"

The blindness, what was it? Nothing more than a further development of her seeing. Narrowing down. Winnowing out. She had to look at it that way, as part of the process, not as an ambush, in later years. She reduced people, yes. What artist didn't, to make a statement? This is not Tyke, she said to him when he protested her depictions of him; this is a photograph of Tyke; it is an analog. Not the you you are, or choose to be. But an occasion for my *saying* you, for what I say about you.

She remembered him facing the camera in a thin T-shirt

and cut-off shorts, but naked really, his collarbone visible, sharply curved like the jawbone of a fish, his eye sockets hollow, a wild animation in his smile, a feverish happiness dampened, there in the eyes, by early wisdom. His body so taut and tender. There was nothing extra, just his sunburned buttery blond skin with its white boy-hairs; his shoulders, strong for his age and rounded, not angular, but almost chiseled. The sun had loved him, it followed him, lasted in his eyes, in his laugh, on his shoulders, after it had gone from the water and the rocks. She'd seen statues in Italy like him. But they had been wrapped in sacking against the bombs.

Later, Tyke refused to let her photograph him. Said she was stealing his life, he did. She hadn't understood.

But now he was stealing hers.

Retrospective! Who wanted to look back? And who could afford it? Her mother used to quote Pope: "In vain the Sage, with Retrospective eye, would from the apparent What conclude the Why."

When she told that to Tyke he laughed: "Mother you're so secretive! For an exhibitionist, especially," he protested. "Who lived her life in public. Made everyone else public." But if she let go of all the threads of her life, if she let them all know her secrets, she would no longer belong to herself. She would be their creature. And she had never wanted to belong to anyone but herself.

What she wanted was to find that sun-blessed boy again. She wanted to tell him she was sorry, she wished she hadn't left him. (Yet she had to leave him; she would not be who she was if she hadn't left him.) Somehow, she hadn't understood that his life, too, had its imperatives, that he couldn't stand still and wait for her wars and assignments and dates with whatever destiny.

If she could catch him off guard, surprise him again, as she'd done that day. He'd run up the rocks as he did then, and she would hold out her arms and call, "Tyke!" the cameras slapping at her side.

The Well
Christopher Woods

Forget, for the moment, the women who gather there talking, waiting to fill pitchers. And forget for now the dirty-faced children who twist their mother's skirts, who spit at one another, and who toss laughter wildly in the air. Forget all that.

What matters now is this one man, bent and nameless, who has slowed there, so close to the well. For him, now, even walking has become a curse. What he thinks about as he walks is the agony that, until now, he has resisted thinking about. Breathing deeply, he swallows one child's laugh, then another.

Slowly he circles the well, feels it pulling him into its bosom. Nearby, sitting on benches, are other old men. Maybe they have been there forever. He remembers running past them when he was still a child.

He never had time to stop, to talk to them. Or as a man in middle age, passing but not really seeing them. And later, his own hair and beard white, he had looked away rather than think about them. He would have no part of all that.

Until now. He circles until he finds a place to sit. He is lucky. The bench is still warm from someone else. He wonders whose place he has taken, where they have gone. Away for a few minutes? For eternity? And he wonders how long he will remain there, within the pull of the well, the lure of its depth. All that.

Maybe, he thinks, it won't be so bad. Feeding on the circular darkness that grows out of the earth. Watching children passing, the older men who look away. Even the other tired old men who stand so near to the well, all of them waiting patiently for a seat.

Retired
Daniel Green

When he could no longer work he sat
bewildered, wondered what he was supposed
to do, his work was life, his life, work,
he felt undone, bereft of being the man
he used to be, a cracked stone jug, empty.

Bringing home a workman's pay was his
solid base of dignity, responsibility fulfilled,
the roles of husband, father, guide, and judge,
earned and justified.

Even pensions, truly earned, did not qualify
as pay. Tolerance was not a substitute
for respect. His opinions about the day's events
were not asked, took comfort in soliloquy.

The tasks at home he'd never done became
the day's routines—at kitchen sink, supermarket,
shuffling behind the vacuum cleaner,
hanging wash, all women's work—he learned,
resigned to do with grace.

He thought he'd earned for keeps the badge
of "Mister," but that, too, slipped away,
became a thoughtless "Pops," a nothing name.

Emmaline
Willa Holmes

Emmaline's cheeks felt hot. Surely they were flushed and he would notice. She steadied her fingers against the handle of the coffee pot.

"Want some more coffee?" Her voice sounded high and funny to her, but if Howard marked the difference, he didn't let on.

"No," he said. "I've got to be on my way. I promised Roger I'd stop by the office and show them how I handled the Newton account. Then I'll get a haircut."

Retirement hasn't changed him, she thought. Keeps time better than a clock.

"The salesmen down at the office really think I've got it made, coming and going as I please." Howard gulped his orange juice and dipped egg yolk off his plate with a last bit of toast. "When you go out, pick up my cleaning, will you? It's two suits and a sports jacket. Oh, and take my black shoes in for new heels. I left them out next to the bed. I'll be back home by twelve-thirty for lunch."

Emmaline carried the dishes to the sink and lowered them into hot soapy water. Howard didn't think it was worth getting a dishwasher for just the two of them.

"Why don't you let the dishes soak while you go up and make the bed?" Howard said. "More efficient that way."

"I've done it this way for years," she said.

"Just trying to be helpful, Emmy." She watched him go out the backdoor and down the driveway toward the car.

"He hasn't called me Emmy since Dora and Tim were little," she thought. Then she stiffened her back. "Won't make any difference." She put the last cup into the drainer and squeezed water out of the dishrag. She stretched it out over the edge of the sink to dry. Funny to think she wouldn't be there to use it again. To wash the lunch dishes or the dinner dishes.

"Won't be any lunch. Or dinner, either," she said aloud to

the kitchen. When the phone rang, she knew it'd be Addie. Addie'd come over or called almost every day for the ten years she'd lived next door.

"Morning, Em," Addie said. "How's it going?"

"Hard," Emmaline answered.

"Changed your mind?"

"No. Yes. I don't know. What should I do, Addie?"

"I told you what I thought. Have it out with him. Tell him that big house is too much for you now, and having him in and out all day is driving you crazy."

"Wouldn't do any good. He doesn't hear what I say."

"Well, then, what's it to be?"

"I don't know. The house. Howard. It's hard to leave. And I've been patient, haven't I? Patient with all his ways?"

"Of course, you have. You've got the best, most patient disposition of anyone I know. In fact, if you'd just get mad once in a while..."

"That's not my way. And it's not Howard's way to be any different than he is." She stood, holding the phone. Then: "I'll do it. I'll move to my new place today, just like I planned."

"Are you sure? I don't know how you can live in a rented room. Not after having your own house and all."

"I'm sure. Anyway, it's a one-room apartment. There's that little kitchenette in what used to be a closet. I thought I'd put up a drape so I can pull it closed if somebody comes. So they couldn't see the dirty dishes."

"You with dirty dishes? That's not like you."

"Maybe it will be."

Em took off her apron and looked in the hall mirror, fluffing up her grey hair. Best get going before Howard comes back. She reached into the hall closet for a light beige coat and a small suitcase, the same one she'd packed with clean nightgowns for herself and with baby clothes and diapers for the new baby the two times she'd gone to the hospital.

"Time to get out of here," she told the hall. She shifted the suitcase to one side as she closed the door and twisted the knob to make sure it locked. She'd picked the day carefully.

She rented the room over the bakery nearly a month before, but she waited to make the move on the day she knew Dora would be driving in to go to the dentist and to spend the rest of the afternoon with them.

The clock in the room over the bakery ticked so loudly she turned and looked at it. Two o'clock. By now Howard had come home and found no lunch waiting. Dora was through with her appointment with the dentist and had walked up the steps to the front porch. Would Howard be standing there, looking down the street, fuming because lunch was late? Or would he be sitting at the kitchen table, waiting for her to come rushing in, apologizing for the delay, taking mayonnaise and sandwich meat out of the refrigerator and bread from the bread box on the counter?

They wouldn't call the police, would they? Not this soon. Would Dora think to call Addie, to see if she knew where her mother was?

Emmaline told Addie, "Just Dora. If it's Howard that calls or comes over, don't tell. Just Dora."

The rocking chair creaked beneath her. Been hard to get it out of the house. She'd waited until after dark on the night Howard went to lodge meeting. Addie'd backed her son's pickup to the garage door. Emmaline had gathered together all the things she planned to take to the new place and covered them with a tarp at the back of the garage. Howard didn't go in there much since he'd hurt his back and hired a yard man to mow the grass.

The ticking of the clock matched the creaking of the stairs. Someone was coming. She turned the rocker away from the window and faced the door, rocking faster, in time with the ticking and the creaks.

She waited for the raps on the door. "Mom? Mom, are you in there?" Dora's voice sounded anxious.

"I'm here. Come on in."

The door swung open and Dora pushed in past it. "Are you all right? Has something happened?"

"Didn't Addie tell you?"

"She said where I could find you is all. And not to bring Dad. Have you two had a fight?"

"No. Nothing like that. Sit down. Take that chair at the table by the window. Remember it? It was your Grandma Rose's. I found it up in the attic when..."

"You've been planning this? You've been going through the attic looking for things to bring here? This is—*premeditated?*" Dora's voice grew shrill.

"It's OK, Dora. Really it is. Sit down and I'll explain."

Dora pulled the chair out into the room and sat down in it, fanning her face with her hand. "Really, Mom, this is crazy. It's just insane."

Emmaline recoiled inside. She hadn't imagined they'd think she was crazy. They couldn't make her go home, could they?

"How will you get along? How will you manage?" Dora's face was red and she looked as if she'd cry.

"I'll do just fine," Emmaline told her. "I've got it all figured out. As a matter of fact, that's what made up my mind for me. Your father took me down to the Social Security office before he retired. They had me sign papers, too, both of us about to be sixty-five."

"But just because you get Social Security..."

"Don't you see? A separate check came to me. It had my name on it. I never knew they did it that way. Howard had me endorse the first check, and he put it in the bank. That's when I knew."

"Knew what, Mom?"

"I knew that check was mine. It was meant for me. I went back to that office and put in a change of address as soon as I found this room." She sat up straighter. "I have my own income."

"But what if it isn't enough to live on? Dad has a retirement fund, a pension plan. You'd be so much better off." She looked around the room and frowned. "If you're really going through with this, Dad'll probably have to give you money."

"Either way, I'll be all right," Emmaline said, smoothing her skirt across her legs. "They told me at that government office how much money I can earn before they take away part of my check. Mrs. Morgan in the bakery downstairs says I can work behind the counter for her Monday and Wednesday mornings. And I've already found a baby-sitting job two nights a week, but I told them I don't do housework and I don't do dishes."

Dora pulled the hair back off her face. "What am I going to tell Dad?"

"Tell him…" Emmaline paused, but for just a second. "Tell him I've retired."

Photo by Katie Utter

A Free Man
Judith Bell

Part determination, part habit, Bradford Clemmons jostled his way through the press of commuters waiting for the city-bound train on the platform outside Melmont station. He liked being up front, leaning out over the tracks, keeping watch on the point in the distance where the parallel lines of the rails seemed to narrow, the cross ties disappearing. There was something about that first sighting of the train rolling out of a still languorous morning haze, its great round light sweeping clear the way into the city, making him feel life was right on course.

But this morning his eyes strayed from that particular bend in the track, wandered over the people keeping watch beside him. Not that he knew any of them. They were mostly the ages his children would be if he had any, and he tended to see them as such. The number of his peers catching this train had steadily dwindled these last few years, leaving him to feel like the last hanger-on.

His immediate neighbors had all retired long ago. He saw them on his way to the station each morning, puttering among their flowers, walking their dogs, padding down the flagstones in slippers and robe for the morning paper. He pictured them going back inside, having that second cup of coffee, and then being lost, totally lost, the way he found himself on Sunday afternoons. After the paper had been read section by section, a televised golf tournament watched—he'd never had the time to take up the sport—Bradford was ready to be back at the office, away from the calm and quiet of his own house. "Your problem," Jen, his wife, liked to say, "is that you equate leisure with idleness."

"Brad!"

Bradford ignored the call. No one but Jen called him Brad anymore, and she was so busy with her painting, with the children's art classes she taught, it was possible she hadn't noticed how the name no longer fit him, how, with his expanded midsection and achromatic hair—no longer black, not exactly grey—he had settled into the solidity of the uncle for whom he'd been named.

"Hey, Brad!"

There it was again, sounding insistently in his direction. He looked further down the platform, stared with contextual blindness at a young man waving his newspaper at him. Why, it was Davis Thurman from his accounting firm. What was Thurman doing in an established community like Melmont? Of course Bradford was only twenty-two when he moved here, but he had been married with a baby on the way.

He remembered driving down street after street of Colonials, Tudors, and Victorians built in the 1920s and 1930s, chafing against the suburb's settledness. He'd grown up in old Richmond in a sprawling Victorian maze of dark rooms. Up North, out on his own, he developed a decided preference for the impermanent, the new. "My husband likes subdivisions," Jen had offered to the real estate agent in explanation of his silence.

"If it's any comfort, Melmont was built by developers. Of course, after thirty years houses take on an unavoidable grace." The agent let them into a fieldstone house she affectionately referred to as "the Irish cottage." "Natural air-conditioning," she offered when Bradford complained about the outdated kitchen, the oil furnace. Jen ran her hand along the deep windowsills, traced the molding in the casement windows. Pregnant, she had taken on a new vulnerability, a softness that made him rush to please her. And he could see she wanted this house with an intensity of desire he was only capable of feeling for her.

Bradford sensed the agent watching him watch his wife's face flush with pleasure as she traced the toe of her sandal delicately along the pattern in the parquet floor. "It's a quick walk to the station, a thirty-minute ride to Grand Central. And remember, Melmont is small, it lacks name recognition. Prices here will be a full twenty percent lower than Scarsdale or Larchmont."

"We'll take it," Bradford had said, grateful she had continued to appeal to his practical side even after seeing his weakness.

"Brad." Thurman was suddenly beside him. "Thought you'd thrown in the towel, old man." He cuffed Bradford's shoulder, offered his hand for shaking. "Just closed on a condo." He pointed his paper in the direction of the commercial district.

"Yes, the condos, of course." They were considered an eyesore by residents of Bradford's neighborhood, Melmont Manor. Thurman wore the uniform sported by all the young additions to the firm: khaki pants, navy blazer, loafers. Like them, he expended a great deal of energy on putting himself on equal footing with the senior staff. It wasn't enough that they took the liberty of calling you, uninvited, by your first name, they went further, as if by shortening your name they could make you less substantial, less of an obstacle.

"So anyway, hey," Thurman tapped him with his newspaper, "you're a free man. So what are you doing here with the working stiffs?"

Bradford repositioned himself to resume watch, but young Thurman, who had the bulk of a boy who had not that long ago excelled at college ball, moved with him. "I've been taking this train for forty years. I always promised myself the day after I retired I was going to get dressed, walk to the station, wait for the train, watch the rest of you get on, watch the train pull out, and go home."

"That's wild," Davis said, which was what he seemed to say about everything. Bradford wondered if this was a pat phrase among athletes like "There you go!" had been in his college days, and the not knowing made him feel his age. He waited for Davis to say something more, but judging from the pleasantly blank look in his eyes, he would not.

"Why aren't you playing pro ball, Thurman?" Bradford said, shifting the focus of the conversation from himself. "My hunch is right, you did play in school, didn't you?"

Davis sucked in a middle just beginning to soften. "That's

right. Quarterback, Penn State. Knees." He looked down, buckling his joints slightly. "Lost it all in one sack. Wild, huh? Hey, there's the train."

"So it is," Bradford said, irritation edging into his voice at having his ritual upset.

"Have a nice retirement," Davis waved his paper over his head, stepped through the doors opening in front of them and disappeared, digested by a shifting mass of grey and blue suits. The commuters around Bradford surged forward, and he found himself caught in the undertow. Familiar morning smells greeted him inside the car: coffee, aftershave, perfume, mouthwash. He breathed deeply, overriding the catch in his throat. It would be so easy to wait for the conductor's call of "All aboard," to yield to the backward press of the crowd as the doors closed, to adjust to the list and sway of the car as the train pulled out of the station. He could stay here unnoticed, anchoring his attaché case between his legs, holding his folded newspaper in front of his face.

The specter of Grand Central Station came to mind. He saw the passengers fan out, absorbed by the larger crowd, all of them with a destination, a place they belonged. Even the panhandlers at Grand Central had a reason to be there. The prospect of facing his own aimlessness sent him hurtling toward the Melmont platform.

"Coming out," he cried, his voice lost in the screech of the conductor's whistle. He stopped the meeting of the doors with his attaché case, landed on the platform. Free of the train, he watched it glide out of the station, silver and perfect, the faces of the passengers forming a band of unbroken color behind the seamless ribbon of glass.

"You miss your train?" A young man in a custodial uniform emptied the ashtray beside Bradford.

Yes, Bradford thought, watching the custodian drop the bowl of the ashtray roughly in its holder, *I do miss my train.* Instead he said in the hearty voice he used for talking to other men, "Retired just yesterday. Thought I'd come down, watch the rest of them hit the grind."

"Man, this is the last place I'd be if I was retired."

"Where would you be?" Bradford waited, ready to endow the impending answer with revelatory meaning.

The custodian tapped the end of a cigarette he took from his shirt pocket against the back of his hand, lit it. "I'd be on some island, man, Jamaica maybe, sitting on the beach, doing nothing."

"So you'd travel?"

The custodian flicked ashes into the ashtray he'd just emptied. "Yeah, sure. People's all through expecting you to do things. Time to do something for yourself."

Bradford shifted his gaze to a splashy poster announcing an art exhibition that had just opened at the Met. He could look for Jen at the art center where she taught two days a week. They'd go into the city, look at things he hadn't taken the time to see, do the things she'd given up trying to share with him.

He tried to think of when she had first changed, when she gave all the attention she'd focused on him—on the babies she'd never managed to carry to term—to her art instead, to her students, transforming her pleas for closeness and understanding into unreadable blobs and smears of paint. After one of her trips to the doctor, he had come home to find her in tears, furiously rolling white paint over the yellow walls in the room they had intended as a nursery. "This is my studio," she'd announced, wiping her eyes with the back of her fist, smearing paint across her face. "If I can't create physically, I'll create aesthetically."

At first she had simply invited neighbor children in to play at making art, but he put his foot down after coming home one day to find the lower half of the back of the house transformed into a giant mural of flowers and trees and hovering butterflies, the porch columns ribboned with paint. Watching him scrub her afternoon's work away, Jen never argued once. She had simply set about organizing support for a community art center in the old Laury School behind the post office.

Outside the station, the sun blasted him with a directness

unfamiliar to a man accustomed to spending his days in an office building. Shielding his eyes, he rushed past storefronts, imagining idle shopkeepers watching him, speculating about his business in town on a Thursday morning.

Climbing the steps to the Laury Art Center he noticed they were beginning to crumble, that paint peeled from the windows and gutters Jen and her volunteers had painted a cheery red. Day lilies just past their bloom bordered the walk. Donated and planted by the local nursery, the failing blossoms drooped forward into beds choked with weeds. What could Jen be thinking of, walking past this neglect day after day? She had never managed to pick up that life was serious business, that there were things that had to be attended to. Whatever fool thing she or "the children" as she referred to her students, took into their heads to do was all that mattered to her. She didn't see the clutter that began in her studio, inched its way into the hallway, the spare bedroom, and beyond; she didn't notice the disrepair of the art center and what's more, she seemed to pride herself on this failing.

From the door of the airy classroom where she taught her preschoolers, he watched her, dressed in jeans and a paint-smeared denim shirt, crawl from the work of one child to another. She stopped to retie the ribbon holding back her straggling grey hair. In her flushed face he was surprised to see the fresh beauty he'd remembered just this morning, thinking of her and the day they'd first looked at their house. She was the same as she had always been, all her life building on that moment when she had the courage to paint the nursery walls white. In comparison his own life felt segmented, compartmentalized, and now, abruptly broken.

"Brad!" Smiling, Jen scrambled to her feet, clapped her hands. "Children, look who's here. Mr. Clemmons has come to look at the worlds you've made."

A boy charged into Bradford's legs, leaving a brown hand print on his trousers. "I'm drawing a planet with chocolate rivers and silver trees. What's yours like?"

"What a great idea, Simon! You come make something, too,

Brad." Jen took his attaché case, hid it behind her desk.

The children begin to giggle, some of them looking at him from behind their hands, others holding their drawings over their faces.

"Jen, I hardly think…"

"Oh, come on. Draw what you know. Draw the Manhattan skyline, show the kids where you work."

Before he could object, she rushed off to the far end of the room to comfort a crying child whose chalk had broken. She had forgotten yesterday was his last day, forgotten he no longer had a place to spend his time.

The children watched him in expectation. He took a piece of paper from the supply table, selected a coffee can filled with broken pieces of pastel crayons. He chose a seat, arranging and rearranging his bulk to fit within the perimeters of the small chair. Ignoring the gaping stare of his tablemate, he told himself he was doing this for Jen. Any moment now, she would surely announce snack time, a bathroom break, or recess, and he would be free to leave, to go on about his day. The boy beside him went back to his drawing. Glancing over the child's small hunched shoulders, Bradford made out a castle. A pink sun emitted yellow rays showing pink on the grey walls.

He stared at his blank paper, thinking of snow, of the mountains of Korea, and of a fear like the one he was feeling today. He'd been too young to go to World War II, so when the Chinese stirred things up in Korea he was glad to go, spoiling for the fight he'd missed. But each day in Songjin he awakened crying, went out and watched boys his own age fall dead. There had been nothing between him and the war except the little he'd experienced of life. Now there was nothing between him and his retirement except all that he had lived through in between.

"You want to try my crayon?" The boy beside him held out a piece of pink chalk. "It makes drawing easy."

Goldie, Jen's retriever, wandered over, settled her greying muzzle on Bradford's knee, her watery gaze questioning his presence. Bradford gave her a reassuring pat, awkwardly closed his fingers around the moist pastel.

    Enveloping, encouraging, Jen's voice rose and fell between the unconscious breathing of children, the muted rasping of chalk. Bradford ran the stick of saturated color along the edge of his paper. Watching it soak in, his eyes opened wide, trying to feel the color. Dragging his fingers down the waxy smoothness, he stared transfixed at the elaborate pattern of whorls thrown into relief along his fingertips, at the pastel crayon, settled now in the curve of his fingers. His hand began to move to the imagined pulses of the children.

Photo by Katie Utter

Meditation for Twilight
Albert Huffstickler

Sometimes, far out in space,
I feel my sexuality blossom—
like a hot flash or like
a belated Fourth of July display.
Lights blossom far beyond
my body's reach then
linger on the air
like a remembrance of youth,
of love's first promise
never quite fulfilled, then
fade as slowly as an old man's
hopes—which seem, for better
or worse, to outlive all
the body's capabilities.
And so, I put the coffee pot on
and think of the things remaining
and smoke my pipe and wonder
how I might have delayed
time's reckoning and watch
the smoke plume upward
to my low ceiling, thinking
of all the men who have
thought these thoughts before me
and feel for a moment that
kinship richer than blood,
deeper than time, that thing
that brought us here so
very long ago and caused us
to stay and continue—some
faith we don't even remember
and can never, even now,
really touch.

Washing Helen's Hair
Anne C. Barnhill

Helen kneels on the oak stool in front of the bathroom sink. Her knees, lumpy with arthritis, hit the faded red cushion with a soft thud. Almost dizzy, she rests her head on the cold rim of enamel. With her left hand, she caresses the familiar grain of the wooden legs, feels the varnish and where it has thinned in spots. It is her stool, the one her husband, Alonzo, made for her years ago. She smiles.

"I'm ready, Lon. Waiting." Her voice cracks, not from emotion but from the strain of yelling for him to come to her. He's on the back porch, shucking corn from the garden. He planted only one row this year after she refused to freeze the surplus. She is tired of his garden, tired of the peeling, boiling, cutting, chopping. She needs rest.

"I'm starting without you." She turns on the faucet, letting the water run until it's warm. This resting on her knees isn't as easy as it used to be. But she'd rather feel her feet go numb and walk on prickles than give up her hair day.

She listens for his step, then turns the water on with more force. He'll hear that, certainly. Alonzo could sense waste even with his bad ears. He might pay no attention to her voice, but he'll high-step it into the house to see why she's running so much water.

Sure enough, the slow gallumph of his steady stride up the hall vibrates the floor. She raises her head and spies him in the mirror, watches as he ambles toward her. His face is tanned from hours spent in the yard, digging roots, poking his fingers in to test the soil. He puts his old felt hat on the hall dresser, then heads to the bathroom. She notices how bent he has become, yet he straightens when he realizes she is watching him. She winces and lowers her eyes. She thinks how his back is now shaped like the sewing needle her daddy used to stitch people and animals back together.

He wears his old white linen jacket, a Sunday morning uniform of years gone by. She used to tease him about looking like the ice cream man, and he'd laugh that gruff chuckle of his, put his arm around her waist, his muscles ropy, like a lasso.

Now his hair, sparse and grey, streaks across his crown in thin pencil lines. Yet he still cuts a fine figure, and her heart beats faster as she watches him, his large, veiny hands hanging at his sides.

"Had to finish the corn. Water hot enough?" Alonzo tests it with his fingers, then bends around her to wash his hands with soap.

"Feels just right." Helen gives him a thorough search, ogling his reflection in the mirror, looking for any corn worms that might have strayed onto him. She does hate a worm.

"Ain't any on me, missy. I got 'em all." He unbuttons her collar, then pulls down the zipper on her dress. She lets the front drop to her waist. He slides the straps of her slip off her shoulders so that he can touch her.

Slowly, he begins to rub the white flesh, kneading gently, ever so gently. Her shoulders, her neck, the back part of her head. He continues to massage the dimpled skin until he hears her "Ah." That's his signal to start taking down her hair from the French twist at the nape of her neck. Carefully, he removes each fancy comb, then gingerly loosens the hairpins.

"I'm tender-headed." She makes a face at him in the mirror. She sees his dark brown eyes crinkle with fond exasperation.

"I know, missy, I know." Her grey curls fall and cover his hands. The strands wind through his fingers. The hair, stiff and wiry, is the color of pewter, and she imagines he's remembering how blond it had been years ago. And how soft.

Helen hands him her brush made of pig bristles. She holds her head straight as he combs through the long rope of her hair.

"Still pretty. Soft like a silk shawl." He bends over, buries his face in her hair, the smell of it sweet and fresh like warm milk in a pail, the kind he used to carry up from the barn when he was a boy. He's told her this before, many times, confessed his love for her smell. He begins to wet her hair, cupping his hands under the faucet, then pouring the warm water onto her scalp.

"Feels so good." Helen leans over the sink, the weight of the water pulling her. Without him to hold her, she thinks she might fall down the drain, like in that silly nursery rhyme: "Oops, there goes Helen down the hole." Alonzo's fingers support her and he begins to make whirls all over her head.

She smells strawberries when he opens the shampoo. Alonzo surprises her with a new brand every so often, and she likes the changes, loves to think of him at the grocery store, pouring over the different bottles, deciding which one she might enjoy.

He begins to hum. A hymn, one of the old ones, "When the Roll Is Called up Yonder." The feel of the suds, the sound of his voice remind Helen of the first time he washed her hair.

She remembers how embarrassed she'd been, a girl barely fifteen and him a man of twenty-three. They'd married in 1935 with little more than a suitcase of clothes to move into the hotel room they'd let from old Mrs. Abernathy. Helen laughed.

"What's so funny, missy?" He still scrubbed her head, cleaned it good, the way she liked.

"Oh, nothing. I was remembering how scared I was of you back when we were first married." She placed her hands on her thighs and pinched to get some feeling there. Not ready for him to stop, she hoped to delay the inevitable numbness.

"Scared of me?"

"Yep. Especially on our wedding night. And when you wanted to bathe me and wash my hair, I didn't know what to do. It's kinda funny now." Helen grinned. Thinking back took her mind off the pain creeping into her legs.

She could see him as he was then, a tall, gangly man with dark curly hair and a black mustache. She'd been in the bathroom, sitting on the edge of the claw foot tub, her fingers poised above her head, ready to take down her hair. She'd felt his strong hands on hers as she reached for the combs.

"Let me help you." He removed them, then ran his hands through her hair, his thick fingers easing out the snarls.

"Be careful, Lon. My scalp is real tender." She felt the familiar bunching of her muscles, her whole body tense against his touch.

"I won't hurt you." She realized she stood before him in the light, wearing only her undergarments. A hot blush began on her chest.

"I'll bring in a chair. You'll strain your back leaning across the tub like that. We'll wash your hair in the sink, then I'll run your bath water." He raised her up, brushed the hair away from her eyes. While he went to get the chair, she wanted to slip into her robe, the one she'd embroidered for their honeymoon. But she just stood, her bare feet against the cool linoleum floor.

"This'll be a lot easier. Sit down and lean over the sink. That's it." With her back to him, she felt her neck bend, thin as a bird's. Her head heavy, she felt him take the weight of her skull in his hands. He stroked her crown first, then began to wet her hair.

"Your hair's the first thing I noticed about you. Yellow, shimmering in the sunlight." Lon had never been a sweet-talker, hadn't ventured much conversation in his lovemaking. But now, his voice was soft, easy. She relaxed into it. He began to hum that Steven Foster ditty about the girl with brown hair, one he used to sing under his breath when they'd courted in her parent's front parlor.

Soon, her head full of bubbles, Alonzo raised her to a sitting position and piled her hair in a variety of shapes on top of her head. They laughed at the "hairdos," a long spike, a blob with a curl at the tip. Later, clean from her bath, her hair slightly damp, he'd taken her to their bed.

The sound of his voice snaps her back into the real world, the world where her knees ache and her legs, no longer smooth and pearly, are speckled with blue splotches. The world where her golden hair is now the dull color of storm clouds.

"Tired?" He's already rinsed her hair and now holds a large yellow towel slung across his forearm. Yellow's her favorite color, and he always uses the big fluffy one he gave her several years ago.

"My legs are as numb as rubber and my feet have gone plumb to sleep."

"We'll manage, missy." He smiles at her in the mirror.

Helen catches his hands as he starts to wrap her head in the towel. They are rough hands, familiar. Age spots, brown and ragged, ride the veins. These are hands she can trust, hands she has trusted for most of her life. Helen notices a trembling in him. He is tired, too. She brings the callused fingers to her mouth and kisses them, her dry lips leaving a hint of moisture.

"Thank you." She whispers the words, not certain he can hear her.

He gives no reply, just pats her shoulder and leads her to the overstuffed chair on the back porch where he will towel-dry her hair, the drying faster there in the sun.

Helen allows herself to be led, her hand in his. She sinks back into the chair. He lifts her feet, one at a time, onto the hassock, then rubs them for a moment until they are buzzing with warmth. Then he begins to comb her hair carefully, so as not to pull a single strand.

The Fallout Fantasy
John Laue

(After reading Joseph Campbell)

The kids think I'm an old man
in his dotage,
and I'm old all right
compared to them
and even most of their parents;
but I'm not really old
as old goes.
And I won't give up teaching yet.
At least another year,
I've said for a few years now.
And the years build up
like mountains I climb
growing higher and steeper.
I've made a tentative wish
for the very last one
to be a volcano.
When I reach the top
I'll dive into its crater
and shoot out. Yes!
My spirit will float
light as thin ash
all over this marvelous world.
It'll coat the eyelids of fine women,
get in their husbands' armpits,
lodge in the navels of those people
whom I'm curious about,
be eaten and passed
by animals, fish, and birds,

penetrate hell again and heaven
and all places in between.
And when it's traveled enough,
been part of many lives and deaths,
it'll gather, coalescing
into a me without ego, fear, or fantasy.
Then I'll be a new man!

Laundry
Grace Butcher

At the home of the man whose wife has died
laundry flaps on the line,
lively and colorful.

He has it all figured out now,
the moves one makes
to make things clean and usable.

The blue work shirts, the flowered sheets,
the green and white towels
billow in the warm wind,
collecting something of the sun
for him to fold away later,
filling the closet with fading light.

Everything is pretty much the same
though only half of what it used to be.

No dresses brush against the shirts.
The towels will wear out soon,
and then those young colors will be gone
and he will buy maroon and brown.

He doesn't think about it, he simply tromps
down into the dimness of the basement
she used to call "the dungeon" with a laugh,
pulls the pile of damp clothes out
and carries them up out of darkness toward the sun.

And suddenly he stands as if struck
by the thought of her emerging from this dark:
year after year her body rising toward the sky,
the basket of clothes that had been renewed,
to be hung like prayer flags, offerings of love,
to a god who should have responded.

And now all he, the man, can do
is stand at the top of the steps
between the basement and the yard,
the basket in his hands, half blinded by the sun,
the light surging around him as tangible as water.

This is where she stood each week,
rising from the dark below as if
from a grave, over and over again,
never thinking about not being able to do it
one more time. He squints against the sun,
hangs the clothes. The sheets take the wind,
their faded flowers suddenly so bright
they hurt his eyes.

Photo by Roger Pfingston

The Chance of Snow
Kathryn Etters Lovatt

Dawson gave Russell Owings his blue speckled cup with the rooster on it. He kept the yellow one, a mama hen with three biddies, for himself. Neither man offered his hand. Dawson, a farmer his life through, grain and vegetable to start with, all timber in the end, had gotten enough handshaking these last couple of days. It had not once come natural to him. For a young man like Russell, who routed wood and mixed stain, Dawson guessed it was about the same. His palms were probably as thick as hide.

"You needn't have come out," Owings apologized. Etta's old hound pawed the fencing like he was ready to climb over. Nothing Dawson did kept him down.

The young man squatted into a bare patch alongside the pen and rubbed behind the dog's ears. "My wife sends regards. Too cold, you know, to bring the baby out."

Dawson nodded in agreement. A brood of sparrows huddled at one end of the power line, not a twitter between them. "I do believe we're in for it," he said.

Russell blew at the rim of his cup, and a breath of coffee with real cream and half a spoon's worth of sugar wrenched a warm, sweet hole in the air. "Sure feels like it."

"We got a fire made."

The Dawson house, set this summer for a coat of paint, looked as sad as the afternoon. Smoke barely topped its chimney before being swept up by the day's weather. "You're welcome to come on inside and get warm." Dawson stopped short of offering food. Etta always fixed a ham to take to the grieving family, a fresh ham and a big dish of candied potatoes. Dawson's mouth flooded with the memory.

He could picture his wife as she moved about, sink to stove, making everything by idea and pinches. Inside the lap of her flowered apron, she would wipe her hands of cloves and sorghum, grated orange rind. Dawson imagined butter melting between her fingers, new crop pecans on her breath. He saw her lift the roaster out of the oven, the steadiness of her strength surprising him. It never ceased to surprise him.

How Dawson longed to bring this beanstalk of a boy into that very dream, Etta in her kitchen, let her fatten him up.

"I'm not dressed to visit," said Russell. "I just walked over to see how you were fixed for the night. I could wrap your pipes."

"Not but one outside," said Dawson. "I got it cut off." He studied Russell, who looked shy of twenty, though Dawson knew he was way past. He couldn't judge anymore; everyone looked young to him. "You're fine," he told Russell.

Russell always looked fine. Etta used to say what a wonder he was. "A cabinetmaker," she mused, "and him so neat and clean all the time. Not afraid of his height either." The last jab went to Dawson, who argued he couldn't help his slouch, that his spine had buckled from stooping over fields all these years.

Dawson studied Russell. No trace of gall about his face, there was no spite in the boy's eyes. He tucked his shirts inside his pants, wore lace-up boots. He didn't seem to care about a watch. Dawson so strongly approved of all he saw that he forgave Russell his twenty-odd acres. He repented every oath he'd sworn when Russell bought it out from under his nose. Paid asking price. Asking price. Ah, he was just a kid. A kid who wanted to be out of town a little ways and saw his chance. Dawson felt he knew something about that now, felt he knew all manner of things about his neighbor.

After a day's work, for instance, right before supper, Dawson would bet a sou the boy rolled his sleeves beyond his elbows, that he lathered his arms and scrubbed with a vengeance about his neck. Dawson figured this out the other night when he stood helplessly in back of Russell. He watched the boy's head bend to Etta's, his mouth covering every trace of hers, watched as he wrestled her poor bosoms like yeast dough. He blew into her, blew, blew, blew. Blew, even though, maybe, Etta was already gone.

Russell's neck didn't have a lick of dirt around it, Dawson took note of that fact. What's more, his red flannel shirt held dampness at the wrists, and his collar lay soaking wet all around. He wore an undershirt with a clipped label. Factory second. Dawson had a few himself. Funny, thought Dawson, what you see when you can't think. Funny, how you remember a body's shoulders free of sun, a button hanging on a thread.

"It might be snow to start with," predicted Dawson. "Sooner or later, it'll turn to ice."

The cold went through his one suit, wool, chaffing him in the stride. It settled on his head, and he wished for a hat. When he was as young as this fellow here, he had a fine crop of hair himself, browner though, much browner than Russell's, and wavy. It began to grow thin about the time he turned sixty, thin but silky, and white as a petticoat. "Etta was scared to death of ice," he said. "Afraid she'd fall and break her hip and never be right again."

When Russell rose up, the dog gave a long, plaintive whine and laid his head on the rim of his food dish. He had a bowl of scraps he wouldn't touch. "Damn dog," thought Dawson, because he was used to saying it to Etta.

"Damn dog," he'd say when it would rain and she would bring him in. He stunk up the house like a barrel of wet burlap.

"Lewis Dawson," Etta would click, "you know good and well you love that old mutt."

"An animal can tell when things aren't right," Russell said. An orange streak of dry pine needles caught in the cuff of his jeans; he picked them off a couple at a time. "He's trying to put it together."

"I reckon you heard him the night through," said Dawson. "He's got a howl to wake the dead." Dawson's heart clenched. Oh, hell. He could feel it coming, another swell of despair working its way to the surface. He put his cup on the gate post and took out his handkerchief. He wiped his eyes clean. Old men's tears, he noticed, came thick with matter.

Russell kept his own eyes low. He pressed his lips together

so hard they turned white.

"I don't think it's even hit me yet, not truly. Me here alone. Etta down there."

"I can understand how you feel," allowed Russell. "Somebody sweeping the yard one morning, gone the next. I can hardly believe it myself."

"She's not buried half a day," Dawson drew in a last mild sniffle, "and here comes the devil." The two of them crooked their heads sideways to see up between the tree branches, loblolly pine and bare oak.

"Heavenly days," said Dawson. Russell and the dog both came to attention. "A saying of Etta's," he remembered. "She'd forget the iron. Or leave her peas boiling. She'd see how late in the day it was getting and what she still had to do. 'Heavenly days,' she'd say. The same thing in the same voice every single time. And then, all in a bustle, she'd have to run off and mind things."

The entire sky looked like one huge field of wet cement this afternoon. No place to fall but down, and by the time it hit ground, the ice would be merciless, and every bit as hard as mortar. That little tent the funeral home had left over Etta's grave would be no match for sleet. The canopy would fall under the thrash of the storm, fall on the flowers and on Etta. And he, too, would be cold tonight. The extra blankets, wherever they were, would drown him in camphor. They would weigh him down without warming him through.

Dawson felt his grief lift a little when he considered all this. A certain vexation even came over him. He felt irritated at Etta herself, leaving so abruptly. On the brink of the weekend, to boot, so the service fell on a Saturday. Worse, on this particular Saturday, a winter storm overhead.

She died in the evening, which counted. They calculated those few hours into a whole day, and so the first day was lost. Friday, the second day, had been one question after another. Caskets, flowers, what would she wear? Who would carry her? And there was the obituary, all that straining to remember who

Etta's original people were and who might be left among them.

Every waking minute till today, until the service itself, he had something else to think about. And now, the chance of snow. This mix of circumstances, Dawson realized, undermined proper mourning. They took away from Etta's dying.

People's minds were on slick roads and the supermarket. They looked ahead toward hazard, then on to thaw, and further still, to where the world fell back to normal. Dawson knew there was no chance of that for him. Nothing would ever be the same.

"Etta," he thought, "how could you?"

Under Thursday's perfect skies, she had hung two loads of wash on the line. Dawson had watched from the backdoor window. It was so bright out, everything acted like a mirror. Even Etta's sheets, fresh out of Clorox, glared. Her duster had never been so yellow.

"Take advantage of this," she had warned her husband. "Get up and do what you can, while you can."

Maybe she had done too much.

She never could sit still. She wouldn't listen either.

"Things can sure change in a hurry," he told Russell, who shook his head in melancholy agreement. Dawson realized he'd been accorded his first genuine silence since Etta had fallen out at the supper table.

"She never did say she felt bad," he confided finally, softly. He fingered two pennies in his pocket, a black walnut.

"Maybe she never did feel bad, Mr. Dawson. Maybe she never knew what hit her."

It would have been a good thing to hear if Dawson hadn't known better. He kicked a pine cone, a hard green one. He felt it on all his toes. As much as he gave for these dress shoes, and no more leather than that.

"She knew," he said. Pain had knocked the breath clean out of her. She had looked across to Dawson with such surprise, her hand not to her heart, but at the hot blade of her shoulder. He saw the pain all right, saw that she understood the truth of pain like that, what it meant, and he saw that she did not fight against it. "I wish I'd been up the road checking the saplings," Dawson confessed. "I'd rather have found her already gone."

"I don't guess you ever get over it," Russell said.

"You go on," said Dawson, who had a war behind him.

"I don't see how."

It came to Dawson all of a sudden how bad it had been on the boy, him seeing the meanness of death, kissing it. Seeing Etta's death at that. She had helped rock the colic out of their newborn.

"You want to go first if you can," Dawson warned him. "It's better all the way around."

Dawson opened the gate and slapped his hand on his knee for the dog to come on. Both of them needed to get out, go walk, if not up to the mailbox or over toward the creek, then just stretch their legs around the yard. Russell fell in line next to Dawson; the dog wedged himself in the middle.

"Had it been the other way around, Etta, she would be inside that house there. She'd be holding up everybody else," said Dawson. Russell admitted it was probably so. "Me, I'm a worry to them. No one knows their duty. Who's to stop me now, they wonder—I wonder it myself—from doing as I please?"

Russell stopped and checked one of the red shutters. It hung a little off. "Just what is it you want to do?" he asked.

"Son," Dawson said, "you haven't been married long enough."

The dog went straight for the front porch and sprawled across the welcome mat. His jowls flapped over his huge front paws. He looked a sight, sick to the heart.

"It's nothing I want to do exactly, it's what I get a mind to do. Wild hairs." Dawson could tell he wasn't getting through yet. "Say there comes a pile of snow tonight."

"There's a snow," said Russell. "All right."

"And tomorrow, I think I'll dig out."

"Go on."

"Why, Etta, she would call me a fool to my face, an old fool. She'd say, 'You'll drop dead, Lewis Dawson. Mark my words, you will drop dead, and I'll die trying to drag you in.' I would get the shovel out of the barn anyhow. Maybe I'd get outside and go to work. Etta would fret at the door. She'd see my mistake and walk out a little piece—no sign of a sweater or nothing over her shoulders—she'd stand there with her arms wrapped in front of her, shivering, and she'd holler out, 'Stop, Lewis. Please stop! You are giving me the sick headache.'"

"And?"

"And then I could cuss and throw down my shovel, and I could come inside the house."

"Ah," said Russell. He had to laugh. Dawson too.

"Men don't have half the good sense a woman does," Dawson admitted. He hoped Etta felt satisfied somewhere, hearing him say it.

Neither man's coat was enough with this wind, whipping as it did right into the porch well where they stood. The window panes to the living room trembled trying to hold against gusts that backed up and divided and slid in through the cracks anyway.

Some of the children, not Dawson's grandchildren, who had brains to know better, but children of cousins and children of people who called themselves cousins, were sitting in those funeral parlor chairs right before the windows. So was Willis, Dawson's brother. A half-brother he was, from their father's second wife. Stiff as a brush, his shrunken hands propped on his Masonic belt buckle, he had fallen into a wide-mouthed sleep. Willis was living proof of where loneliness could drive a man.

Dawson could see all his company from here, the only thing out of eye's view was the right arm of the kitchen and the two dim bedrooms behind the hall.

"Not much of a house," said Dawson.

"It's a good house," said Russell and petted the boards under his hand. He moved by the window and looked in as well. "I've always liked this house."

"Not much to keep up. A little dark maybe, but easy on Etta's eyes. They were giving her a fit."

"Too late a frost this winter." Russell wiped the glass. "Hard on anybody allergic."

"They were old, that's what she said." Now Dawson wondered what it really meant, why her whites began to burn, why her irises turned so tearful a grey they were practically see-through. "She should have seen about them."

"More food." Russell pointed to the pasteboard bucket Dawson's oldest girl put on the table. Dawson came close and looked in again.

"They take turns getting after me to eat. All I have a taste for is buttermilk."

Out came coleslaw, rice, and gravy; those wipes for your hands.

"You ever eat any of that chicken?" Dawson asked.

"Once in a while."

"What do you think of it?"

"Beats nothing," said Russell. He smacked his lips.

"Could be," said Dawson, who realized then, that when it came right down to it, a Kentucky fried drumstick might be better than no drumstick at all. "Things sure can change in a hurry."

"You ought to eat," Russell said. "Everybody will stay after you till you do."

"Hmm," said Dawson. "You see anything decent?"

"There's a pie or two. Real tins."

"Widows," said Dawson.

Russell went in closer yet, right at the glass, his breath fogging it. "A cake of some sort. "

"The good ones aren't interested in another husband," said Dawson. "I used to ask Etta, if something was to happen to me, would she marry again."

"What'd she say?" Russell cupped his hands about his eyes and stared hard, but Dawson backed away.

"Oh, you know, different things. 'Lord have mercy, Lewis, you have got hardening of the arteries.' She favored that one. Or she'd say, 'Oh yes-sirree, by all means.' That her next husband was going to be young and rich. A doctor maybe."

"Sounds just like her."

The temperature was dropping fast. Dawson was considering closing the dog in a back room. He'd make a racket, for certain, until he was let in the kitchen. Then he would whine in the kitchen because Etta was gone, and the grandchildren wouldn't be able to stand it and they would cry, "Grandpa, can't we please bring Noodle in front of the fire?" And when they had begged enough to satisfy him and Dawson didn't think he seemed too easy, he would say, "Do what you want. Take him home for all I care."

Maybe then the dog would eat a chicken breast, pulled piece by piece off the bone, offered in a soft little hand. He would have to eat something sooner or later or he'd have to lay down and die.

"Etta wouldn't marry again," he told Russell. "She could have done without me."

If Russell wouldn't come in, Dawson knew it was time for him to go. The air stung to breathe it. Every once in a while, Dawson thought he caught a flake of snow, like a tiny white feather floating from a nest. Everybody would leave soon. They needed to get where they were going before it was too late.

"We're just across the field," Russell said as they came up on the backyard and to the path that would take him home. "You come over any time. You need anything, you pick up the telephone."

There was the moment of parting, which was awkward. It had the two of them bowing and nodding and waving back and forth. Dawson reconsidered the value of shaking hands. If that brief touch could offer some grace around these comings and goings, he was all for it.

That evening, he shook everyone's hand who offered it. He let his daughters kiss him over and over, and he let them fix him a plate of food and put it in the oven.

When they were all gone, even Willis, who would have slept the night through if they had left him be, Dawson remembered Etta. He made himself remember she was not in the next room, but gone for good. What would she would do on a night like this?

She would bathe in the sink, he thought, with a nappy

washcloth and Dove soap. She would pull on her gown, still in the drawer, and her robe, on the bathroom hook, and she would borrow some of his long wool socks. She would fill milk jugs with fresh water, just in case, and when she looked outside she would see a fine white veil falling in the porch light. The trees would be leaning forward, every inch of them heavy with ice, and there would be no walkway, only white, the whole world dangerous, but white and brilliant. She would bring in more wood then, and not let the fire go out.

Widow
Eleanor Van Houten

Tomorrow I will take out the dead flowers.
They have faded and withered this long week.
I will wash and return the casseroles
and cake plates to sympathetic friends.
I will go to the market and shop for one.
Tomorrow I will take the dog for a walk
and weed the garden. Tomorrow I will
begin to get my life in order again.

I will not pack away his clothes, just yet.
Standing in his closet I smell his scent,
stroke my cheek with a woolen sleeve,
remembering how it once felt
encircling my shoulders.
On his dresser in a blue Japanese bowl,
a handful of coins from his pocket
and a tangle of old keys.

Choices
Nancy Robertson

He tells her
he cannot take her
home for Christmas dinner.
Too many stairs.
His fingers fuss
with the handles
of the basket
that held the present.

Got to go
busy
lots to do
pats her hand, bye Mom,
leaps from the couch
strides down the corridor
forgets the basket
in his haste
to get away
from this place.

Her chin quivers
face distorts
tears stain
her best dress.

Later
when she sits
at Christmas dinner
with the others left behind
she says,
My son came
to see me today
but I didn't want
to go home with him.
Too many stairs, you know.

Flying Time
Elisavietta Ritchie

"He asked me to fly to Bangkok with him,"
giggles the nurse. I picture my father's
wheelchair sprouting aluminum wings,
his skeletal shoulders growing feathers—
scarlet, vermilion, green—
like a swan sired by a parrot.

"I hope you agreed to fly with him,"
I answer. "He was a famous explorer."
She laughs, slaps her plump palms
against her white uniform.
"Lord, what a spaced-out
i-mag-i-na-tion your daddy's got!"

His blue eyes watch us. I smooth
wisps of hair like down on his skull.
My mad daddy. Here are
the springs of my imagination.
At eighty-four may I too
have license for madness.

Meanwhile, I wheel his chair
to his place at the table
between old Mrs. Silverman
screaming "Sugar! Coffee! More milk—"
and Muggsy sloshing soup on his neighbor.

I set the brakes, fasten his seat belt.
Although my father insists that this trip
he would rather have curry and beer
or smoked eel and vodka,
I spoon pureed liver and unsalted limas
into his mouth quickly before
his fingers explore the plate.

Downstairs, in the Ladies,
by mistake I enter the oversized stall
with handrails, high commode,
the blue-and-white Handicapped sign.
But will there be space enough here
for my wings?

Photo by Robert Ullman

Can Opener
Dianna Henning

The cat food is
a small hill in the middle
of nondescript ooze
only the comfortable
dare call gravy.

With palms flat
on his upper legs
the old man bows in
simple thanks. He has
again coaxed open the can,
set the card table;
a Kleenex folded under
the knife and fork.

Tonight it's Friskies Beef
& Liver Dinner,
saltines set to the side,
a mug of warm tap water
to wash it all down.

The man's gaze is tight
to his plate where he carefully cuts
the mound into smaller portions,
prompts with his fork
tidbits of Friskies
onto a cracker he then
mops through the caramel liquid.

Later, his aching hands
find their way into a pan
of the good warm water.
This medicinal soak
tides him over until his next check,
and he's grateful
to have gotten the can open
without help from
the pensioner next door.

The World of Dolores Velásquez
Eliud Martínez

It saddens me not to know what the doctors and nurses talk about when Isabel is not here to tell me in Spanish...*me da mucha pena...me da vergüenza y me da coraje*. More so, it infuriates me that in all my eighty-two years I never learned to read and write, not even in Spanish. What are they saying? *Estas enfermeras y los doctores, ¿qué están diciendo?*

I don't understand these nurses and doctors, or even my own grandchildren. I remember when my sons Antonio and Eduardo used to drop their children off to keep me company, when they were very little, before they started school, and later, after they started going to school, when they were ill and could not go. The children are grown now, but when they were little, I remember that taking care of them used to make me sad, to be sitting in the same room with my own grandchildren, like persons from different countries who are not able to speak the same language. Mexicanos lose the language in this country. I suppose it is bound to happen. Sometimes I would say something to the child in Spanish, to Michelle, for example, and she would blink her eyes and shrug her shoulders, and the same with Eduardo's little boy, or Antonio's girls, though they speak Spanish, but Michelle and her brother would say, "I don't understand what you're saying, *'buela*." Some of the others, too. Well, at least they knew how to say *grandmother* in Spanish.

The doctor told Isabel that I have to stay here. Isabel, Isabel, I want to leave this hospital. I want to go home, but the doctor told her that I am too ill. He says I need medical attention that I can get only in the hospital. Isabel always wanted us to move in with her, but we were stubborn. She offered many times to take her father and me. When I wanted to move, Antonio did not. "I have too much work, *mujer*." At his age, nearly ninety years old, and still wanting to work!

And the times when he was agreeable about moving, I hesitated, thinking about my mother in her old age. Getting old makes trouble for others, better to stay where we are, I thought. So we never moved in with Isabel and Vicente. Antonio and I could never agree. Is it too late, now? Am I going to get well enough to go home? Isabel is such a good daughter, no one could ask for a better daughter. *Sí, ella tiene razón, pero*...but I still want to go home even though she is right...*pa lo que me queda*...with what life remains to me, why not let me die at home?

I must have dozed off. Isabel is here almost all the time, but when she has to go to the bathroom, or when she goes to the cafeteria for lunch or to the house to sleep, these nurses don't listen to me. To them I am just a dying old woman. They probably think there is nothing more they can do, and they don't speak Spanish either. People in this country should at least know Spanish. There are so many of us who cannot speak English, but for us it is too late to learn. Not for them, they are young, and they should try to learn.

El doctor MacKenzie told me I have to stay here. He is a good young doctor...*es muy bueno*...and he speaks Spanish. *Habla español*...he doesn't need anyone to translate for him. I told him I don't like it in the hospital, and he says, *"Lo siento mucho, señora Velásquez, pero usted está muy enferma."* He and Isabel, I know they are right, but I still wish I could go home.

Here in the hospital it is hard to get a good sleep. Sometimes I get drowsy, and just when I manage to fall asleep a nurse comes and wakes me up to take my pulse or to tell me I have to take a pill. Or a nurse comes in and sticks a needle in my arm while I am sleeping soundly and wakes me up. I look up and there is the white uniform, always one of them here to bother me. Except when I need them. No matter how many times I ring for them, that's when they don't come. I hate it when they don't come to take me to the bathroom and I soil myself. Then they take their time about coming to change my clothes and change the sheets. Is this any way to treat an old woman? Isabel gets angry with them. I don't know what she says, but when Isabel is talking and waving her arms and gets angry, the nurses listen!

Sometimes I wake up during the night and I don't know where I am. Isabel said that she found me in the bathroom the other day, cleaning the bathtub, thinking I was home. I don't remember, but she said so. During the day my sons and their families visit. Usually they take turns and sometimes they come at the same time. With their wives and sons and daughters. At times, the room is filled with visitors. My daughters-in-law, my sons, and my grandchildren, my great grandchildren, but Isabel is always here. Sometimes I don't know who it is that comes up to me and kisses me and says, *"¿Cómo está, 'buela?"* What am I supposed to answer? Depending on my mood, if I feel like making them laugh I will say, *"Bien."* Then I say, *"Bien fregada."* All worn out, ha, ha! Ahh-a-ah! What a wretched life!

They see that I am dying, but they love to make me laugh with their constant joking. Especially my youngest, Eduardo, *¡Que lindo, mi consentido!* I used to scold him when he didn't visit me for a long time, always too busy with his work. He's a very important businessman, always dressed up, suit, tie. "I could die here at home," I said to him, "and you wouldn't even know, Eduardo. One day you'll come to visit and you'll find me dead." And in his playful way, he made me laugh, as he always does. "Of course I would know, Mamá, I would read about it in the newspaper." *¡Ah qué m'hijo!* So silly. Always acting up. Here in the hospital I was remembering the other day, how right after he was born, when the nurse brought him to me to breastfeed, she said, "This little one gave you big trouble, a very difficult time, Mrs. Velásquez." A Mexican nurse translated, *"Este muchacho va a ser muy travieso."* He's going to grow up to be full of mischief. He is my last born. We were very poor in those days. He was going to be the seventh, but I lost the one before him. All of them boys, except Isabel. "No more after this baby," I told Antonio. "We can barely feed the large family we already have."

They grew up so fast. Now I wonder where the years went. How did we get so old? Who would have known that Antonio and I would live so long? Who could have imagined we would have such a large family! Every day they come to visit. Except for Miguel, he is too far away. If only he would write.

"¡*Isabel!* Has Miguel written?"

"No, Mamá, but he telephoned. He's coming to see you, and this time Natalie and Sara and Becky are coming with him. Next week." *Vienen la semana próxima, los cuatro. Los periódicos dicen que viene un norte y que va a hacer mucho frío.* She tells me that the weather reports say a bad norther is bringing some very cold weather when they come.

"This is one of the worst winters in Texas in a long, long time. And you know, Mamá, *Sara habla español.* You'll be able to talk with her in Spanish."

Que bueno, hija.

Last night I was thinking about what it was like to be a girl in the old days. For a long time I could not get to sleep. I was aching all over. *Pobrecita* Isabel. She had fallen asleep in her chair. If sleeping in a bed is uncomfortable, it must be much more uncomfortabe to sleep in a chair. I finally fell asleep. Just before I closed my eyes I was thinking about Miguel's daughters. When the little one was five or six years old, I don't remember exactly, they came to visit. Her sister is a little older, two years, I think. Maybe they were a little older than that, but they were little. One evening the little girls made me laugh so much. I was sitting in my armchair, Miguel and I were watching one of the telenovelas on the Mexican television station. I heard them laughing, and out of the corner of my eye I saw them in the hall. Then I turned my head and saw them. They were laughing, holding hands, going into the bathroom to take a bath, all by themselves, and they didn't have any clothes on. Oh my heavens! *¡Diocito mío!* There they were, little Sara and little Rebecca, just like on the day they were born, and I could not help laughing aloud. Miguel asked me why I laughed. He was sitting on the sofa and could not see his little girls. He asked me again. "*¿Por qué se ríe, Mamá?*" And I told him. "Your little girls, *tus hijitas,* Miguel, they just went into the bathroom. I saw them in the hallway, without any clothes on, just like on the day when they were born, and they were not at all embarrassed about their bodies." Miguel told me that he and Natalie were bringing up their daughters to respect their bodies, to know that there is nothing shameful about the body, and that day, I thought, oh, how different it used to be for girls, for women in the old days! My mother was always telling us girls to keep our knees together, to sit properly. She used to get so angry about the way we would sit. *¡No anden enseñando sus vergüenzas! No se sienten como los hombres.* "Don't sit like the men do. Keep your legs together!"

So I am glad for Isabel, for my daughters-in-law, and for my granddaughters that some things have changed for women. They went to school, they learned how to read and write, and their daughters are in school now. The next generation of women will have good jobs too. My granddaughters take pride in their jobs. Whenever one of them buys a new car she drives it over to show it to me. "Look *'buela,* I bought a new car." *Sí, me da mucho gusto por ellas*. They have good jobs. They buy nice clothing and dress nicely all the time. Yes, they speak English and they drive their own cars and they have their own money to spend. When a woman can drive, she does not have to depend on a man to take her anywhere. Things were much different in the old days. Even so, I always found it very annoying when any of my daughters-in-law or my granddaughters would sit down at the table to eat before the men, or expect to be served, as if they were men. *¡Me daba mucho coraje!* I could not help it. I never could get used to it. How dare they act as if they were men!

"*¡Isabel!* Did you prepare something to eat for your brothers?"

"Mamá, *estamos en el hospital*. We're in the hospital. *Los muchachos* ate before coming to see you."

Wisdom Women
CB Follett

Old women, you were the lattice
for new growing vines, used to tell
how fire was kindled, blazed,
how the years turned and seasons
swelled with new growth.

Dark eyes nearly hidden
you kept the secrets. Waited.
Planned when to fish, plant,
harvest the tall grain. You
instructed girls in the mysteries

of blood and sex,
birth, children. You held the moon
on a silken thread, tugged it
around Earth so cycles interwove

with songs you sang by dark-night
while the moon slept, the sky lit
with thousands of stone fires.
You chanted our histories,
how we moved
across land and streambed to come here,
and when we moved from here, as spring
heated the land, this too would you braid
into the story, spinning it out
in thick plaits.
Now, old women don't tell us
what is carried in their wisdoms.
They live silent,
separate from the rest of us
and the long call of the owl is far.

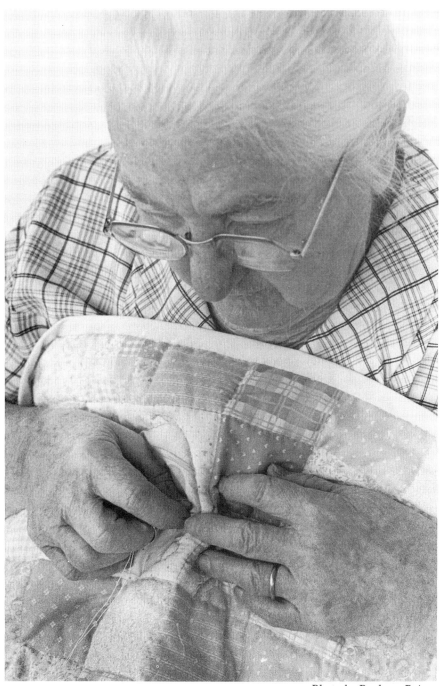

Photo by Barbara Beirne

Prayers for My Aging
Arupa Chiarini

1.
May my body be
an old tree
inscribed by rain,
one rumpled breast
held high
to feel the sun,
one low,
to nurse
the landscape of the earth,
sienna rose of evening time.

2.
May I grow old
with the cypress
by the ocean.
May I be rocked
by the waves,
while my sparse hairs
dance and gossip
with the wind.

3.
May I be the silver birch,
may I stand through the winter,
may I reflect light,
may my desires be written
in black lace calligraphy
on white parchment,
may the universe rejoice
in my beauty.

Romance in the Old Folks' Home
Michael Waters

First he offered to read to her,
but she was afraid
he spoke as Bible-thumper, so declined.

Then he steeped several
herbal teas for her table—
she sipped without looking up.

He scissored photos from weeklies
and taped them to her door,
little windows into the past:

couples skating on Highland Pond,
dancing four days in a marathon,
sleeping on roofs above Flatbush Avenue.

She knew she was being spoken to
in a language long forgotten,
like Latin lost after school.

When she found the horned shell
near her lounge on the lawn,
she pressed it to her ear
to hear the ceaseless *hush*,
knowing longing had replaced
the sluggish creature housed there.

The next evening she appeared
with freshly-washed hair
pinned with an ivory comb,

and brought that shy spirit
her favorite book—
The Marble Faun by Nathaniel Hawthorne

who liked to brood on sin—
while the faint widows flushed
and whispered her name—oh, Anna!—

and she asked him please to begin.

Photo by Teresa Tamura

Her Game
Floyd Skloot

The nightly round of gin
rummy and shot of schnapps.
They both play to win.
The TV, one of their props,
flickers unwatched, the tints
wrong, the sound low.

She is eighty-eight. He hints
her mind and wits are slow
now, no match for his. This
is false and he knows it. Another
prop, such banter; it's his
specialty. He calls her "Mother"
when he is close to losing,
Rosie when winning. She'll shake
her head and say, "Choosing
you was a serious mistake."

The time he had fare
left for one only,
she said she did not care
to walk, rode the trolley
home herself, and made
him walk the mile through rain.

She underknocks. Played
perfectly. It's still her game.

Drying Apricots
Maggi Ann Grace

Earlier than light
they coax a stepladder
and pails stained black
to the far corner
of the orchard
where once they wrapped
themselves in blankets
and moonlight, would
have melted into each other
if they could. But now,
branches arc over the ground
that breathes the ripeness
of wounded fruit.
The reach is easy.
It is fruit they have come for,
and they fill their buckets
with echoes of the hollow
sound of flutes,
darkening into fullness.

They carry their harvest,
now heavy between them,
to sawhorse tables.
Their task is familiar

(they have been at it for years):
to discard the stone
that alone seems to couple
this fruit. Wife on one side,
husband, opposite.
Their fingers split the pick
easily without a blade
until their hands web
with juice. And the halves
are arranged to dry
on wooden trays branded
by the process, day after
day after week in a season.
Sun-seared apricots thicken
to a new meat—tougher
than the whole, and sweeter
on the tongue.

Photo by Barbara Beirne

Dance
Lynne Burgess

The phone is ringing. The old woman lets it. She sits still in the rocker looking out over the tall August field to the end of the coulee. It is going to be hot again. Hot and humid. Out the south window, Catback Ridge curves still and shimmering green against the pale morning sky. A cloud of dense air rises as the day heats, climbing to blue. The old woman needs to watch it evaporate to nothingness.

She wants to be a plant. A dandelion. So that at the browning end of this life, now that the wind has blown her seed away, she can wilt back into the earth, unnoticed. Not a mother, a grandmother, an old neighbor, a widow. Just a plant. Her bones are light and porous, her short white hair so thin her scalp makes it look pink, her skin dry as summer dust. It is time to loosen her roots from this farm. The old woman sits in the rocker and tries to still everything that moves within her—heart, breath, bowels.

The phone starts ringing again. The old woman gets up and pulls the phone jack out of the wall. She lowers herself stiffly to the kitchen floor and lies spread-eagle, sun warming her, relaxing her. Nan, her oldest, is the hardest to shake free. It is probably her on the phone just now, calling to see about groceries. At least that is the pretense. Really calling to check on her.

Nan doesn't understand. "No, Mother," she always says when the old woman presses a fifty into her hand. "You need it more than I do." But that isn't the point.

The old woman has systematically given away the contents of her savings account, has emptied her closets, keeping only the most essential cookware, blankets, and furniture. Every time someone stops by, they leave with something. It can be a blue bowl, a red sweater, a pile of embroidered pillowcases, or a worn wing-backed chair. The picture albums have been divided up, old letters tied in bundles according to sender, books offered to the children who have loved them best, mementos given to the grandchildren. The old woman has burned her notebooks filled with years of private thoughts. With each load that leaves the house, by hand, by fire smoke, or by failures of memory, the old woman feels lighter, closer to what she seeks to be.

She keeps only the white cat. And the land. These are two things she doesn't truly own. The cat chose her. And the land, well, the land. She remembers when Henry first brought her to this coulee. She felt like she was absorbing every wren song, every pine scent, every goldenrod, every line of leaf against sky. She hushed Henry's voice and walked into the field where he planned to build their house. Still vivid in her memory are the small yellow butterflies spiraling over spikes of vervain swaying, purple, in the wind. As she breathed, she was soaked by the deep sense that this farm was where she had always been.

The sunlight shifts from east to west, slowly. The old woman feels sweat pool over her upper lip, soak her armpits and crotch. The white cat lies stretched full body along her side. Gravel crunches under tires in the driveway. The old woman's heart speeds up. The cat is instantly on all fours. A car door slams. "Dammit," the old woman mutters. She rolls to her side, then to her hands and knees. Blood pounds in her temples, and she nearly blacks out. The kitchen screen opens. The old woman pulls herself up and sits heavily in the rocker. Nan sets a bag of groceries on the table.

"Your phone isn't working, Mother."

The old woman doesn't answer, just starts rocking.

"Mother, you look flushed. Are you OK?"

The old woman narrows her eyes.

"Mother, please talk to me. Are you OK? I tried to call…" Nan grabs the disconnected phone jack coiling on the wooden floor. She shakes it at her mother. "What if you get sick or hurt? What if something should happen to you?" Her voice is squeaky as if her vocal chords were being squeezed by tongs.

The old woman sighs. They have been over all this before. Something is going to happen, is always going to happen. It is this inevitability that gives her all the courage she needs to live alone, not preserved like a jar of pickles in the safety of her daughter's home. But Nan has always tried to take care of things, control things. When she was a teenager, she nearly killed herself by not eating. The old woman remembers holding Nan's hand across the kitchen table, saying, "Eat this honey cake. It's your favorite." It didn't get better until she stopped thinking it was her job as a mother to make Nan's life right. We are too much alike, the old woman thinks. This daughter wants to intervene in what cannot be stopped. And it feels to the old woman like meddling. So she concentrates on the sound of a morning dove cooing in the pines. The cat settles in for a nap on her lap, sleek and warm.

"All right, don't talk to me." Nan's voice enters her. "A cooked chicken is in the foil bag. I'm putting it in the fridge. If you don't want me to come around tomorrow, you'd better answer your phone." She slams the door harder than is necessary. The white cat looks up, startled.

It has been a long time since Henry died, almost forty years. Some days it seems as if the years they spent together belong to another woman, that when she buried him, her life became something new. On those days, she barely thinks of him. Her memories and dreams arch right over her marriage to her youth. She had lived a restricted city life as an only child in a literary family. She remembers white dresses with eyelets and satin sashes, black hightop boots with pointed toes, afternoons when all would retire to their rooms and read. Most evenings were spent in polite attendance to dinner guests. She had no special friends, even at school. Schoolgirl whisperings and crushes seemed vaguely ridiculous and, more to the point, impossible for her. She lived, solitary, surrounded by adults who liked to argue the fine points of Joyce and Elliot, while sipping sherry.

Henry changed everything. And ever since the white cat squeezed through the backdoor as she was closing it, she has been remembering him. What the cat has to do with him, she doesn't know. How can this slender green-eyed female have anything to do with the big, hard-working farmer who brought her to the coulee and gave her five children? About the only likeness was its mystifying insistence on staying with her even before she began putting out dishes of milk-soaked bread. No matter where she went, outside or in, the cat would find a place to sleep nearby. At night it liked to sleep with one paw on her arm, purring like the distant engine of a mower.

"Henry," she said, years ago, "let's dance." The music on the radio was filling her legs with an unexpected longing to move, to find a way back to the first days of their courtship. She put down the iron and waltzed over to tug the loose straps of her husband's overalls. Henry never danced in public. He even blushed when he had to pass the collection plate at church. He hated standing out in front of anyone. He would move with unusual speed to the men's room if an insistent dowager came after him at a wedding. No, Henry did not like to put his barn of a body on display. The memorable exception was their wedding day. The woman supposed he'd become numb to embarrassment after having stood before the entire town and all her stuffy relatives and said, "I, Henry, take thee, May," so publicly. And then he kissed her. She'd been surprised at the tenderness of his kiss. He was sweating, his face red, his collar looking two sizes too small. But he took her hand, held it in his clammy one and kissed her in front of everybody. And that day he danced, awkwardly at first, but his solid frame found the rhythm of the fiddle. It was as if a spring had welled up through an alfalfa field, irrepressible and pure. And that night, years later, children grown and gone, she remembers that Henry, tired and still sweaty from field work, took her in his arms, and they swayed to the radio music. Until she remembered the hot iron and pulled away to finish pressing out the wrinkles in his Sunday pants.

The cat is warm on the old woman's lap. When had Nan left? It is common for her, these days, to get lost in a daydream. The day is slipping toward evening. The old woman knows that the night sky will be bright with the full moon.

She stands, and the cat drops gracefully to its feet, taking the opportunity to clean its forepaw. Yes, she thinks, there will be enough light. She finds her old work boots in the dusty closet and ties them on. The worn leather brings back a memory of haying so strong she can smell the drying windrows. The ridge appears close, possible. Nothing else needed but the starting out.

The trail to the ridge has narrowed to a deer path now that Henry isn't around to keep it mowed. But it is still there. Blackberry canes tear at the old woman's skirt and skin. The fruit's purple juice mingles with blood from the thorns' scratches. It is a soft dusk. The day's heat works its way up through the birch, cooling the woods. A wind blows gnats and mosquitoes away. The white cat has slipped out with her into the evening air. It follows, tail straight up, luminous against the dark underbrush. The old woman has to stop every few yards to let her racing pulse slow. The cat leans against her tired legs, waiting for her to go on. Now she is remembering Nan when she was a toddler. She sees her, blue of eye, silky hair shining like a halo in the sun, squatting by a small grass snake, its head crushed by a car in the driveway. "No no no no no," her daughter was chanting. She watched from the kitchen door. It was Henry who gently lifted the snake, let his daughter stroke the soft brown scales, then threw it into the tangled gooseberries.

A loud whippoorwill startles the old woman. Keep on climbing. Slow and steady. All the time in the world. Her legs are quivering and her shirt sticks to her skin when she finds the place. She rests against a sandstone outcropping until the dizziness passes. Then she turns. Behind her the full moon is rising, vibrating in the sky. Before her the layered ridges deepen into greys as the sun's rose light slips beyond them. Her pumping heart slows. There is a rhythm in the night, of arteries flowing, pulsing crickets, wind rocking trees. The white cat calls to her its lovely query. Down below the old woman can see the farm house, small lodestone beyond whose pull she has climbed. The kitchen light comes on.

"Let's dance, Henry," May says into the night.

Front Porch Partners
Elizabeth Crawford

They suit one another, rocking
together; she in polished oak
spindles, he in overstuffed
maple covered by blue afghan
crocheted in years past.

She hums a song someone
played at their wedding
while he daydreams of dancing
with their prettiest guest.

He reviews images of work,
playing cards, hunting, fishing;
hears creak of wooden oars
cutting through cold morning mist.

She sees an old trundle sewing
machine, the vegetable garden
bordered on all sides by favorite
bright-colored flowers,

and remembers platters of fresh
fish dragged through flour
then fried to golden crispness
in the hot oil of a black iron skillet.

When a frown strains her forehead,
he pats the back of her hand
which slowly turns upward
palming his fingers, reassuring
that she is still there,
still aware of his presence.

Photo by Martha Wright

Acknowledgments

Grateful acknowledgment is made to the following publications which first published some of the material in this book: *The Poet from the City of the Angels* (Bombshelter Press, 1995) for "Hands" by Michael Andrews; *Corrales Comment,* Vol. XIII, No. 4, April 9, 1994 for "Spring Without Burpee Seeds" by Jean Blackmon Waszak; *Pebbles,* Vol. 1, No. 3, Fall 1994 for "In the Autumn" by William Borden; *For Truly to See Your Face* (Black Hat Press, 1996) for "Dance" by Lynne Burgess; *Karamu,* 1996 for "Nearing Menopause, I Run into Elvis at Shoprite," by Barbara Crooker; *Sou'wester,* Vol. 14, No. 3, Spring/Summer 1987 for "At the Reunion" under the title "Reunion" by Mark DeFoe; *The MacGuffin,* Vol. VIII, No. 1, Spring 1991 for "Manon Reassures Her Lover" by Martha Elizabeth; *Psychopoetica, Remembering and Forgetting,* Spring 1995 (University of Hull, UK) for "Wisdom Women" by CB Follett; *Pinehurst Journal,* September 24, 1993, for "Retired" by Daniel Green; *Plainsong,* Vol. 6, No. 1, Winter 1985 and *Where We've Been* (Britenbush Books, 1989) for "Nothing's Been the Same Since John Wayne Died" by William Greenway; *Willamette Week,* December 17—23, 1992, for "Emmaline" by Willa Holmes; *Coffeehouse Poets Quarterly,* November 1992, for "Meditation for Twilight" by Albert Huffstickler; *If Death Were a Woman,* Spring 1994 for "Instructions for Ashes" by Ellen Kort; *I Know It Isn't Funny But...* (Sunflower Inc. Publishing, 1995) for "Pebbles and Crumbs" by Ric Masten; *St. Petersburg Times,* December 9, 1986, *The Orlando Sentinel*, November 2, 1986, and *The Columbus Dispatch*, March 1987 for "A Woman Like That" by Peter Meinke; *Literally* (Writers' Center of Indianapolis), Fall 1994 and *The Village Sampler,* November 1994 for "Harvest" by Shirley Vogler Meister; *The Work of Our Hands* (The Muses' Company, 1992) and *The New Quarterly,* Vol. XI, No. 4, Winter 1992 for "Spring Cleaning" by Sharon H. Nelson; *With Respect for Distance* (Black Rock Press, 1992) for "For an Anniversary" by Gailmarie Pahmeier; *The Southern Anthology* (Southern Artists Alliance, 1995) for "Queen of Cards and Powders" by William Ratner; *Home Planet News,* Vol. 6, No. 3, Issue #25, 1988, *A Wound-Up Cat and Other Bedtime Stories* (Palmerston Press, Toronto, 1993), *Flying Time: Stories and Half-Stories* (Signal Books, 1992 and 1996 ©Elisavietta Ritchie), and *The Arc of the Storm* (Signal Books, 1996) for "Flying Time" by Elisavietta Ritchie; *Room of One's Own,* December 1995 for "Choices," previously titled "The Mount" by Nancy Robertson; *Prairie Schooner,* Vol. LVIII, No. 3, Fall 1974 for "Her Game" by Floyd Skloot; *Plexus,* Issue #55, May 1995 for "The Man Who Loved the Woman Who Loved Elvis" by Terry Amrhein Tappouni; *Porter Gulch Review,* Spring 1995, for "Widow" by Eleanor Van Houten; *Ms.,* Vol. III, No. 5, March/April 1993 and the *1992 Frederick County Poetry Contest Winners Anthology* for "Reflections in Green Glass" by Davi Walders; *Poetry,* Vol. CXLIX, No. 3, December 1986 and *The Burden Lifters* (Carnegie Mellon University Press, 1989) for "Romance in the Old Folks' Home" by Michael Waters; *Gypsy,* No. 17, 1991, *Mind Matters Review,* Summer 1992, and *The Plaza* (Tokyo, Japan), Issue #25, August 1995 for "The Well" by Christopher Woods.

Contributors

MICHAEL ANDREWS is cofounder/publisher/editor of Bombshelter Press and *ONTHEBUS*. He has published nine poetry books and three poetry-photography portfolios, and he has coauthored a book of poems about Vietnam. He has also finished two novels and a book of philosophy, *The Gnomes of Uncertainty* (Waking World), which is being digitally published on the World Wide Web. He has traveled around the world and is currently living in Los Angeles. *p. 32* §

DORI APPEL is an award-winning poet, playwright, and fiction writer, whose work has appeared in four previous Papier-Mache anthologies. Of her eleven produced plays, *Girl Talk*, coauthored with Carolyn Myers, was published by Samuel French, Inc., in 1992. "Friendship," a monologue from *Female Troubles,* is included in *More Monologues by Women, for Women* (Heinemann, 1996). *p. 50* §

ANNE C. BARNHILL lives in Kernersville, North Carolina, where she writes freelance for area newspapers and magazines. She began writing seriously in 1989, and she won an Emerging Artist Grant in 1991. In 1993 she received a writer's residency from the Syvenna Foundation in Linden, Texas. Her fiction has appeared in several literary anthologies and magazines, and she's been selected as a Blumenthal Writer/Reader for 1996. *p.137*

BARBARA BEIRNE of Morristown, New Jersey, has exhibited her photography in numerous museums and galleries. She has written and photographed six children's books. She is an adjunct professor at County College of Morris, and is currently pursuing a photography project in Appalachia. The Thanks Be to Grandmother Winifred Foundation has recently awarded her a grant to help fund this project. *p. 171* and *179*

JUDITH BELL lives in Arlington, Virginia, with her husband and son. Her novel, *Real Love,* won the 1989 Washington Prize for Fiction. Her stories have appeared in many journals, including *The Washington Review* and *Snake Nation Review,* and in the anthologies *Farm Wives and Other Iowa Stories* and *A Loving Voice.* An art historian, she writes for *Art and Antiques*, *Elle*, *Omni*, *USAir*, and *The Boston Globe Magazine*, among others. *p. 127*

JEAN BLACKMON is an essayist and short story writer whose work has appeared in publications such as *Puerto del Sol*, the *Dallas Morning News,* and *Tumblewords: Writers Reading the West*. She won a first prize for short fiction from *Writer's Digest*. She lives in Corrales, New Mexico, where she and her husband own a grocery store. *p. 85*

WILLIAM BORDEN's novel, *Superstoe,* was published by Orloff Press in 1996. His short stories have won the PEN Syndicated Fiction Award and have appeared in numerous magazines. He is Chester Fritz Distinguished Professor of English at the University of North Dakota and is Fiction Editor of the *North Dakota Quarterly. p. 6* §

LYNNE BURGESS lives in rural Wisconsin. Her writing comes in batches that correspond with time off from teaching adolescents. "Dance" is included in the collection, *For Truly to See Your Face,* due in 1996 from Black Hat Press. *p. 180*

GRACE BUTCHER is Professor Emeritus of English from Kent State University's Geauga Campus. Her most recent book, *Child, House, World,* won the Ohio Poet of the Year award for 1991. She has been competing in track for over forty years. *p. 144* §

ARUPA CHIARINI is Playwright in Residence at Acrosstown Repertory Theater, a grassroots, multicultural theater in Gainesville, Florida. She is proud to be part of the Writers in the Schools program. She has lived in Vermont, Oklahoma, Hawaii, California, and Florida. *p. 172*

PETER COOLEY has published five books of poems, the most recent of which is *The Astonished Hours* (Carnegie Mellon, 1992). He teaches creative writing at Tulane University and lives in New Orleans with his wife and three children. His poem is from a new manuscript to be called *Sacred Conversations. p. 4*

ANN COOPER, a teacher-on-the-trail, has written six natural history books for children, including the 1992 children/young adult Colorado Book Award winner. Her poetry and essays have appeared in the *Christian Science Monitor, Sistersong, Frogpond,* and *Poet Magazine. p. 47*

ELIZABETH CRAWFORD earned her BA in history and English with writing concentration at the University of Wisconsin. She has had poetry published in the *Wisconsin Poet's Calendar* for the past three years and works as the general manager of a bookstore that specializes in gently used, collectable, and new books. She recently began facilitating workshops on Courting Creativity. *p. 185*

BARBARA CROOKER has published over five hundred poems in magazines such as *Yankee, The Christian Science Monitor, Country Journal,* and in over forty anthologies (including four by Papier-Mache) and five books. She has received three Pennsylvania Council on the Arts Fellowships in Literature, raised three children, and is still dancing. *p. 12* §

CORTNEY DAVIS coedited *Between the Heartbeats: Poetry and Prose by Nurses* (University of Iowa Press, 1995) and authored *The Body Flute* (Adastra Press, 1994). Her poetry book, *Details of Flesh,* will be out in spring 1997 (Calyx Books). A recipient of a 1994 NEA poetry fellowship and two Connecticut Commission on the Arts poetry grants (1990 and 1994), she lives in Redding, Connecticut, and works as a nurse practitioner in women's health. *p. 15*

MARK DEFOE is a teacher/administrator at West Virginia Wesleyan College. His two chapbooks are *Bringing Home Breakfast* and *Palmate.* His work has appeared in *Poetry, Paris Review, Sewanee Review, Kenyon Review, Yale Review, North American Review,* and many other publications. *p. 16* §

MARTHA ELIZABETH grew up in Virginia, lived in Texas for ten years, and is now a writer and artist in Missoula, Montana. Her poetry collection, *The Return of Pleasure* (Confluence Press, 1996), won the Montana Arts Council First Book Award. *p. 1*

CB FOLLETT's poems have appeared in numerous magazines and anthologies, including *Calyx, Slant, The Taos Review,* and *Verve.* She recently won the 1994 New Press Literary Quarterly poetry contest and the 1995 Portland Festival Prize, and she received a Marin Arts Council poetry grant in 1995. She has published two poetry collections, *The Latitudes of Their Going*, 1993, and *Gathering the Mountains*, 1995. She is also a painter. *p. 170*

MICHAEL S. GLASER is a professor of literature and creative writing at St. Mary's College of Maryland, where he directs the annual literary festival. He edited the anthology, *The Cooke Book: A Seasoning of Poets* (SCOP Publications), and his own poems are gathered in *A Lover's Eye* (The Bunny and Crocodile Press), now in its second printing. He has five children, serves as a Poet-in-the-Schools for the Maryland State Arts Council and lives in St. Mary's City, Maryland, with his wife, Kathleen. *p. 17* §

MARIANNE GONTARZ is passionate about people, particularly the aging process, which she expresses in both her work and her photographs. Her work has illustrated many books, including *Ourselves Growing Older* (Boston Women's Health Collective), *Growing Old Disgracefully* (Hen Co-op), and Caroline Bird's *Lives of Their Own: The Secrets of Salty Old Women.* A transplanted Bostonian, she now happily resides in San Rafael, California. *pp. xvi, 27, and 45* §

KATHERINE GOVIER is an Edmonton native who has lived in Calgary, Washington, D.C., and London, England, and now lives in Toronto with her husband and two children. She has taught at Ryerson and York University in Toronto and at Leeds University in England. She has published three short story collections and four novels. Her recent novel, *Hearts of Flame,* received the 1992 City of Toronto Book Award. Her next novel, *Angel Walk,* is due out in the fall of 1996. *p. 112*

MAGGI ANN GRACE is a poet and fiction writer living in Chapel Hill, North Carolina. She teaches creative writing in the most unlikely settings, but also in schools, summer camps, and through adult education programs. She holds an MFA from the University of North Carolina, Greensboro, and is happy to have her work included in this anthology, her third from Papier-Mache. *p. 177* §

DANIEL GREEN, a social worker for many years, was the executive director of the Red Cross in New York. He started writing poetry at age eighty-two, several years after being widowed. He has since published numerous poems in many journals, and has three collections in print, *Late Start* (1989), *On Second Thought* (1992), and *Better Late* (1995). Now eighty-seven, he is remarried, and he and his wife travel extensively. *p. 120*

WILLIAM GREENWAY is a native of Atlanta and is Distinguished Professor of English at Youngstown State University. He has published five collections of poetry, the latest of which is *How the Dead Bury the Dead*, from the University of Akron Press. *p. 44*

ROSE HAMILTON-GOTTLIEB's recent publications include "Forty Acres" in *Farm Wives and Other Iowa Stories,* plus stories in *Room of One's Own* and *The Elephant Ear.* The theme for *Grow Old Along with Me,* combined with her experience cycling, inspired "Aerodynamic Integrity." *p. 35*

ROBERT L. HARRISON has been published in books such as *At the Crack of the Bat* and *Slam Dunk* (Hyperion Books for Children); *Baseball: A Treasury of Art and Literature* (Hugh Lauten Levin Associates, Inc.); *The Best of Spitball* (Doubleday); *Mudville Diaries* (Avon Books); and *Green Fields and White Lines* (McFarland & Company), his own book of baseball poetry. He now resides in East Meadow, New York, with his wife, Dorothy, and their two sons, Roger and Kevin. *p. 29*

DIANNA HENNING holds an MFA in writing from Vermont College of Norwich University. She was awarded the 1994 fellowship to the Writers' Centre in Ireland, sponsored by Eastern Washington University. She has recently been published in *Sing Heavenly Muse!, Slant, The Lullwater Review,* and *Staple* in England, and her essay on William Butler Yeats was published in the twenty-fifth anniversary issue of *Psychological Perspectives*. *p. 163*

LOIS TSCHETTER HJELMSTAD is a Colorado piano teacher and author of award-winning *Fine Black Lines: Reflections on Facing Cancer, Fear and Loneliness.* Other work has appeared in various publications, including *The Rocky Mountain News, American Medical News, Health Progress, Your Health, Colorado Woman News,* and *LinkUp* (England). *p. 89*

WILLA HOLMES, a writer, retired high school teacher and, years ago, a reporter/photographer for a weekly newspaper, has four children and ten grandchildren. Her husband, Tom, a retired college counselor, is definitely not the model for Howard in her story. She lives in Troutdale, Oregon. *p. 121*

EUNICE HOLTZ lives on the edge of Cherokee Marsh in Madison, Wisconsin, where she is aware of nature daily. She uses poetry and journaling to hold onto the precious ordinary things of life. "What Do Old Women Talk About" was written in response to the death of a dear friend who chose never to talk about ill health. *p. 108*

ALBERT HUFFSTICKLER, a native Texan, graduated from Southwest Texas State University. Now retired from the University of Texas Library, he is sixty-seven. A Texas Senate Resolution recognized his contribution to Texas poetry in 1989. His last collection, *Working on My Death Chant,* was funded by the Texas Commission on the Arts. *p. 136*

ALLISON JOSEPH is the author of *What Keeps Us Here* (Ampersand Press, 1992). Born in London, raised in Toronto and the Bronx, New York, she currently lives in Carbondale, Illinois. She teaches creative writing at Southern Illinois University at Carbondale. *p. 2* §

PHYLLIS KING has lived many lives in her seventy-five years: college student, mother of four, display manager, librarian (recently retired from New York Public), and finally poet. In the last seven years, she has been published in numerous small magazines. She is married to James L. McPherson. *p. 63*

ELLEN KORT, from Appleton, Wisconsin, received the Pablo Neruda Poetry Prize, authored twelve books, and teaches writing workshops for cancer survivors. Her work has been performed by the New York City Dance Theatre. *p. 98* §

JOHN LAUE, former editor of *Transfer* (San Francisco State University) and associate editor of *San Francisco Review,* and also a paranoid schizophrenic, is a widely published prize-winning poet who taught and counseled high school students for twenty years. His poem, "Fallout Fantasy," is from his manuscript, *Wasted Roses,* about his teaching experiences. Now retired, he coordinates readings for his National Writers Union local and is on its steering committee. *p. 142*

KATHRYN ETTERS LOVATT, a South Carolina native, lives and writes in Hong Kong. She has an MA in creative writing from Hollins College, and her stories and poems have appeared in a number of periodicals and anthologies, including *I Am Becoming the Woman I've Wanted* (Papier-Mache Press, 1994). *p. 147* §

ELIUD MARTÍNEZ, novelist, surrealist artist, and amateur photographer, has published a novel, *Voice-Haunted Journey* (1990, Bilingual Press, Tempe, Arizona), the first of a projected trilogy titled, *The Notebooks of Miguel Velásquez.* "The World of Dolores Velásquez" is excerpted from the second novel of the trilogy. A Texas native, he received his PhD in English and comparative literature from Ohio University, Athens. He teaches fiction, film, and creative writing at the University of California, Riverside. *pp. 87 and 165*

RIC MASTEN was born in Carmel, California, in 1929. He has toured extensively over the last twenty-six years, reading his poetry in well over four hundred colleges and universities in North America, Canada, and England. He is a well-known conference theme speaker and is a regular on many television and radio talk shows. He lives with his poet-wood carver wife, Billie Barbara, in the Big Sur mountains. He has thirteen books to his credit. *p. 95* §

JAMES LOWELL MCPHERSON, former college teacher, former village postmaster, former Poet Laureate of West Virginia while soldiering overseas in World War II, author of *Goodbye Rosie* (Knopf 1965), has been writing poetry for seventy of his seventy-five years. He is married to Phyllis King. *p. 62*

PETER MEINKE is a poet and short story writer who lives in St. Petersburg, Florida. He read his story, "A Woman Like That," winner of a 1986 PEN Syndicated Fiction Award, at the Library of Congress in December 1988. His book, *The Piano Tuner*, won the 1986 Flannery O'Connor Award for Short Fiction. His latest book is *Scars*, a collection of poems. Retired in 1993, he most recently has been Writer-in-Residence at the University of North Carolina at Greensboro. *p. 68*

SHIRLEY VOGLER MEISTER is an award-winning Indianapolis freelancer with prose and poetry in diverse US and Canadian publications. Her poetry's been in print more than four hundred times, including in Papier-Mache's anthologies, *When I Am an Old Woman I Shall Wear Purple, If I Had My Life to Live Over I Would Pick More Daisies,* and *I Am Becoming the Woman I've Wanted. p. 84* §

SHARON H. NELSON's eighth book of poems, *Family Scandals* (1994), follows *The Work of Our Hands* (1992) and *Grasping Men's Metaphors* (1993) in a series about the constructions of language, sexuality, and gender. She writes essays and political analyses and edits nonfiction in Montreal. *p. 82* §

GAILMARIE PAHMEIER coordinates the creative writing program at the University of Nevada. She is twice the recipient of an Artists Fellowship from the Nevada State Council on the Arts. She is the author of *With Respect for Distance* (Black Rock Press, 1992). *p. 65* §

MARY ELIZABETH PARKER is a poet, essayist, and fiction writer in Browns Summit, North Carolina. She has two published chapbooks of poems, including the prize-winning *Breathing in a Foreign Country*, and has authored several published or soon-to-be-published essays and short stories, including "There's a Place Named France," accepted for broadcast on National Public Radio's *Sound of Writing. p. 76*

ROGER PFINGSTON teaches English and photography in Bloomington, Indiana. His poems and photographs have appeared in numerous magazines and anthologies, including *New Letters, Yankee, Artful Dodge, Camera & Darkroom, American Photo, Shots,* and *The Party Train,* a collection of North American prose poems. *pp. 46 and 146*

WILLIAM RATNER lives in Los Angeles with his wife and two daughters, works as a voice-over actor, has published fiction in *Pleiades* and *Taiwan Fiction,* essays in *Coast Magazine* and *TV Marquee,* and reads aloud for a public school literacy program. *p. 51*

ELISAVIETTA RITCHIE's *Flying Time: Stories and Half-Stories* contains four PEN Syndicated Fiction winners. Some of her other books are *Elegy for the Other Woman: New and Selected Terribly Female Poems, Tightening the Circle Over Eel Country* (Great Lakes Colleges Association's 1975–76 New Writer's Award winner), and *Raking the Snow* (Washington Writer's Publishing House 1981–82 winner). She edited *The Dolphin's Arc: Endangered Creatures of the Sea. p. 160* §

NANCY ROBERTSON lives in Prince Rupert, British Columbia. Her writing has appeared in a wide variety of publications including *Room of One's Own, Gallerie: Women's Art, Prairie Fire,* and the anthology, *Gifts of Our Fathers* (The Crossing Press, 1994). *p. 158*

SAVINA ROXAS, former Clarion State University professor, writes award-winning poetry and fiction, and has recently been published in *Green Fuse, Poets On:, Whole Notes,* and an anthology, *Grandmothers Through the Eyes of Women Writers.* She has a poetry chapbook, *Sacrificial Mix,* and her novel, *A Rocky Shore,* is with Lee Shore Literary Agency. *p. 90* §

SARA SANDERSON is an Indianapolis essayist, book reviewer, lecturer, and poet, having written commissioned lyrics for internationally performed music. A Meredith Fund, Texas, grant enabled her to travel to the Pacific Northwest, now often the setting of her poetry. *p. 93*

DEIDRE SCHERER grew up in New York state in a family of artists. She received her BFA from the Rhode Island School of Design in 1967. A cloth book she made for her three daughters inspired her to substitute cloth for paint, and she has since worked with fabric and thread for more than twenty years. Her images of aging have appeared in more than ninety individual and group shows throughout the United States and internationally. Her work has appeared on the covers of several Papier-Mache books. *cover* §

PAT SCHNEIDER's books include *Long Way Home* (poems); *The Writer As an Artist: A New Approach to Writing Alone and With Others;* and (forthcoming) *Wake Up Laughing.* She is director of Amherst Writers and Artists and AWA Press. *p. 88* §

FLOYD SKLOOT's books include the poetry collection *Music Appreciation* (University of Florida Press, 1994), two novels, and a collection of essays, *The Night Side: Seven Years in the Kingdom of the Sick* (Story Line Press, 1996). He lives in Amity, Oregon. *p. 176* §

TERESA TAMURA, a third generation Japanese-American, is a photographer based in Seattle, Washington. She is an MFA graduate of the University of Washington. Her work has appeared in newspapers, magazines, books, and museums. She was born and raised in Idaho. *pp. 5, 28, 81, 111, and 175* §

TERRY AMRHEIN TAPPOUNI is a poet, novelist, reviewer, essayist, and mother of six. Her chapbook, *Lot's Wife,* from Skin Drum Press, is in its second printing. She is an active member of the Undead Arts Collective, a collaboration of visual artists, writers, and musicians in the Tampa Bay area. *p. 13*

ROBERT DANIEL ULLMAN has been a freelancer working in photojournalism, fine art, and editorial photography since 1974. He has had both one-man and group shows in New York City. His background is in fine art, which is the foundation of his work. Born in New York City, he continues to live in New York. *pp. 18 and 162*

KATIE UTTER lives in Westerly, Rhode Island, and has been taking pictures for most of her life. Two of her photographs appeared in Papier-Mache's *I Am Becoming the Woman I've Wanted.* Being able to capture the spark of a person's true personality in a black-and-white photograph, she believes, is her gift. *pp. 64, 94, 126, and 135* §

AMY UYEMATSU is a sansei poet from Los Angeles. Her first book, *30 Miles from J-Town* (Story Line Press, 1992), won the 1992 Nicholas Roerich Poetry Prize. A second book, *Nights of Fire, Nights of Rain,* is due in 1997. *p. 66* §

ELEANOR VAN HOUTEN is a retired speech therapist who lives on the central California coast with her husband who, despite the content of her poem "Widow," is alive and thriving. Some of her poems have been published in the *Porter Gulch Review. p. 157*

JANE AARON VANDER WAL, born in Hopkinsville, Kentucky, in 1937, lives, paints, and writes on the Bay of Fundy shore, Nova Scotia. She has an MA in painting from the University of California, Berkeley. Her husband is a painter. She has one grown daughter: a jazz pianist. She has been published in *Poetry Canada, Antigonish Review, Fiddlehead,* and other Canadian literary magazines. *p. 49*

LISA VICE's novel, *Reckless Driver* (Dutton 1995), will be issued as a Plume paperback in 1996. She has received a PEN Syndicated Fiction Award and a Ludwig R. Voelstein Foundation Award. She lives in Thermopolis, Wyoming, with the writer Martha Clark Cummings. *p. 99*

DAVI WALDERS is a writer and education consultant. She initiated and works actively with writing groups for battered women and parents of HIV-infected children. Her work has appeared in many publications, including *Ms., Seneca Review,* and *Cross Currents.* Mother of two adult daughters, she and her husband of twenty-nine years also canoe and watch for eagles at their cottage on Maryland's Eastern Shore, where they plan someday to grow old together. *p. 19*

MICHAEL WATERS teaches at Salisbury State University on the Eastern Shore of Maryland. His five books include *Bountiful* (1992), *The Burden Lifters* (1989), and *Anniversary of the Air* (1985), all three from Carnegie Mellon University Press. His awards include a fellowship in creative writing from the National Endowment for the Arts. *p. 173*

SALLY WHITNEY is a writer, mother, wife, and collector of dreams. Her short fiction has appeared in *Catalyst, Common Ground, Buffalo Spree*, and other magazines. She is currently working toward an MA in English with writing concentration at the William Paterson College of New Jersey. *p. 21*

BAYLA WINTERS is a professional portrait photographer, performance poet, media reviewer, columnist, and literary consultant. Widely published, she is a 1996 Pushcart Prize nominee and award winner of the International Women's Writing Guild, New York City. She is the author of five contemporary poetry books; her sixth, *Seeing Eye Wife,* is due out in spring 1996. *p. 31*

CHRISTOPHER WOODS lives in Houston. His plays have been produced in Los Angeles, Houston, and New York City. He has published one novel, *The Dream Patch,* and has completed a new novel, *A Woman on Fire. p. 119*

MARTHA WRIGHT has lived in a small city in the finger lakes area of New York for over thirty years. She brought up three children there and practiced as a psychotherapist for many years. In "retirement" she has turned her attention to photography and poetry. *p. 187*

MARION ZOLA is a screenwriter, book writer, and most recently, a producer. Her first love remains poetry. She worked under the poet John Malcolm Brinnin, and has had her poems published in poetry magazines and several anthologies, including *The Diamond Anthology* and *Poetic Voices of America. p. 67*

§ Denotes contributors whose work has appeared in previous Papier-Mache Press anthologies.

Papier-Mache Press

At Papier-Mache Press, it is our goal to identify and successfully present important social issues through enduring works of beauty, grace, and strength. Through our work we hope to encourage empathy and respect among diverse communities, creating a bridge of understanding between the mainstream audience and those who might not otherwise be heard.

We appreciate you, our customer, and strive to earn your continued support. We also value the role of the bookseller in achieving our goals. We are especially grateful to the many independent booksellers whose presence ensures a continuing diversity of opinion, information, and literature in our communities. We encourage you to support these bookstores with your patronage.

We publish many fine books about women's experiences. We also produce lovely posters and T-shirts that complement our anthologies. Please ask your local bookstore which Papier-Mache items they carry. To receive our complete catalog, send your request to Papier-Mache Press, 135 Aviation Way, #14, Watsonville, CA 95076, or call our toll-free number, 800-927-5913.

"In stories, poems, and photos, 66 exceptionally talented women share their deepest feelings—of joy, despair, acceptance, coping—indeed, of myriad 'ordinary' experiences rendered extraordinary by their creators' abilities to draw us in. . . . This volume offers a collection of riches, women with whom we empathize because in them we see ourselves."
　—*Sojourner*

"*If I Had My Life to Live Over* is an anthology bound with centuries of wisdom. . . . These works are filled with love and life, death dealt with, sickness shared, and the golden daisy petals of beautiful maturity. . . . This work is a quiet celebration of the victories and tragedies of life. Reading it is like spending a quiet afternoon, sitting on the deck, watching the sun set."
　—*Nebo, A Literary Journal*

"Then you buy a copy . . . to give to a friend, because you have to share it and you can't bear to part with your own copy. Your friend says the same thing . . . and so the chain goes."
　—*Encore Magazine*

"The writings and the emotions behind them are honest and thought-provoking."
　—*Greensboro News*

"The selections cut across a spectrum of age, race, and ways of life, from young girls reflecting on relationships to old women reflecting upon their next meal. . . . an honorable and thought-provoking companion volume."
　—*Kirkus Reviews*

Other anthologies edited by Sandra Haldeman Martz

When I Am an Old Woman I Shall Wear Purple
If I Had a Hammer: Women's Work
The Tie That Binds

If I had my life to live over
I would pick more daisies

Edited by Sandra Haldeman Martz

Papier-Mache Press
Watsonville CA

Copyright © 1992 by Papier-Mache Press. Printed in the United States of America. All rights reserved including the right to reproduce this book or portions thereof in any form. For more information contact Papier-Mache Press, 795 Via Manzana, Watsonville, California 95076.

00 99 98 97   16 15 14

ISBN: 0-918949-24-6 Softcover
ISBN: 0-918949-25-4 Hardcover

Edited by Sandra Haldeman Martz
Cover art, "More," fabric and thread, Copyright © 1992 by Deidre Scherer
Cover design by Cynthia Heier

Grateful acknowledgment is made to the following publications which first published some of the material in this book:

Passages North, vol. 3, no. 2, Spring/Summer 1982 and *A Decade of Good Writing, Passages North Anthology* (Milkweed Editions) © 1990 for "Old Friend Sends a Chain Letter" by Therese Becker; *Common Touch*, vol. 2, no. 2, Spring 1992, © 1992 The Straub Association for "Life Support" by Dorothy Howe Brooks; *Kinnikinnik*, vol. 1, no. 5, December 1990 for "Small Life" by Lizabeth Carpenter; *Phoebe*, vol. 3, no. 1, Spring 1991 for "Broken Vows" by Joan Connor; *Bluff City*, vol. 3, no. 1 © 1992 for "It Is Enough" by Ruth Daigon; *Spectrum* for "If I Could Begin Again" by Sue Saniel Elkind; *The Torch*, August 1991 for "Eating Cantaloupe" by Midge Farmer; *North Dakota Quarterly*, vol. 59, no. 1, Winter 1991 for "On Loving a Younger Man" by Alice Friman; *Bachy*, vol. 15, Fall 1979 and *My Self In Another Skin* (Drenan Press) 1981 for "A Palsied Girl Goes to the Beach" by Nan Hunt; *Poetry* vol. CLX, no. 3, June 1992, © 1992 The Modern Poetry Association for "Adoption" by Alison Kolodinsky; *Midwest Poetry Review* vol. VII, no. 2, 1986, and *Catching the Light* (Pocahontas Press, Inc.) 1989 for "Counterpoint" by Lynn Kozma; *Open City*, no. 257 (1984) and *Pudding Magazine*, no. 15 (1987) for "Vietnam" by Jennifer Lagier; *The Vincent Brothers Review*, vol. IV, no. 3, issue #10 for "The Scorpion Wore Pink Shoes" by Janice Levy; *Crosscurrents*, vol. 10, no. 2, Spring 1992 for "Ripening" by Joanne McCarthy; *Tucumcari Literary Review*, August 1990 for a different form of "The Sacrifice" by Shirley Vogler Meister; *February Caprice* 1991 for "Art As Life" by Ann Menebroker; *The Cooke Book: A Seasoning of Poets* (SCOP Publications) 1988 for "A Woman's Choice" by Jacklyn W. Potter; *Ita* (Capricorn Publishing Pty, Ltd) © 1990, 1991 and *Fair Lady* (National Magazines) © 1990, 1991, 1992 for "Cauliflower Beach" by Carol Schwalberg; *Morning of the Red-Tailed Hawk* (Green River Press) © 1981 for "October Fire" by Bettie M. Sellers; *The Montana Review* and *Stalking the Florida Panther* (The Word Works) 1988 for "The Keeper of Spaces" by Enid Shomer; and *Nebo: A Literary Journal*, vol. 8, no. 1 and 2, Fall/Spring 1989-90 and *Tucumcari Literary Review*, vol. III, no. 1, issue 13, January/February 1990 for "Mother Land" by Linda Wasmer Smith.

Library of Congress Cataloging-in-Publication Data

If I had my life to live over, I would pick more daisies / edited by
    Sandra Haldeman Martz.
    p. cm.
    ISBN 0-918949-24-6 (pbk.) : $10.00.—ISBN 0-918949-25-4 : $16.00
    1. Women—United States—Literary collections. 2. American
literature—Women authors. 3. American literature—20th century.
I. Martz, Sandra.
PS509.W6I4   1992
810.8'09287—dc20   92-34059
                                                                             CIP

*To the women who inspired me to make wiser choices
and the women who comforted me when I made foolish ones.*

Contents

xi	Foreword
1	If I Had My Life to Live Over *Nadine Stair*
2	Requiem *Martha B. Jordan*
3	Loving Jerry *Jan Epton Seale*
8	Small Life *Lizabeth Carpenter*
10	Broken Vows *Joan Connor*
18	A Palsied Girl Goes to the Beach *Nan Hunt*
21	The Keeper of Spaces *Enid Shomer*
22	Adoption *Alison Kolodinsky*
24	The Sacrifice *Shirley Vogler Meister*
27	Holy Places *Stephany Brown*
37	Morning News *Maggi Ann Grace*
39	Getting Ready *Catherine Boyd*
43	Spiderplant *Terri L. Jewell*
44	Life Support *Dorothy Howe Brooks*

48	Art As Life	*Ann Menebroker*
50	Résumé	*Dori Appel*
51	Mother Land	*Linda Wasmer Smith*
52	A Woman's Choice	*Jacklyn W. Potter*
54	Máire, Who Feeds the Wild Cat?	*Pat Schneider*
57	Imaginary Bonds	*Bonnie Michael*
58	The Scorpion Wore Pink Shoes	*Janice Levy*
68	Good Intentions	*Doris Vanderlipp Manley*
69	Sunspots	*Barbara Lucas*
70	On the Nature of Sin	*Sandra Redding*
83	The Woven Wall	*Kennette H. Wilkes*
84	White Horses	*Tricia Lande*
94	October Fire	*Bettie M. Sellers*
95	One Last Time	*Lori Russell*
107	It Is Enough	*Ruth Daigon*
109	Five Years Later	*Maril Crabtree*

110	Praying in the Dark *Gailmarie Pahmeier*
111	A Weaver *Barbara L. Thomas*
112	Orchards and Supermarkets *Rina Ferrarelli*
114	Divorce *Ellin Carter*
115	Vietnam *Jennifer Lagier*
116	Getting On with It *Grace Butcher*
117	Cauliflower Beach *Carol Schwalberg*
127	The first time I married *Karen Ethelsdattar*
128	Good-Bye Prince Charming *Claudia Van Gerven*
130	Old Friend Sends a Chain Letter *Therese Becker*
132	Woman *Lillian Morrison*
133	The Choice *Lesléa Newman*
134	Bittersweet *Fran Portley*
135	Forbidden Lover *Susan Eisenberg*
136	The Life I Didn't Live *Joanne Seltzer*
137	Swamp *Kirsten Backstrom*

147	Amazing Grace	*Susan Vreeland*
161	If I Could Begin Again	*Sue Saniel Elkind*
162	Shopping Expedition	*Elisavietta Ritchie*
167	Hot Flash	*Linda Keegan*
170	On Loving a Younger Man	*Alice Friman*
171	Ripening	*Joanne McCarthy*
173	Eating Cantaloupe	*Midge Farmer*
174	The Woman with the Wild-Grown Hair	*Nita Penfold*
175	Strawberries	*Leslie Nyman*
186	Old Women's Choices	*Ruth Harriet Jacobs*
187	Dearest Margaret	*Eleanor Byers*
190	Shrinking Down	*Janet Carncross Chandler*
192	Keepsakes	*Elaine Rothman*
198	Counterpoint	*Lynn Kozma*
199	Salamanders	*Randeane Tetu*
205	Advice to Beginners	*Ellen Kort*

Foreword

If I had my life to live over...

At some time almost everyone has reflected on life's crossroads and wondered what the outcome would have been had we chosen different paths. Especially when viewed from our later years, we often feel a sense of having sacrificed some of the quality of life in order to achieve material goals or in some other way meet public expectations.

It is in that horizon of our imagination—where the unlimited possibilities of "what might have been" form a background against which our understanding of "what is" emerges—that we find the universal appeal of this anthology and its title piece, "If I Had My Life to Live Over." The version included here is attributed to Nadine Stair, an eighty-five-year-old woman from Louisville, Kentucky, but the work can be found in many forms and often with no ascribed author. This small prose piece, with its commitment to a fuller life, a life with "more ice cream and less beans," has inspired many to pen their own visions of a life relived. It thus provides the perfect starting place for a word journey through women's experiences, exploring the spectrum of women's choices.

With poems, stories, and photographs chosen from more than 3,000 manuscripts received over a two-year period, *If I Had My Life to Live Over I Would Pick More Daisies* moves from childhood to adulthood through old age, reminding us that our options are both limited and extended by personal belief systems, ethnic and cultural identity, class and economic status, age, and gender.

Our choices are seldom simple or straightforward: right or wrong, yes or no. They are more often complex and conflictive and intertwined with the decisions made by others. And while the larger, more public choices such as education or career paths or political activism may have the more obvious impact on our lives, it is often those small private moments of decision, known only to ourselves, that live vividly in our memories. It is this latter group of choices that constitutes the core of this collection. My hope is that this book will touch the hearts of readers as it has touched mine.

SANDRA HALDEMAN MARTZ

IF I HAD MY LIFE TO LIVE OVER I WOULD PICK MORE DAISIES

Photo by Lori Burkhalter-Lackey

If I Had My Life to Live Over
Nadine Stair

I'd dare to make more mistakes next time. I'd relax, I would limber up. I would be sillier than I have been this trip. I would take fewer things seriously. I would take more chances. I would climb more mountains and swim more rivers. I would eat more ice cream and less beans. I would perhaps have more actual troubles, but I'd have fewer imaginary ones.

You see, I'm one of those people who live sensibly and sanely hour after hour, day after day. Oh, I've had my moments, and if I had it to do over again, I'd have more of them. In fact, I'd try to have nothing else. Just moments, one after another, instead of living so many years ahead of each day. I've been one of those persons who never goes anywhere without a thermometer, a hot water bottle, a raincoat and a parachute. If I had to do it again, I would travel lighter than I have.

If I had my life to live over, I would start barefoot earlier in the spring and stay that way later in the fall. I would go to more dances. I would ride more merry-go-rounds. I would pick more daisies.

Requiem
Martha B. Jordan

For Angel Camacho

When the last from childhood dies
the heartbeat slows
to a dry leaf rustle
no one calls you
niña
and
tu
or whispers charms
like river water rushing
over moss
and fish
and pebbles
sana, sana, colita de rana.

Loving Jerry
Jan Epton Seale

I have been wondering since the second grade what it feels like to fall in love. Then I get the note on Monday: MEET ME AT RECESS BY THE WATER FOUNTING.

Jerry McCondle is one of the few people, boys or girls, in the whole fourth grade that fills up his T-shirt. (My mother says, "Nelda, you are so-o-o scrawny," when she pins me into a dress she is sewing for me.)

The other boys have sharp, bony shoulders and their T-shirts hang on them in wrinkles, showing their mothers have not flapped them before hanging them on the clothesline. (One time when my mother made me wear a shirt a little bit wrinkled, I cried. She said, "Nelda, only real pretty girls have to have everything perfect.")

Anyway, Jerry's shirt even looks bulgy. And his jeans make a soft, swishing sound when he comes up the aisle.

He drops the little triangle-folded note in my lap as he comes back from collecting last Friday's spelling test. I leave it there and take off my glasses, holding them up like I'm wondering if they need cleaning. If I hold them a certain way, they are like a mirror, and I can see Jerry behind me wadding his spelling test into a little ball and chucking it into his inkwell.

At the fountain, Jerry is careful to be five people ahead of me. He waits beside the water, saying things to each kid in line, sometimes slapping the water up into a person's face, especially if they are wearing glasses.

When my turn comes, I try to wipe my mouth before I raise my head but the icy water makes my lips numb and I can't tell whether I've gotten them dry when I raise up. In a way, I hope I haven't. The models in my mother's magazines all have wet lips.

"Hi," I say, feeling silly because I've been in the same room with him all morning. He doesn't splash my glasses and that makes me wonder if he is in love with me. He turns and walks beside me, not saying a word, just looking out at the baseball diamond where Rosemary and John are choosing their teams.

We stop behind the backstop. "We're going to sit there," he says, pointing to the old bleachers.

When we are settled, Jerry holds out his arm. On the inside is a big blue heart that looks a little like the beautiful tattoo my Uncle Charles came home from the war with. It could be from the blue pen we have to use for English. The arrow could be from our red arithmetic correction pen. How would I know?

"Nelda," Jerry says slowly, "on Friday I'm going to have them put a girl's name in this. On Friday."

"That's nice," I say, staring out on the field where nothing much is going on yet. I figure I should probably know who "them" is.

When we go back inside, the health lesson is on the alimentary canal, and my best friend Maydean and I glance through the chapter and count *body* four times and *bowel* twice. (Maydean has been in love I don't know how many times since last year when she moved to our school.)

Of course, the teacher calls on me to read aloud. She always calls on me. One of my paragraphs says *body*, and it makes me so nervous I start grinning when I get to that line, and by the time I get to the word, I laugh out loud, put my hand over my mouth, and start coughing. Across the aisle, Maydean clamps her hand over her mouth too.

Miss Schumaker stands and stares at us. "May I ask what is so funny?"

I shake my head and continue to cough. There is no way to tell Miss Schumaker that Maydean and I *know* that *body* is a nasty word.

Tuesday morning Jerry is waiting for me when I come up the walk. His hair is parted a little crooked but it is all combed with Vitalis. I check whether his heart has washed off. It is there, and I'm still thinking about whether he took a bath last night and redid the heart, or whether he did not take a bath at all, just put on a clean shirt, when he speaks to me.

"Meet me again today, same place," Jerry says as we pass into the front hall where Mr. Jenkins, the principal, is standing in a brown suit with his arms folded.

"Shhh!" I say.

Jerry glances back at Mr. Jenkins. "To hell with him," Jerry says, but quietly and right in my ear.

Maydean writes me a note during lunch-count: DO YOU LOVE JERRY? YES ____ NO ____ .

Before I can answer back, the teacher starts the six-weeks spelling review. I put Maydean's note in my desk.

Before recess, I check my socks, that the backs of them have not worked down inside my shoes. Jerry is waiting for me, and we walk out to the bleachers again.

"Yep, Friday," Jerry says when we're settled. He's looking at his heart. He digs in his pants pocket and offers me a stick of Juicy Fruit. I say, "Thanks," and unwrap it slowly, thinking about what I might make out of the foil. Jerry takes two pieces for himself, unwraps them, rolls them together, says "Watch," and throws them in his mouth like popcorn.

We stare out at Rosemary and John's teams, who are playing for real today. Once, I forget and clap and scream "Yea!" when Sharon hits the ball into right field.

She throws down the bat and runs to first base. "She's deader 'n a doornail," Jerry says. "Shit! Ten to one, they've got 'er."

I'm thinking whether Jerry should have said that to me when he scoots a little closer. I have my hand on the seat, with my skirt spread over it, and now he runs in his hand and gets hold of mine. His hand feels real warm and rough and a little wet. The wet part surprises me. I look back toward the building, checking if Miss Schumaker might be looking at us out the window.

Now we sit staring at the ball game. Jerry is concentrating, you might say. But I am trying to memorize everything about Jerry's hand to check out with Maydean later. Am I holding it too tight or too loose? Suddenly, Jerry doubles back his middle finger and starts rubbing it slowly inside my hand.

I look at Jerry. He is looking extra hard at the ball field, his eyes kind of scrunched. I think he must have seen something awful and I look. Nobody is even up to bat.

On Wednesday it rains in the morning so we stay inside. When that happens, the girls play jacks in the corners of the room and the boys play rubber horseshoes in the hall.

Jerry waits for me after school, and we ride our bicycles side by side until Bluebonnet Grocery, where he fishes in his pocket for two dimes, tells me to stay with the bikes, goes in, and comes out with two Grapettes. We drink them there under the dripping trees. I try not to get any around my mouth. Jerry fits his lips inside the bottle on purpose.

So his whole mouth is purple. "Want a kiss?" he asks and smacks me before I can decide for myself.

"Je-e-rry!" I say, like I know I'm supposed to, and turn away. He laughs and carries the bottles back in.

When I get home, Mother asks me why I'm late. "I had to go back and get my speller." I am careful not to open my mouth too wide. I race through the house to the bathroom. Anyway, the speller is partly the truth.

Thursday when Jerry goes to the board to diagram the sentence Miss Schumaker has assigned him, he drops another note in my lap. When Miss Schumaker gets all mad because Jerry has put an adjective on the subject line, I open the note. It has I LOVE NELDA written a billion times on it, from one corner sideways, over and over, to the bottom. At the end it says, IF I DECIDE THEY RITE YOUR NAME ON MY ARM, YOU GET ONE OF THESE EVER DAY AFTER THAT—FOREVER.

I refold the note and put it in my desk. I take off my glasses and fold them. I cross my arms and lay my head on them. It seems like all I am doing is folding things. I am too tired. I roll my head and pick out Jerry at the board.

He is all fuzzy around the edges but I can still see that some of his hair has gotten loose and is sticking straight up in back. I begin to think how my mother calls a cowlick a turkey tail, and which name is right.

Jerry is erasing his sentence after Miss Schumaker has told him to start over and do it right this time. He's not erasing neatly. He's doing it like swipe! swipe! making puffs of chalk dust. I squint and try to see the heart on his arm, but I can't. I don't know if it's because he's moving his arm too fast or because I don't have on my glasses.

I raise up and reach inside my desk. I feel Maydean's note and bring it out. I press it out on my desk and uncap my pen. I check NO.

Small Life
Lizabeth Carpenter

It was March first. Outside the land thawed imperceptibly under harsh easterly winds blowing over the plains.

Lakota City lies along the Big Yellow River, on the alluvial plain south of Granite and Larchwood. In the spring, if you hike the river's muddy banks downstream, through its wild westward thrusts and counter curves to the east, you'll need insect repellent and long pants—the soil of the floodplain breeds gnats, chiggers, hornets, ticks, cockleburs, snakes. Every other decade a bull moose is sighted far from its native mountain rangeland, thrashing through cattails and cornfields, lumbering across Highway Five. But this is the exception; most of life here, in its abundance, is small and unnoticeable, deceivingly safe.

Marly left school at noon. Chunks of ice floated on the river, its steep clay banks soft and treacherous, patterned with tiny bird prints. She stepped carefully on matted wet leaves at the top of the bank. Wiry shrubs poked her hands and sides and slapped against her face. She progressed slowly. She climbed up one side of an eroded ditch with her hands braced against the muscle over each knee—"knobby knees," Clayton called them—and stumbled at the top over half-buried timber. Last night she and Clayton had parked on War Eagle's Bluff and opened all the car windows to the warm spring breeze. When they'd kissed, he had touched her knobby knee under her skirt. His hand was trembling; she became very still. Her instincts had abandoned her. The city glowed blue-white on the southern horizon as a slow warm river crept through her legs and arms and chest. The car was quiet except for their breathing, the rustle of clothing, leather seats.

Suddenly, fiercely, she pushed him away.

Clayton rested a moment against the steering wheel. "Blocked shot," he said. He laughed shortly, started up the Beetle, and drove Marly home.

Remembering this, Marly froze again, her hand gripping a thin willow tree. Behind her, upriver, five bridge supports like huge cement doorways stood spaced across the water, awaiting construction of a new state highway. Between here and the city it seemed pastures vanished monthly, the land slipping away like snowmelt, sprouting boxy new prefab or brick-fronted homes.

A warm wind pushed through the leafless branches and lifted the hair off Marly's forehead—the air so dry and clean, so settling, she was afraid to imagine a world without such untouched lonely places. She didn't know how she would live.

Broken Vows
Joan Connor

I stand before the mirror in the chapel hall, fidgeting with the chin strap of my veil. I see my parents behind me, reversed in the mirror. I have a queasy feeling, like car sickness, as if I were traveling backward. The floral scent of my bouquet—of the flower arrangements, the lilies and glads and roses—intermingle, heady and cloying. The chin strap cuts into my neck. The images in the mirror blur, and a memory surfaces, entire.

Summer vacation. I can smell Mom's perfume and some peanuts she is munching. I slide the bead on my hat strap up to my chin. We crossed the California state-line six road signs and at least that many backseat tussles ago. Kyle and Jamie are scrapping their way cross-country. The scuffle picked up in Minnesota when Jamie drew the battle lines right down his third of the backseat, using the khaki strap of his canteen for a marker. Outside Minneapolis, I moved out of the front lines into the front seat between Mom and Dad. Jamie nudged the canteen strap into the center of the backseat, and he and Kyle have been at each other ever since. Today is particularly bad. Dad has warned them to cut it out four times. His knuckles look almost blue against the shiny black of the steering wheel. Dad is humming, but the hum sounds tight, forced. I try to ignore Kyle and Jamie, train my eyes on the road ahead, but the road here pushes itself on like a drudge through a round of chores. No roadside distractions. Only great overarching trees and their shadows.

Sometimes Dad and I sing to drown out the boys. I love it when Dad sings to me, slightly off-key and very deep. My favorite is the song he's humming now, "Clementine." The hum breaks into words. "Dwelt a miner, forty-niner, and his daughter Clementine. Oh, my darling," he wails, "Oh, my darling."

Mom taps out the time or her impatience on the dashboard.

"Oh, my darling, Clementine" I join in, high and sweet. I tug the brim of my Deadwood cowboy hat over my eyes. Dad bought me the hat, red with white embroidery, in South Dakota. I love it. In Yellowstone, the hat blew off and landed on the crusty edge of a bubbling hot mudpot, two yards out, just far enough so that my father couldn't reach it. While I cried and my mother screamed, my father hopped the boardwalk fence, tiptoed past the Danger sign, and retrieved the hat. You've got to harmonize with someone who would do that for you. I chime in as Dad starts, "You are lost...," but the boys' voices cut the song short.

"It's mine," Kyle wails in a pitch that crawls up my spine.

"That's it," Dad yells. "Enough. I've had enough."

The boys lurch forward in midsquabble as Dad jumps on the brake.

"I asked you to stop bickering half a state ago. Now get out. Get out of my car." His voice surprisingly soft, he thumps the steering wheel as he speaks.

"Duncan," my mother protests, "they've been cooped up in the car all day."

"Then uncoop," Dad answers her. His eyes sight the length of the car's hood like a gun barrel. "All I asked for was a little peace while I drove. I just asked you to keep them quiet. So uncoop," he repeats, and adds, "now."

"But Jamie crossed the line," Kyle whines. "He started it. He put his tomahawk on my side of the seat. See?" Kyle asks. "Look."

I tip my hat back off my head and twist in my seat to examine the evidence.

"I don't want to hear it, not one whine of it, not one explanation. Just get out of the damn car," Dad says.

"But there's nothing here," Mom says, scanning the area, "just a rest stop." Dad does not even turn to look at her. She sighs. Without another word, she yanks the handle on the passenger side. The boys tumble out, grumbling. I start scooting across the seat toward the open door, but Dad touches my forearm. "Except you, Molly," he says, turning. "You can stay if you want. You weren't in it."

I stare at my father's blue eyes. They waver, hazy, like car metal, hot in the sun. I hear Kyle behind me, whining, "It isn't fair," as Mom shoos the boys away from the Galaxie. My hat cord cuts into my neck. My chest tightens. I glance at Mom and Jamie and Kyle standing on the shoulder of the highway. I look back at my father's eyes and consider this offer. I blush.

"Go or stay, Molly," my dad says, "but make up your mind now." He turns his attention back to the hood of the Galaxie.

The sun bounces off the windshield, stunning me. I cannot see my father's face in the glare. My heart bangs in my left side, the side close to my father, the side that wants to remain on the seat. My right arm lifts and reaches toward the passenger door, the handle. My right hand hovers there. The moment suspends itself. How can he make me choose? Then Kyle whimpers. Ready to cry myself, and without realizing that I have made a choice, I reject my father. The vinyl seat smooches the hot backs of my thighs as I inch across the seat to the door. I slam the door shut. I want to whisper, "I love you, Daddy." But the Galaxie squeals off. Mom stares at the rear license plate as it recedes, her eyes following the Galaxie to the vanishing point.

"Wow. Look at the patch of rubber Dad laid, Mom." Jamie admires the tire marks, parallel black zippers, a shade darker than the tarmac.

But Mom does not respond. Her face composes itself in some expression that is almost no expression, drying like papier-mâché into a mask. "Come on. Let's cross the street." She takes Jamie's and Kyle's hands and guides them across the highway as if she were stemming traffic. But the road stretches empty and quiet like a road nobody lives on, a road whose only purpose is to connect at either end with other roads.

"You really done it now," Jamie says, craning around Mom's leg for a shot at Kyle. "Dad's gone off and left us for good."

"No sir," Kyle says. "No sir. You did it, James Patrick. I told you to keep your junk on your side of the car. Didn't I tell him to keep his junk on his side of the car?" Kyle asks looking up at my mother.

"Stop bickering," Mom says and tightens their wrists in her bracelets of fingers.

"Ouch. Stop it. You're hurting me." Jamie tugs, but Mom keeps walking across the road. As I follow them, my hat thuds rhythmically between my shoulder blades. In the rest stop on the other side, some picnic tables rot in the shadows of the giant firs. Mom releases the boys, drops her shoulder bag on a bench, and sits in a mound of pine needles at the base of the tree. Jamie inspects some graffiti carved in the table top. Kyle slumps against a trash barrel, curling up very small. "Is he coming back?" Kyle asks my mother.

"Yes," my mom says, "he's coming back." She trickles some pine needles into the palm of her hand, lets them sift through her fingers. I wonder how she knows Dad is coming back, how she can be so sure. But when she raises her eyes, they meet mine, patient and certain.

"When?" Kyle asks.

"When he's ready," she says.

"Today?"

Mom shrugs. "I think probably." Her lips curve into the merest smile.

"Where'd he go?" Kyle asks.

"Who cares? Stop being such a baby," Jamie says.

"I imagine he went to see the sequoias," Mom answers Kyle, talking over Jamie. "Your father's wanted to make this camping trip, coast to coast, since he was a boy himself."

"Good going, Jamie," Kyle says. "Now we'll never see the sequoias; will we, Mom?"

"Shut up," Jamie says.

"Yeah, shut up, Jamie," I second.

"You," Jamie sneers. "You should have gone with him. Daddy's widdle girlie-whirlie."

"Yeah, well maybe I should have," I say. I pick a prickly pine needle from my ankle sock.

"Stop bickering," Mom says, but the command has no air in it. Her voice sounds tired as she asks, "Don't you kids ever learn? Why do you think we are sitting here on the side of the road?"

Kyle flops down on the ground in a sulk. Jamie lies on his stomach on the picnic table, tracing anonymous monograms with his fingers. "Anybody got a knife?" he asks, but no one bothers to answer him. I sit next to Mom and watch her nudge the pine needles into ridges, mound them into mountains.

"What if he doesn't come back?" Kyle asks.

"He'll come back," Mom says. She rubs a smutch of pitch from her forefinger with her thumb.

"What are the sequoias like, Mom?" Jamie asks.

"I've never seen them," she says, tilting her head back against the tree trunk. "But I imagine they're like this. Only bigger. Bigger and older."

We all look up through the tree branches, higher than anything we could have imagined back home in Maine. The morning becomes afternoon, golden and dusty. Jamie and Kyle build castles in the pine needles. When Kyle grows cranky and hungry, Mom scrounges around in her pocketbook, producing three sticks of Juicy Fruit, a few peanuts, and some restaurant packets of saltines. The crackers are dry and gum my tongue like communion wafers. Mom rests. Kyle falls asleep with his head on her leg. Jamie complains. We pretend not to be listening for cars until a drone small as a bee's grows louder, more mechanical as it nears. Jamie twitches, then leaps up yelling, "I knew he'd come back. I knew it." But the drone precedes a truck, loaded with scabby logs, its claw clanking on its crane as it passes. The roar recedes, and Jamie's face reddens. But he won't let himself cry; he's twelve-and-a-half years old. "Made ya look," he mutters as he sprawls on the ground.

Later, when I cry, Mom finds a packet of tissues in her purse. She comforts me as she pats my back. "Your dad's just tired of camping, sleeping on the ground, driving all day, being cooped up in the car. He just needs a break. Time and space to walk around for a while. Away from us," she says.

I recognize the truth of these explanations. We've been camping cross-country since June. But I'm not crying because I'm on the side of the road in a place that has no name or traffic. I'm crying because I chose, and nothing will ever be the same again, because I looked into my father's urgent blue eyes, eyes so near to mine that I can almost see his world through them, and I turned away from them for two boys sniveling in red crew cuts, boys most of the time I don't even like very much, and a woman in a faded madras skirt. Like "The Farmer in the Dell," I stepped inside the family circle while my father, the last, unchosen player, stood like the cheese at the song's end, alone.

This is what I try to tell my mother as I cry, but the words garble themselves. She hushes me. I think she does not understand. But her palm on my cheek hesitates with an almost imperceptible impatience as if, here in this stand of secretive old trees, she understands the choice perfectly, completely, and can just barely restrain herself from hastening the moment along.

"Stop your blubbering," Jamie says, and he butts my shoulder, one of his rough comforts. He flushes when I smile at him. Mom eases me off her shoulder.

I sit upright and wonder how we must look to a stranger driving by, a misplaced family of four, unwashed and unfed, huddled at the roots of these titanic evergreens. We must look stunted. Small. Observed by this strange eye, I let the fancy draw me in, pretending we are characters illustrating the frontispiece of an old wives' tale.

We listen to the wind stir as the day dims. Dusky, we huddle around the table. Small stars spin out, pinwheeling orphans. Out of time and place. My mother, my brothers, and I sit on the damp benches. A meager congregation. Is this the image the Galaxie's headlights catch in the beams of my father's memory?

When we clamber, sleepy and sheepish, into the car, my father does not apologize. And my mother asks him no questions. But we do not go to a campground. We spend the night at a Holiday Inn. My father brings paper sacks of hamburgers to the room. And he does not complain when Jamie and Kyle tussle and tumble on their rollaways or turn the hotel TV up too loud.

But I have trouble falling asleep, listening to my mother's breath keeping time with my father's. When I close my eyes, the floor of my dream collapses. I fall through. Everything skews. I land, wholly awake, in an old, known place, but I am totally new.

In a few years, "Remember the sequoias" will become a family joke, the wry alarm Dad sounds when Jamie won't say where he's going or when he expects to be back, when Kyle won't submit to a haircut, when I take too long picking out a dress for church, when Mom's defense of our misdeeds becomes too strident. "Remember the sequoias," the reminder that family ties can stretch to the snapping point, transforms itself into a unifying anecdote, a family rallying cry. Our in-joke. Kyle, Jamie, and my mother learn to laugh with my father, but I cringe. My memory differs from theirs: Dad ordered them from the car, but I decided to go. Worlds tilted at that decision. I declined the man, the pull of his gravity, wobbled away and aligned myself in a safe system of familial orbit. I don't know if he ever realized the scope of that choice, or its repercussions. I do not know if, in that instant, I hurt him, and, if I did, if he recalls it. But I changed forever. I realized that life entailed a series of compromises of the private self to the public, a slow accommodation to ordinariness, to convention's momentum. I had vowed to resist being trundled along by the ongoingness of life. But I did not. I do not.

I make this coward's choice again on my wedding, fidgeting before the mirror, knowing that at the end of the aisle a man my father doesn't like, but at least doesn't hate, waits for me. The memory subsides. My father's face attends me, pale, almost blank, as if he'd like to be somewhere, anywhere, else. Maybe in a Galaxie, alone and racing against the clock.

On the periphery of my vision, I spot my mother, trumped up in a silly blue-lace gown. Her face, pink and happy, stings me as I understand for the first time her joy today and her patience as she sat on roadsides for twenty years, certain that my father would always return but that I one day would stand in this corner with my father about to usher me off. I startle at the nearness of my father's face and realize he is speaking to me.

"Remember the sequoias," he says.

My mother laughs abruptly and too loudly. Tears sting my nose, pungent, piney. The phrase has been a family adage for years; it shouldn't surprise me now. But it does.

"Don't worry, honey," he says to my startled face. "Your old man wouldn't desert you now." Clumsily, he kisses my cheek. "You made the right choice," he whispers.

I wonder which choice he means; which choice, judicious, stands alone. But in an instant all the choices blur, seem one long attenuated and inevitable choice I've been making all my life. I close my eyes on my confusion, and I see a shower of shooting stars on the dark domes of my eyelids. All the scenery I missed that summer unrolling beyond the Galaxie window, while I, nearsighted, looked in the wrong direction, unreels in tangles on the floor. I wonder what became of my Deadwood hat, what trash can I stuffed it into, what friend's house I left it at, what carton, what moving van I failed to pack it in.

"It's time," my mother says as the organ cues us. And my father wheels me around and guides me down the aisle. The walk stretches long and empty as if its only purpose is to connect one point of departure with the next. My feet choose the way, and every step, every choice is an exclusion of possibility, a diminution of the boundless self. I'm dressed in white, a flutter of lace and satin ribbons, glittering like the votive candles in a liar's eyes. At the end of the aisle a man in black tails waits.

A Palsied Girl Goes to the Beach
Nan Hunt

Empty now of voices except
my duplicating hum of loneliness
my room is airless; and I crab-crawl
my way downstairs where
children, their questions raw and
open, stare at my praying mantis-stance.
But the adults snap to attention
shift and shadow out of reach.

I would clutch them back
just to fence the cruelty.
My mind must put the lid
on their revulsion (clambering inside
like spiders under glass)
their dread that between us lies
fate's mere flirting finger-snap.

Each step of mine is a tightrope test.
The signal to the muscle shoots
a devious, interrupted race
and when my foot sways down
my will must   stalk it
until it comes to place.
Jerk and twitch   I get there.

I offer my dangled limbs
for the sun's hot benediction
fingering shells as rosaries
for the dear struggles wet

in living things.
And, braced against the curling surf
I, inconsequential as coquinas
scoured over, stay the waves.

And more than stay—
resist.

Photo by Marianne Gontarz

The Keeper of Spaces
Enid Shomer

I am the keeper of usually
vacant spaces. I am the one
who notes how bare the swamp oak grows
as it opens its arms to the wind
in early fall. I notch
the southern skies with gray
before the migratory birds
fly past.

It is not voids
but possibilities I see:
the ribbed hull of a leaf
where tea scale gains
its barnacle grip,
the scalloped calyx cup
where mites drink dry
the bloom.

I am the one who, looking
at my hand, sees not a shape
but all the places
where the hand must go,
and the spaces between fingers
where life like sand escapes
even as I make
a fist.

Adoption
Alison Kolodinsky

I stitched us together by night
in the rocking chair, marveled
at your fingers, the foreign navel,
memorized the sweep of your eyebrows,
unraveled your language.
Having accepted the unfamiliar,
I kept watch
for proof of our union.

Tonight I inhale as I kiss
your perfect face, moist
from busy dreaming. Your fragrance
marks me—that fingerprint
only a parent can read.
I crawl in beside you, grateful
and patient, to dip us
with even breath
in this night's ink.

Photo by Anna Tomczak

The Sacrifice
Shirley Vogler Meister

A child is growing somewhere
    in this weary world,
    an innocent unwary
    of emotions shattered,
    a child whose life around
    mute hearts is curled,
    who'll never know how much
    his being mattered.
Lovingly, she chose to yield
    at birth the son
    she bore with courage
    in her unwed prime.
    Clearly, she saw
    paternal lack of worth
    as parent or as spouse:
    poor paradigm.
Reality pressed close
    and she perceived
    how only hope
    was left to give her son,
    that good intent would not
    their needs relieve:
    the sacrificial web
    was firmly spun.

Adoptive keepers now
    assume his care
    and fill his time
    with wonders far removed
    from lineal love
    that evermore still dares
    to grow—a selfless love
    already proved.

Photo by Marianne Gontarz

Holy Places
Stephany Brown

Oh, honey, don't hurt me. I'm too old. This is what my mother used to say to me all the time when I reached the age when girls become smart-alecky to their mothers. I realize now that she wasn't old then, just prematurely gray. "Early silver," my father used to say as he held on to a hunk of her waist-length hair. But it worked. I wasn't unkind to her like my friend Sally was to her solidly brunette mother and Anne-Marie to hers. I figured Mom just couldn't take it, the old being more fragile than the young.

And she wasn't unkind to me either, even when I broke all the rules and got pregnant at sixteen. I should have been smart enough to figure out that if she could handle an out-of-wedlock baby, she could handle an unkind word or two. But by that time I'd lost the urge to be smart-alecky. I had other things on my mind.

Mainly Jeff. Jeff in his white Spitfire, one hand on the steering wheel, the other somewhere on me. He'd turn on the Motown station and if the top was down and we were on a country road he'd turn the music up loud and sing along with the Four Tops or Mary Wells or Smoky Robinson and the Miracles. When we reached our cornfield, all the sounds would stop, and it would seem for a minute that we'd entered a church. And after a time the cornfield always seemed like a holy place to us, even if there hadn't been any noise on the way there.

It wasn't our cornfield, though, neither his nor mine. It was almost an hour away from our neighborhood and it was farmed by people we never saw. We only went there at night. Jeff loved the drive there, the long straight road lined with tall trees and farms. When the night was bright enough we could see the outlines of old silos. He'd go way too fast, seventy-five or eighty, but I didn't have the heart to tell him I was scared.

Sometimes there'd be straw in my hair when I got home. My mother, who'd have been reading on the couch or playing backgammon with my father, would pick some of it out and say that I'd missed curfew again, that she couldn't help worrying when I was late. "And that little car is so flimsy," she'd say, "it would protect you no more than a tuna fish can; what if a truck hits you?" I told her once that Jeff was saving up for a Cadillac that would protect us, but I said it nicely, the old being unable to handle sarcasm.

My sweet father, for the most part, stayed out of these conversations. Sometimes he would nod and say, "Your mother's right, honey," or echo something she had said. He figured it was some mother-daughter thing. Or he figured sex was involved. Or maybe he just saw my mother as wiser than he.

She was wise. She knew I was pregnant before I did and before any test had been done. She could tell by my face, she said, by the way it puffed out a little. I was horrified and expected her to be mad but she said she knew I loved Jeff and that Jeff loved me and that out of such love babies are born. She was so calm. I relaxed and figured she would take care of everything. But no. The next day she said she'd support me in any decision I made. But she had no advice. She'd help me find an adoption agency or an abortion. She'd drive me to the Florence Crittenton home for unwed mothers or buy a new silk mother-of-the-bride dress for my wedding. She'd let me live with her and Dad and be a single mother, but she wouldn't take care of my baby for me. And she insisted on this: I had to tell Jeff. The baby was half his. I promised her I would, but I couldn't. I was afraid it would spoil things, and I couldn't stand that.

Three months passed and Jeff and I kept driving down country roads and I kept pretending to be carefree. By then it was too cold to lie in the cornfield, but sometimes we'd bring blankets and lie there anyway. We'd point out constellations and tell stories. Jeff liked to point to the east and tell me about Andromeda, who, in Greek legend, was the daughter of an Ethiopian king. For some offense, some boast about beauty that her mother had made, Andromeda was chosen to be sacrificed to the gods. She was chained, naked except for some jewels, to a rock at the edge of the sea. Jeff told me about Andromeda's rescue by Perseus, how Perseus beheaded a sea monster to free her. He told me how that was nothing compared to what he would do for me. I'd stare at the stars, trying to see the configuration in the shape of a much-beloved woman, and believe him. I'd imagine him slaying some monster for me, protecting me, freeing me, loving me forever.

We'd talk about constellations or we'd talk about our pasts or we'd talk about our future together. We didn't know when we'd get married but we knew that we would. We'd talk about which tall tower of apartments we wanted to start our life out in and how we'd decorate our kitchen. We'd talk about names for our babies—Laraine, Melanie, Sabrina. The first would be a boy, he'd be named Jeff. I showed him the bits of leftover yarn my grandmother had given me. I showed him the pattern in her knitting book for a many-colored baby blanket. We'd plan our wedding. Anne-Marie and Sally would be bridesmaids in fuchsia dresses. The best man and ushers would wear cummerbunds to match.

And then one night he found my pants unbuttoned and made a joke about too many french fries. That was the night I told him I was pregnant. I was surprised at his reaction. After I blurted out the truth of it, he grew quiet. This was unlike him. We had always talked.

Afterward, he was silent for days, pretending he hadn't heard me. And then he told me this: He couldn't face it; he'd enlisted in the army. His father had signed for him; he'd leave for boot camp on his eighteenth birthday, only a few months away. He wouldn't even wait for graduation. "No," I screamed, "What about my yarn? What about our wrought-iron kitchen table with matching chairs? What about the map of the stars that would hang in our baby's room? What about me, your beloved, the one you'd kill sea monsters for? What about the Magnavox stereo in our living room where we'd play Temptations albums and Martha and the Vandellas and the Supremes?" I begged him and beat on his chest with my fists but he was steel. He didn't even say he was sorry. Or ask me what I was going to do.

"There's a war going on. My country needs me," was his answer. He turned into a stranger. He was no longer the boy who sang into the wind. Suddenly he was all involved in the Vietnam War and stopping communism. It was a subject that had never come up, all those nights in the cornfield and in the car. All that talking we did, that incessant talking, and he'd never mentioned the war or patriotism or serving anybody but me.

For a week I grieved. For some reason I spent most of that week with Jeff's mother, not with mine. We'd sit on her couch drinking Cokes and eating potato chips and she'd promise me he'd come to his senses and "do right by you, honey." And if he didn't, well, then, "God would punish him." He was acting more and more like his dad, she said, stubborn and selfish. I didn't know if Jeff was more afraid of me or of his mother but he spent the rest of the time, before he went in the army, at his dad's efficiency apartment, a sordid little place full of overstuffed used furniture. It didn't even have a radio. Losing Jeff like this was a heartbreaker for his mother. She didn't get to be with her baby before he went off to war.

I wanted to die that week but then something happened. I started to feel calm and I gave Jeff up in my mind, his music, his pain, his Greek legends. I didn't throw his picture away but I took it off my dresser and put it in a drawer, under my scarves. I ceremoniously laid all his gifts—the opal ring, the cameo brooch, the gardenia corsage from his junior prom—in a box covered with quilted ivory satin and stored it high on a closet shelf.

By then, by the time I was free to think about my baby, it was too late for an abortion, so at least I didn't have to picture what that would entail. That's what my mother said anyway. Perhaps that was her way of expressing the opinion she claimed to refuse to express. Another refusal to pose as the authority in my life. Another chance for me to take responsibility for myself. And I was relieved that I could check off another option, to shorten my list of choices, a list I didn't want to face.

But I did. I faced the list. I decided to give the baby up. I decided it one morning after I'd had a dream about being a mother. My brown hair was bleached blond and stringy and heavy black eyeliner was on my eyelids. Me and the baby lived in a small efficiency full of used, overstuffed furniture with no radio. In the dream I was using a knife as a microphone and doing an imitation of Diana Ross singing "Baby Love, My Baby Love." My hips were swiveling and I felt real cool. My baby started to struggle. I had laid him facedown in a big chair and he started to sputter. The blanket under him had gotten all wadded up around his face and he couldn't get his breath. I knew he might die and I planned to get him, but I wanted to finish my song first. I woke up before either the rescue or the death, but I took the dream as a sign that I wasn't ready.

I stayed in school until my stomach got ridiculous. Then I made an appointment with Sister John Gabriel, the principal. I told her that my family was going to be moving because my father had been transferred. She put her hand on mine and her eyes went soft and understanding and she said she knew the truth of the matter, she had eyes to see and she was sorry. She said she knew this was a painful time for me. I hadn't expected her to believe me, but I had expected her to be cold and cruel. Her kindness took me by surprise and tears washed down my face. She took me in her arms and held my head against the side of hers, and I felt how stiff her starched white cap was under her veil. I cried and cried and she just held me. When I was done, I thanked her. I said I hoped my tears hadn't wilted her habit. She offered me a bar of the World's Finest Chocolate, with almonds, which we sold every year as a fund-raiser.

That was my last day at school. And it was the day I told Sally and Anne-Marie the whole truth. The story I had made up, and that they had believed, was that Jeff and I had broken up because I'd seen a cheerleader from the public school riding in his Spitfire. I had explained that the loss of him made me feel so empty inside that I was filling up with food—hot-fudge ice cream cake, onion rings, Milky Ways, cheeseburgers, whole jars of olives. I couldn't stop eating. They'd given me their pity and their understanding. Both confessed that grief made them overeat too. They were just lucky they hadn't blown up like I had. They were both on the basketball team. I was the sedentary one. We'd talked about it quite a lot. Almost every night on the phone I'd produced a litany of the food I'd consumed that day. They had tried to help: "When you get the urge to eat, drink three glasses of water to give you the sense of fullness," "Always have peeled carrot sticks on hand." They had been into my story.

The truth floored them. Anne-Marie kept covering her face with her hands and saying she couldn't believe it. Sally called Jeff a shit-head over and over. Neither of them had known a pregnant person before, so they had lots of questions. Sally wondered if they should get everyone in our class to sign a petition begging Sister John Gabriel to let me stay in school.

"No," I said. "Just don't forget about me. Without Jeff, without school, I'll really have nothing to do. I'll just be home watching game shows and soaps," I said, "and reading Victoria Holt and Mary Stewart."

But that's not what happened. Our television broke and my mother said we couldn't afford to have it fixed. Even then I knew that was a lie, but I accepted it. I didn't like TV that much anyway. She probably broke it herself, got a screwdriver and took the back off, unscrewed a tube or unhooked a small wire. "Well, no use sitting around here," she said. I'd feel better if I exercised, she said—a radical notion for those days I realize now, but I obeyed her. Every day but Sunday we went swimming at the YWCA pool. I'd move slowly through the cool blue water and imagine that my baby was doing the same thing, moving slowly in the water in my womb, waving his tiny arms, kicking his tiny legs, holding his tiny eyes closed tight. My little swimmer.

We didn't have *in utero* photographs back then, but there were sketches. I checked out a book from the library called *Expectant Motherhood* and learned the words for all my parts, words I'd had introduced to me in sophomore biology but that had seemed to belong only to married women: *fallopian tube, cervix, vaginal canal, uterine lining*. I learned that my bones were going to loosen up, I'd be split, sort of like an earthquake, when it was time for my baby to be born.

Our library didn't have books on how to put your baby up for adoption. I don't remember where we got the phone number that led me to Mrs. Quinn, who told me all about a Catholic couple one state away. She didn't say which way. The man was a member of the Knights of Columbus and the woman was active in the sodality. I bet the number came from Sister John Gabriel. The man was a lawyer and the woman a homemaker who loved to bake and do needlepoint. They'd been married for seven years and God still hadn't given them a child. I thought they sounded OK. I thought about it for a few days, and then I called Mrs. Quinn and told her they could have my baby. I filled out forms.

I got down my bag of yarn and asked my grandmother for the knitting lessons she had promised me. Knit one, purl one. It was soothing to sit in the wing chair in my mother's sewing room and knit. I thought the least I could do for my baby was to give him a many-colored blanket for a birthday present, a going-away present.

My mother's sewing machine was across the room from me and as I knit, she sewed, humming away, making me maternity clothes. My mother made a ridiculous number of dresses for a person who hardly ever went anywhere except the library and the YWCA. But she kept buying great swaths of flowered material and designing me these tents. She didn't want me to get depressed.

My father brought me something every day, just something from the newsstand by his bus stop: a box of lemon drops, a bag of salted peanuts, a strawberry twirler, a *Time* magazine. He'd ask me how I was feeling and smile kindly, but he never mentioned the baby directly. He taught me how to play backgammon and let me help him build a birdhouse down in the basement, at his workbench.

Sister John Gabriel had implored me to keep up with my schoolwork, "to keep your mind alive." I had planned to do a little algebra every day, a little chemistry, some French, religion, and English, but I got lazy. I remember I read some French plays, one by Corneille and one by Racine and one by Molière. I read each one out loud, alone in my room. The rhythm of their verses put me in the same mood as swimming did. It was soothing, like a lullaby. For some reason it made me feel close to my baby.

My English class the semester I dropped out was British Literature. The only entire novel we were assigned was *David Copperfield*. I read that alone too, in my room. My class hadn't gotten to it before I left. When I first began novels in those days I always had a dictionary and a notebook at my side. Once I got hooked I never bothered to look up a word, but for the first thirty pages or so I was alert for words whose meanings I was unsure of. *Caul* appears on page one of *David Copperfield*, and that was my first entry in my new vocabulary notebook.

So when my baby was born in a caul, I wasn't shocked or appalled. When the doctor pulled away the veil, the membrane, and I could see him more clearly, he didn't look much like the graceful swimmer I had pictured during my pregnancy. He was wrinkled and red faced and greasy.

The next day my mother made me visit him. She walked me down the hall to the nursery and made me look at him through the glass. His eyes were closed, his lips parted in a smile. My mother motioned for the nurse to meet her at the nursery door. The nurse wasn't happy with what my mother said, I could see, but she complied. She handed her a gown and a mask which my mother then handed to me. I put them on. Then she led me into the nursery and told me to sit in the rocking chair. The nurse was mad. She told my mother she was cruel, the baby was being adopted out, what was she trying to do, punish her daughter for getting pregnant in the first place? My mother didn't seem to hear her, she just took the baby from the nurse and gave him to me. She unwrapped his blanket and told me to feel his skin, his hair, and to be sure I was ready to give him up. "Kiss him on the forehead when you're ready to say good-bye," she said.

I put my finger on his arm and moved it up and down. A petal. I touched his black hair and studied his toes. I laid my hand on his stomach and closed my eyes. I tried to conjure up the girl in the efficiency pretending to be Diana Ross. I even hummed her song, "Baby Love, My Baby Love," but I never saw the girl with the heavy black eyeliner and bleached stringy hair. She just wouldn't appear, even though I'd written about her vividly in my journal.

I kissed him on the forehead, but I didn't say good-bye. I held him for most of that day and stared and stared at his face. I called Mrs. Quinn the next day and told her the deal was off. My mother got my old bassinet out of the crawl space and put it next to my bed at home, and she went to a department store and bought him kimonos and diapers and rubber pants.

A few days after we got home I called Jeff's mother and told her my news. She was shocked. I had been so firm in my resolve to give the baby up, she wasn't at all prepared to deal with having a grandbaby. But she was kind and told me she was sure I'd done the right thing, and the next day she came over to visit. She brought a blue sweater-and-bootie set for David (I had decided against naming him Jeff), and she brought a nightgown for me. She brought along Jeff's last letter, full of the rigors of boot camp, and a photograph of Jeff I barely recognized; his head was almost shaved. That day, for the first time in three years, I felt no love for him. When he looked like a soldier, he was a stranger to me.

But the love came back in a few months. I even put his picture back up on my dresser for David to look at. And I kept imagining that he'd come to his senses, that a grenade would explode in front of him in the jungle outside of Da Nang and knock him to his senses, and he'd come home and marry me and move us to our favorite tower of apartments. On Sundays the three of us would picnic in the cornfield.

He did come home before his tour of duty was completed. He was wounded by "friendly fire"—a buddy's gun had gone off accidentally and the bullet had hit Jeff in the leg. His mother called me in secret to tell me he was home. She had written him everything. She was trying to persuade him to at least visit me. He didn't have the courage, it seemed.

David was walking by then. I polished his white high-top shoes, dressed him in a cute sailor outfit, and took him over to meet his father. I had my figure back by then, and my hair was still long. I thought the two of us would be irresistible, sort of. My mother said later that maybe I should have left David with her, if I had really wanted Jeff back.

I don't know if I really wanted Jeff back that day. As I climbed the steps to his mother's door with David on my hip, I saw through the picture window that he was there, sitting at the kitchen table with his mother. He looked anguished. His chin was in his hands. His eyes were closed. His hair was still short. I guessed that they were talking about me.

He didn't kiss me, but he was real nice to me. He told me he was sorry and he even wept a little. He kept staring at David, looking for himself I guess, and trying to make contact with him. But David had found the cupboards with the pots and pans and was much more interested in making a racket than in making a relationship with his long-lost father.

So Jeff wasn't the man of steel he had made himself be when he'd said good-bye to me all those months before. But he wasn't the same as he'd been in the cornfield, either. I could see it on his face—faraway eyes, set teeth, a line beginning between his eyebrows. I guess war changes a person, the way having a baby does. So by the time I said good-bye, by the time I threw my arms around his neck and told him I'd always love him, and told him that having his baby was the best thing in my life, I knew that it was over. I knew there'd never be a wedding with Anne-Marie and Sally in fuchsia.

And having his baby is still the best thing I ever did, nineteen years later. I tell my mother that, and I ask her if she had known it would be, if that's why she insisted I hold and touch his newborn self. But she swears not, she shakes her head adamantly, and says no, she thought that giving him up was the right thing to do. She thought I should have my own life. She didn't want me to be tied down at sixteen, tied down by love and obligations.

My mother is old now, but there are hardly any lines in her face. Her hair is a bright white. She braids it and winds it into a bun at the back of her neck. Her skin always looks tan with her hair so white. Her eyes are a clear blue, like the water in a swimming pool. We sometimes go together now to that YWCA pool where I first pictured David inside me. We do laps side by side, slowly. It seems more meditation than swim sometimes. It seems like a holy place, the swimming pool, like a cornfield, like a church, like a room where a baby is born.

Morning News
Maggi Ann Grace

I hold the paper
sliced in early light,
read past the trial of a father
who powdered
his toddler's disposables with Drano
to inside pages
where an infant was found
locked inside a pickup truck
sucking a beer-filled bottle
while the teen mom window-shopped.
I flip to the back page
where the eight month old found
in an unheated Chicago apartment
won't need amputation after all,
only treatment for frost
and rodent bites.

My coffee is glue
sliding down my throat
and I must dress to pass
parades of mothers,
robeless judges
who tow chapped kids,
balance signs that talk of rights,

not of adolescents
not of men and women
who make mistakes
but rights of the results:
unborns who may be dropped
like bread crumbs on church steps,
in toilet bowls or scalding baths.

Getting Ready
Catherine Boyd

The temperature, as it often does on muggy, overcast days, continued to rise as the afternoon rolled toward evening. About halfway between the big white house and the end of the vineyard, Margo bent over, fitting one shiny irrigation pipe into another. She wore a beige T-shirt, spackled with mud, a navy-blue one-piece bathing suit underneath. Her skin was tanned dark; the working muscles were wet and they flashed in the gray light.

She walked to the end of a twenty-foot pipe, resting in a muddy ditch between two rows of tiny grapes. She inserted the pipe into the next one, gave it a hard twist followed by a test pull. She sloshed along the ditch to the unattached end, where another pipe waited. Instinctively, she felt someone coming. She looked across the field of green leaves and saw Eric walking her way.

He waved and smiled. "Hello there!" he yelled, waving a second time.

"Hello," she called back. "I was hoping you'd find me." Starting at her bare feet, she traced the warm mud to her hips and waist. She laughed nervously—not because he was seeing her like this—but because of what she planned on telling him.

When Eric reached Margo, he took her in his arms and gave her a long kiss. "I missed you," he said.

She wrapped her hands around the back of his neck, moved with his hug, and stared at the playground of her childhood, a one-acre pond. These last three weeks, awake every night, sweating so much the sheet had become pasted to her breasts, Margo would throw a towel around herself, sneak out of the house, and walk along the grape rows to the pond. She would swim freestyle to the other side, take handfuls of silty black mud and rub it on her stomach, trying to decide what to do.

She patted his sides and stepped back. "Let's go to the pond. It seems cooler there." She reached for his hand, and they walked to the wooden diving dock.

"Where's your mom?" Eric asked. "I didn't see her car."

Margo let go of his hand and sat. Her feet dangled in the water. "She went to the store. Whenever you come, it's like suddenly we have to eat big meals."

He kicked off his shoes and socks, and sat next to her, legs in the water. He took a deep breath. "You sure it's OK for you to be doing work like this? In your condition?"

Her head dropped back and she watched a turkey vulture glide a slow, wide circle. "I feel strong as a horse." She turned to him, threw out her right arm and flexed the bicep. "What do you think?"

His foot touched hers. "I think we should be talking about it. Once your mom gets back it will be nothing but social stuff."

Margo pulled off her T-shirt and shook out her hair. She dropped into the water.

His feet kicked involuntarily. He said, "I feel like something's wrong."

She grabbed his ankles, holding them still. "There is something I've got to tell you."

He leaned forward and touched the tops of her shoulders. "Before you say anything, I want you to know there's no hurry. I'm not going to try to push you either way."

Standing in the oozing silt, she looked across the vineyard at the slow up-and-down vibrations of the heat waves. She held on to him and quietly spoke: "I went to town last week, and I had one."

He was sweating heavily. He swallowed hard, swallowed again. "You had one? What the hell does that mean?"

"I had it last Friday. At a clinic in Stockton. Don't worry, I used a fake name."

Eric looked blankly at the pond. "Jesus, Margo, I just talked to you on the phone *yesterday*."

"It's not the kind of thing you tell someone over the telephone."

"But I would have gotten a day off work and met you there. I would have gone *in* with you." He rubbed his forehead. Almost to himself, he said, "Oh, I get it. You needed to do it alone."

Margo held her mouth tight, to keep from trembling. She turned around so she wouldn't have to look at him.

Eric took off his shirt and joined her in the pond. They swam across to where a four-inch pipe delivered pumped well water. They took turns pressing their bodies against the cold current. Margo took care to not let the powerful flow hit her low on the belly.

Without speaking, she headed back. Eric followed. They climbed onto the dock and, faces down, stretched out on the baking planks. They dried quickly in the sun.

"Did you ever think about what it would look like? If it would be a boy or a girl?" Margo asked.

"A little, sometimes. But not as much as I thought it could foul things up for us—in the long run. You know what I mean," he said.

"It seems to me a baby would be pretty innocent as far as messing up our lives goes."

Eric turned and wrapped his arms around her. He kissed the back of her neck. "I wish you would have called me." He hugged her tightly from behind.

Margo reached over the side of the dock and trailed a hand through the tepid water. She wanted so badly to hear him say he had wanted the baby, but that it just wasn't practical, or realistic, or smart. She wanted to hear him say that part of him wished she could have had it. She wished to God he would tell her he felt the same way she did.

"Listen to me," he said. "You did the right thing. The *best* thing." He stayed nuzzled against her. "Margo, please, talk to me. Tell me what you're thinking."

She turned and looked at him. "I think it's different for women."

"It must be. It can't be easy to give up a piece of yourself."

Her thoughts sped out in all directions, stretching the already worn fabric of her mind. She started to cry—and said, "I'll be all right. I'll be fine."

"Of course you'll be all right. It's just going to take time. There's always a certain shock afterwards with something like this."

But she had lied to him. She hadn't gone to Stockton. She had lied to him because ever since they had found out she was pregnant he had acted more like a close friend than a father. He'd given her advice, and little else. She needed him to take a stand. She needed to know what he really felt before she went ahead with her decision. "It's funny it bothers me so much." She choked on her choppy breathing, started again. "It's not like I'm against abortions, not at all. It's just that I'm not for them. No matter how many times you turn it over in your head, it's bad either way."

Eric ran his hand down her spine. "It was the only thing you could do, Margo. I feel lousy about it too."

Although she had known all along that she would make the trip to the clinic in Stockton, and use a fake name, she hadn't been able to get herself to feel ready. Now she was close to ready.

"C'mon, let's go inside and take a shower," Margo said. They helped each other up from the dock. "My mom's going to be back pretty soon and I want to help her with dinner."

Spiderplant
Terri L. Jewell

i watch you
push out earth
thick yellow anchors
shove unwilling babies
into air
along slim tendrils
bearing fruit
and flower
i choose a
golden barrenness
while full of seed
plant a prudent crop
libations to the south
dream my own acreage
of sacred ground

Life Support
Dorothy Howe Brooks

It has been only three weeks since she first came to this room, this intensive-care neonatal unit, yet it seems to Cynthia that she has had no life outside, no life before. The clock on the wall of the newborn nursery, visible through the glass partition beside her, is her only contact with the passing time. The fluorescent daylight begins at 6:00 A.M., ends at 9:00 P.M. John brings her a newspaper each day when he stops in for his early morning visit, and this way she keeps track of the days. If it weren't for John she would have to chalk a primitive mark on the pure white wall behind her each time the lights went on.

Beside the chair where she now sits, there is a cot. Nearby, a small, black-and-white television, a writing table where she eats, and a bookcase with well-read copies of *McCall's, Science Today, Parent*. Directly in front of her, not quite close enough to touch, is the machine, the large steel structure with the glass womb where her baby, Michael, lives. He wears patches to preserve his eyesight, and a miniature diaper. Wires and tubes taped carefully onto his tiny body connect him to receptor points in the machine. Above the glass housing are dials, switches, and a glowing console with regular graphic patterns appearing and disappearing to measure and regulate his breathing, his heartbeat, his nourishment. Just above his diaper, the oversized stub of an umbilical cord, almost healed, shows Cynthia how recently her own body gave him life support.

It is seven-thirty. John has just left for work. Cynthia stretches, stiff from another night on the hard cot. John wants her home, says he needs her, but she can't leave. Her body is mending. The swelling in her stomach is gradually returning to normal, her breasts, large with anticipation of the child to nurse, have lost their milk. She places her hands over her empty womb as she often held them during the past eight months when she could feel the new life quicken beneath them, and looks to the infant. She has never held him.

She gets up and goes to the glass incubator. She reaches her hands through the openings designed to ensure that even these sick babies feel their mother's touch, and strokes his forehead. He never responds. The doctors say he may already have been deprived too long of oxygen, may never respond. They do know that without this machine he would be dead. Cynthia thinks maybe he is already dead, maybe he died, alone, in a moment that she cannot now recapture.

On the table is the form John brought her this morning. It is a consent form for surgery. The tests they have been doing for the past three weeks have finally yielded a tentative answer. His heart is defective. His only hope is surgery, delicate microsurgery on his heart. His chances are not good. She and John must consent. They hold him in the balance. Her choice this morning is to consent or watch him in this glass bubble forever.

Cynthia feels there must be other choices. She wants to unplug the machine, snatch her baby back, and cradle him. She longs to hold him to her barren breast and rock him, to sing to him all the lullabies that she practiced when he was safe inside of her. But there is no plug, no master attachment she can safely sever to steal back her child. And there are nurses around the clock looking in who would save him from her.

In quiet moments Cynthia thinks back to the night in the delivery room when her nightmare began. It seemed a normal birth. The black hair of the head crowned. John squeezed her hand in his excitement. One more push and the infant emerged, covered in white mucous and bits of blood. But he wouldn't cry, couldn't breathe. The doctors whisked him away. A nurse gave her a sedative, asked John to leave. When she awoke in the recovery room, John told her their baby was alive but only barely. She lifted up in the bed and reached for John, held him close and tight, and they cried together.

Though she can see the well babies in the next room, she can hardly imagine that only three weeks ago they expected, even assumed, they would have such a child. A child peacefully sleeping, breathing on his own without the aid of the steel machine. It is difficult even to imagine such a child, though she sees them every day. Looking at Michael, it seems impossible that such a tiny thing could exist on its own, disconnected, apart from any life support, just as it seems impossible to suppose that she and John had a life before this room.

She picks up the consent form and reads it again. "Little or no anesthesia..." A stumbling block. The doctors explained that his chances were so slim they couldn't risk putting him to sleep. They would use some local anesthetics to reduce the pain, but they couldn't know what he might feel. They told her the latest research indicates newborns feel very little pain. Very little pain. She repeats the words to herself as she walks again to the tiny body. She reaches her hands in again to stroke him. Very little pain. Who is to measure the pain?

This morning, John hugged her and said she must sign. He said he knew how difficult it was for her, it was just as difficult for him, but she must sign. It was their only hope, Michael's only hope. We have to do what's best for Michael, he'd said. She has been a mother only three weeks yet her child is depending on her to know what is right, to do what is best.

Her instincts are false. Her instincts tell her to grab him, to hold him, and that would kill him. Her reason must prevail. Medical science must prevail. She looks up at the dials, the green monitor charting its regular course. Life in the steady, rhythmic patterns. She looks at her child and it feels like death, not life, the machine is preserving. A death machine, postponing death, altering it, shaping it.

She sees the form on the table waiting for her, demanding her attention. She knows she will sign. But she will sign the way she has done everything these past three weeks, as if she was in a fog, groping. She wishes she could sign with courage, with conviction, with hope.

As she lies back in the chair and rests her head on a soft pillow, she has a dream. It is not quite a dream for she is not quite asleep. It is a scene that comes to her in those suspended moments between waking and sleep. It is this: She is in labor again. The head crowns and the infant emerges, covered in white mucous tinged with blood. His eyes are shut against the light, but his breathing comes, shallow but steady.

She opens her nightgown and John takes the infant and places him directly on her breasts. Skin touches skin. The umbilical cord extends but is not yet cut. She strokes the tiny head, the cap of black hair, holds the tiny body close and tight against her. The limp form, so newly come from the womb, molds itself to her, to her large breasts, her rounded belly. The tiny head burrows into her, searching instinctively for the nipple. She finds it and brings it to his lips and he sucks, though there is no milk yet to nourish him. Then his movements stop, his breathing becomes faint, his chest no longer pulses in its regular rhythm. He looks as if he is asleep but Cynthia knows he is not, knows he is gone. She is calm. She doesn't cry out or call for help because in the dream—and this is how she knows, finally, that it is a dream—she is certain of what he needs.

Art As Life
Ann Menebroker

It's about stillness,
a feeling for the primitive spirit,
displaced structure,
and someone listening, lying
in her single bed
by a window
shadow and light
making canvas figures
upon the walls,
breathing slowly,
taking it all in
as if she were, for this moment,
the only person on earth
who finally hears
what is being missed,
who finally sees
what has been overlooked,
who touches herself
slowly, to feel who she is
through flesh, this minimal
product
of skeletal remains,
who then turns sideways
from the view,
closing her eyes, but
retaining the image, sleeps
with a smile on her lips.

Photo by Lori Burkhalter-Lackey

Résumé
Dori Appel

When her life seemed
too demanding, my mother often
claimed it was her sole ambition
to stand in some monotonous
factory line, watching cans
of beans roll by. She wouldn't
mind the pay because
her simple job would be to drop
a piece of pork
on top of each. On better days
she craved a business
of her own, some classy place
with her name on the awning that
she ruled in a good gray suit.

Now the direction of her gaze
has changed. She focuses on what
she hasn't been—a faster reader,
better shopper, thin. As she recites
her litany of disappointment,
I see her in that scheme she once
imagined: A conveyer belt
is humming, and a thousand cans are
floating by like objects in a dream.
Beneath the cool fluorescent lights
my mother lifts her hand—a girl
with a paycheck coming,
and nothing but
this moment on her mind.

Mother Land
Linda Wasmer Smith

I knew that place like the freckles I tried to bleach
With lemon juice across my nose. I knew
The geometric grace of fields that reach
Beyond the point where green caresses blue.
I knew the fertile Mississippi muck
That sprouts soybeans and weeds that spread like fire
Through hay. Sometimes I believed I might be stuck
Forever, deep in that tenacious mire.
I never really came to know that place,
I never knew the life-force in my blood
That slows all movement to the seasons' pace.
I pulled myself free like a shoe from the mud
And left. Now from books, my children understand
The concept Farm. They'll never know the land.

A Woman's Choice
Jacklyn W. Potter

1.

The black coat. *It's the key to fashion.*
She wants it. The one with the collar
that won't quit, the midcalf, pure wool
black coat—the limit, the essence,
half-price, the black coat. She wants it.

She tries it: the perfect coat.
She is particular, precise,
she is the woman in the black coat.
See her seduce the bay!
See her lie in iridescent foam!
Soft wool rides the waves.

Now she gives it
back to the rack.

2.

As she watches the boats
that go for clams and scallops,
the wind slaps her,
the wind that wears kid gloves.
She has consumed
many heads of lettuce,
she has picked
at many bones of fish.

Each day she repeats
a thousand motions,
she gathers her heart and body
at last, home, to the place
of her solitary choosing.
The sea gulls wing before her window screen.
She wears her skin alone to bed.

Máire, Who Feeds the Wild Cat?
Pat Schneider

For Máire O'Donohoe

Behind the convent a wild
cat is ill. She sleeps
in a fine mist of rain
on the warm hood
of a cooling automobile.
She's sick, poor thing,
you say. You say
she's too sick to run away.

And you are cloistered here
uneasy now in all
the old, familiar habits,
awkward in the raw world,
its own severe conventions,
language of fashion,
innuendos. Rules.

From the window of the guesthouse
I study the convent walls,
the remote third floor
where no one may go but
nuns of your particular order.
The wall is fortress high
and fortress thick. Inside,

the sisters smile, repeating
and repeating one another's names:
Rosario, Saint Ambrose, Immaculate.

Outside, where a mist of rain
has chilled the bone of this day,
a wild cat watches,
too sick to run away.

Photo by Lori Burkhalter-Lackey

Imaginary Bonds
Bonnie Michael

Like rings around Saturn
the furies of her life encircle her.
Not knowing she is the planet,
she gives them power.

Her prison sky looms endlessly.
Her other lives were long ago;
she cannot seem to remember them,
cannot seem to find their moons.

When the time is right, she will know
the galaxy is more than Saturn—
she is not held by imaginary bonds
nor blinded by falling stars.

The Scorpion Wore Pink Shoes
Janice Levy

"*Despiértate,* wake up, Soledad!" Clara hissed.

Soledad groaned and rubbed her eyes.

"Come on, *ya se hace tarde,* it's getting late, and we have a lot to do."

Squinting through one eye, Soledad saw that Clara was already wearing her gray dress and white apron, the name Harrington Hotel stitched over its top pocket. Crescents of sweat darkened the cotton uniform under her arms. Soledad stretched slowly, her aching legs sticking up under the white sheet of her cot. She coughed up the phlegm that stuck in her throat like lumps of glue. She felt like a leftover meal.

As Clara pushed her cleaning cart filled with disinfectants, toilet scrub brushes, and plastic bags out of the basement, she gestured with her nose at Soledad to hurry. The housekeeping staff lived in the basement of the Harrington Hotel in New Hampshire, with sheets hung across the ceiling to separate the cots. Soledad's bed was closest to the row of washing machines. She stared at the clothes spinning around and wondered how it would feel to be sucked up and tossed about until you became just a blur of color.

She threw off her blanket and walked stiffly to one of the dryers to take out some pillowcases and sheets. She rested her head on top of a whirring machine and imagined herself slow dancing, her body pressed against the warm chest of a handsome man. The deep, soothing noise of the machine reminded her of Geraldo's humming in the shower, while she lingered in bed and inhaled his scent from the sheets. But that was a long time ago, when she had been almost as young as her daughter, Gabriela, was now, and there was still a reason to linger.

When Clara's friend, Mr. Jones, came to Costa Rica looking for women to bring back to the States with him, Soledad left her job at the factory where her boss stood with a watch to make sure she scaled and gutted fifteen fish an hour. She asked her mother to take care of Gabriela. "You'll see, *Mamá*, I'll send you money so the doctors can take the veins out of your legs and Gabriela can go to the *universidad* to study."

She told her daughter she would come back in a year. *"Te prometo,* I promise." Gabriela had stared at her with lizard eyes. Mr. Jones wore a toupee that looked like a dead pigeon and his cheeks were the color of an emery board. He got Soledad a tourist visa and a social security card that changed her into "Maria Rivera," a Puerto Rican from New York. When she started working in the hotel, she sometimes leaned against the door of a room before knocking and strained to make sense of the words that shot out in English as fast as gunfire. But after six months, she could say little more than, "Good morning," "Sorry," and "Room clean?"

Clara learned English because she cleaned Mr. Jones's house on her day off. Soledad saw her friend and Mr. Jones coming out of the service elevator together early one morning; Clara's face had been flushed and her hair messed up. Clara said you could make fifty dollars in four hours, but you had to be smart.

Every Sunday night, Soledad made a three-minute phone call to Costa Rica, covering one ear with her hand to block out the noise from the hallway. While waiting their turns on the long line that snaked down the hall, the maids passed around letters and pictures. Soledad's mother had sent her a picture of Gabriela, standing with Gabriela's father, Geraldo, in front of a neighbor's house. Gabriela was, at fourteen, as tall as Soledad, and already wore her mother's shoes and clothes. In the photograph, she stood slumped forward, her fists rolled up under her chin, her head tilted away from her father. Geraldo had one hand on her shoulder. Soledad couldn't make out her daughter's face clearly, but she knew how her daughter was feeling. Gabriela didn't like to be touched. By anyone. Ever.

Geraldo faced the camera, mustachioed and heavy-lidded, with his hips jutting forward. Soledad remembered how just touching his thigh lightly with her fingertips used to make her legs turn to jelly. In the six months Soledad had been in the United States, she had received one letter from Geraldo, the handwriting smeared and running up and down the page like crawling worms. Soledad heard he had remarried. She wondered if he hit his new wife in the face after yelling at her.

On the telephone, Gabriela spoke excitedly about her upcoming *quinceañera*. In another month she would be fifteen years old. Gabriela thanked Soledad for sending the money to buy fabric so *Abuelita* Rosa could make the dress for her big party. But now the problem was finding a pair of matching shoes.

"I've looked everywhere, in all the stores, and I can't find anything I like. They have to be perfect."

Soledad could picture her sullen daughter pacing up and down and frowning.

"I want shoes that a princess would wear: princess slippers, with high, high heels. And pink. They've got to be pink."

When Soledad asked if she had chosen an escort for her party, she heard Gabriela take a deep breath, and she knew her daughter was tapping her foot up and down.

"Yes, *Mami*. I asked Juan, but don't worry because we're not *novios*; he's just my friend. But, so anyway, about the shoes, you won't forget to send the money for them, OK?"

Soledad wiped her eyes when her daughter used up the last moments of the phone call with kisses.

Soledad knocked on the door of the first room she had to clean. She opened the door with her key and pushed her cleaning cart into the center of the room. Holding her breath, she emptied the overflowing ashtrays. She put clean glasses with paper tops on the dresser, replaced the stationery in the drawers, and filled a little wicker basket in the bathroom with bottles of shampoo and conditioner. As Soledad filled a vase with water and added a red carnation, she thought of her mother's house, where she had returned after Geraldo had left her lying on the kitchen floor. The house was small, and the color of tarnished silver. The roof was wooden; the balcony a slab of colored stones. On the front porch steps, Soledad had placed red flowers in brightly painted tin cans. She painted the cans herself, with images of fuchsia-feathered roosters and scampering little black pigs, all of the things she saw while she sat on the porch and waited for Geraldo to make it all good again.

When he did, it was always the same. He'd bring *Mama* Rosa some flowers, swing Gabriela in the air, and toss his hat across the room for Soledad to catch. Soledad would cook his favorite dishes and wash his clothes. She'd stroke his face and lay her head on his chest. Once, Geraldo stayed for a few weeks and they took a trip to Póas, the volcano, outside the city of Alajuela. As the taxi huffed its way on the winding roads, through the green fields and small farms, Geraldo chewed on her ear and played with her hair. They walked, arms around each other, up the trail to the crater of the volcano. As they walked through the forest of clouds, Soledad matched her breathing to Geraldo's and thought his face looked like *un ángel del cielo.*

Soledad sighed and threw off the sheets and put them in her laundry bag. She remade the bed and put on fresh pillowcases. She hugged a pillow and closed her eyes. Those were the times to remember, she thought. Not the times when Geraldo paced the house and scratched himself like a dog in heat, went out at night and came back stumbling and falling against things. He'd come back later and later, until Soledad knew he was finally gone, because the only sounds in the house when the sun came up were the muffled sobs of Gabriela and the ticking of a clock.

Soledad pushed her cart down the hall to Suite 710, the best accommodations on the floor, with a living room, a fireplace in the bedroom, and a telephone in the bathroom. She picked up the breakfast tray from the floor and put the leftover rolls and packets of orange marmalade in her pocket. Several bottles of perfume, all opened, sat on the bathroom sink, their tops lying nearby. A makeup case floated in the half-filled bathtub, forming lily pads of greasy rainbows on the water's surface. False eyelashes swirled like drowning spiders under the faucet. Soledad shut off the dripping water and walked into the living room. Three fur coats were rolled up on the couch—they looked like drunks holding their stomachs. A purple suede hat with a corkscrew stuck through its brim sat in a bucket of melted ice on the bar's countertop. Soledad looked at the wine stains on the bed sheets and the broken champagne glasses on the hearth. She suddenly felt tired and looked around for a clean place to sit down.

Flung over the back of a chair was a man's tuxedo and a pink gown with a neckline of white feathers. She ran her hand down the front of the dress, over a big orange stain, touching sequins and beads and pearls, some hanging by loose threads. A cigarette had burned a hole over the left shoulder.

As a bead from the gown fell into her hand, Soledad thought of her daughter's *quinceañera* dress. Gabriela wanted a traditional dress, down to the floor, tight on top and full at the bottom, with a skirt shaped like a wedding bell. She mailed a sketch of the dress to Soledad, along with a piece of material, and for weeks, Soledad kept the swatch of pink satin with tiny white rosebuds on it in the pocket of her uniform. When she touched it, she could almost see Padre Vargas, the pastor at the *Iglesia de Cristo*, giving her daughter the blessing at the *quinceañera* mass, just as he had blessed Soledad, sixteen years ago, making the sign of the cross as she knelt in front of him. Soledad remembered her own *quinceañera* and her tall, handsome escort who danced a kind of waltz with her, weaving in and out among the other fourteen girls and their escorts, forming small and then big circles, like the ripples on a pond. She had stood with all the girls on the sidewalk outside the church, giggling when a car drove by and made a great poof that made their full dresses fly up. Soledad fingered the cross around her neck and thought of the *Iglesia de Cristo*, with its hard wood pews and a ceiling so high it made her neck hurt to see its top. The stained glass behind the altar glistened in the sunlight like multicolored dewdrops. Soledad wondered if Padre Vargas still kept a pail hanging outside the side door of the church for the children to deposit their bubble gum in.

Soledad held the pink gown against her body and looked in the mirror. Her tall, dark escort had flirted and danced with all the girls, but he caught her eye with a look, quiet and still, like a gift held just out of reach. In back of the church, against a tree in the woods, he took her hair and tied it under her chin so it framed her face like a bonnet. He held her so close that she could feel his eyelashes on her cheeks.

"*Te necesito,* I need you, Soledad," he had pleaded.

Soledad had let him find his way past the bows and ties of her dress, under the satin slips. His face had looked like a wounded bird, so she had held him and stroked his head until he shivered and stopped.

After they were married, Soledad and Geraldo lived with his parents in Sarchi, northwest of San José, the capital. Geraldo worked with his father building ox carts that the farmers used to carry their coffee beans. *Turistas* liked to watch them work in the open sheds. Soledad painted geometric designs on the ox carts and listened to Geraldo practice his English with the men in baggy shorts and gold watches, men with cameras around their necks. Geraldo told them the wheels he carved made music as they turned.

He winked and smiled at the overdressed ladies in high heels and ropes of jewelry. He took them by the hand and set them down in his handmade, wood rocking chairs. He took off his hat and fanned them, using a mixture of Spanish and English to describe their beauty. Almost always the men bought something, if only to get their wives out of the rocking chairs, because Soledad knew the señoras could sit there forever, giggling and running their fingers through their hair.

Once Geraldo caught a man with a big belly and baseball cap wiping paint off Soledad's cheek with a handkerchief, then opening his wallet and pointing to her. Geraldo had grabbed Soledad by the back of her neck and dragged her behind the shed. He covered her mouth so she wouldn't frighten away the *turistas*. Many hours later, Geraldo pinned her against the bed and squeezed her wrists as if he were stapling her to the sheets. He pushed his weight against her again and again until he had felt the blood rush down her legs and then he fell asleep with his legs across her hips. Soledad rolled out from under him and walked outside to sit in the darkness. She wondered if the man with the big belly and baseball cap was showing his wallet to other women that night or if he made love gently and so quietly that his wife wept. When she counted back, she knew that was the night Gabriela was conceived.

With a heavy sigh, Soledad began wiping the mirrors with glass cleaner. As she pulled down hard on the curtain cord to bring in more light from the high windows overlooking a little terrace, she tripped over a pair of shoes that lay behind the curtain.

The shoes were pink satin with tiny white rosebuds. The toes of the shoes were open except for a transparent lace covering that looked like a bridal veil. The inner side of the shoes curved toward the middle like the waistline of a young girl. Little silver chains of pearls were strung around the heels, which were several inches high. Soledad cradled the shoes in her hands and noted the soles looked clean and a piece of the price tag had not been scraped off one of them.

"Maybe he carried her all night," she said to herself. "Maybe in his arms like a *princesa*." Soledad looked to find the size of the shoes. She slipped them on her feet and smiled. She held out her gray uniform and curtsied to the mirror. Soledad spun around the room, her arms moving like the waves of an ocean. As she arched her neck and pointed her toes, she pretended she was a rich lady, having returned to Costa Rica. She imagined she was making the eight-hour train ride with a lover, from San José to Puerto Limón, to vacation by the Caribbean Sea. They would dangle their hands out the windows and pass through the shoulders of huge mountains, into tangled jungles, along the Reventazón River with its rapids and high rocks. They would see white sand and blue seas and palm trees that looked like feather dusters as they swayed in the wind. Her lover would buy her peanuts and *papas calientes,* hot potatoes, from the small boys who jumped on the trains and sold them down the aisles. The barefooted ladies who wore aprons would call her Doña Soledad and stand before her selling yucca and hot fish. Her lover would snap his fingers in the air and a man would run over with a paper cone filled with bits of ice, berry red with fruit juice. Soledad and her lover would share one and lick their lips, melting the ice in each others' mouths with their tongues. She would put her feet in his lap and he'd take off her pink shoes with the white rosebuds and lightly kiss her ankles, never taking his eyes off her face.

Soledad caught sight of herself in the mirror, her hair messed and swirly. She untied the belt of her uniform and her stomach protruded forward. Soledad shook her head as she took off the shoes. *"Ay, Soledad, que tonta eres,* how silly you are," she said. She thought of her serious, amber-eyed daughter and wondered if Gabriela still believed in the magic of such things.

Soledad heard voices coming from the hall and quickly put the shoes behind the curtain, in the same corner where she had found them. She looked at the clock and realized she would have to work extra fast to finish cleaning all the rooms on the seventh floor. Soledad jumped as a man walked into the room, stumbling as if he had a third leg that kept bumping into the other two. A woman wearing a bathing suit and clumps of jewelry at her ears and throat pushed past him. Soledad thought she looked like a doll whose hair grew when you pressed its stomach, a doll she had once bought for Gabriela. The woman looked at Soledad and scrunched up her eyes, nose, and lips. She shook her fingers in the air as if shooing away pigeons. She threw her purse on the floor, kicked her shoes off, and fell back on the bed. The man said something to Soledad and then repeated it louder. He opened his eyes so wide his eyelashes reached up to his eyebrows. He pointed around the room and spoke louder and louder, his earlobes turning as red as the rising liquid of a thermometer. Soledad bit her lip and said, "Good morning, sorry, clean room?" in one fast breath and quickly pushed her cleaning cart out of the room.

That night, Soledad dreamed of two scorpions mating. The male and female moved back and forth, front legs gripping front legs, mouth parts locked together. The male whipped his tail forward and stung the female again and again, dragging her thrashing body around a dance floor. The female wore pink shoes with white rosebuds. A band played a waltz; then the music switched to mariachi sounds and the female, heavy in her ruffled dress, bit off the male's head and kicked it with the point of her shoe.

Soledad woke up, sticky with sweat. She stood on tiptoe to look out the basement windows. A light snow was falling, the first snowfall Soledad had ever seen. The branches of the trees, stiff under the flakes, made her think of crinoline; the patches of frozen pond reminded her of icing on a cake.

As she watched the sun scratch away the night, Soledad covered her cheeks with her hands and tapped the sides of her head with her fingers. She pushed her tongue hard against the back of her front teeth. Soledad dressed quickly. As she pushed her cleaning cart out into the hall, she saw Mr. Jones walking toward her, waving a piece of paper. Bulky in his dark fur coat and hat, he looked like a circus bear to Soledad.

"*Buenos dias,* good morning," he said. "Getting an early start today?" He spoke in broken Spanish. "There's been a change in one of your rooms. The people in Suite 710 had some kind of an emergency and they checked out late last night. I think they flew out to Canada. The new guests are checking in early, before noon. So start on the suite first."

Soledad nodded and Mr. Jones reached out and pushed a strand of her hair behind her ear. "I hear you've got a daughter who wants to go to college? If you're looking to make some extra money, let me know. Your friend Clara tells me you're real smart."

Soledad jerked her cleaning cart forward and bumped into a standing ashtray. She could hear Mr. Jones laughing as she reached the service elevator. Soledad took the elevator to the seventh floor. The hall was quiet, except for the sound of a baby crying. She ran to Suite 710. She saw the Do Not Disturb sign lying in a breakfast tray outside the door. Soledad pushed the door open. Wet towels stuck like leeches against the chairs. Orange juice from a pink-rimmed glass dripped onto the pillows. The floor looked like the bottom of a hamster cage, with its piles of ripped-up newspapers and bits of half-eaten food. Soledad quickly made her way across the room to the windows that overlooked the terrace. Biting her knuckles, she drew open the curtains and looked into the corner.

"*Soñadora,* dreamer," she said, spitting out the words. "What did you expect?"

Soledad straightened her shoulders and roughly tugged at her gray uniform. She thought of Mr. Jones and shivered. She looked at the top of the dresser for a tip and brushed aside some dirty tissues and empty cigarette packs until she found an envelope. Soledad put the three dollars in her pocket and walked toward the door to get her cleaning cart. She threw the empty envelope at the garbage pail, but it landed on the floor. She bent down and stuffed the envelope, hard this time, into the pail. It was then that she felt the blood pound in her ears as she pulled out the pair of shoes—princess slippers, pink with white rosebuds, and high, high heels.

Good Intentions
Doris Vanderlipp Manley

Someday you will tell your children about a woman
who left behind a trail of abandoned projects

husbands never sure of ownership
children never certain of devotion

carvings begun in heat and left unfinished
until discarded in another move

paintings she intended to redo
to catch the true brilliance of the scene

friends she wanted to help in time of trial
but managed only to blow a poem their way

dresses she started making but by the time
she finished them her taste or the weather had changed

cookies burned to a crisp and cakes that fell
when the housewife was submerged by the scholar.

From this conglomeration which makes a life
what will you remember? A woman no more

substantial than a cloud—yet one who caught
the sun.

Sunspots
Barbara Lucas

The late afternoon sun makes islands
across the winter lawn—
spots of time, I call them—
somehow more intense
than the great swaths of summer.
The light enters me, filling dry wells
until I become my own sun.
My fifty years flare to corona
and I walk in a body of gold—
my nuptials to winter.

But I know I can't live on islands.
I must cross their blue borders
into the slashed eye of wind
and ululation of brown leaves.
Whatever I've conceived
must be born into this cold.
Women who choose islands
also choose the sea.

On the Nature of Sin
Sandra Redding

"Have a toke?"

I look at the cigarette my son holds out to me. "Don't think so. Might be a sin."

"You're a hoot, Mama Grace. You know that?"

Some might think my son peculiar for believing in square-shaped planets and polka-dot aliens, but not transgression. "We all have our dark side," he's tried explaining. "But the dark side has nothing whatsoever to do with wrongdoing. It's like right and left, up and down. It takes some of each, both light and dark, to form a person."

John Willis spends most Sundays reading science fiction. I suppose that's where he gets his pagan notions.

He's not the only one confused. Some of those church women have it muddled too, only the exact opposite from John Willis. According to their crazy quilt way of thinking, almost anything a person decides to do, including movie watching and shag dancing, is S-I-N.

Ginny Ledbetter's one of them. Has been for more than twenty-five years. She teaches a Bible study group, I understand, and testifies regularly about wrongdoings here in Spero. Every Sunday morning, she and the rest of the choir dress in maroon robes and sing love songs to Jesus.

With her adoration finished, she prisses about the churchyard, robe still on, plain-faced, not even a smudge of lipstick, spouting off *my* transgressions, as if she really *knows*, to anyone who hasn't already left for home and fried chicken.

"You something, you know that?" When John Willis grins, I gladly forget Ginny Ledbetter and her sanctimonious sisters. Smoke from his funny-smelling cigarette drifts my way. I sneeze.

I know he makes them from papers he keeps in a tin box decorated with silver stars and gray crumbled leaves and seeds he keeps in the bottom kitchen drawer. Most turn out skinny and bent.

He is not the only young man in Spero who smokes these cigarettes, but most keep such business from their mamas. Not John Willis. If he wants to do something, he does it come pestilence or flood. He claims it's my fault. "Guess I take being willful from you," he's often told me.

I can't deny.

John Willis took a shower before I brought the chicken casserole, but his longish hair and beard still haven't dried out. At the moment, he wears bright yellow bathing trunks and green flip-flops. In the summertime it's his usual way of dressing. If he decides to go to the pool, he adds dark glasses, coated purple to protect his eyes from cancer rays, and a shirt covered with orange parrots and palm leaves.

My boy turns up the volume of the puny radio he carries in his pocket. After placing the earphones back over his ears, he begins strumming an invisible guitar. Soon, he's hopping and gyrating about the room, his belly bouncing. When he finishes such shenanigans, he starts in on me again. "Won't hurt nothing," he says. "Why deny yourself a simple pleasure?"

"Pleasure *always* has a price," I remind him before crunching on a cube of ice from my tea glass.

I puzzle on why he's being so insistent. Usually we do not pester one another. John Willis does whatever he fancies and I do whatever I fancy, but today he seems hell-bent on converting me to his way of thinking. Talking on about the merits of those cigarettes, he becomes almost as fanatical as Ginny pandering her negative religion. He speaks of bright colors and powerful smells. His mind, he says, has been sharpened, expanded so that a single thing slows, as if it might go on forever.

I'm almost sixty, I tell him. I can't afford slowdowns.

"Ah-law," he says, finally giving up. He pulls out a chair and sits down at the table with me again. "Certainly enjoyed the casserole, Mama. Certainly did. None better. Not in all of Spero."

"I'll bring macaroni and cheese tomorrow."

"You'll spoil me."

"Already have."

The room we sit in contains a sleeper-sofa that's a putrid shade of green, but John Willis has brightened it up with zebra-striped pillows. On the mosaic cocktail table, rescued from a dumpster, he's placed a robust philodendron that snakes down the side. There's not much else. Only the table we sit at and a park bench, paint peeling, knife-carved names still visible, a stop sign, and a bigger than life-size poster of some bare-chested female. I don't know who.

My boy, I suppose, does the best he can.

Because he's enrolled in refrigeration courses at the technical college, he now works only three nights a week at the Handy Pantry, so he hasn't much money for furniture, or food. What little's left after rent, he probably wastes on music tapes and smoking supplies.

When John Willis smiles, his eyes close, forming slits that resemble new moons. He gets that from my side, and the way the skin between his eyebrows scrunches, forming two lines when he frowns. His lankiness comes from me, too, and ears that stick too close to his head. Also the small sliver of birthmark shaped like a dragonfly wing. Mine, dark as a Damson plum, lies flat against my belly; John Willis's hovers near the base of his neck, curved up, as if flying for his chin.

I can't help but wish he looked more like his daddy. At least his hair's the same as Ray's—dirty brown with red glints. They share the same laugh, too—a lighthearted, almost musical sound that tumbles out, free-fall.

If John Willis had been around Ray more, other similarities might have sprouted. It's always good for a boy to see how a man does things, especially when the man's his daddy, but Ray couldn't be there often. He had other obligations.

Though the church women might tell otherwise, I could have married Ray if I'd wanted. He offered to leave Ginny even before John Willis was born, saying he'd move his clothes and woodworking equipment into my trailer that very night, and, soon as he could arrange a divorce, we'd make it legal, changing my name from Grace Cunningham to Grace Ledbetter.

"No." That's what I told him as I reached out touching the stripe of moonlight that silvered our bed sheet, and it wasn't because of any sympathy I felt for his wife that I said it. God knows, though I'm ashamed to admit, I've never felt much of anything for holier-than-thou Ginny in her spotless maroon robe. "Whatever this is between us," I told Ray, "is the best I've ever had with any man. Truly more than I expected. A hundred times better than when I ran off and married Buddy Haskins at sixteen and better than when I left Buddy for Foster Cunningham ten years later. I'm not willing to take chances again, Ray. No use tampering with what feels right."

Reaching up, he cupped my chin in the wide span of his hand. Slowly, with his other hand, he removed the pins that held my dark hair. The only sound, besides the faint ticking of a clock, was his breathing and my own. As he took out the remaining pins, setting free the final strands, I felt suddenly hallowed and peaceful, as if the two of us were in a large church, bathed by multicolored light streaming through stained-glass windows.

I often felt like that with Ray. Never with Buddy Haskins. Never with Foster Cunningham. Only Ray.

Back then Spero wasn't much more than a gas station, an elementary school, two churches, and a combination beauty shop and service station, co-owned by Angelene Johnson and her husband, Jimbo. Because of the smallness of the town, there was no place to hide my swelling belly after John Willis's conception. Right away, the whispers began. At the service station, I could imagine them joking, trying to guess who the father might be between guzzles of Cheerwine. Angelene, pouring rotten-smelling permanent solution and blue-tinted dyes over old women's heads, probably made a soap opera plot of my predicament, and the church women, egged on by Ginny, surely deemed me worthy of hellfire and damnation.

But I never admitted, except to John Willis, that Ray was his daddy. Still they suspected.

Especially Ginny.

"Well?" John Willis asks, holding his cigarette stub up to my face.

"That ropey smelling stuff's illegal. If I wind up in the jailhouse, who'll cook for you?"

He laughs, and I laugh. I thought he'd offer me his cigarette again, but when he doesn't, I pick up his yellowed T-shirt and sour-smelling socks from the sofa and fold the newspaper scattered about on the floor. "You should live better."

"I know."

"It might be those cigarettes making you so careless."

Soon as the words fly from my mouth, he reaches out, touching my shoulder. The hangdog way he looks makes me feel ashamed for acting like his mama even though that's what I am.

"Why, Mama Grace, I'm truly surprised. It's not like you to criticize what you don't know." He turns from me, holding what little's left of his "herbs" daintily between thumb and index finger. I surprise myself by taking the foul thing from him. "Don't I get one of my own?"

"Well Lordy be. Anything you want. Anything atall." As he takes a thin paper out of his tin box, sprinkling it with gray leaves, I almost change my mind. Something doesn't feel right. There's a nag in my head telling me *no*. But ignoring my better judgment, I inhale the old one anyway, then blow out. Lowering myself to John Willis's rag rug, I lean back against the sofa.

I sit there, cross-legged, for the longest while, feeling purely content. Smoking one of my son's funny cigarettes is not a harmful thing to do, I tell myself. A person needs to keep up with what's going on in the world. I've tried kiwi and mangoes. Even tried sushi once, though I almost gagged. Nothing more peculiar than eating raw fish. I close my eyes. When my thoughts backtrack, I think of Ray...

"Hold it," John Willis instructs.

"I am holding it," I say. "See. I'm holding it just like you—between my thumb and the next finger."

"The smoke. Hold the smoke."

With the fresh cigarette, I do as John Willis instructs, leaning back, waiting until my lungs feel pumped up as inner tubes before letting go.

Handing it back, I tell John Willis I feel swimmy-headed.

He laughs. "Maybe you ate too much chicken casserole."

"Any left?"

"Uh-uh. All gone. Want some popcorn?"

"Believe I might."

Before he goes to the kitchen, he hands the cigarette back to me and I get reacquainted. As I study the design on the rug, the blue pieces of cloth begin to grow, joining up with the yellow. Colors have never looked quite so bright before. I wonder if it's what I'm smoking, or my imagination.

Ray told me once, "Why, lady, I bet you could dream up about anything."

He wasn't wrong.

I've always been blessed with visualizing. Yet despite my gift for invention, I could never quite make Ray there when he wasn't. Though I could close my eyes and think it, I could never make it quite the same. No warm imprint of his fingers on my skin. No touch or smell of him—pine shavings mingled with spicy aftershave, and the direct way he had of looking at me, almost as if he knew my thoughts before I had a chance to think them through.

"But I am there, don't you see?" he told me when I tried to explain. "I'm there cause that's where I want to be."

I knew it to be at least partly true.

Even after all these years, he's never left. Not completely. He rarely comes by the trailer anymore, but I still see him—at softball games, in the cabinet shop he owns down on Main or at Phil's Pizza, where I work evenings.

At Phil's he usually orders the salad bar and a bottle of Miller High Life. Because of stomach troubles, he rarely eats pizza anymore.

"How you been doing, Gracie?"

There is something uplifting in the sound of Ray's voice. And I swear, a blaze of pure light radiates from his blue eyes, connecting us still. Sometimes, I even forget that I wait tables and live in a mobile home and that I've never owned a microwave nor traveled any further than Myrtle Beach. All that matters is that Ray sits there, watching as he gives his order, and that I write all the words down in big block letters across my pale green pad.

"How's our boy?" he sometimes asks, if no one's sitting nearby.

Bending my head over my pad, I tell him about the A John Willis made in refrigeration and about those crazy stories he reads, but I never mention that he smokes funny cigarettes. Other times, we speak of an impending storm or fishing conditions over at Piney Lake or all the new construction going on down in Asheboro.

Before our conversation ends, he gets personal: "I'm glad you still wear your hair long," he might tell me, never mentioning how it's now sprinkled with gray. Or, "You have the most delicate hands, Gracie," or he might mention how I've managed to stay slim or the way my cheeks dimple when I smile.

Sometimes, rarely but sweetly, he brings up the past, all the crazy things we used to do. "Still play cowboys and Indians?" After asking, he ducks his head shyly and plain as if it happened that very minute; I envision the snakeskin boots, dyed a soft coral color, he once bought me. Boots with feathers and spurs attached, and him in a black-banded Stetson, never admitting completely to being good or bad.

There was no need to admit. Not to me. I knew the man soul and bone. Every inch. Every scar. Even those that couldn't be seen.

I don't do as well with talking. Sometimes when he's near, I feel too full of the sight of him to remember what I'd intended to say. Sometimes all I manage is, "How you, Ray?"

He grins when I ask. "Just tolerable."

Other times, when I manage to be more talkative, I remind him that I know he is the same, the way he's always been. "Heard you helped out old Miss Cranford," I told him the last time he came by. "Heard you planted her tomatoes. Heard you repaired her rickety fence and painted it bright yellow."

Our conversations form brief wisps of brightness, breaking up the monotony of our lives. And on those days when he does not come, I carry him in my head, recalling conversations, word for word, from a previous time as my worn-out shoes make roads across the restaurant floor.

After we finish our talk, I go about my business, waiting other tables, pouring drinks, refilling shakers with Parmesan, oregano, and hot, dried pepper. The whole while I'm conscious that he's looking at me. When I don't feel the burn of his eyes anymore, I know he's gone.

Later, when I clear his table, I find a ten dollar bill, sticking crisp as celery from the empty beer mug.

I do not need the money, and Ray does not have that much to spare, but I put it in my pocket anyway. That's what he intends. It's part of what we do.

John Willis helps me eat the butter-drenched popcorn. We giggle.

"I ought to be ashamed," I confess, "whiling away the afternoon. I need to be at Phil's by four."

"You work too hard, you know that?"

John Willis's hair sticks up. When I reach out to smooth it down, an odd feeling creeps over me. I suddenly have a fresh suspicion I shouldn't have puffed on those odd-shaped cigarettes. "I'm not sure why I'm doing this," I confess. "I'm certainly old enough to know better."

"You're doing it cause you're a liberated woman. You make your own decisions."

"I'm serious. Maybe I'm just trying to catch up. Maybe I'm just feeling desperate, not wanting the world and its doings to leave me behind. Maybe I'm afraid of getting old, John Willis."

"Never knowed you to be afraid of nothing."

"Maybe that's because I never wanted you to know."

Before I leave, I rinse the bowl that held the chicken casserole, watching khaki-colored sprigs of broccoli dog-paddle for John Willis's drain. There are no paper towels, and the only dishcloth smells sour, so I leave the dish draining on the kitchen counter. "I just might fix apple cobbler tomorrow to go with the macaroni and cheese," I tell him. "Want me to bring some over?"

"You're too good, Mama."

"Earning stars for my crown, that's all."

"Don't fool yourself. Ain't no place for crown wearing. There's only here, only now."

Noticing how solemn he looks, one part of me wishes he didn't believe that way, but another part of me remains proud that he believes however he wants without my interference.

"We all don't think alike," I say to him, sounding puffed up, even to myself, "and the way I think isn't necessarily the way you think."

After I finish my spouting off, I wonder: what do I believe anyway? I halfway know, but it's like stars—bright, shining, yet somehow too distant for proper acquaintance. I've always meant to study on it more, to clarify the fuzzy spots, but being John Willis's mama hasn't left much time for pondering.

At the door, I hug him bye. Because he's greased himself with tropical suntan oil, he smells like fruit salad. Even after I get behind the wheel of my faded-blue Pinto, whiffs of coconut remain in my head.

I turn on the ignition, and find the country station on the radio. I sit there, giving the cloud in my head time to loosen, as I listen to Willie Nelson sing about blue eyes and rain. John Willis's screen door opens. He sticks his head out. I wave to him. I continue to smile at my son as I shift into reverse.

He frowns. He tells me something, but for the life of me I can't make it out.

"What?" I ask, but I suppose he doesn't hear me through the windshield, so I keep backing up.

John Willis comes running then, both arms waving. Too late, I understand. *Stop.* That's been his message. The back wheel of my car humps up. "Lord forgive me," I say out loud.

John Willis rushes to the back of the car, squarely facing the results of my transgression.

"Mercy," I say, dreading that I must get out and look too.

Soon as I get there, I bend and peep beneath the bumper, but all I see is John Willis's hairy arm reaching for whatever I've hit. What he drags out is a blond puppy dog with long, curly ears and a twisted mouth, blood outlining the bared teeth. The animal does not move, not even a twitch. His tongue, hanging sideways from his mouth, resembles a limp ribbon. Then, about the time I've resigned myself to his being dead, he lets out a pitiful howl, and one of his eyes, the iris dark and gloomy, opens.

"Oh, dear Jesus." My hand trembles as I reach for John Willis's arm. My fingers feel numb. "I shouldn't have smoked that cigarette."

"Don't be foolish, Mama. Could've happened to anybody."

He takes me by the arms, wanting me to see the situation his way. "The two aren't connected. The damned dog didn't have sense enough to get out of the way, that's all."

If it hadn't been for that puppy's accusing eyeball, I might've accepted John Willis's explanation. "It's actions and reactions," I say to him, though I'm not completely sure what I mean. "Smoking that cigarette was a sin, at least for me. A voice deep inside told me so, but I went ahead with it anyway."

"Ah-law," John Willis says.

When a couple of blue-tailed flies begin to swarm over the cocker's carcass, John Willis fans them away. He pokes the dog gently with his bare toes. "Still breathing."

The open eye of that hurt animal continues to power-drill through my heart. My son bends down, balancing on the balls of his feet. He touches the dog. When he gets back up, puppy blood covers the palm of his hand. "Back's broken," he says. "Must be all messed up inside. Guess I've got to shoot him."

"We don't even know where he came from. We don't know who he belongs to."

"Don't reckon ownership matters now, Mama. No need to let an animal suffer."

I walk back to the driver's side of the car. My stomach churns. My head aches. Though I try not to think about the cocker, I keep remembering the bright smear of his blood on the pavement.

When John Willis comes out of his apartment, he holds his hunting gun. Purple sunglasses protect his eyes from what he is about to do.

My son, I suppose, is right. Mercy requires that the dog be shot, but I am right too. The animal's death rests on my head.

I do not go with him behind the car. I do not want to see, but when the gun fires twice, I jerk as if the bullets pierce my own skin.

Once back inside the apartment, John Willis brings me a Coca-

Cola. "Now calm yourself, Mama." He speaks gently, places his large hand on my shoulder.

"Now don't be treating me like a child. I'm not tottery yet."

He smiles, kisses my cheek. When he stands straight again, I notice the wing mark decorating his neck. The first time they brought him to me in the hospital, I searched his seven-pound, four-ounce body for something wrong. His head had been round as an orange. Ten fingers and ten pink toes. Nothing missing. Nothing extra. All parts accounted for. No sin marks. Not one single blemish except the tiny, harmless birthmark holding him from perfection. I took it as a sign: God's approval of me and Ray. Only a pencil dot against us.

"The accident happened because of my wrongdoing," I say to John Willis.

"You toked a joint. That's all. What you did has no relation to that dead dog."

"Everything's related," I say to my son, though I doubt he will believe. "Everything's connected. Everything means something."

"Ah-law."

"Do you know what it spells backwards?" I ask him.

"You are just upset."

"Well, go on. Tell me. What does it spell?"

John Willis scratches his head. "What does *what* spell backwards?"

I focus my eyes, my vision making a straight line to him. "*Dog*," I say, slowly, precisely, so there'll be no mistaking.

Despite his deep summer tan, John Willis pales. He turns away from me. "That's silly, Mama Grace. You're beginning to sound as ridiculous as those church women you're all the time criticizing. That's the way they carry on. They claim if you play rock and roll records backwards, you hear devil messages. They claim to know when the end of the world's going to be and the time they say comes and passes and we're still here and then they come up with some new time. Now they've even come up with a devil brand of washing detergent."

John Willis uses heavy ammunition to dissuade me. He knows I object to the ways of those church women. He, more than anybody, knows the harm they've inflicted on me and his daddy.

"It's not as if I search for meaning," I tell him. "No need searching. It's there in the shape of a thing sometimes, or the way it's spelled, or a sound."

John Willis refuses to let it rest. He keeps blabbering, trying to make what I'd seen not be so. Finally he gives up. "Guess I've got no business arguing with my own stubborn mama, now have I? You ought to know what's right for you, now isn't that so, just like I know what's right for me?"

"Yes, and we shouldn't be trying to confuse one another."

When John Willis grins, I swear, light seems to radiate from him—powerful light, the same light that falls from Ray's eyes.

Soon as I see the light, I know my son will be able to ferret through his own rights and wrongs.

I hug him. "You're natured like your daddy, John Willis, despite whatever peculiar notions and habits you might have."

He ducks his head, grins. His glow becomes my own.

Not a godly glow, mind you, but *goodly*. The same with something extra.

Gradually, the picture of the dead dog, though still stuck in my mind, fades from full color to brown tones.

Photo by Lori Burkhalter-Lackey

The Woven Wall
Kennette H. Wilkes

I have stolen a strand
of the spun gold you wear
so lightly at your heart
and with my tight weaving
constructed a wall between
me and my doomsdays.

I am safe. I can break
my alliance with death
and read theology
in a children's book.

Forget my tales of alienation.
I am engaged in the erotic act
of looking at myself peel
the Bible pages off, verse
by verse.

White Horses
Tricia Lande

The first time I saw Dorothea Lange's photo, *Migrant Woman*, I was ten years old and thought it was a picture of my Aunt Vergie. Aunt Verg, who at forty-five talked to spirits and saw white horses in the night, gutted tuna for a living, pulling her sharp knife upward in the fish's soft underbelly that shined mother-of-pearl under the fish market lights.

The picture of that migrant farm woman was in *Life* or *Look*, one of those photo-heavy magazines so popular in 1941, and I ran with it through the clapboard house I shared with my grandmother and aunt.

Aunt Vergie and Grandma sat on the glassed-in front porch where they always spent their evenings. They would talk quietly, or stare off down our hill toward the west channel of the Los Angeles Harbor. Aunt Verg always curled up on the old black car seat someone had pulled out of a '36 Ford, and my grandma sat in her wooden rocker, where she would fit a light bulb inside a cotton sock, making a hard surface to work her darning needle against, taking small, careful stitches.

My grandma must have heard me coming because she said something like, "fans...silly in November." Then she yelled, "Soody, don't you all let that screen door bang," a second before I pushed through the door, letting it slam behind me.

Then she said, "Sue Donna," as if that was all she needed to say. Sue Donna was my real name, but I was only called that when a family member was irritated with me.

"Look here what I got. Aunt Vergie, you got your picture in a magazine!"

Vergie sat fanning herself. She had a red-and-white fan with a peacock outlined in gold on its face, and I had one just like it. She and I had been given those fans by the Japanese man that owned the only

Chinese restaurant in San Pedro. That was where we lived then—San Pedro, the waterfront area of Los Angeles.

I sat down next to Vergie on that hard seat, laid the magazine across her lap, and she put the fan down on the apple box that served as a coffee table. Vergie stared at that picture for minute, then outlined it with her finger.

"Well, Soody baby, this ain't a picture of me. It looks like me, but it ain't. Hell, she looks like all of the Bybee women."

The woman in the picture held one hand up so that it lightly touched her cheek, and Vergie said, "She even got cotton-picker hands. Look at them scars." The picture was not in color so the marks on the woman's hands showed up as dark blotches as if the film was flawed.

"How do you get cotton-picker hands, Aunt Verg?"

"Get bad scratched from picking cotton. You out in the fields all day you cain't clean the cuts proper, so they don't heal right. That's why I'm glad I got me a different kind of job now."

The marks on my aunt's hands matched those in the picture, only Vergie's were red. On days I had gone to the fish market after school just to be with her, I had watched those scarred hands work. They moved so quickly, scraping the sides of fish with a knife, sending scales flying like a shower of blue-green sequins that turned dull moments later. I could see those scars when Vergie held up the picture to my grandma.

"She looks like us, don't she Momma?"

Grandma pushed her glasses up on her nose and looked at the picture. "Well, let me see the thing, Vergie."

"Yep. Just like a white Indian. Look there, Soody. See, them too-close-together eyes and that little thin nose is what comes from being part Cherokee. That skinny hair," Grandma pulled her own fine white wisps behind her small pink ears, "that's what comes from being Scotch-Irish. Scotch-Irish got terrible bad hair."

Grandma rarely wore her teeth, and she had a habit of pulling her lips inward, rubbing them against her gums before and after she spoke.

That soothed her gums, she once told me, and she did that now.

"Do you think she's kin, Grandma?"

"Probably. Woman's probably from Arkansas so she's probably a Bybee. Bybees married everybody in the whole damned state, then started marrying each other. Whole damned place is related."

The intermarriage of my grandfather's family, a group of people Grandma considered to be completely depraved, was one of her favorite topics of conversation. The truth was that she and my grandfather were also related. But somehow that was different in her eyes because they were related on their mothers' side of the family and their last names were not the same. Usually, she would go on for sometime on this subject of intermarriage, but Vergie stopped her.

Vergie laid the magazine in her lap and began fanning herself again. "I seen a white horse last night."

"You never done that, Vergie."

"Yes I did, Momma. I looked out the window about midnight. And there it come yonder flying through the night sky."

"We left all that back in Arkansas. All the white horses. They don't have no white horses in California."

"Grandma, I seen white horses at the Fourth of July parade. They was real big and they had silver saddles like the Lone Ranger's got."

"Don't mean them kind of white horses. I mean omen white horses. Spirits. Somebody in the family sees a white horse in the night and it means somebody in the family going to pass on. But them spirit horses stay in the country. They don't go by salt water. It makes them dissolve."

Grandma leaned across me as if being closer to Vergie would help her get her point across. "That's why you cain't see no white horses in California."

"Well, you didn't let me finish, as usual, Momma. It was a white horse, but it was a white sea horse and it was swimming through the sky. Its tail was curling and uncurling and it was just streaming along."

Grandma leaned back in her chair, rocking twice as fast as before. "Soody, I want you to mind what's being said here, because this is just what comes from cousins marrying each other for about five generations.

It makes the kids, and grandkids, and their kids peculiar. That's just what's wrong with the Roosevelts. Eleanor and Franklin is cousins. Then they raised all them peculiar kids and him getting the paralysis and all."

By now Vergie was fanning just as fast as my grandmother was rocking.

"I want to know something, Vergie. And I want a straight answer. Where did you all get that fan?" Grandma rubbed her lips against her gums.

"I want her to tell more about them sea horses," I said.

"I don't want no more nonsense about no sea horses. I want to know about that fan."

"You know damned well where I got the fan. Hiro give it to me at the restaurant."

"The child's got one just like it. You taking the child with you when you meeting this man?"

"We didn't meet him. We just gone in for lunch. He give them away to everybody what goes in for lunch."

"I don't want you taking Soody in there again. Feeding a child fish heads is a shameful thing, Vergie."

"I didn't eat no fish heads, Grandma."

"Man ain't got no sense anyway. Whoever heard of a Japanese man owning a Chinese restaurant. Don't make no sense."

Vergie fanned harder. "He tried running a Japanese restaurant, but folks around here is ignorant about Japanese food and they wouldn't come in."

"Folks around here know enough not to eat fish heads."

"Jesus, Momma." And with that Vergie got up and stomped off into the house, taking her fan with her.

My grandmother and I sat on the porch for a time longer, listening to the sound of a tug whistle in the channel, a lonesome long sound that was carried up the hill by the wind. With it came the dead fish smell from the canneries on Terminal Island, that listless sandbar that sits in the middle of the harbor. Finally, my grandmother moved her lips together twice, and said, "This ain't going to turn out well."

The next day was a Sunday, my aunt's one day off a week. The two of us always spent that day together—I should say the three of us, because we would see Hiro Ikeda on Sundays.

Sundays, Vergie would braid my blond hair, weaving red or pink ribbons through the plaits, and she would put on her soft green dress with large white polka dots and wear white cotton gloves on her small hands, rubbing the red scars with lotion first. We would walk down the hill to the wharf, passing bridal shop windows with mannequins in long white dresses. Past bars with peeling signs that said names like Longfellow's and Shanghai Red's. Women stood at the bars' entrances wearing gaudy black dresses trimmed with shiny sequins. Those women, their heavy faces made up in white, would smile at me with maroon lips. Vergie would say, "Soody, they ain't bad women, really. Just lonely inside. You do sad things when you're lonely inside."

As we walked, my aunt told me stories about her only sister, my long-dead mother, or about how things had been back in Arkansas when my family left ten years before. The story she told most often was the one about my great-great-grandfather, and the telling never varied.

"He didn't want to go in the army, Soody. Didn't want to go in no man's army, blue or gray. But the gray coats come and got him. Said, 'Boy, we going shoot you for sure if you don't join up,' and him madder than a hen at Sunday dinner. They made him build bridges. Built bridges all across Georgia. Well, he built them bridges all right. But just as soon as one got built, it got blowed up and burnt down during the night, one after another. All his gray coat officers, they never could figure out how the hell them Union soldiers was sneaking across their lines to burn down them bridges. Them crackers never did figure it out." Vergie would laugh as if she had been a part of my great-great-grandfather's scheme.

And I would always ask, "But if he blowed up and burnt all them bridges how did he get back home?" Vergie would shake her head and say, "Soody baby, you got to learn to dream."

But that particular November morning, the last Sunday in that cold month, she didn't tell any of her usual stories as we passed those wooden brides in the store windows, or the washed-out women dressed in black, but said she had seen the white horse again the night before.

"It come streaking through the sky and its hooves pounding against nothing, but sending up sparks just the same."

"I thought you said it was a sea horse. Sea horses got no hooves to pound."

"I only said that to get on Momma's nerves." Vergie pulled her gray cloth coat closed at her throat. "Her and her hissy fits. She don't believe nothing I say anyway."

"That's because sometimes you tell wrongful stories, Aunt Vergie. Like how we come to get them fans."

"Lord, Sue Donna. You getting just like her. You all want to hear the rest of it about the horse or not?" Then she went on as if I had said yes.

"You know who was on the back of that horse? It was your Momma, Modene Folton. Modene Folton, big as life and wearing a long flowing dress. She says to me, 'Vergie, it gets real lonesome sometimes.' It's an omen for sure, Soody."

Vergie's voice trailed off at the end. Then she was quiet, and no matter what I asked she said no more until we reached the docks.

Hiro Ikeda stood on the wharf, which smelled of creosote and diesel fuel from the tugboats docked nearby. His small white launch with its blue-and-white striped canopy was there too, lightly bouncing against a pylon. That launch was always clean, its white paint perfect. He took great care with the little boat and was as gentle with it as he was with my aunt.

It was overcast and cool that morning, and Hiro wore his navy-blue pea coat. He was a small man, no bigger than my aunt, and when he wore that pea coat with the collar turned up it hid even his nose, so that it seemed he looked at the world peering from a shell, checking to make sure things were safe before he completely emerged.

Hiro was just a kind little gray-haired man who drank lemon tea and ate steamed dumplings—vegetables wrapped in dough and drenched in sweet, thick honey sauce. To hear him tell it, nothing ever happened in his small life of work and sleep. Nothing more than a storm now and then that would blow up from Baja, and the three of us in his launch would ride the swells while Hiro gripped the small boat's wheel as if it were all there was between us and eternity.

I don't know how long Vergie and Hiro had been meeting for these Sunday launch rides, only that it had been going on as long as I could remember, and they always took me with them. That morning they greeted each other as they always did. Vergie held out her cotton-gloved hand—I never saw her remove those gloves when he was around—he took it in his small brown fingers, and bowed slightly at the waist. "I am happy to see you, Vergie." He always said it in a way that made it seem there was some doubt she would come.

Vergie, who could string enough four-letter words together to make a sailor blush, smiled and softly said, "Thank you, Hiro. It's so nice that you all asked us."

Then, as always, Hiro repeated the ritual with me, taking my hand and saying, "Little Miss Soody. You look so sweet today." He touched my hair so softly that it seemed more like the touch of a gentle breeze.

The sea was smooth that morning, and it did not take long to reach the rocks of the breakwater. We dropped anchor just inside the harbor so I could watch the fat seals that lay on the gray boulders, and the pelicans that would glide so low their bellies seemed to skim the water's surface. This was my favorite part of our voyage because Hiro would let me sit at the wheel.

Vergie and Hiro sat in the back of the boat, each wrapped in a blanket, speaking softly. Hiro said, "We could try, Vergie. If we just tried."

"Where would we live? Ain't nowhere we could live in peace. Then there's the child. I got the child to think about."

"You know how I feel about the child, Virginia. Besides, it's too late to have our own."

"It ain't too late just yet, Hiro." And my aunt laughed what sounded to me a young girl's laugh, light and soft like my friends at school. "But then we'd be in a real fine mess for sure, having a mixed-blood baby." Then she laughed again, but this time she didn't sound young at all. "Well, Momma's always yelling about the misery of family marrying family. Guess she wouldn't have nothing to yell about on our account."

Vergie said no more for a minute, then, "I got to think on it some."

"Vergie, we don't have half a lifetime left, and it seems like that's how long you've been thinking about this." It was the first time I had ever heard anger in Hiro's voice. After that he moved away from Vergie, came forward near where I sat and leaned over the railing.

I looked at him over my shoulder, and I could see that Hiro Ikeda was crying. Not loudly; there were no sobs, no deep throaty sounds. Just large drops of water that hung on his cheeks. We came home early that Sunday, Hiro and Vergie not speaking on the way in, and Vergie silent on our walk back up the hill.

That next Sunday, for the first time in my memory, Vergie and I did not go out in Hiro Ikeda's launch. That Sunday was December 7, 1941. That day Vergie Bybee cried and my grandmother rocked in her wooden chair, but did not darn socks.

The following Sunday Vergie did not put on her soft green dress, but a black one. She braided my hair, but did not weave pink ribbons into the plaits. She did not wear her white gloves, but held that red-and-white fan with the gold peacock on its face in her bare hand as we walked down the hill to the center of town and stood on the sidewalk with a crowd of other people.

A flatbed truck with wooden stakes around the sides of its bed sat idling in the street. Hiro stood in the midst of fifteen or so other Japanese men at the back of the truck, their belongings tied in white sheet bundles at their feet. There were other men too. Large white men in dark suits and wide brimmed hats. Vergie and I watched them as they yelled orders at the Japanese. We watched as they shoved this one and that. As they demanded that the small brown people climb onto the truck, Aunt Vergie leaned into me.

The crowd on the sidewalk yelled too. "Hang them! Send them to hell! Sneaky bastards!"

When Hiro climbed aboard the truck, Vergie held the closed fan over her head, not high, but just inches above her light brown hair. If Hiro saw her signal he gave no sign, but settled against the back of the truck cab and stared off toward the channel.

The truck filled with men and belongings tied into bundles and moved off down the street. Vergie said, "We ain't going see him again, Soody." And even at that young age, I knew that to be true.

I ran across that picture, *Migrant Woman*, last summer. It was in a book, *Collected Works of Depression Era Art*. I looked again at the picture of that stick-thin woman with fine brown hair parted in the middle, pulled back behind tiny ears peeling from too much sun. I saw the way her scarred hand lightly touched her cheek, and that look in her eyes which haunts me. Far off, as if she could not stand seeing what was in front of her. Her small mouth, lips, made straight by anguish.

In that picture I see the image of my aunt, see her scrape at the sides of those tuna with their sequin scales that turned dark over time. And I think about how it must have been for Vergie on that hard-edged day when she could no longer dream, and decided there would be no more for her than putting that sharp knife in a fish's underbelly, pulling it upwards so that what gave the creature life spilled out on a hard white metal tray.

Photo by Jude Keith

October Fire
Bettie M. Sellers

In the churchyard, flames, the Burning Bush,
a maple touched to fire, by autumn fanned.
Were I possessed as Moses was, the hush
might speak, Jehovah's voice resound. I stand
uncertain, questions wrinkling my face:
Should I kneel, is this some holy ground?
Or is it just the usual for this place
that maples turn, a season come around?
And as I ponder, November rain
gathers wind from lowering eastern skies
to strip the maple of its leaves. The stain
of scarlet filters down before my eyes.
I wait too long; I watch the moment pass
till only ashes stir upon the grass.

One Last Time
Lori Russell

"I want to go back to Yosemite one last time," Mac said looking at me with eyes the color of his faded-blue hospital gown. His skin pulled taut over his cheekbones like yellow leather. Silver and black whiskers sprouted on the ridge of his jaw. "Well, what do you think, Doris?"

I stared at the green plastic tubing that wound from Mac's nose over his ears to a socket in the wall. It hissed a constant exhale of oxygen. How much time had passed since the doctor met with us? Five minutes? An hour? I pressed my fingernails deep into the flesh of my palm. White half-moons appeared on the skin under my nail tips, but I felt nothing. "OK, Mac. If you think you can make it to Yosemite, let's do it."

Mac's thin fingers reached for the plastic basin beside him. His shoulders shuddered as he retched. Then, wiping his chin with a tissue, he whispered, "When do we leave?"

We first came to Yosemite on our honeymoon. Money was tight then, so we stayed in a cabin and ate boxed cereal and milk for breakfast. Each morning I hiked to the bathroom with a terry cloth robe pulled tight over my new lingerie. We packed picnic lunches and spent the days hiking the trails above Tuolomne Meadows and Wolf Creek. At night, we watched from the valley floor as the rangers pushed a huge bonfire off one of the nearby cliffs. The embers cascaded in a fiery waterfall.

When the kids were small, we had camped out each summer in a canvas tent that smelled of mildew, and rolled out our four sleeping bags on air mattresses. Mac and I always zipped our bags together because I loved sleeping next to him, feeling the warmth of his skin and the curve of his hip against me. Mac taught Kathy and Jim how to thread a pink salmon egg on a hook and fish for trout in the Merced River. When the fish weren't biting, we'd ride our bikes through the redwood groves on the valley floor.

Mac and I returned to the cabins after Kathy and Jim left home. By then, they had been remodeled to include a bathroom and shower. That was as much luxury as Mac would allow. I'd always wanted to stay at the Wawona Lodge at the south end of the park. I imagined sitting in the shade of the pines watching the people. Mac thought I was crazy. Some things just weren't worth the fight.

It was a Thursday in late October when we left for Yosemite this time, one of those warm golden autumn mornings when the sky is bluer than you ever thought possible. The leaves of the apple tree had begun to curl around the last of the red-skinned fruit and the dew was still wet on the ivy.

I packed the car: the thermos of coffee for me and the wicker basket we once filled with dry salami and Swiss cheese for Mac. Today it carried Gerber's strained carrots and chocolate pudding, a can of high-protein strawberry-flavored liquid, and some crackers. Mac had lost his appetite for most foods.

He watched me from the porch chair.

"Put the suitcases in first," he commanded as I opened the trunk. I hoisted his beige leather case first, then my blue Samsonite.

"Doesn't fit with both of them," I called.

"Yes it does. Jiggle the blue one until it fits in the back."

I shoved hard against the case, then bounced it up and down. It wedged on top of the spare tire. The leather case slid in easily.

In the backseat I put the bag of Mac's pills: one for nausea, another for diarrhea; morphine, sleeping pills, pills for agitation, and heart and blood pressure medication.

Mac shuffled to the car. He stood for a moment, hooked his cane on the door, and fell back onto the front seat. Slowly he picked up his left leg with both hands and slung it into the car. His breath was quick, his upper lip shone with sweat. Picking up his other leg, he heaved it into the car.

I slid onto the seat easily and turned the ignition key. Mac had driven on all of our vacations. It was one of those unspoken agreements we made in marriage, like who made the morning coffee and who bought the stamps. Since Mac had started chemo, I'd been driving more. He just didn't feel up to it. I'd also been doing all the grocery shopping and errands, jobs Mac had readily accepted when he retired. My usually generous husband reveled in seeking out bargains and triple coupon savings. But now, six T-bone steaks and eight chickens lay thick with white frost in the freezer. Mac had lost his taste for meat about a month ago.

The traffic was light leaving the city.

"Look at the new condos," Mac said, pointing to the cluster of white stucco buildings with red-tiled roofs by the curve of the freeway. The condos had actually been built about the time Mac began treatments but for the last year he had only gone between the house and the hospital.

We rode on in silence. Red tipped the branches of the trees as if the color came to the ends first and worked its way inward toward the trunk. The car strained as we drove up to the pass. The brown hills were patched with black where the grass had been burned.

I didn't know what it was to lose a husband. I had watched friends go through it, watched them hang on to every shred of hope, seeing only what they wanted to see. I wished I could have been that way. Instead I saw Mac's every change: the luster in his eyes dulled by medication, the dark hollows of his cheeks, the pale yellow of his skin. His stomach had started to swell, like a pregnant woman's. Sometimes he became so short-winded he had to stand up to draw a full breath. He was filling up with his own body fluid, the doctor said. Drowning.

I placed my hand on his leg. It was thin like a child's, the kneecap bony and angular in my hand.

"Remember when we used to stop and buy a block of ice for your feet?" Mac asked as the car eased downhill from the pass. "That was when we had the old green Chevy."

"And no air-conditioning!" I laughed, remembering how it had been hot on our other trips through the valley. Wrapping the ice in a towel, I had rested my feet on top of the block and stayed cool.

I followed the Airstream trailer in front of us down the two-lane highway past plowed fields. The earth had been turned upside down and large clods of dirt lay drying in the sun. A lone patch of cornstalks stood tall like yellowed bristles of a toothbrush. There was so much brown this time of year. The hills were dark like the tanned back of a field hand.

I had hoped for autumn color—gold, orange, crimson, cinnamon—like at home, but here there was only an occasional rusty-needled pine to add some color. Abandoned cars decayed under trees and against fence posts. Roadside signs beckoned: Almonds, Pumpkins, Mexican Curios for Sale. We passed knee-high ceramic ducks, skunks, and teddy bears standing in neat rows waiting to be purchased.

"Remember when we came through here and got that flat tire?" I said to Mac. "Kathy was just a baby."

"Yeah, I walked five miles down the road to the gas station. God, it was hot." He rolled down the window and stuck out his hand, testing the air like water in a bathtub. "I don't think it's as hot today." He turned toward me. "Doris, I don't care what else you do, but after I'm gone, buy yourself a fancy car, OK?"

"Right, Mac...like a Mercedes or BMW? Honey, that's just not me, you know that."

"How do I know that? We've always had to worry about money, for the kids, the house, whatever. With the money from the life insurance policy you can get what you want."

I gripped the steering wheel. How could he sit there talking about my life after he is gone? Of course we had talked about this before; what married couple hadn't? But those conversations were theoretical musings made when we were both healthy, when cancer was something that happened to other families and "until death do us part" seemed a romantic notion.

Mac coughed into a yellow-stained handkerchief. His body seized as he exhaled, then was still. Seconds passed. Tears poured down his pink cheeks. He drew a rattled breath and coughed again.

"Slow deep breaths Mac, slow down," I said, grabbing his shoulder. He breathed slowly and the yellow color returned to his face. I pulled off the road. Mac closed his eyes and pressed his head back into the seat. I heard him exhale slowly.

"I'm OK."

"I'll find a place to stop and get something to eat. Give you a chance to get out of the car for a while."

He nodded.

As we approached the next town, I pulled into the parking lot of the Pine Cone Restaurant. I held his arm as he struggled out of the car. Inside, we sat down at a red Formica-topped table. I rummaged through my sack and pulled out a fat pill bottle.

"Take one of these before you eat anything."

He waved me away with the back of his hand. "I don't feel nauseated. I don't even feel hungry."

"Mac, please. The doctor said you're supposed to take them before every meal, you know that."

"I hate these things," he said, pushing two small white pills into his mouth.

"What can I get for you two today?" said the waitress who was now standing beside Mac.

"I'll have the cheeseburger—no onions, fries, and a Diet Coke."

"And what about you, sir?" she continued, flashing a wide smile at Mac.

"Nothing thanks. I brought my own food." He nodded toward the canned protein drink and strained carrots I was pulling from the wicker basket.

"OK. Ma'am, that cheeseburger will be just a few minutes."

I leaned back into the chair. My shoulders felt stiff and sore. A throbbing pain had lodged over my eyes. "Mac, remind me you need your morphine before we leave."

I put the bottle on the table next to the salt-and-pepper shakers. The waitress returned with my Diet Coke.

"I thought you could use these," the waitress said to Mac. She placed a bowl, glass, and silverware in front of him. "For that gourmet meal of yours," she said smiling. "Now all of our customers are going to want what you're having."

Mac's mouth softened into a grin. "Thanks."

She nodded and walked behind the counter to pick up two plates from under the cone-shaped warming lights.

"I'll be back in a minute, honey," I said, and walked toward the back wall to the rest room. Inside, I leaned against the cool white tile. In the reflection of the mirror I saw my wrinkled blue sweatshirt and jeans. Caring for Mac left me no time to worry about what clothes I wore. My skin looked gray and my cheeks sagged into jowls. The circles under my eyes had become darker. How long had it been since I'd slept through the night?

The waitress served my food as I returned, then lined up the ketchup, mustard, and relish jars with the morphine bottle on the table.

"Anything else I can get you?"

I ate in silence while Mac took an occasional bite of the chocolate pudding or a sip of protein drink. After paying the waitress, I took Mac's arm. I held tight to him as we walked to the car.

As we continued, the land spread out between the houses until barbed-wire fences were the only divisions. I followed the telephone poles, giant wooden crosses strung together with wire. We passed through several small towns, each with a liquor store and single gas pump.

After an hour I pulled the car onto the gravel shoulder. "OK, time for your morphine," I said reaching behind Mac's seat for the paper bag that held the medicine.

Mac's eyelids fluttered but didn't open.

I sorted through the plastic containers. Where was the morphine? I counted the bottles...four. There had been five when we left the house. I opened my purse: wallet, Doublemint gum, Kleenex, lipstick. Then I remembered the bottle sitting on the table in the diner. "Mac, did you pick up the morphine off the table?"

"What?"

"At the restaurant, did you pick up the morphine bottle off the table?"

"No." He rubbed his eyes then yawned.

"Damn! Well, it's not here."

"You forgot the morphine?" His eyes widened. "Doris, how could you?"

"I forgot because I'm taking care of everything. Everything Mac. Every pill, every meal, the driving, you, everything. Can't you help with just one little thing like the morphine?" I clenched the wheel and stared straight ahead.

"No. I'm sorry, but I can't."

His words hit me like a slap. I turned toward him stunned. Tears flooded his eyes.

"Damn it, Doris, I can't remember anything anymore. Half the time I don't know if it's day or night. I just wake up, take the next pill, and go back to sleep. I hate it." He pressed his lips together as if trying to stop the flow of words.

"I know you can't help it," I said, beginning to cry. "It's just so much to deal with…to see you this way." I slumped against Mac's shoulder. How many tears had I held in during the chemotherapy sessions—the loss of hair, the vomiting, the suppositories, the pain. I hated the way we endlessly tracked every bodily function, and then waited—for the next side effect, the treatment to stop, the inevitable death. Was this all there was?

"I don't want you to go. You just can't die," I said sniffling. "I'm sorry, I've tried to be strong, be the good wife, but it's not fair. It's just not fair." My sobs erupted again, rushing out and echoing off the car windows.

"I'm here with you now, Doris," Mac said softly. His body began to shake.

The sound of muffled cries filled the car. I didn't know where Mac left off and I began. All I felt was warmth as I slumped into his lap. Our breaths rose and fell together. I wanted him to assure me things would be all right, that I would be all right after he was gone. He said nothing.

Mac fished a handkerchief out of his pocket and handed it to me. "Let's just forget the morphine."

"Come on, Mac, you know we can't do that."

"Why can't we? Why can't we just leave it behind, leave all the pills and the cancer too?"

I kissed his neck. "Because it's a part of you now, a part of us. We can't get away from it."

I turned the car around and headed back toward the diner.

As I entered, our waitress, standing behind the cash register, smiled warmly. She held up the brown bottle, shaking it so I could hear the morphine tablets rattle.

"Got 'em right here," she said. "How far did you get?"

"About an hour out of town. Thank you so much. I don't know what we would have done if I couldn't find them."

"Your husband's really sick, isn't he?" She looked straight into my eyes. I remembered the way she had placed the silverware in front of Mac as if he had been a paying customer. I wanted to tell her.

"Yes. He has cancer. We're on our way to Yosemite so he can see it for the last time."

I searched her face for the familiar pained expression I'd seen when we had told our friends of Mac's condition. I expected the words of false hope I'd heard from our families.

"I'm so sorry," she said quietly. "How terrible for you." The lines around her eyes softened. She reached across the counter and placed her hand over mine. It felt warm and moist as if she had just taken it out of the dishwater.

"I lost my husband two years ago. Thought I was going to die right along with him... but I didn't." She squeezed my hand gently. "It won't always hurt this bad."

I began to cry.

"Do you want to sit down for a while? I'll get you a cup of coffee."

"No, we're already late. We won't get into the park until after dark and Mac needs his medicine."

"I'll fix you a cup for the road then. It's on the house."

When I returned to the car Mac's eyes were closed. I touched his shoulder.

"How about that morphine?" he said. "I'm hurting." He took the pills with a slurp of coffee and was snoring before we reached the town limits.

I rolled down my window and tuned the radio to the local country western station. There was something about a long drive that made me crave songs about wayward love and big rigs. Mac liked classical music and occasionally some jazz. Usually he'd howl if I turned on a "hick station" as he called it, but since he'd been taking the morphine, he could sleep through anything. I edged the volume up a little higher.

Shadows lengthened on the red rock beneath the manzanita bushes as we drove into the foothills. Gray-green spikes of grass grew in clumps along the side of the road. I pushed down on the accelerator hoping to make up for the time we had lost. The car's engine strained, lurched as it shifted into another gear, then settled back into a soft hum. As I braked around yet another turn I realized there was no quick way to drive through the mountains. Lost time was just that...lost.

The sun shone in my rearview mirror. I watched it drop into a pool of orange beyond the edge of the valley. Ahead of me the sky was washed in lavender and the plants became dark silhouettes on the landscape.

Mac moaned softly, folded his arms across his chest and then was quiet. I hummed to the music on the radio as I drove. Finding my way to the park was easier than I had expected. Maybe I would come again someday and stay at the Wawona Lodge. I could sit on the lawn wearing my straw hat and peer over the edge of a fat book at the golfers and tourists. At night I would sit at a corner table in the restaurant and watch the faces of the couples in the candlelight. I'd wear that green dress with the pink roses Mac thought was too gaudy.

I looked over at Mac. Could he read my thoughts? Did he know I was fantasizing about being alone? He lay next to me sleeping softly.

I drove on until we reached the entrance to the park. A short man with wire-rimmed glasses shone a flashlight into the car.

"You folks know your way?"

"Yes," I said, then stopped. Mac had always driven during the daylight. As a passenger, I hadn't paid much attention to how to get to the cabins. "Can you just tell me how to get to Yosemite Village?"

"Follow the signs. You can't miss it." He handed me a map. "Just in case."

I drove along the pine-fringed roads, following the beam of the headlights. Pinholes of light dotted the dark curtain of sky. The cloudy trail of the Milky Way spread out before me. I felt giddy from the smell of pine and dried leaves, excited about greeting an old friend. The road turned gently downward toward the valley. I pushed on the accelerator and we rushed into a tunnel bored through the granite. The car tires thumped and whined. As we emerged from the mountain, the white moon greeted us. It hung round and complete over the valley. I stopped the car, pulled Mac's down jacket from the backseat and got out of the car quietly. At the edge of the road, the valley spread out before my feet. I saw the pewter crest of Half Dome and the steely ridges of the canyon walls in the moonlight.

Mac's jacket smelled of him. I pulled it around me like a warm hug. We had returned to the beauty of the park, to our memories. For Mac, it was the last visit. I would come back again and again. Spreading my arms I embraced the wind as it swept over me. I breathed in, tasting the freshness of the air in my mouth. Looking into the face of the moon I saw no pain, no suffering. I watched until my ears ached and my toes felt numb in my sneakers.

Mac opened his eyes when I slid into the seat next to him.

"Mac honey, we're here. Look. We made it."

Photo by Lori Burkhalter-Lackey

Photo by Marianne Gontarz

It Is Enough
Ruth Daigon

It is enough to lean against
the fabric of your flesh.
It is enough to lie
in the domestic morning.
It is enough to watch light
expand through windows—
rising and falling
between our bodies on this bed,
this room, this continent.

We grow wise watching leaky faucets,
faded wallpaper, mismatched socks.
The coffee boiling on the stove
prepares us for the network news,
shopping malls, miracle cures
and tomorrow always sitting on our bed.

But in this rush of years,
we have not lost the pure imagined past,
the here-it-is, the pitch, the pinnacle
of time shining from within a million
summers or the music so intense   it disappears.

We invent a lifetime out of small things,
free the air between our fingers,
diagram the stars   dream them into
daylight and admit the future
which is here   always here
like a clock that runs forever.

Photo by Marianne Gontarz

Five Years Later
Maril Crabtree

To a Former Lover from a Married Woman

What can I say to you,
who loved the unknown bits and
pieces of me into being
and watched the fragments
weave themselves into another
whole with no more room
for a divided love?

The warp and woof of my
existence lie now
in my own hands,
steadier and wiser with the
passage of my inner time,
knowing more now of what I
chose than when I chose it.

Yes, I would choose again
the same end, but in a
different way, not out of
desperation and the need
to cling to clarity, but out of
freedom and the need to find
my own soul's fabric.

The beginning?
I would not change
a single breathless moment
nor do I fail to savor
all the sharpened memories of it
this hot July night.

Praying in the Dark
Gailmarie Pahmeier

For James Whitehead

Having gone alone to her hotel room after the conference,
an aging professor suffers through her prayers:

Lord, forgive me my common
dreams, my daily deceptions.
Forgive that I have feigned to bless
those books that give me bread,
that I have written save few words
which shine with any soul,
that I have somehow earned a place
solid, certain, removed from blood,
hunger and heart.
Forgive that I no longer have to pray.

And Lord, forgive me my love of the boy,
the one who sings the country songs
with clarity and calm,
the one who reads every book I recommend,
the boy whose memory holds my poems
in place.
Lord, if you can forgive me this, protect him.
I promise to pray again. Amen.

Amen.

A Weaver
Barbara L. Thomas

 Once
contemplated
  a disturbing
    fray
  before
choosing the

 way
the pattern
   should continue
    She
  taught
the shuttle

 symmetry
and rose from
  the loom
    clothed in
  beauty of her
own

 fashioning

Orchards and Supermarkets
Rina Ferrarelli

1.

My thumb doesn't leave a dent
in the avocado.
The undersides of the bananas
are still green. The pears,
Bosc and Bartlett,
have the hardness and heft of rocks.

I stare at the grapes, I look
at the price. The higher it is,
the more sour they are.
I turn a bag of red Delicious
over and over in my hands
looking for a yellow cast.

It's either too soon
or too late,
and I wait, defer, make-do.
Was it always like this,
or have I learned patience at last?

Or is this what wisdom ever was,
being happy with what you can have,
when you can have it?

2.

If I found myself in an orchard,
would I know, did I ever know,
how to pick the fruit
right off the branches?
Would I recognize
the color of ripeness,
the aroma?

But what orchard, what plantation
would ever do?
I want apples and pomegranates,
cherries and pears, oranges
and plums, each kind
suspended in its own season.
It would have to be
a garden of delights.

Divorce
Ellin Carter

Trailing fingers in cool grass
she considers the delicate spirea,
its old names—the bridal wreath,
hardhack and meadowsweet—this tracery
and desiccation after all.

Over her head a pear tree in full
noisome bloom whispers in Middle
English of "The Merchant's Tale,"
of *blisse in marriage,* how beauty
and decay may intertwine.

Then, rising, she lifts up a branch
to carry indoors to the fireplace,
where sparks will kindle quickly, for
pear is the most ardent wood, and white
or green will wither and blaze forth.

Vietnam

Jennifer Lagier

For David

For a decade
we took Da Nang and Cua Tung to bed,
rubbed napalm over shrapnel scars,
calling it love.
For the first two years,
I held you through the nighttime sweats
which scattered hot opiate hallucinations,
fragging holes in your sleep.
Till hostilities went guerrilla.
While the decoy stayed topside,
terrorism tunneled deep underground
and I wore Vietnam like a totem
in this Hanoi Hilton
we built for ourselves,
becoming your hooch mama,
accepting all aggressions,
until Cambodia imploded inside my mouth
and was no longer contained.
Banging my head,
I kamikazied against
your stark white barrack walls,
slipped and ran,
refugee free,
through the dead marriage mud.

Getting On with It
Grace Butcher

When the heart stops oozing blood
& the outpouring is clear as water
(so to speak) then you know you've
turned the corner & will be well.
When you look inward & all the pathways
are no longer dark but clearly lighted
& shine like transparent drinking straws
then you know you'll find your way alone.
When the gray morning has nothing to do
with you & doesn't weigh you down
like a heavy blanket, then you know
that moving will be easy again and
your body will flow through time
like the river it really is, smooth & deep,
no rocks, no shallows to smash or catch you,
keep you from moving on.   When the heart slows
to its normal rhythm and the beauty
of birdsong at dawn doesn't make you cry
because you are alone listening, then you
know that everything has happened that is
going to for now, and you can get on with
your life & everything about it that was
yours alone and always finer than
anyone could ever imagine it would be
without him.

Cauliflower Beach
Carol Schwalberg

They met at Christmas over a goose.
She remarked on his teeth.
He blinked in reply.
She told him to call her when he needed crew on his boat.
A week later, he invited her to watch whales on land.
They had their first dinner in a shopping center four blocks from her house. He sipped martinis before his steak, she mentioned liking wine but he ordered none.
He thought that she was small and had electric hair.
She considered him a mountain of a man, twice her weight and over a head taller. His navy blazer was fine, but his white shirt needed bleach, ironing, and a necktie.
Fearing to be rude, he stared ahead without looking at her and sketched his life story. Missouri-born and Texas-bred, he was a widower without children and a homeowner without a mortgage. He explained that he was an engineer who tested fixtures on spacecraft, which explained nothing at all.
Looking at his profile, she expanded on her work history and skimped on her personal life. A fourth-generation New Yorker, she had zipped from art school to art direction and later drifted into free-lance design and illustration, becoming a visual Jill-of-all-trades. She mentioned divorcing a minor talent with major neuroses, but omitted anything about falling in love with a series of the same. Nor did she say that in Los Angeles, she had twice set up housekeeping with marginal misfits.
Four years before, she had resolved to seek out men who were both sane and solvent. She had found dates who met these requirements, but her times with them seemed the dreariest of her life. Just two weeks before, she had met a friend's reject, a widowed stock market analyst

from the Beverly Hills flats. The man sat in her living room for an hour detailing the reasons he was not mourning his wife, a depressive who might go months without speaking. Characterizing himself a paragon of mental health, he nevertheless insisted that any restaurant they selected must be on the near side of Lincoln Boulevard, for he could rarely bring himself to cross major streets.

Tonight, Frank had chosen the very same restaurant as the stock analyst, and he also was saying he did not mourn his wife. When the check came, Annie thought to forestall a list of his wife's failings by suggesting a turn around the shopping center.

Frank smiled, "I've gone to London and Paris, but I've never toured a shopping center before."

After the third shoe store, the stout engineer drew to a halt, "You mean there's more?"

When she nodded, he said, "Next time we have to be brave and cross Lincoln Boulevard."

The stock analyst again, Annie thought, and flashed a look of absolute horror.

"That's a joke," he said. "We can go anywhere you like."

Annie laughed.

They ambled on, Frank joking and Annie laughing, at one point stopping dead in her tracks to double over. Whee, I'm having fun, she thought.

Frank deposited her back on her doorstep at ten-thirty. "I'm baby-sitting a test," he remarked enigmatically. "Seven days a week. Whoo, but am I tired!"

The next Saturday, he turned up wearing the same navy blazer and unironed shirt, but carrying a large package. "I had some tea I wasn't using."

Tea? She reserved tea for advanced stomachaches.

True to his promise, they crossed Lincoln Boulevard to dine at a mediocre but expensive restaurant. By this time, Annie realized that Frank was impervious to hints, and when he ordered his martini, bluntly asked for wine.

He responded with grace. "You know, I've hardly dated at all these last few years. I guess I'm not acting civilized."

He started to make her laugh almost instantly. Once again, he never looked her way and took her home by ten-thirty, without so much as brushing her lips.

The following Saturday, he arrived at the dot of six-thirty, carrying a skillet. A second-hand skillet? Open packages of tea? He must be cleaning house.

They returned to the same steak house. He announced that he would be going to Paris in the middle of February. "I've got to buy clothes!" He sounded so emphatic she could hear the exclamation point.

"You do need clothes," she agreed, not trying to be sarcastic.

"Yes, I have to maintain my position as a fashion leader."

They laughed together and the following Saturday, he arrived in a gray tweed Norfolk jacket. "Handsome," she said. "What else?"

"That's it."

Clothes, one jacket? Annie was puzzled.

This time, when he said good night, he kissed her lightly. She hugged him in response and invited him to dinner the following Saturday. "I'll ask the Creamers, too. I never paid them back for Christmas dinner."

"I'll come at four to help," Frank promised.

He showed up at three-thirty.

In the middle of dressing and running late as usual, Annie threw on a robe and tied the sash carelessly. Frank noticed a flash of bra and inferred that she must like him.

After Annie finished dressing, Frank perched on a stool in the kitchen while Annie sliced and diced, sautéed and simmered. He never made a move to help. Why did he come early, she wondered.

Annie had thought to give of herself and prepare a dish her father's family had brought from Hungary. She thus turned dinner into disaster. Ian Creamer proved allergic to paprika, Janine could not abide sour cream, and Frank picked out each piece of green pepper. "They're against my religion," he said by way of joke, but to put a good face on the matter, added, "That was a delicious meal. I always like French food."

Annie noted with dismay that he was serious.

The Creamers left early to tend Ian's outbreak of hives. "Don't go, Frank," Janine said. "Help Annie clean up."

After Frank displayed a dishwashing skill far beyond her own, Annie suggested adjourning to the sofa. They kissed and kissed and kissed. At the stroke of ten-thirty, Frank jumped up. "Another day of work."

"Let's continue our...um...conversation tomorrow," Annie suggested.

He arrived at five. After going out for a quick snack, they returned to become lovers. There was a small technical failure.

"You're just excited," Annie told him.

He left to go home and feed Max. "He's a wonderful cat. You'll have to meet him. But he really likes to eat."

"Like his master."

"Go to hell."

She expected never to see him again.

He called the next day. "I've been thinking over our technical problem, and I think I found a solution."

On Tuesday evening, the engineer proved himself correct. Both of them satisfied, he stayed on in bed. "I left food for Max," he said.

He had acne scars, a bald spot, and more body hair than most primates. She had bunions, knock knees, and enough belly to pass for pregnant. Yet they had an endless appetite for each other.

Wednesday passed in a blur of warm feelings and exhaustion. When Frank called, Annie suggested that they try sleeping the next time they got together. He considered sleeping a huge joke and wanted to see her that evening.

"Sorry, I have a meeting."

On Thursday, they bolted dinner and raced to bed.

He was leaving for Paris on the following Friday. She offered to drive him from his home to the airport.

"Get there early," he instructed.

When she arrived at three, he said, "Don't waste time. Get out of your clothes." They made love until an hour before flight time.

He told Annie to come to his house as soon as he returned from Paris. He gave the precise day and hour.

She feared that he might forget her and sent an aerogram to his hotel. When she received neither cable nor card, she began to believe that the affair was over. She had a sour, stale taste in her mouth, a familiar feeling of betrayal. He had seemed sincere, but then so had many others.

Upon his return, she thought to phone before leaving for his house. "Do you still want me to come?" she asked nervously.

"Of course!" he bellowed.

Frank had come back with black silk panties and less of himself. "I missed you so much I couldn't eat," he said. His eyes looked naked, like peeled grapes.

"In Paris, the world capital of good eating?"

"My niece said I was turning anorexia into a life-style."

They fell into bed.

Between bouts of lovemaking, they agreed on philosophy, politics, and the world order, everything but how to manage daily life. At home, Frank set the thermostat at sixty. Annie shivered in the cold. When night came, he piled his bed with a dozen blankets. "There's going to be a headline, Couple Crushed Under Weight of Blankets," Annie complained. Frank subscribed to the intermittent, although affectionate, school of slumber that involved periods of wakefulness ended by touching the bed partner. Annie rolled into a ball and fell into an aloof but deep sleep that could be interrupted only by a piercing alarm or human touch. Frank persisted in touching her whenever he woke.

"I really love you," he would say.

"I really want to sleep," she would growl.

She realized that the polite response should have been "I love you, too," but she wasn't sure what she felt. Her work load was so heavy that she hardly had time to think. She ricocheted from design class at the university almost an hour's drive away to clients at scattered points all over Greater Los Angeles to her drawing board. Making love with Frank seemed like just one more activity, although pleasanter than the others. He was very nice, she knew that—bright, funny, boyish, and totally without guile—but did she love him?

Her busy schedule prevented her seeing Frank every night.

"Sometimes I think you actually like to work," Frank said.

"Like my work? I adore it. Gee, there's some I would do even if they didn't pay me a dime."

"That's hard for me to understand. I work for a paycheck, not for fulfillment."

Annie considered the cabbage family a hardship of early childhood. Frank was immensely fond of cauliflower, not just the florets but also the stems, which he sliced and ate raw. After considerable teasing, Annie presented Frank with a notepad in the shape of a cauliflower, and extended her cooking repertoire to *chou-fleur Mornay* and *chou-fleur aux tomates fraîches*. Annie complained that Frank wore so many white shirts that she would fall prey to snow blindness. He sent away for stripes. Frank glanced at Annie's much-laundered jeans and asked, "Did you buy those new?" She gave them to charity.

After he introduced her to Max, they alternated the venue of their lovemaking between her place and his. His house betrayed the dust and decay that came with five years of widowerhood. His year-old refrigerator appeared virginal except for diet drinks and frozen dinners. Both went into the trash when she discovered he had high blood pressure. "These aren't good for you," she declared. He seemed to welcome the attention.

A day later, driving on the freeway, she realized that she must love him for she worried about his sodium intake and cared what would happen to him.

She told him she loved him.

He looked up from his cauliflower soufflé and beamed. "You've got to meet my niece and her husband. I know what we'll do. We'll all get together on my boat."

Thrilled that she would finally go out for a sail, Annie ran out to buy deck shoes. On the day of the sail, the wind came up, and the Coast Guard issued a small craft advisory. Although Frank and Annie drove to Alamitos Bay, the boat never left the slip.

His niece, Lisa, looked like a magazine cover, and Annie thought that she was out of her beauty league. Then the redhead played show-and-tell with her handbag, producing a hot-water bag, a pair of wire cutters, and a can of garbanzo beans. Lovely she was, but comfortably eccentric.

Annie worried that he had no bathrobe and bought him one.

Frank worried that she had no health insurance and one morning, as they were tangled in sheets, pointed out, "If you marry me, you'll have major medical."

Major medical? The veteran of perhaps a dozen proposals, she had never had one both so unromantic and so loving.

She was touched and confused. They had known each other less than three months. Their backgrounds met at no points whatever. His father had been a Lutheran pastor, hers was a Jewish butcher. She agreed with Frank on world problems, but they argued about blankets and lights and schedules.

The thirtieth or fortieth time Frank asked Annie to marry him, she said, "Max is very sweet, but I'm allergic to cats."

"I'll give him to my niece. Lisa has two of her own he can play with."

"But we hardly know each other. Let's try living together a couple of months."

"I don't want to be on trial," he insisted.

"How about vacationing abroad for a couple of weeks?" she countered.

"On our honeymoon," he said firmly.

Before they went anywhere, Annie arranged a much-postponed trip to New York. She would dredge up assignments, talk to her sales rep, visit what remained of her family, and laugh with old friends. Most of all, distance would allow her to think, to make a decision about Frank without consciously making a decision.

Even when Annie was a continent away, Frank wanted to stay in contact. "Call me collect," he said.

She talked until his phone bill went into triple digits.

They rarely left each other's thoughts or conversation. Even though the pair never sought opinions, they came anyway.

"She's an artist. You're an engineer. She'll make you change your life-style," argued Helen, Frank's sister.

"How can you consider a man with so little interest in your career?" asked Alan who had been selling Annie's work for years.

"Three months? You need to live together for a year," decided Susan of the five marriages.

"Are you trying to prove you can catch a second husband?" asked Winnie, a psychotherapist who had never married.

"What do you have to lose? Isn't California a community property state?" counseled Paula, whose business faced bankruptcy.

"Grab him. A plain girl like you, how many chances will you get?" advised her beautiful cousin Judy. "Incidentally, have you thought of buying mousse for your hair?"

Annie returned with smoother hair and her customary indecision.

The proposals continued. One evening, after she prepared a cauliflower curry, Frank displayed a sheaf of papers, smoothing them and saying, "See. This is what I can offer you."

The papers described his pension plan, and showed both the projected monthly payments and the lump sum that would come to him upon retirement. Frank ran his hand over the papers again as though the pages were pearls and rubies.

She glanced quickly through the pages without focusing on the numbers and then looked up at his earnest face. No one this good should have to offer anything at all, she thought. It was perhaps the most touching, poignant moment of her life.

Before she had time to formulate an answer, rain began to fall. Annie told Frank about her fear of rain. He held her closely, "You have me now, honey."

They went to bed.

It rained all that night and continued for days. At first, the thirsty ground sucked up the moisture, but as the rain continued to beat down, canyon rivulets turned into torrents, carrying soil, rocks, and trees in their wake. In the flatland, storm drains failed, and water rose, cresting the sidewalks and the lawns.

Annie fled low-lying Mar Vista for the higher ground of Santa Monica. Even north of Montana Avenue, the rising waters invaded the houses, forcing people to leave their sodden homes. They sought refuge in the basement bars, golden oases of light and warmth where the supply of pizza and hot dogs never ran out, and the kegs of beer and wine never became empty.

The bars took on a carnival atmosphere. Singles clustered in groups to sing and dance. Families gathered together, the old reliving tales of their youth and playing with the young. The children enjoyed their reprieve from school, and adults reveled in an unexpected holiday. It was a time of gladness, but Annie felt closed in and restless.

One day, during a break in the weather, Annie ventured into the street, shoes in hand, wading cautiously, the water lapping gently at her shins.

The streets were empty, and the air felt fresh for the smog had vanished. The cars had stopped floating and were now still. Under a gray sky, Annie kept moving to stay warm. She headed toward the ocean to look at the pier. It was empty and soaked, the snack stands closed and the carousel at rest. There was no sound but the surf. The world seemed empty and new.

Annie went down the stairs to the beach and saw that the storm had changed the shore. In place of the sand, there was an unbroken field of snowy white cauliflowers, stretching from the ocean walk to the sea. The cauliflowers were soft underfoot and miraculously dry, and although there was neither shelter nor people, she knew that she had found a safe haven.

When Annie awoke, she smiled at the sheer looniness of her dream. Flooding in Mar Vista? The area had fine storm drains. Basement bars in Santa Monica? There were few bars, and none in basements. Almost no one had a basement in Southern California, nor were people likely to rejoice when rain flooded their homes. But the cauliflower beach could only mean Frank.

She rose on her elbow and peered down at the big man. Frank lay on his side, mouth open, gray hair askew. Sensing her movement, he stirred and his eyes fluttered open. When he felt her breasts brush his back, he reached behind to draw her close.

As they lay together spoon fashion not saying a word, his body hairs prickling her skin, she felt protected and happy and totally loved. Without deliberation or conscious thought, she suddenly realized that she could not possibly imagine a future without him.

The first time I married
Karen Ethelsdattar

The first time I married
I took my husband's name for mine
& added Mrs.
I pulled it over my ears,
a woollen cap,
even when it scratched in warm weather.
I was his falcon, hooded.
I was his pigeon, banded.
I sank into his name like a feather bed
& neglected to rise in the morning.
I crept under his wing
like a fledgling
too small to spread its own feathers.

Now I add your name to mine,
proud & frightened.
This time I keep my own,
I surrender nothing.
Still this act
reminds me of captivity—
sweet & dangerous.
Forgive me when I grow fierce
& understand
when I seek wild mountain meadows.

Good-Bye Prince Charming
Claudia Van Gerven

she thought she was done with all that
had turned all the mirrors to the wall
given up meat, taken possession
of her gray hairs
but the story reasserts itself
persistent as the green joy
that rises in the lilac
winsome and upright as the sex of young boys
she hears it thumping through the night
trying to undo the latches
to break into her glass house
her windows loosening
like spring water

what should she do with the answering tattoo
gray hairs breaking loose from the snood
do they remember the fire dance
are they still red at the roots
how can she call his name
no longer being princess, no longer
being poor, what can he give her
but those same cold slippers dreaming
among the dust puffs behind the closet door
they would shatter in such tarantella
shards mining the threshing floor

where will she find her beauty now
not in the eyes of boys
clear as streams rushing over boulders

nor in the dark glass of downtown
office buildings where the King slinks
among his portfolios

it is easy enough to say
let her sing her own song
let her find her own way
among budding willows
on the creek bank, through
the predatory traffic of
the alleyways, will her words
rise up the glass walls
will the magpies peck them away

if she says I am beautiful
will lilac laugh
and laughing will she kiss
sleeping buds awake?

Old Friend Sends a Chain Letter
Therese Becker

"This prayer has been sent to you
for good luck. It has been around
the world nine times. The luck has
now been brought to you."

You open the envelope and people
begin to spill out on the kitchen table:
an arm, a leg, and poor Joe Elliott
who lost his four hundred thousand
all because he refused
to circulate the holy chain.
And worse, there's General Welch
who lost his life only six days after
he failed to pass on the prayer,
the chain letter sent to you by a friend,
and begun by a holy missionary
from South America
for those of us in need
of a salvation we could buy
at the post office.

The list continues like a voodoo obituary.
You pour a second cup of coffee,
gaze into its dark circles;
all the small lives link before you,
people cutting up rosaries
at night in their garage,

snipping necklaces off the necks of young girls
as they wait in line for a burger,
large dogs set free
with one clean snip of the wire cutters.

Their chain fetishes gone mad
attract them now into armies;
they begin to hack down
rows of chain link fences,
work their way toward your neighborhood,
your fence, your dog, your daughter.
You rise to latch the chain
on your front door
and the old ritual rises with you,
taking you back to the kitchen table
where you take out your pen,
reluctantly, and address the first envelope.

Woman
Lillian Morrison

After the thousandth insult
she wakes up to fury

having waited ten thousand years
like the people of India
under their yoke of acceptance
assaulted again and again
by barbarians.

She was Saint Sebastian
bleeding from arrows.
She has become Saint Joan

a determined guerrilla
in the centuries-old, undeclared
war against her.

The Choice
Lesléa Newman

You can carve out a life for yourself
just as your bones have been carved
from some larger bone
your flesh peeled from some larger flesh

Or you can lift the paring knife
from the kitchen drawer
and free the veins
that rise to meet the skin

There is no one
save the poems you might write

Bittersweet
Fran Portley

Dried acacia flowers share a crystal
vase with bittersweet berries
in my neat New Jersey living room.
Put the quilt back in the guest room,
friend, you know I'm too Victorian
to share your waterbed. Your music
and my poetry never made it together.
Still, I fell in love with something,
the steep walk down to your beach,
eucalyptus trees. Maybe talking
to you mornings in the cluttered
kitchen over a mug of reheated coffee.
The kiwifruit I buy in my supermarket
never taste as sweet as the ones
I picked with you in California.

Forbidden Lover
Susan Eisenberg

The forbidden lover beckons.

I refuse to follow until
nightfall cloaks
           my heart-tracks
and all eyes are turned aside.

In daylight we pass each other coldly.
We wear dark glasses.
We speak in tongues and riddles,
our lovepoems coded in casual conversation or
passed under tables in large raised letters that
must be swallowed before we part.

Islanded
raised in dark barrooms and parking lots
nurtured on subterfuge our love grows
deformed. Plans orchestrated in
hushed phone calls mis-
communicate. We grow distrustful. We grow wary.
Voices of propriety
raise haughty heads in snickering chorus:
no blossoming   without daylight
without daylight   no blossom.

The Life I Didn't Live
Joanne Seltzer

I wish I never married
I wish I had fewer children
I wish I were a lesbian

I wish I ate less meat
less dairy
more *Umeboshi* plums

I wish I talked less on the telephone
celebrated fewer holidays
paid less for cosmetics
dropped more in the poor box

I wish I found less time
for shaving legs and underarms
more for visiting planetariums

I wish I lived in a hermit's hut
surrounded by edible berries
instead of lawn

I wish the loon called to me more often

Swamp
Kirsten Backstrom

There is a swamp behind Jillian Bremen's house. Sometimes, she imagines that she inhabits a fairy-tale castle, surrounded by a wilderness of lurking exotica. Sometimes, she takes a more practical approach and appreciates that she bought the twelve soggy acres for a song. The swamp breeds mosquitoes, but Jillian can tolerate minor aggravations. She has established herself here; she has made a commitment to this place. The house sprawls graciously on ground composed mostly of sandy landfill. The house and the land accommodate each other. But recently, they haven't really accommodated Jillian.

She designed the house while she was still a credulous college kid who believed she could create anything that she could conceive. She lived in a crummy studio apartment for nine years until she could afford to buy land and build. Now, she runs her own architectural firm, and her home is a project for her spare time. The house is her indulgence, her headache, her conception, her nightmare. It has sloping solar panels in the south wall, a spiral staircase at the core, a multi-leveled living area, and a practically separate basement apartment for her son.

She and Danny have lived here together for half of his life, but he has never taken much interest in the ongoing construction. Lately, he's preoccupied with his stereo, his girlfriend, and especially his car. The car is a green bug that squats with its greasy guts exposed in the carport under the house. Danny seems to see it as a puzzle to be solved rather than as a vehicle to be driven. Jillian worries about his tendency to putter ineffectually; she also recognizes the same tendency in herself. After all these years, the house is still under construction.

When she stands at the breakfast bar in the kitchen, she can look up through the bare lattice framework of the ceiling into the bathroom above. For years, she's been meaning to do something about the plumbing. Her ex-husband, George, insisted on installing the toilet, tub, and sink himself. She's not sure what he did wrong, but the pipes groan ominously whenever the taps are turned on, and the toilet has a tendency to overflow.

The rest of the house is in a state of perpetual transition and malfunction as well. She and Danny have grown accustomed to maneuvering around stacks of lumber and drywall. They put up with plaster dust on the furniture, in the food. They eat on any available surface, sit wherever there is room. The arrangement changes all the time. Interior walls have been torn down and rebuilt so often that it is like living in a maze.

Since the start of his senior year, Danny has been increasingly annoyed by this chaos. He retreats to his own domain. He is getting ready to leave home and feels no personal investment in the house. After he has gone, the choices and changes will be Jillian's to make, alone.

She is in the habit of working late nearly every night. On weekends, there's time for Danny, if he's around. During the week, she keeps herself too busy to think about how things will be different when he no longer lives here.

Jillian's half-hour daily meditation is her only real time to herself. If Danny and Stu and her job did not exist, she imagines that her whole life would seem like one endless meditation. The day's distractions would drift across her thoughts, but she would not attach herself to them. Invariably, she'd return to the gentle transitions of her own breath: inhale to exhale, moment to moment.

After work, she hurries through a gourmet microwave dinner. She scrubs off her makeup and changes into a sweatshirt and jeans. When she thinks about herself at all, she thinks, objectively, that she is in pretty good shape. She has always been thin, and her work burns the calories. Though she's almost six feet tall, she carries herself without slouching or apologizing for her height. She wears her long hair loose and casual. Jillian cultivates a kind of hectic, windblown professional appearance which elicits both respect and protection from those who work for her. She is known to be brisk and absentminded. She is known for her look of perpetual distraction.

No one at work would ever imagine Jillian meditating. It is something she does to reclaim herself from their expectations. She tries to forget all commitments: to her job, to her image, even to her house and son. Whenever possible, she meditates outside, despite the mosquitoes. The swamp is not comfortable or beautiful, but it is the one place where no one bids for her attention, where no one challenges her self-possession.

As she douses herself with mosquito repellent, the citrus astringent smell makes her think of how she used to hold Danny's wrist so gently while she splashed the stuff on his pudgy arm. If she got a drop in a raw scratch, he wouldn't wince at the sting but open his eyes wide instead with astonishment and indignation.

She wants to explain to him and to herself that parents and children can't help hurting each other. Thinking of Danny, Jillian wonders if she should postpone her meditation tonight and try to talk to him, even though he has made no effort at all to talk to her. When Danny doesn't want to be disturbed, he locks his door. Jillian has no such option, since there are few doors in her part of the house. Of course, she and Danny make a deal when Stu sleeps over. If Jillian asks for privacy, Danny smiles conspiratorially and stays downstairs. But when she's just meditating, he often interrupts. She doesn't quite feel justified telling him she needs this time to herself, so she meditates outside, where no one is likely to come looking.

Now, she decides not to knock on Danny's door. He probably wouldn't be able to hear her anyway. The floor is throbbing with his music. Jillian feels the pulse through the soles of her sneakers. The blunt thrum of the bass line prods at her. The noise makes her tense, although she doesn't really notice it any more than she notices the tarps that have covered the living room furniture for a month. The fireplace would be finished sooner if Danny would help, but Jillian is going to have to hire someone to do the masonry anyway. She stops to write herself a reminder on the pad by the telephone. The top sheet is scribbled over with the lush grotesque doodles that Danny draws while he's talking on the phone. The words *Dad* and *graduation* are engulfed almost completely in a welter of twisting vines and leering faces.

Like Jillian herself, Danny is a very private person. When his father called him suddenly after a five-year silence and offered to buy him a new car for a graduation present, Danny didn't tell his mother the details of the conversation. Jillian assumes that father and son will get together to shop for the car, and probably have dinner.

She wishes that she could warn Danny about George. She doesn't want him to be disappointed by his father again. She admits to herself that she is also worried on her own account. George might take advantage of this difficult and vulnerable time, to steal Danny's loyalty from her.

She knows that she can't press her son for answers. She can't criticize his father. She can't question his decision to use part of his college fund to travel around the country for six months. She can't ask him whether he approves of Stu, whether he feels crowded out of his home by the presence of a new man. She can't ask him if he's sleeping with Cheryl, if he's taking precautions. She can't be a mother for fear of compelling him toward his father, for fear of losing him. And yet she also knows that she is ready for him to go.

Tonight, Jillian really needs to meditate. She changes her clothes and finishes her dinner even more efficiently than usual. She decides not to pester her son with questions, not to distract herself from her essential time alone.

Outside, the dusk reverberates with the stuttering discourse of crickets and peepers. A bullfrog groans periodically. She holds her breath, listening. As the door bangs shut behind her, Danny's music vanishes. The mosquitoes flock to Jillian in a whining cloud, brushing her cheek and neck.

The house is surrounded by mounds of sand, an island of dry ground in the midst of the swamp. Danny used to be the only little boy in town with an acre of sandbox. When he started tunneling into the sandbanks, Jillian had to make him stop. He could have been buried alive. Sometimes it seems that his whole childhood, her whole parenthood, was a succession of narrowly averted accidents. This place was always dangerous, but something kept mother and son both safe.

The landscape changed over the years. Parts of the yard were leveled and cultivated. Enormous rolls of turf were spread like carpet around the front deck, and four truckloads of chipped bark were dumped along the flagstone paths between the house and the garden. If all goes according to plan, Jillian will have the backyard finished this year, and the stark sand will be replaced by a fragrant brown slope of bark all the way to the muddy shallows of the marsh.

Now, Jillian's sneakers fill with sand as she slides down the slope to the path. She doesn't stop to empty them. In fact, the cushions of sand feel soft under the arches of her feet. She was pacing a building site all day, exercising her best manners on the contractors who ignored everything she said. She could feel them winking at each other as she turned her back to roll up the blueprints. At least Jillian has the last word on their work. If they disregard her specifications, she can always make them tear the whole thing down and start over. She's never actually done this, but it helps to know she can.

The path into the swamp is spongy and ridged with roots. Everywhere, shallow water laps around the ankles of the trees. The swamp is a dark-green mirror with a dusting of pollen and pond scum. Sculptural crags of deadwood protrude at odd angles, reflected to create an eerie shadow-architecture of pillars which support no ceiling and stand upon no floor. The smell of vegetable decay is rank, warm, and sweet. Stagnant water leached through peat smells bitter as strong tea. And the soil itself has a loamy chocolate smell.

One year, Jillian and Danny dug chunks of the black mud from the bottom of the marsh, to fortify the garden. They waded knee-deep, stirring clouds of silt. The legs of their blue jeans looked green through the yellow water, and their feet kept sinking when they stood still. As they lifted their full shovels, much of the mud melted away. They mounded the rest onto a tarp and lugged it back to the house. It made the garden grow jungle lush, but they didn't repeat the project because of the leeches they found sucked on to the backs of their legs when they stripped off their wet jeans. Danny was only eleven, but he knew how to salt the leeches and scrape them loose. Jillian was proud of his coolness, his independence, but horrified at the same time.

Jillian's meditation spot is provided with a sturdy cedar bench. She sits, adjusting herself to settle her spine against the hard frame. She can feel all the angles of her own taut body and wishes that she were built of flexible amphibian cartilage instead of blunt bone. She takes off her sneakers and folds her legs into the lotus position. She takes three deep breaths, holding each as long as possible, releasing each as completely as possible. A mosquito settles on the side of her neck. She slaps it, feels distracted, draws three more breaths.

First, with her eyes closed, Jillian imagines herself saturated with dark water, absorbing tranquility through her skin the way that a hibernating frog breathes by osmosis in the mud at the bottom of a frozen pond. Then, with her eyes open, she takes in the whole surrounding swamp. She closes her eyes to disappear, she opens them to be aware, to be nowhere but here.

She always focuses on the mossy grotto of the embankment where a great drowned oak tumbled over years ago, its splayed roots ripped up from the ground. A curving earthwork of root and dirt still rises on the edge of the marsh, poised like an enormous clawed paw. The fallen tree bridges an expanse of still water. Moss has overgrown the embankment. An abandoned muskrat den between the roots yawns dark and empty.

As night permeates the marsh, the mosquitoes become more difficult to ignore. Jillian's skin feels itchy, clammy. She stares into the intricate wet network of twisted roots looming over her, and remembers the nightmare Danny had when they first moved here. He dreamed he was digging a tunnel into this embankment, scooping with his plastic beach pail. The hole was so deep that he had to extend his whole arm inside to scrape the bottom. And then the hole became the mouth of a snapping turtle. He was reaching down its throat while it choked and writhed.

Jillian blames George for Danny's nightmares. He was always teasing the boy. But the snapping turtle dream might have come from another source. The agent who sold Jillian the land boasted that he and a group of guys from the neighborhood had rid the swamp of vermin to make it more marketable. They marched in with hip boots and pitchforks to rout out, overturn, and skewer nine snapping turtles. The largest was a dinosaur the size of a Thanksgiving turkey; the smallest was no bigger than a soup bowl. Even the little ones could take your finger off, the agent claimed. He offered to do the job again if the turtles returned, but they never did. She would never have called him anyway. He told the whole story in front of Danny.

Jillian can't concentrate tonight. The distractions sweep her up and carry her along. She keeps imagining Danny's dream as she looks at the embankment eclipsed by spreading shadow. The roots appear to squirm, and the doorway of the old den gapes at her. She shifts her gaze to the swamp itself, to watch the water striders skittering over the skin of the water. Their feet make dents as though they were skating on gelatin. They don't weigh enough to break through.

A small frog lies in shallow water, quite close. Jillian didn't notice it before, and only just happens to notice it now. Its eyes protrude like floating bubbles. She can barely make out the suggestion of its shape, its legs trailing as it hangs suspended at the surface. She tries to concentrate on the frog. Although the darkness makes it difficult to see, she imagines it is watching her, with round amber eyes as intent as her own.

Memories bob up again, relentlessly. When Danny was a baby, Jillian would lower him into the bath and steady his wriggling body, while he flailed and frog-kicked. His plump belly balanced heavy in the palm of her hand as the water buoyed him up.

Jillian realizes that she is not meditating very well. She keeps forgetting to breathe. She unfolds her legs and finds that her foot has fallen asleep. She massages it for a moment, feeling as though she is warming a slippery animal in her hands. It is numb and rubbery. It is distinct from herself. It tingles, then stings, as she tugs on her sneakers. She leaves the laces loose, takes a few steps, and crouches by the edge of the swamp for a closer look at the small frog.

The frog is just out of reach. For some reason, she wants to see it swim away, to be sure that it is alive. She imagines that it would be safer overnight in deep water, rather than here near shore. She doesn't know why she can't leave it alone, but she picks up a waterlogged twig and reaches, just to touch it lightly, just to prompt.

The big frog comes out of nowhere. It lands with a splash between Jillian and the small frog. It actually jumps toward her, with a squealing croak like the creak of a clogged pipe under pressure. Jillian drops her stick and stumbles backward. She is reminded, absurdly, of her dread of overflowing toilets, that horrible embarrassment, primal panic, ridiculous guilt. She wants to explain, to escape. She's not really afraid of a bullfrog anymore than she's afraid of a toilet, but she is taken by surprise. She steps on her shoelace, trips, and staggers hard against the bench. Automatically, she scrambles around to put the bench between herself and the advancing frog.

It must have been hiding somewhere in a dark pocket of the mossy embankment. It is as fat as a guinea pig, leaping in clumsy lopes. Jillian knows that her reaction is irrational. The big frog couldn't really be defending the small frog against her. But there is no doubt that she is being challenged, threatened. The bullfrog squats, poised to leap again at any moment.

It is dark by now. She can't even see the small frog from here. The mosquitoes are fierce. Her meditation has not been a success. Ordinarily, she'd keep trying, but tonight she decides to do herself a favor and give it up. She considers stooping to tie her shoes, but the bullfrog makes another lunge.

Jillian turns and walks quickly up the path. The ends of her laces flap loose, ticking against leaves and roots. Her heels flop in and out. Somehow, her untied sneakers make her feel like a naughty child, hurrying home late.

She was not trying to hurt the little frog. She only wanted to be sure that it was all right. She only came here in the first place for some time to herself. This is her land, after all. She is no intruder. No one can chase her away. No one can blame her.

Ahead, the sloping south windows of the house gleam watery yellow between the black pillars of the trees. Jillian can't remember if she left the lights on herself. Maybe Danny has emerged from his basement to wait for her, to talk to her. She hopes he won't be able to see how foolish she feels.

The house looks angular and awkward, looming on the bare hill of landfill. Somehow, it doesn't seem to belong here. Jillian is a fine architect, but she has to admit that her own home is not quite right. Maybe the design was wrong all along. Maybe she should listen to Stu and sell the place. Maybe she should marry him, or move out on her own, now that Danny is old enough to be going away. Maybe she should do whatever she wants for a change. This seems to be the first time in her life that she has had a choice.

Actually, Jillian wants to go after that damn bullfrog with a pitchfork. She wants to flush the ugly thing down the toilet. She wants to fill the swamp with bark, just for spite.

Or maybe, instead, she wants to be an ugly, unreasonable frog herself, to swim down through murky water and hibernate in mud while the whole world freezes over.

At the back steps, she stoops to tie her shoes. She tugs the laces tight, as if she is tying up all the loose ends in her life. And she walks into her own house as though it is really hers.

Photo by Jude Keith

Amazing Grace
Susan Vreeland

My parents aren't waiting at the baggage claim so I walk out onto the street. Twenty minutes pass. I should have told them I'd take a cab; they've just turned eighty. I don't dare leave curbside to phone them, afraid they'll come just then. If they don't see me, they'll panic, think I missed the plane and am still in Los Angeles.

Eventually, I spot Mom's white bubble hairdo and Dad's side-to-side sway, his shuffling feet planted wide apart for each step, a walk perfected more than fifty years ago for stability on the rocking decks of oil tankers. He looks jaunty in his Greek wool sailor's cap, with Mom in mint-green polyester pantsuit, knocking shoulders with him as they walk, and all at once my resolve melts away.

"Sorry we're late," she says. "He wasn't in the right lane so we had to go way around." Her voice carries a perpetual irritation, a fact that she's always denied.

I hug them and rediscover how short they both are. I look down at Dad and feel again the shock at seeing the mauve-colored surgical scar peeking out his open shirt. "Happy fiftieth."

"Thanks for coming, Annie," he says.

On the way home Mom "helps him," as she calls it, telling him when it's safe to change lanes. I try to ignore it. "Don't forget. Turn on Oakdale this time, not Rupert," she says.

"She knows best," he says, then turns to me in the backseat. "Always."

"Watch where you're going, Stanley." She turns back toward me. "It's just that we never drive this far from home. Only to the grocery store and church."

"And senior center for Friday bridge," he adds. "Don't forget that."

Obviously an airport trip was too much for them. Mom looks at my face and her eyes narrow. I turn my attention to something out the window so she will too. "You look different," she says.

The wig—it's a fine effort, the same middle brown color, but a little too full. "It's the glasses," I say. "Did I have these frames when I was here last?"

"I don't know," she says. "It's been so long." She smiles her wistful, round-faced smile. For a moment I see her as I remember her from childhood—nourishing my brother Greg and me with tapioca and time. Trying to keep hothouse flowers alive in Philadelphia winters for Dad's homecomings from sea, there being nothing green and growing on board ship. Telling me that if you can do something for someone and you don't, you're never quite whole.

Dad's driving becomes more sure in our own neighborhood. I recognize streets where I played kickball, and houses of playmates. We turn onto Berkshire Street, the first address I ever memorized. Riding behind them, I feel I am again their child, holding the weight of an untold secret in my lap, a piece of news they will unwrap like a grotesquely empty present. The leaves carpeting the lawns on our block remind me of my childhood duty every autumn. Guilt for not always having done it lies like a dark pool in my chest.

"My God, the eugenia has grown so much you can barely see the house," I say. The hedge is wild and sprawly, over five feet high. "I remember when Greg used to jump it."

"Before it finally outgrew him," Mom says.

"It makes the house look kind of secretive hiding behind it," I say. Dad scowls slightly and makes an abrupt turn into the drive. The rear tire bounces over the curb. We lurch sideways but he pretends it didn't happen.

That evening Greg calls from New York. At the last minute he can't make it. Pressing business. I half expected that. His executive success excuses him.

She's gushy to him on the phone, but after she hangs up, she speaks bitterly against him for not phoning earlier so she wouldn't have told her friends he would be there.

"He probably couldn't help it," I say, by now a family refrain.

"He doesn't call as much as you do. Sometimes it's two weeks or more." In this way, she lets me know how often I've been expected to call. I haven't met the quota either.

We say good night and I walk down the hall to my girlhood bedroom, close the door, and look at the doorjamb. The secrecy lock they indulged me when I was twelve is still there. The latch is stuck, repainted a couple of times. With a nail file, I chip it loose. Ivory paint flakes off to show the salmon color I had in high school, the powder blue of elementary school. Maybe they'll never notice. I get the lock to work, take off the wig, and avoid the mirror above the dresser. I want to be in control of how and when I'll tell them.

Before we leave for the party the next evening I hear Mom's voice in their bedroom. "You're not going to wear those baggy pants. They make you look like an old man."

"Why, certainly not," Dad says. "What would you like me to wear? You tell me and I'll put it on." I wonder if Mom hears his sarcasm. She never appears to.

The living room of the neighbor's house is decorated in gold crepe paper with a Happy Golden Anniversary banner hanging over a dozen casseroles and Jell-O salads laid out on card tables. There are mostly people from church, a few from Dad's union.

"After fifty years, how many dinners have you cooked?" Mom's friend, Helen, asks.

The hostess gets out a calculator. "It comes to 18,250," she says.

"And every one was delicious, too."

Approving laughs at Dad's comment. Mom shakes her head. She can't accept a compliment.

The sheet cake has gold bells and Estelle and Stanley, In Love Forever written in script. Mom gets teary when she sees it. There's talk about the decades and the children's births, Greg's marriage, the two grandchildren. Helen asks her when each of us was born. "Greg was in '46, just after the war. September 20, a Friday at three o'clock in the afternoon. And Annie was March 6, 1949, a Sunday at eleven at night."

"Incorrect, Mrs. Burnside," Dad says. A smile streaks across his face but he does not look at her. "Greg was at eleven at night and Annie was at three in the afternoon." Everybody laughs. Mom looks confused, doesn't want to be wrong. I don't know who's right. Privately, I'm rooting for Dad, but know better than to take sides.

The collective present is a VCR and a membership at the Video Palace. The guests beam in pride. "Now you can smooch at the movies right in the comfort of your own living room," one man teases.

"And we will, too," Dad says on cue.

At home after the party I see Dad standing watch at the open kitchen door, saying his nightly good-bye to the sky, a personal ritual deeper than habit, left over from his days at sea. When he was home as I was growing up, he'd take me with him for this quiet observance on my way to "tucking in," the dark expanse releasing my childish news of the day. My heart turns over to see him still do it. I had forgotten.

I am convinced that when Mom is in repose, she rehearses the times she perceived herself to have failed, to have been found wanting, rearranging the circumstances to be more comfortable, whereas Dad, I'm just as certain, remembers moments when a pale star hung off the tip of a crescent moon or when the sky was a smear of purple above the open ocean.

I walk over and stand next to him, the cool air making me hug my arms. "It's still there, Dad. Your sky."

"Cloudy," he says. "No stars tonight. The night before you came I saw the Milky Way."

"Has it changed any in all the years?"

"No. Most things don't."

I cannot bear to dislodge his comfort in that thought, so I kiss him on the temple and go to bed.

In the morning Mom and I linger after breakfast, reading at the kitchen table. Dad fills the hummingbird feeder. He works methodically. "They're thirsty little creatures," he tells me. "And they depend on me. You look." He holds up the plastic tube with red sugar-water. "This will be nearly empty tonight." Carefully, he wipes up some red drips on the counter.

Mom reads again the wealth of greetings written on anniversary cards.

"Would you like another cup of coffee, Mrs. Burnside?" It's the name he uses in moments of mock gallantry or easy peace. He leans forward slightly at the waist, with the polish of a butler in slow motion. "To go with the cards?" She says yes and he takes a painfully long time to decide where the parts of the coffee maker go, even though he's done it every day for years. It's his job, just like taking out the trash. "Have you collected some trash for me, Mrs. Burnside?" he asks every afternoon.

He slides his feet across the kitchen linoleum. "Pick your feet up," she says. I wince. He doesn't hear her.

He pours the coffee and mutters, not a question, "What's the point of picking them up if they're going to come back down again."

I notice that the microwave I sent them last Christmas still has the instruction book and warranty sitting in it, even though it was the simplest one I could find. I go over its operation with Mom. She's distracted, wants to tell me news about the children and illnesses of each person at the party. I try not to listen, until I hear about someone taking prednisone. I go into my bedroom and zip mine into my suitcase.

Later I hook up the VCR to the television and try to explain to Dad how it functions. For the time being, it sits on the floor. Mom frets over not having the right furniture to accommodate it.

The paperboy comes to collect and Dad goes into the bedroom for his wallet. He's there a long time. Eventually Mom follows him. "Don't keep him waiting, Stanley."

"No, no, I wouldn't think of it."

"Well, what's the problem?" He mumbles something I can't hear. "You can't find your wallet? Again?" Her voice has the edge of a scalpel. "Isn't it here on your dresser?" I hear drawers opening. "If you put it in the same place every day, you'd always know where it is."

"Why certainly, you're absolutely right."

His voice is steady. I wonder if his wounds had formed scars so completely that he had no more feeling close to his heart.

"I'll go pay him." Mom bustles to the front door with her purse, pays the paperboy, and whispers to me, "Do you see what I have to contend with? He can't do anything anymore." She returns to the bedroom. "Did you find it?"

He mutters a no. I wish he had.

"You've got to take care of your things," she says. "I can't do everything. Where'd you put it last?"

He must not remember; that's why he doesn't say. I go into the bedroom to help them look—under the dresser, the bed, the chair.

"Maybe it slipped behind the dresser," he says. I step toward it quickly to pull it out. I don't want him doing it. The wallet isn't there.

"Is it still in the pants you wore last night?" Mom asks. We look in the pocket. Not there. We fan out through the house. I spot the wallet on the counter by the kitchen door.

He is baffled. "Isn't that something? How could it get there?" And he's embarrassed. In front of his wife of fifty years and his own daughter. I give Mom a quick look so she won't say anything more. We watch as he goes outside. I know that it is to be alone.

I avoid eye contact and retreat to the bathroom, where I splash water on my face and ache. The cool water is soothing and I bury my face in terry cloth.

Mom corners me when I come out. "A few weeks ago he turned left into the pharmacy right in front of an oncoming car and the driver swerved and yelled something awful to him. He moped around for days, but he did drive me to my hair appointment when it was time."

"How long has it been since you drove?"

Mom lowers her eyes, looks serious. "I know, I know. I'll practice around the neighborhood."

"Maybe while I'm here I should drive with you a little."

She shakes her head. "I'll do it."

Hours later the sound of Dad's harmonica croons through the hallway. Mom freezes, listens. A few notes in and we recognize "Amazing Grace." We tiptoe through the kitchen to hear better. Her eyes get watery. I tease her with a smile. "I can't help it," she says. "When he does those fluttery parts, it's just beautiful, but lonesome, too." As the music continues she intones the words, "That saved a wretch like me." Shyly she reaches for my hand. "It's the getting old," she says in defense of her tears, but the melody is haunting to me, too. I nod because I do not trust my voice.

The next day Mom and I look through the Sears home catalog to choose new drapes for the den, my gift to them. We settle on a silvery gray. "Don't you want to ask him?"

"No. He'll like this. I'll show him later." The conversation moves to where it left off the day before. "All he does is read both newspapers, watch CNN, and worry about the world," she says. "He falls asleep in his chair and he forgets to take his medicine."

"Ssh, Mom. He's right in there."

"He can't hear us." Her shoulders and chest heave in a great, tired sigh. "He puts too much salt on his food and it's not good for him. I try to cook fish. Dr. Morris said I should, but I hate to. It smells up the house and it's more expensive."

"You can afford it, Mom."

She shakes her head. "I try to take care of him, but everything's on my shoulders. When the water heater broke last spring I had to call the repairman—he couldn't do it, he never calls anyone—and I had to make the decision between a thirty-gallon and a forty-gallon tank."

I feel I've got to know everything, so I ask, "What else?"

"I make all the appointments. I figure out the medical insurance forms."

I know she's been saving all this up to tell me. "What else?"

"He forgets to feed the hummingbirds. I have to remind him. He used to do it like clockwork every morning."

"What else?"

"He says he's going to leave me."

She stares at the Sears catalog. Both of us are silent, in respect for the words just said. She shifts position in her chair.

"You don't believe him, do you?"

"He says he'll go to the Seaman's Home."

Below her pinched mouth, her chin quivers. All she's done for others, all the lunches packed, the laundry, all this seems to have melted away without due recompense and left her empty and confused. Lines tighten around her eyes, which plead for me to do something.

"I'm sorry, Mother. You shouldn't have anything to worry you." I take her hand in mine. "If I could do anything in the world so you wouldn't have any worries, I'd do it."

"I know." She pats my wrist. "Wait here." She grasps the armrests of her chair and pushes herself up and into the bedroom. In a minute she returns, her large-freckled hand in a fist surrounding something small. She says nothing, her lips pulled in tightly, but motions for me to hold out my hand. I do. She uncovers a satin ring box. I look up at her, aghast. She gives a vigorous nod. I open it and see the ruby ring Dad gave her on their silver anniversary.

"You should be wearing a nice ring," she says.

"No, Mom." I know she's making reference to my still-unmarried state.

She nods again, more firmly. "I've worn it twenty-five years. Time for it to be moving on." The lines in her face bow into a luminous smile and her eyes gleam. "Put it on."

I slide it on and feel the weight of its elegance. "It's lovely." I venture on shaky ground. "You didn't give each other gifts this time."

"No. Under the circumstances." She sighs. "Or maybe we're just tired." She pulls a handkerchief from her sleeve and blows her nose. "Is there anyone special you're seeing?" she asks, it finally dawning on her that she hasn't asked me anything of my own life—my friends, my job, my condo.

I shake my head. "But that's OK, Mom. I've been doing a lot of things I've always wanted to but used to put off. I go to plays whenever I want and I take a walk on the beach every day."

Her mouth registers approval. She looks at the ring. "Stanley was right. I figured it out. You were at three in the afternoon."

"Why don't you tell him?"

"He doesn't care. He's forgotten it."

Greg calls to see how the party went. I talk to him on the den phone after Mom hangs up from the living room. "They're old, Greg. You haven't been here. You don't know. You'd better start coming around more."

"I know. You're right."

"I can't be the only one they depend on anymore."

"I know," he says, impatient.

I lower my voice. "Greg, I can't talk now, but I'm going to have to call you. We have to talk. Seriously. They're going to need you, Greg."

"Sure, whenever." His breeziness is irritating.

"Do you remember them bickering when we were growing up? Did they hide it or what?"

"Come on, Annie. Don't tell me you never noticed it before. It's been going on forever."

"But it's worse. It's as though all these years of living without us made them careless about keeping it private."

"Look, just don't let it get to you. You can't do a thing about it."

"It's pretty pathetic, really. Two old people, still after fifty years trying to learn how to live with each other." I make him promise to call them more often.

That afternoon I hear the high whine of a motor. In the kitchen Mom and I look up at each other, wondering what it is.

Out the front window we see Dad step up onto a ladder and whack at the eugenia hedge with the electric clippers. He's so short it's a reach for him. Mom marches out the front door and I follow.

"Stanley, what do you think you're doing? You can't do this. Dr. Morris laid down the law."

He doesn't answer her, but takes another pass at the top of the hedge. The teeth of the blades grab at a tough branch and he staggers back, but hangs on, and it cuts through.

"Stanley. Stop it." She pounds on his thigh.

He wheels around above her on the ladder, the blades slicing the air two feet from her head. The motor rips through the neighborhood. They hold the pose for a threateningly long minute, the blades vibrating. His mouth is a straight line, his eyes narrow. He looks foreign to me, strangely tall and menacing. "Go back in the house, Estelle."

Mom's quick glance across the street checks the neighbors' windows. She is aware of the picture this gives. She backs away. With a quick flip of her hand she motions me to follow her; she's always thought proximity implies allegiance.

"This is ridiculous, Dad. You don't have to do this." He has turned back to the hedge and can't hear me above the grind of the motor. I retreat to the house.

Peering out the living room window, Mom says, "See what I have to contend with? See? He shouldn't be doing that. Dr. Morris told him to slow down."

"But when he does slow down, you complain he's not doing anything."

Mom glares at me, then begins to cry and her eyes plead. Like so many times before, I take her round soft form into my arms and bend over her. "He doesn't hold me anymore," she whispers, and in that moment I know that any added ounce of worry would catapult her over the edge.

"We'll get a gardener," I say. She shakes her head. "Why not?"

"He won't have it."

"The same way you won't have a housekeeper?"

"I can't sit there while someone else cleans my house."

"Then schedule it on Friday when you go to bridge." Another head shake. "Why not?"

"Not when I'm not here."

I walk into the kitchen to get the Yellow Pages. She pads behind me. I turn to the H's. She sulks. "He's not dressed warm enough either. He only has on that thin cotton jacket." She scours the sink as if it were alive with vermin, and runs the water full force. I see in her slightly puffy face a sad, worn love, wrenched by confusion.

We hear the motor roar wildly, the crash of metal hitting cement, the ladder falling against the sidewalk. Mom and I bump hips getting through the front door.

Dad is lying in a tangle of cord and ladder. Above his left eyebrow a gash is bleeding. His eyes are open but he is dazed and unfocused. I'm conscious of Mom screaming, "Do something. Do something."

I disconnect the hedge clippers. "Get a dish towel," I say. Mom moves as if fifty years had rolled back. I stanch the wound, which is more messy than deep, and we get him into the house. He refuses to go to the emergency room.

"I told you. I told you you shouldn't be doing that." Deftly, happy to be in charge, Mom cleans and wraps the wound and puts him to bed. He looks pathetic and angry. Against his protestations, Mom serves him dinner on a bed tray. We all eat in the bedroom. When she leaves to take the dishes away, he admits to me quietly that he "had a spell or something" on the ladder.

"Did you have heart pains?" I ask. He shoots me a glance, then looks away and shrugs. "Why won't you go to Dr. Morris?"

"I don't like him much anymore. All he does is run tests, and he doesn't tell me anything, and then I get a big bill, so what's the point?"

Better than he can guess, I understand, and let it go.

The week is over and I'm due back in California. Mom insists we leave for the airport two hours before my flight. "He might get lost," she says. I counter her, saying I'll take a cab, as much to show her how simple it is as to avoid an ordeal.

Part of me would like to stay to help them—to hire a housekeeper, a gardener, take Dad to Dr. Morris, give Mom driving lessons or hire a driver. But part of me is glad to escape into the world of competence and reason.

The cab comes, and we walk by the butchered eugenia hedge, some of it a foot shorter than the rest, most of it with wild branches growing askew above the mass. Better the hedge than each other, I think.

We hug. "I like your perm. Meant to tell you," Mom says. Then, "Get in, get in," afraid the meter is running already.

"Don't worry about us," Dad says, a square of gauze taped to his forehead.

As the cab nears the corner, I look out the back windshield. I had hoped I would see that it wasn't worth it, that all those years only brought bitterness, that I wouldn't miss much. Instead, I see them clawing to hold on, two tiny figures leaning against each other in front of the hedge.

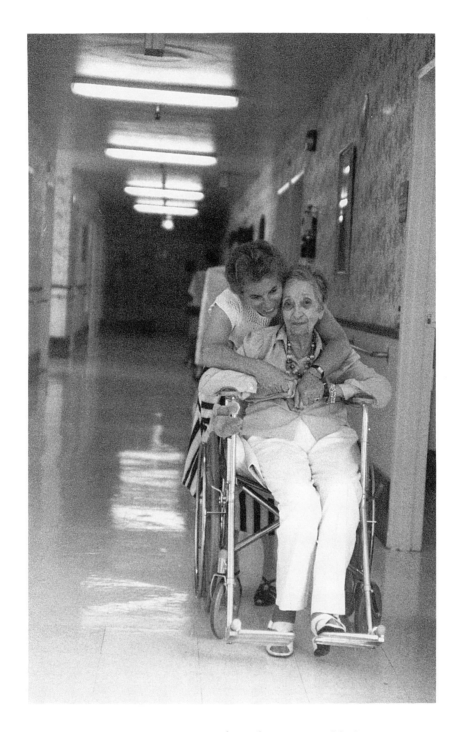

Photo by Lori Burkhalter-Lackey

Photo by Marianne Gontarz

If I Could Begin Again
Sue Saniel Elkind

grow
as a speck of dust would grow
then let me begin
by being a better daughter.

Let me begin by understanding
the silence of your life;
by showing you the sounds of
sight:
how a peach full in the sun
might be the sun,
how a flock of starlings
fanning the sky
is like one large wing,

by remembering Dad's gentleness
his quiet but deliberate way
of speaking, so easily read by you.
Let me begin with patience—
that I need not shout,
simply face you
when I speak.

Shopping Expedition
Elisavietta Ritchie

"Summer is a dead season," the motel owner says.

What tropic rampage of life around his pastel pillboxes: scarlet hibiscus and purple bougainvillea entwine with pale clematis, innocent honeysuckle and Virginia creeper mingle with poisonous pink oleander.

My mother's neighbor is waiting outside in his sapphire Lincoln Continental. I watch him from inside, here by the registration desk. He does not seem to notice me. Perhaps he feels it indiscreet to be observed leaving a motel with me. He was kind enough to come here for me. He is vain enough to comb his waxy silver hair for me.

My brother took over my mother's Volkswagen when he flew in this morning. He is also not afraid to sleep in her bed tonight. This afternoon he is meeting with her lawyers.

The motel owner is flipping the Yellow Pages for the closest coffin store. His first time to have to look up this item. Also mine.

Finally, among Fruits & Vegetables (Wholesale), and Fuel Ejection Systems, Fund-Raising Counselors, and Furs, we find numerous Funeral Directors.

I write down six addresses, thank him, walk out to the car. After the motel gloom, the sun is terribly bright, and I am warm in the black silk dress borrowed from my mother, or rather, her closet. Strangely, it fits.

My mother's neighbor gets out, shakes my hand solemnly, opens the other door for me. He squeezes my arm, as if to offer condolences, or something else.

We have talked long on my previous visits. Fortunately, now he is saying he does not know what to say. I show him my list of addresses.

"They are scattered all over the suburbs," he points out, "or in the seedier sections of town."

I think of certain foreign cities where one whole street, fragrant with pine shavings and incense, devotes itself to the craft, and funeral revelers gong full blast all across town so everyone knows and in some way shares in the celebration.

She would have shunned such exotic show, as well as funeral parlors.

Cold in the car, I roll down the window, welcome the heat which billows inside, licks the white leather seats with its stream.

"That doesn't help the air-conditioning," he murmurs, leaning toward me. He keeps squeezing my hand.

"That doesn't help your driving," I murmur back.

He continues to careen through the streets as if late for a wedding.

The first showroom stands among beauty parlors and package stores, used car dealers and billiard halls, in a neighborhood my mother would not have frequented. Nor would my mother's neighbor. He is busy unfastening my seat belt with more than condolent warmth.

Terribly cold in the showroom. The salesman, large in a dark shiny suit with a faded carnation in the lapel, extols the value of velvet linings.

"But my mother hates velvet. Besides, velvet's too hot for this climate."

"Then rayon? Or satin? Or best of all silk; see how nicely striped—"

Like Grandmama's love seat, I think.

"Feel here," he says, "how soft this padding is. And see here, these handles are hinged for ease of pallbearing."

I think how my brother and my mother's neighbor and her lawyer and maybe her dentist will all together give a jolly heave ho, even a *Yo, heave ho....*

"And let's consider oak versus walnut—"

Or whatever wood lasts almost forever, and with age might improve.

"My mother insists on cremation. No point in sarcophagi at $4,995."

The salesman inhales. "For a dignified burial service—"

Distaste on his florid face. He doesn't want his coffins in the fire. He shows me the line in the catalog that guarantees imperviousness to groundwater.

No, as far as he knows, twenty years in the business, there are no reusable coffins.

My brother and I divided the chores: Should I have left this one to him?

The salesman steers us from coffin to coffin. Each appears more substantial, more plush than the last. Some have handles of brass.

I remember the Mother's Day card of padded satin trimmed with pink lace I sent her once, in part as a joke, but also.... It reached her in the midst of her myriad causes. She scribbled back on a plain prestamped post office card: *Why waste your money on kitsch?* I never sent her another.

In her sensible striped beige dress she is still lying cold back home until they come for her. My brother left the air-conditioning on High. That will also keep the flowers from wilting.

She would be annoyed at the stiff bouquets. "Sympathy gifts," she often said, "should go for worthier purposes. And lilies are so depressing, gladioli so rigid."

On the way home, we will surely pass a field or empty lot. I will gather her favorite daisies, as if for a bridal bouquet. I won't let them burn.

"Black is becoming to your fair skin," my mother's neighbor's whispers caress my hair. "But you're pale today beneath all those freckles. As soon as we've finished this business, I'll take you to lunch, feed you a juicy steak, or better, calves' liver, washed down with a good burgundy. You need extra protein and iron to carry you through this ordeal."

How my mother's neighbor sounds like my mother, except that she seldom served meat. It is *she* who lies terribly pale, back there, beneath her freckles of age.

"They'll fix her up nicely," the salesman is saying, "and a pink velvet lining will be most becoming. When the coffin rests open and you approach to kiss her, you'll note the fine workmanship under the lid."

Years since I've kissed my mother. When she was drinking, I couldn't even approach. Despite all her goodness....

I insist that $4,999 is too much. So is $3,999. Even $2,999.

"This coffin is only $2,955." The salesman plumps up the plush. "The Basic Package with Options."

The $2,955 Package lies at the back of the showroom. Brass handles like door knockers. Let me in, let me in, in the dead of the night.

"I know it's a difficult choice," murmurs my mother's neighbor. His fingertips trickle over my forearm. "Shall I help you, honey, make up your mind? And after the funeral is over, and your brother leaves, I'll find an excuse to take you for a few days to the beach...."

The salesman is distracted. His secretary, her coiffure glistening blonde helmet-stiff above her magenta blouse and black patterned slacks, needs him to sign several death certificates. He excuses himself, it'll just take a moment in his office.

Another door leads to a smaller showroom.

"Look over here," I tell my mother's neighbor, who is running his fingers over a gleaming Cadillac of a coffin near the front window. "Absolutely crammed with coffins back here!"

Plain pine in the corner, and what feels like plywood pasted over with wallpaper, or self-sticking shelf paper, to simulate walnut bordered with teak. A smaller coffin, gold foil embossed with dancing lilies, sized for a child.

"Prices are much better here!" I tell him. "And it's warmer, away from that air conditioner."

My mother's neighbor is wiping sweat from his neck with a large white handkerchief.

I finger the Dacron paddings. Orange blossoms and pink roses, forget-me-nots, and here's one printed with blue anchors. I think of the long-ago pajamas, patterned with little green trains, which my mother found at a church bazaar and gave to my brother for Christmas. He swore they were too large, then before he had grown into them, he passed them on to me unworn.

The salesman hurries in. He looks embarrassed. His long arms try to shepherd us back toward the main salesroom. At the threshold he positions himself, arms folded, between the boxes and us.

"These coffins are for Latinos." His voice is low surf.

"But my mother was Latin."

He looks with surprise at my blue eyes, death-white skin, telltale red hair. My mother's neighbor also looks astonished. Both perspire in the moist air which follows us from the back room.

"She was likewise Oriental and Black."

I point past them. "I'll take—that one over there in the corner, daisies printed on oilcloth. My mother will be happy in that, and yes, I know it is plywood."

Think how well it will burn, I muse, and write him his check. Some question as to whether he will accept it.

Back in the icy Lincoln Continental, my mother's neighbor sits very tall, and does not take my hand.

Hot Flash
Linda Keegan

On this hot April morning, spring is like August, seasons changing within seasons. A west breeze blows through the open bedroom window, cools the hot flash that sticks to Mildred's face. Her feather pillow, now twenty-six, as old as her daughter Carla, bursts when she fluffs it, feathers taking to the air as if they had a chance to be geese again.

Seeing years of comfort on the wing, she waves her arms like a madwoman, struggles, tries to catch them, as if she had control over something that had made up its own mind. Some stick to her sweaty face like sucklings, and she is almost grateful. Carefully, she pulls them from her face and lays them in a crystal box on the bureau.

At a time when life is weaning her from the ducts of choice, it is important to understand the reason she chooses to do this; to hold on; to control. Dry rot is a grave deterrent to usefulness, causing its victims to become brittle and crumble into powder. Today Mildred is fifty, wanting babies.

In her green car, Carla comes to visit, to talk, to bring potted flowers for the birthday. "You look young, Mother," she says. "The change is natural." They sit across from each other on the porch, Mildred staring at Carla's face lit lovely by the east sun and framed by the flow of her golden hair. All of spring radiates around Mildred's daughter, blooms as magnificently as Carla herself.

Mildred wells up at the sight, sees lineage, and like a sonogram with an artist's brush, she paints clear portraits of her unborn grandchildren. They are beautiful like Carla, high cheekbones and green eyes. They are holding Mildred's hand in the garden, picking daisies, planting marigolds. They are growing up, riding bikes, listening to stories on her lap, falling asleep with teddy bears on the old feather pillow.

"Mother, please," Carla says, "don't dream about children who don't exist. You'll just make yourself crazy."

Again Mildred glows, damp and blush like sweet crab in the sun after rain. She fans the flying heat, the telltale rose that rushes over her body like embarrassment, spreading dry truth like pregnant seeds, rising, then settling on her face.

"I remember how we struggled," Carla says, showing Mildred her map of life. No babies. Her choice. Maybe later. Maybe. After the comforts are paid for. She doubts it.

"Yes," Mildred answers, "I am listening to you."

Mildred is listening, she's not listening, her own body gone mad with the monthly screaming for blood. No babies, she thinks. Casual. Confident. Like No-Thank-You. Carla's happy to be alive. Yes. No. It has nothing to do with her decision. No, there are no names for what doesn't exist. The narcissus and white tulips, forced in clay pots, hang heavy with blossoms, will not bloom again.

Mildred stares toward the mountain, past Carla, beyond her to where petals skirt around the tiny feet of the magnolia like long snipped curls. She sees her in another time on the lawn, maybe ten, a towel wrapped around her thin shoulders, a bush eager to be a tree: the haircut, the first attempt to honor Carla's choice, uneven in places yet dream-perfect enough for a new young lady. Old memories run free as a mountain brook, ring clear as a songbird's trill.

The heat moves again like a busy chickadee, a sine wave in flight within her body, its peaks and its valleys working their way from the inside out, perching on her face.

"Carla, please," Mildred snaps, "I don't want any pills. My mother never took estrogen, and I won't take estrogen."

"She never had a choice," Carla says. "But you do."

Mildred wipes the sweat, the wet thin layer that spreads like years across her face. She fans again, refreshing her skin with the cool air, pulling the fragrance of the lilacs to her nose. But this shouldn't be; it's too early for lilacs.

"I've ordered central air," Carla says. Hot days like this so early in April, she worries about her mother in the summer. Mildred paints again, imagines the days ahead. She sees herself powder white confined to a cool box to escape the summer heat, cooped up like winter to escape the cold, a thermostat controlling her forever, providing her with all the comforts of life: the bird caught up in the talons of time.

"No," Mildred blurts. "I don't want the pills, and I want fresh air."

Carla stands up preparing to leave. "Well, you think about it," she says as she bends and hugs her mother good-bye. Mildred watches her go, so beautiful in green, so sure of time. She sees her again in another time with her new haircut, handing over her dolls to be held while she wobbled off on the bike they'd found at the dump and painted her favorite purple, the same as the hyacinths. Like then, they wave and smile, blow kisses to each other.

"Yes, Mother," Carla calls back, "I know I'm a comfort to you. Don't manipulate," she scolds. Mildred turns, wondering who will take care of Carla when the heat invades her body on some untimely day.

Back in the bedroom, Mildred recalls the pillow, the comfort, how it molded to her body in another time. On the bureau, the crystal box fills with sun, splashing pretty colors that look like flowers across the wall.

She picks up one of the feathers that had stuck to her earlier, cradles its scrawny body in her hand and strokes the curls on its head. She imagines she's in the garden picking daisies, planting marigolds. As her own body warms, she stares at the life in her hand, sees its eyes opening for the first time, hears it cry, wonders what she should name this little baby.

On Loving a Younger Man
Alice Friman

One day when I am ninety-one
you will look at me from the doorway, leaning
with your head tilted to one side
and I will wonder if you remember
how I too used to lean
and lay my hair down black and whispering on the
pillowcase fresh from the wash, or how
later I would turn
tucking my knees under yours
for the night's insensible hours.
        And if I haven't forgotten—my mind
gone blank as a sheet—I'll remind you then
of the old amazed look your face wore once
at how much your hands already knew,
and I will call you back
from the doorway
to adjust the sweater around my shoulders,
the robe in my lap, and take your hand, upturned
in mine, to show you how that line is still there:
the lifeline I once traced with my nail,
that day on the bench by the Ohio River, that first
time, when I—troubled—leaned my head on your shoulder,
sideways, the way I do now
and you will then.

Ripening
Joanne McCarthy

It is sad to grow old but nice to ripen
—Brigitte Bardot

What she regretted was her skin, folding in
on itself like fabric, elasticity gone. Life-
juice that plumped her cheeks disappeared,
wrinkles cast their fine net across her
face, laugh-lined her mouth. Her eyes deepened.
The hairdresser warned her about the gray.
Leave it, she said, I want to see
what Nature will do. What Nature did
was remind her that ripeness
is all, that autumn is the richest
season, that preparing for snow means
building a shelter, that warmth within
withstands whatever winter howls without.

When the baby laughed, reached for her breast
even though milk had been gone for years,
she remembered sweet burdens of motherhood,
relinquished them gladly, her destiny
now another—grandmother, wise
woman, matriarch. The brain
holds what I am, she said, knowing then
that body was always hers. The heart
holds what I would be, the womb can rest.
She saw her life, and knew that it was good.

Photo by Marianne Gontarz

Eating Cantaloupe
Midge Farmer

I scrape the seeds
from a halved cantaloupe
pare off the thick
veined rind, cut and hold
a wet orange slice. I eat
standing over the sink.

Juice runs across the back
of my hand, drips from my wrist
forearm and chin
even though I quickly suck
and lap as I bite off
each chunk.

The brash color, variegated
texture and gush of juice
from the fruit give me purpose
for this day.

I am the fruit
seeds gone, wrinkly shell
peeled off to reveal
soft flesh covering muscle,
electric-bright mind
and life-juice still rampant
still far from being sucked
away.

The Woman with the Wild-Grown Hair
Nita Penfold

The Woman with the wild-grown hair
finds a metaphor for self-knowledge:

There was a younger time when the Woman
slathered bright paint on old furniture
puttying up the nail holes first
covering the flaws, the imperfections in the wood
praying for a time to do more than make do
knowing there would be a day when
she wouldn't need to cover everything up.

Comes that day she decides to strip
things down to their bare essentials
takes days to scrape layer after layer
of paint off the ancient church pew
oak barely visible through the milk-base
which won't come off no matter what
chemicals the Woman uses and she weeps
in frustration that she can
only go so far and no more.

Strawberries
Leslie Nyman

On the first day of summer Angie went strawberry picking. She had never gone alone before. It had always been Marty's impetus to drive out to the countryside. But this time the heat wave sent her to where cool berries fell like memories into her hand. Humid air, thick and sweet, stuck to her skin. The crease between her eyes relaxed while she searched along the runners for hidden fruit. The heat massaged knots of tension out of her hunched shoulders. She lingered in the sunbaked field until she had picked more than needed. On the drive home she rolled the car windows down to let the warm air rush in and tangle her graying hair.

Her neighbor, Edgar Jackson, was mowing the edge of her property when she turned into her driveway.

"Hey Edgar! Hey!" She ran up behind his tractor-mower.

He shifted the gears into neutral and removed his earphones. Angie could hear tinny music whining from the headset.

"Thought I'd give your lawn a quick going over. You don't want the weeds to get out of hand."

"Thanks, but would you mind leaving it?"

"What?" He turned the motor off. "What was that?"

"Thanks for the offer. It's just that I don't want it mowed. Not yet. That's all."

He surveyed the shaggy grass and sucked his teeth. Then he shrugged, started the motor again, and drove back toward his garage, careful to maintain his evenly mowed lines.

The stillness of the air after the turbulence created by the mower was a welcome calm to Angie. She turned on the radio hoping for Mozart and sat by the window. The smell of strawberries, the warm air soothing her bones, and music surrounded by quiet—June had these moments of perfection that could hardly be found at any other time of the year, especially the year that just passed.

Mechanical rumbling in the distance ruined the moment. "Someone's always got to mow at the most peaceful time of the day," she muttered.

Her neighbors, Jane and Fiona, banged on the kitchen door.

"Can we come in to visit, Ang? It's just us."

"Might as well, you're here. Have some fresh strawberries."

Fiona did not hide her eyes as she took in the two days of unwashed dishes. She fingered the toast crumbs dotting the place mat in front of her.

Jane spoke first as usual, "I'm getting too old for this heat. My Greg says that June is breaking all temperature records." She fanned herself with a magazine. "Is that why Tim isn't here?"

"What?" Angie could not hear across the kitchen table while Jane's husband mowed their lawn.

"We thought your son was coming home this summer to visit."

"I told him not to. It cost a lot of money to come down from Alaska for Marty's funeral. I'll go up for the holidays."

"We understand," she said quickly, "but your first summer alone..."

"We certainly understand," Fiona said with a sharp glare toward Jane.

They were all silent for a moment before Jane cleared her throat, "Oh, yeah, one other thing."

Angie wondered when they would get to the point of their visit. Sometimes it took longer than this.

"If you want one of our men to help with the yard work, like raking or mowing, just say so. Lawns can get pretty raggedy come summer."

"I appreciate that." Angie was inclined to say no more, but Jane perched on the edge of her chair. Angie carried the bowl of berry stems to the sink and, not looking at either woman, said, "I'm enjoying the wildflowers blooming out there, right now. I never noticed those little smooth yellow ones before." She turned around to her visitors, "Thank you, I'll keep that offer in mind."

The street was quiet when Angie and Marty were newlyweds. There was only one other house down the road, and the strawberry farm next door. Over the years this part of town developed into a neighborhood crowded with new houses and laughing children on bikes. Fiona and Edgar Jackson's colonial-style house sat squarely in the middle of the former strawberry patch. He spent every Sunday riding his mower up and down in perfect boring lines over a lawn of weedless grass.

Angie explored her yard in the late morning when she was least likely to meet a neighbor. Colorful flowers were sprouting everywhere. The smell of honeysuckle mingled with an unfamiliar, nose-twitching odor in the garden. She wondered if that was the smell of wild sage. Straggly weeds tickled her knees and up her shorts. From the expressions on her neighbors' faces she knew they were losing patience. Soon an explanation would be required, and Angie was trying to find one.

"Mr. Kelson. I'm glad the Extension Service could send you out on such short notice." She pumped his hand. "Iced tea?"

He had a shy smile that relaxed Angie. It reminded her of Marty's smile, especially the crow's-feet at the corners of his eyes.

"As you see, I've grown quite a garden here."

"Quite a garden, all right." He scratched his head.

The yard was losing its domesticated look, like Marty on vacation when he hadn't shaved for a week. Green shoots struggling between the edges of the concrete steps cracked the little cement back porch. Angie led Kevin through the yard on the flagstone slabs Marty had laid their second year in the house. The stones ended at the hand-built brick barbecue grill. Sunday afternoon cookouts had been a regular event. Since Marty's illness she hated seeing it out there like an unused piece of furniture. Thick-stemmed plants grew around its base. A houseplant ivy left outside and forgotten about, now overgrew its small clay pot and was weaving tendrils around the metal grate.

"You've really got a collection here." Kevin Kelson smiled, showing a mouthful of crooked teeth. "Look, mallow, a nice cluster of mallow. Milkweed and burdock, of course." He walked among the weeds with the familiarity with which she roamed the supermarket aisles.

"There's lots of your clover, gone a little crazy. This is the reason why so many people mow. All this clover in neighborhoods that used to be pasture."

"I hate mowing."

"So I see. I had an aunt who refused to mow any of her property. All kinds of little critters lived in her yard. My father used to say they were the only ones would visit her. My mother said crazy old Aunt Louise had gone to seed. Mom was in league with most of the family to force her to mow." He looked up to see Angie walking away. "Gee, I'm sorry. I didn't mean to suggest that you and Aunt Louise..."

"That's OK. I'm sure many people think I'm daffy. Only, I was hoping that someone in the plant business might understand and, I don't know, be appreciative. But it's not that important."

"No, you don't understand. I was about to tell you that I got interested in botany because of Aunt Louise. Without her I would never have known the natural world exists."

He stooped down beside a white flower, "Look here, you've got bladder campion right next to milk purslane."

"What are these yellow ones?"

"That's cinquefoil, rough cinquefoil. Looks a little like strawberry, don't you think?"

Angie paused by a cluster of purple flowers. "I thought I saw a ram's head lady's slipper here, somewhere. It's endangered, isn't it?" she asked without looking up. "I can't remember exactly where I saw it."

"I don't see any. It would be pretty unlikely to find one in an old pasture." He walked to another part of the yard, "Look, bird's-foot violet. Nice, very nice."

"But not endangered?"

"Sorry." Scanning the plants he asked, "Are you sure you saw a lady's slipper?"

Late the next afternoon Kevin visited again. At the front door

Angie threw a wiggly-fingered wave to Fiona, who was watching from her upstairs window.

"My nosy neighbors are dying of curiosity about you," she laughed.

"I guess I should have called first. But I thought of a way to help save your yard. It goes along with your original plan."

"My plan?"

"Endangered species. It's a good idea. Unfortunately, there really isn't anything endangered here."

Angie laughed, "You caught me at my ruse. It was just an idea. Pretty silly, I guess." She turned away.

"Not really." He lightly touched her shoulder, "Listen, maybe you could make a land donation to the Nature Society. They require complete mapping. Then, they do a site inspection."

"Why would they want someone's yard? I'm not donating my house, too, you know."

"I know, I know, but it is something to buy time. I could map it for you, if you like. What do you say?"

Angie chuckled aloud while looking over her yard. It was a tangle of colorful vines.

"Sure, map away," she laughed.

Kevin came every day, just before sunset. He carried a canvas bag filled with pamphlets about grasses and a large hardbound flower identification book. Angie sat on the steps watching him study the flowers and leaves. Sometimes he held one up for the light to outline the veins. For another he moved it into shade to better determine its true color. Once he shouted out to Angie, "Great, you have fragrant bedstraw," and laughed with delight. She laughed too. Another time he droned, "Lamb's-quarters—God, I hate that. It's everywhere."

The vegetation reached unexpected heights. The unpruned hedge in the front grew taller than Angie, and hid a hornet's nest. Angie walked the long way around the house to avoid it. What had once been lawn was now almost entirely overrun with blue asters, white Queen Anne's lace, and a variety of gangly green spires not yet named.

Five o'clock Sunday afternoon Angie was basking in the unusual silence. Suddenly, the wooden frame of the screen door rattled loosely against the jamb. Edgar Jackson stood in front of her, his smooth face bent into a scowl. She had been waiting all summer for this visit and was not nearly as nervous as she expected.

"It's become an eyesore, Angie. Surely you can see that." His military haircut and ironed trousers suggested someone who did not sweat. "I plan to cut it down for you."

"I would rather you didn't do that, Edgar."

"It's an embarrassment to the neighborhood."

"It's my property and I prefer it like this."

"Like what? It looks like—excuse my French—shit."

"It's natural. The extension agent says there are some unique and interesting flora in my yard."

"That young man? What the hell's he know?"

Angie pressed her lips tightly together.

"We've taken a vote in the neighborhood and I've been elected to tell you we are mowing it down." The stiffness dropped from his voice. "Angie, Marty would have wanted it mowed."

The screen door slammed and Angie heard the mower rev up.

"How the hell does he know what Marty would have wanted. He only spoke to him to ask for jumper cables or cigarettes," she mumbled to herself while dialing the police.

Edgar drove his large tractor-mower up to her front gate and parked there, waiting. The motor idled like a bulldog with asthma. Angie stood on the porch. The machine's reverberations throbbed through her body. Shaking her head slowly from side to side she mouthed the words, clearly, so there could be no mistake. "I will sue you for this." He hesitated. A police car screeched to a stop in front of the hornet's nest.

Edgar looked up, mouth open, eyes wide. "You called the police?" He let out the clutch and turned the tractor into her yard. The grass closest to the street went down quickly. Stalks and stems fell under the roaring motor. A flurry of seeds and petals churned in its wake.

"Stop him! Stop him!" Angie yelled, swinging her arms and pointing. "Stop him. He can't do that. He's not my husband."

The two policemen standing next to their car smiled at each other. One stepped aside to avoid an irate hornet.

Angie ran in front of the mower and stood there with crossed arms. She had no idea what to do if he did not stop. She hoped the police would see she was serious. Edgar advanced, slowly. He waved his hands to motion her out of the way. She stood her ground. The machine's noise grew deafening. She could see he had waxed the fenders and polished the grillwork. Little sparks came out from under the hood. Fat tires rolled over the delicate lacework of leaves. Cinquefoil, mouse-ear chickweed went down.

Edgar's eyes glared blue stone. His face tightened. He was at war. He saw nothing but a stubborn woman standing in the way of his job. He blinked; he saw the two policemen standing beside her. His lipless mouth curved into a smirk and he turned his mower away. Deliberately driving through the middle of her yard, he left a trail of crushed stems and deep tire treads. Angie watched a swarm of hornets follow him home.

"We can't protect you all the time, lady."

"He may do it when you're not home, or asleep."

"Is there anything I can do?"

"Why don't you mow it? It sure could use it."

"I like it like this. I don't want it mowed."

"Better get a lawyer."

Angie stayed home all day and awake through the night, watching to make sure that no one came to mow her yard. She wandered through her house, straightening up the kitchen counters, shaking out rugs at the back door, and enjoying the sweet scents from her flowers. "Why should I have to mow because everyone else does," she said aloud. "I'm tired of doing things to satisfy the neighbors. Marty never liked to mow."

"Maybe we should get sheep," Marty had suggested after coming in from the yard, grass shards stuck to his sweaty body. "They could keep it trim and I wouldn't have to waste my time."

"I really don't think the neighbors would look kindly on us for that. Don't mow it for a while; maybe they won't notice," Angie had suggested.

"The neighbors! We spend too much time caring about what the neighbors think."

"Well, in this world we live with other people, you know."

"Angie, you're always saying that. We live in this world for ourselves too. If you ask me, the problem with this world is too damn many people living too close to each other. Everyone wanting to do their own thing but most of them trying not to get noticed by the damn neighbors. It can't be done. We should have moved way out to the country when we had the chance, when we were younger."

"Maybe so, but sheep in the suburbs is not the way to reclaim our youth. Besides, they'd probably eat his strawberries next door."

"That would be just fine with me. At least someone could have them. He never picks them all. I think he actually prefers planting and weeding to harvesting and eating."

Angie smiled, remembering what a mystery that was to Marty. He loved to eat. He had gained all that weight his last year, and she wondered if she should have let him eat as much as he did.

Hungry, she leaned into the open refrigerator letting the cool escape onto her body. She missed Marty. She could hear herself yelling at him to close the fridge door. Tears fell. She took a yogurt and drifted back into the unlit living room. The streetlight from across the road threw a soft glow over her wild shrubbery. The buzz from the light played its one note song until dawn.

The second page of the "Living" section of the Sunday paper featured a picture of Angie standing chest-deep in her garden of wildflowers. She wished she had not let Kevin talk her into the interview. The story made her sound eccentric. It read as though she were on a tirade about reaping comfort and strength from the beauty of nature.

That afternoon several people drove by, slowing down to stare at her yard.

"Are these free?" A woman stepped out of her car.

"Pardon me?" Angie stood up.

"I'd like some of these purple ones." She reached down and tore up a bunch from the ground.

Jackson roared across the yard. Angie planted herself between the hedge and the driveway. "You'll have to roll right over me," she yelled.

"Get out of the way. This is enough. You have lost all sense of responsibility. You need help."

"What about you, ready to mow me down because you don't like my yard."

"It looks like hell and you know it. Just look around, lady, does anyone else's place look like this? What are you trying to prove anyway?" He dismounted and approached her. "Angie, get out of my way. I'm mowing this today whether you like it or not. If you want to live in the wild go to Alaska with your crazy son. But people in civilization got a right to live in a peaceful environment."

"I could not agree more."

The sun beat down on them. His face grew red and tight like a beach ball. Her face was covered with sweat. He opened his pinched mouth to speak, but closed it again. He stared into her eyes waiting for her to back down. When her only response was a cold stare he raised a hand to her shoulder.

"Don't touch me." She thrust his arm aside.

"Angie, move." He pushed her shoulder until she lost her balance.

Rebounding back to his side, she grabbed his arm and pulled him away from the mower.

He jerked his arm with a force that made her topple backward. Her ankle twisted in a groundhog hole. While she was looking down he leaned his arm across her chest and pushed her to the ground.

Jackson glared, his hands wound into fists, his face daring her to get up.

Angie met his eyes, unafraid. She saw him hesitate, but before she could move Jane and Fiona were tugging on her arm.

"Quick, Angie, come inside." They pulled her up. "He'll kill you for sure if you don't get out of his way."

Angie thrashed to free herself from their arms. As they dragged her up the porch steps her shoes were ripped off. Her ankles were skinned and bleeding.

"Don't!" Her wailing could not be heard above the insistent lawn mower making its quick runs over her front yard.

When it was quiet again and she was left alone, Angie pulled down all the window shades. The destruction made her sick to her stomach. In the cool, dark house she curled on the couch and tried to think about Marty. But the newspaper scattered at her feet distracted her. It lay open to her picture. She stared at it. It was as though she were looking at a stranger. She narrowed her eyes trying to bring it into focus, trying to see it differently. Finally, she noticed the smile. It radiated from the middle of the flowers. It forced her to sit up. The neighborhood was silent when she put up the shades. In the glow of the streetlight her yard appeared unruly and wild.

Monday morning Angie rented a Rototiller. The high-pitched motor echoed through the quiet street. The smell of gasoline filled her nostrils. After the machine had turned over the earth, she spent the rest of the day working down on her hands and knees. She did not wear garden gloves because she liked the feel of the cool, moist dirt in her palms. She liked the way it settled in the lines giving her hands the look of a stenciled leaf.

Late in the afternoon Kevin stood at the edge of the yard. "Oh, my God, Angie, what happened? Are you all right?" His shocked voice unnerved her.

"Yes, don't worry." But his agitation made her see again the broken stems and wilted flowers stacked in a pile at the side of the house. Working in the yard had made it easy not to think about what was lost, now changed.

"What have you done?" he laughed. "I can't believe this." He knelt next to her.

"Strawberries, front and backyard filled with strawberries. Next June it will be beautiful again."

Photo by Marianne Gontarz

Old Women's Choices
Ruth Harriet Jacobs

We keep our thermostats at fifty-nine
so we can give our children gifts
we really can't afford.
We buy bruised, overripe fruit
from the distressed produce
and donate to our churches.

We buy our own clothes at thrift shops
but select grandchildren's presents
from the nicest shop in town.
We eat the same boring dinner every day
because we won't cook for ourselves
but produce a feast for guests.
We never say we need help when we do
but do without, not wanting to burden
those whose burdens we carried.

Some of us break out of these patterns
realize we have rights and choices
to care for ourselves too
but it is hard to forget early teaching.
Even after all these years
we put ourselves last.

Dearest Margaret
Eleanor Byers

Yes, we've agreed, when we grow newly old
to live side by side on your farm in Vermont
where we can raise goats
the small brown kind, following close
and bleating of love.
We've said we want cats, all colors of cats
to play in the shade on hot summer days,
to purr by the stove when evenings are cold.
And, Margaret, remember our plan to grow plants
with long Latin names
and prizewinning Bibb lettuce
for good-tasting salads.
You'll make tabbouleh (you do it so well).
I'll roast a capon (with shallots and beans).
How well we will dine
drinking mint tea or watered white wine
followed by cheese and sweet almonds.
Indeed, we can travel
wherever we like
as long as we're home by noon
to pet the cats, feed the goats
water the prizewinning lettuce.
When winter snow falls
we will pull on tall boots and warm, woolly coats
and slosh down our paths to the tin mailbox
by the side of the road.

To the postman we'll offer our best apple tart
hot from the oven, with cream
in exchange for choice letters.
(We'll write them ourselves!)
Oh, Margaret, let's read *Ulysses*
(again) and this time, patient with age,
unravel the prose of James Joyce.

Photo by Marianne Gontarz

Shrinking Down
Janet Carncross Chandler

Thirty-five pounds and half an inch
so far, in this shrinking of my body.
Homes and bodies sometimes act in reverse.

First, my country home began to flap
loosely around me, like a scarecrow's jacket.
Next, the condominium apartment I bought

felt like too much trouble—why
did I need two bedrooms, two vanities?
So   three weeks ago today

I moved into a retirement community.
All the old-timers welcomed me,
enumerated the years they've been here—

five, ten, even twelve. I watched some of them
move easily between the life outside
and the more relaxed world

of bingo, pinochle, and pool fitted
between breakfast, lunch, and dinner.
My twelfth-floor one-bedroom apartment

feels almost like home, a soft robe
of sunny yellow I can slip on when it feels
chilly outside. The thing I value most

is that tiny slot on my door, showing red
when I'm home and safe inside, clear
when out for the day. It lets the floor rep

know I'm still alive night and morning.
Strong bathroom fixtures prevent my falling.
And should I be attacked by demons

who specialize in old people
(like me) a yank on one of two pulls will bring
help on the run. *This* place seems just my size.

Keepsakes
Elaine Rothman

Someone's calling my name. "Amelia, Amelia, wake up!"

I don't recognize the voice, so I won't open my eyes. She's shouting as if I'm deaf. They all talk very loudly around here as if everyone is hard of hearing, and only some people are. They don't realize how rude they sound. Besides, if I don't know this person, she has no right to call me by my first name.

The sun is warm on my face. It sends silver shafts through my eyelashes. Golden specks dance at the end of every shaft. I hear a radio playing somewhere, and the clack of shoes along the tiles of the hallway. That's another thing they do a lot, walk fast and clump their feet. There's no thought for someone who might be resting.

She's still shouting, something about bringing me my breakfast, and have I forgotten this is bath day. It must be quite an event for her, a bath day. She's going on about time slots, and keeping to a schedule, and how I mustn't make her late.

Now she's calling me Mrs. Cochrane, and offering to help prop me up against the pillows and wash my face with a warm cloth. That's much better. I'll look her over and decide whether she gets a smile or not.

I don't usually care very much for any of the strangers they send to replace Margie. This one looks like a stick of taffy that's been pulled too long, stiff and stale. Margie's all square and deep brown like a chunk of chocolate fudge. She laughs when I tell her that, and says I'm always thinking of candy, just like a child. She told me she'd try to get here by noon, after her little boy's Christmas pageant at school. He's going to play Joseph, a beautiful brown-skinned Joseph.

Just as I thought, breakfast on plastic dishes, artificial eggs, and muffins from a mix. Decaffeinated tea in a paper cup. I ask this new one if she's real, but she doesn't have much fun in her. Real enough, and rushed, she answers. If I don't eat very much of my breakfast, that's all right with her, so long as I take my medication. See, she points to the word *medication* starred right there on her printed instructions. I notice that it ranks right alongside of *bath,* another starred item.

Her name is Frieda, she tells me through thin lips. Fussy Frieda. Says I get a yellow pill, with an orange one to follow. She must think there's no point in calling them by their correct names. Makes it easier all around.

Margie always closes the door softly behind her and whispers, "Amelia, breakfast time, honey." We munch cinnamon toast from real china plates, and sip fresh strong coffee. She doesn't have time to get breakfast for herself at home, so she has a bite with me each morning.

Frieda is pawing through my things, getting bath articles ready. We argue a little bit. Will it be a wheelchair or a walker this morning? I don't want either, thank you. I can use the handrail in the hallway. My strength doesn't usually run out until later in the day. She pretends to admire my red bathrobe.

I'm wearing red so Martin will see me flash like a flame through the woods. My fingers skim the tops of the bayberry bushes. My sandals skid along the slippery hill of pine needles. I must be on time or we will miss the tide. He promised to let me take the tiller once we are safely out in the bay. I can taste the salt spray on my tongue and feel it sting my cheeks.

Frieda sees me tuck the last packet of bath salts into the pocket of my robe and starts another ruckus. The water in the tub won't be very deep, and she's certainly not going to run it hot enough for bath salts to dissolve. There's a long list of residents waiting for their baths today. She'll show me their names posted on the door.

Margie gave me two dozen packets of those salts, all smelling of the spicy woods. She knows the stunted sand cedar. My trees are the tall spruce and balsam. We decided that it was the very same sea that washed both shores where we were growing up.

I hold on to the fragrant evergreen square in my left pocket. I need my right hand to grasp the handrail. We pass an open door where a very frail person is being fed the same stuff that lies untouched on my breakfast tray. The pleasant child feeding her is wearing a pink pinafore.

I once wore a pinafore like that. It had deep patch pockets to hold my favorite lunch, a slice of cheddar cheese, an apple, and a chocolate bar. A nibble of each, one after the other, until they're all gone. The trick is to finish with a single bite of apple, cheese, and chocolate, nothing left over. Wipe your hands on the pinafore when you're through.

I'm moving too slowly for Fussy Frieda. She offers me the wheelchair again. It's true that the walk to the bathing room gets longer every week, but she'll have to be patient. There's no point in working in a place like this unless you're patient.

When Margie gave me the bath salts for my birthday she said she knew I'd especially appreciate the box they came in. It's gray-green with golden curlicues in a raised pattern on every inch of it, and a hiding place inside. It reminded her of the hiding place I told her about, the one that Martin and I used for years.

There was a crevice in the stone wall where steps cut into the rocky ledge slanted down to the sea. I scraped the golden lichen off several stones so no one would guess that one particular smooth stone could be pulled away. I lined the bottom of the hollow with club moss to make a soft spot for the gifts we exchanged. He left me plaid taffeta ribbons for my braids. I left him a rare yellow violet that I found in the woods.

I made a bet with myself that Frieda would show me the list of people scheduled for their baths the moment we got to the door of the bathing room. I assured her that they all know how much I love a leisurely hot soak, and wouldn't mind waiting their turns.

As punishment for my fib, I made myself look into the big mirror behind the nurses' station, something I usually avoid doing. In the mirror I see a little lady hunched like a question mark in her vivid red robe. Wisps of white hair sprout from her pink scalp. Her bright eyes peer at me from between her shoulders. They are the only thing about her that I recognize, the eyes of the supple, silly girl Martin Cochrane married.

I must have worn Frieda down. She filled the tub almost to the rim with water that the bath salts instantly turned crystal green. I close my eyes so I won't have to see her perched on a stool, looking at her watch.

My toes are luminous shells in the pool above the waterfall. I can barely see them over the hill of my belly. Everything floats in the clear sweet water. The striped wool skirt of my bathing suit billows around my hips. My brown hair streams behind me, pulling gently at my temples.

They say it is a dangerous place, so close to the waterfall. The rubber cap that I am supposed to wear whenever I swim hangs on a bayberry branch. Martin knows I come here whenever I can, but he won't tell anybody. He trusts me to know my own limits. That's what counts, Amelia, he always says.

I needed a lot of help getting out of the tub and toweling myself dry. Even Frieda saw how very weak the hot water had made me. She rang for a wheelchair and muttered about having to take my blood pressure as soon as she could get me back to my room.

I am much too tired to put up any fuss. Frieda hovers over my bed looking stern. She nags about the folly of trying to do too much at my age. Then she sits down to read my chart.

I learned to read when I was very small and Martin would leave me messages in our hiding place within the wall. DEAR AMELIA, he would print in big letters, and use easy words to tell me important things. I had to get it right or I would miss the tide for our sail, or the woodcocks whirring their crazy dance in the woods. Before I could spell out many words on my own I would reply with crayoned pictures that said what I needed to tell him.

I feel so tuckered out, I tell Frieda truthfully, that all I want to do is sleep. And if I'm still asleep when Margie gets back, please let her know that I won't be needing any more bath salts, but I do want her to have the box they came in.

She must think I'm raving because she looks at me suspiciously before she draws the blinds and darkens the room. She lets me know she has many other residents to take care of, but that she'll be back when it's time for my medication.

With one foot out the door Frieda shoots an accusing salvo across the bed. "Those yellow and orange pills will be the saving of you, Mrs. Cochrane. They might keep you going forever."

Margie and I have long discussions about what keeps people going. We both know it's a combination of God's will and good memories. That's why we tell each other stories about growing up by the seaside. She says it's a real pity that she and I and her little boy have ended up landlocked. What kind of good memories will he have, she worries.

My dearest recollections all have to do with Martin. I can recall every single surprise we ever left for one another. There were all sorts of love tokens, like the spiral of a purple-tinged whelk, a tiny spring of sea lavender, or a white gull feather.

Of course, once I grew up, there was the large lustrous pearl he would set into my betrothal ring. People could not understand why I would want to marry someone so much older than myself, but we knew it was the right thing for us. We were like two leaves overlapping, all veiny and insubstantial at either end where we lived our lives apart, but bright green and solid where we could share our time.

There was one surprise that did not please Martin at all. It was a spotted newt I left for him one morning. Even though I had punched air holes in the lid of the jar, he was annoyed with me. "Never keep a living thing captive, even for a short time, Amelia," he said. So I stopped collecting fireflies as well.

When Margie gets here around noontime I hope Frieda remembers to give her the bath salts box. Margie will run her fingers over the raised golden curlicues, slide the box open, and lift the paper flap. In the recess she will find the many pills I have saved like bright coins in a treasure chest. It is not a surprise she will like one bit, but we have always understood one another. She will look down at my bed.

"Poor lamb," I can hear her say. "She's really gone for good. I wish I'd been here sooner for her. She looks like she left easy, though."

Very soon I will be standing naked behind the waterfall. I will lift my face to the misty spray and watch the droplets sparkle on my sunbaked arms. My hair will lie in damp curls upon my shoulders. Martin knows where to find me. He will reach for my hand and help me climb the slippery smooth rocks. Together we will float in the quiet pool above the falls.

Counterpoint
Lynn Kozma

Insignificant
as a beached shell
I feel
the indifferent succession
of days
monotonous as ocean waves.

Bleaching with age
I have lost the rage
at my own
unavoidable demise.
But the mind still conjures
eclectic shapes,
the life of things
not seen.
Words dance across the screen
in perfect conjugation—
messengers of a kind.

Death, I know your winter face.
We have met in random places—
legendary landscapes,
halls of sorrow;

I shall wear RED
tomorrow!

Salamanders
Randeane Tetu

"I would not change one stitch, Margaret. Not one stitch in the fabric of my life." The quilt was velvet this time and brocade, and Emma poked the needle into the square she was working with featherstitch.

Wesley had put the bag of charcoal for the barbecue into a chair on the lawn, and when Margaret looked up, she thought it was a person and drew back a little and opened her mouth to say whatever it was she would say as soon as she identified the person and thought what words would be appropriate.

She looked quickly at her own stitching so Emma wouldn't see the mistake she'd made.

Wesley had the orange lawn tractor out now and had taken it across the driveway to mow around the daylilies. Noise and scraps of dry grass made a fog around him. Margaret remembered, in a shift of breeze the day brought, the smell of the sunshine on the dirt between the grasses while she stood, as a child, looking from the garden to the barn where the thin cool line of shadow lay against the stones.

"I wouldn't either," she said.

When Wesley finished mowing, he would take off his T-shirt and use it to wipe his chest and his chin. Chips of grass and dry dust would settle down onto the lawn tractor, and he would go inside and drink water.

She could see clearly the tops of trees and said again, "I wouldn't either," though next Wesley would come out and say, "Well, Margaret, it's a hot one," and swat the T-shirt over his shoulder to scratch his back, a thing she couldn't stand.

Next to the porch, honeysuckle grew on vines, its white and vanilla flowers strokes against the green. Burned-out flowers of the mountain laurel stuck to the laurel leaves. Emma held the thread taut from the square on her lap and reached into her sewing box, but she didn't take out the scissors.

"Now, you see that?" She held the thread and leaned closer to Margaret.

Wesley came to the driveway, and spouts of grass dug up the air, and noise pounded through it, and then the tractor turned away and grass fell down, and Margaret leaned to see. "What is it?"

"Ticket for an opera we never went to. Just before Harold died. And he said go to it. Take someone. But I didn't go. I didn't want to."

"What on earth do you keep the ticket for? In your sewing basket? Doesn't it remind you?"

"Reminds me, yes. Every time I see it. Keep my wedding flowers, too, and programs for the concerts, dresses that I've worn for special things." Emma still held the thread.

"Well, what on earth do you keep it for?"

"I keep it because later I think I'll want to look through and remember."

"Do you ever?"

"Well, I haven't yet. But I may want to. You never know."

"Now, see, it's the things I don't keep that I remember." Margaret leaned across with her scissors and cut the end of Emma's thread. "Like the card for Rubyfruit. I could have kept it, but I didn't, and I can picture that card today. Bright pink."

"And better, probably, than it was?"

"Better? How can a card be better?" Margaret said.

"Well, with all the edges rounded and smoothed over time, glossied and made perfect."

"Oh, I don't know. Do you still keep things now? I mean since he died? Things you want to remember?"

"I'm doing everything wrong now. Not eating breakfast and staying up late to read, and I don't have any concerts, and now it seems all lies. All, all lies and very much the truth."

"There must be something that you'd change though. Some little thing if you could?" Margaret was looking at Wesley on the tractor with the small island of grass ends and dust floating him above the lawn, and she was counting the rows he had left to come to the edge of the daylilies. She reached for a cracker and a sip of tea.

"Well," Emma said, "Laura and Grandma Ruth used to—don't you remember?—beat the rugs over the clothesline? Put them over and whack them hard...the one with the roses on it. And one time they were doing that, and Grandma wanted me to help. But I was doing something else, and I didn't want to help them. But Grandma was ready to get all excited so I told her 'put a lid on it.' And she did, and I hurt her feelings that way."

"Well, we all hurt someone's feelings. There was the time when Wesley and I first married that I was going on about something and nagging a little I guess. So wouldn't you know, he turned to me and said, 'Margaret, just drop dead.' And so I did. Hid, standing up in the closet, and he looked for me—oh, for a long time, and then he finally opened the door, and didn't I just drop out of that closet into his arms. Like to have scared him to death."

"Margaret, you did not do that."

"Oh, yes, I did. And the time that I first met Wesley, and my mother said don't mention.... The first time I met him I must have hurt his feelings awfully. My mother said to me, 'Whatever you say, don't mention his family. He's visiting here with his aunt because his parents just died in a crash.' And wouldn't you know, after we'd talked with him a while, there I was saying, without even thinking, saying, and not knowing that I was doing it, 'Next weekend is Mother's Day,' and what we were going to do. Still not even thinking of it until afterward Mama said, 'I couldn't believe you said that. If I'd been any closer I would have poked you hard with an elbow.'"

"Oh, no. What on earth did you do?"

"And then remembering. I near to died. I near to died, I tell you. And when I remembered how still he got when I said that and how he looked past us at the laurel bushes, why I near to died again of mortified shame and cried with it, I remember, two days, and then I began to feel—I had to do something—I began to feel he liked it. The chance to be dramatic. And that it made him special. He was special. To have to live with that."

"Well," Emma said, "we all have things we want to squeeze our eyes shut about. We are bound to. Don't they gang up on you sometimes—the mistakes you've made, so you want to crawl in a hole and cover yourself up? But you can't go back and make them right so after a while you just keep going, smoothing out the edges the best that you can."

"And then I kind of wonder," Margaret said, "if I didn't have to make that mistake. It really was a big thing to me at the time because I liked him. We had just met and all, but I could tell already I liked him.

"And I wondered, if I hadn't made that mistake and instead had been too careful of him, you know and not mentioned, like everybody else was not mentioning, why, if he'd have noticed me at all. I mean, what if he noticed me because of that stupid thoughtless thing I did, and because he could be dramatic, and it could hit me later, and he could forgive me?"

"I don't know about that," Emma said and took a drink of tea. "But there sure are things I never forgave Harold. Never. Even now. He took us all to family camp one year. And before that we were pretty close. All of us. In a family. He shouldn't have done that, though, taken us to camp so I learned they could do by themselves without me and I could do by myself, too."

Margaret held up a cracker, could see light through it, how it lightened at the prick marks and tightened at the wheat bits. Wesley was behind it.

"I wonder," Margaret said. "I've wondered for a long time if that was my mistake. Or if really the mistake was that I was sorry I had hurt him. And so I fell in love. To make up for it." When she moved the cracker, Wesley was behind it, and she pulled her fingers back so as not to touch him.

Wesley made a wide arc where the corner was too tight, and the lawn mower shot exploding bits of grass around him. Shatters of grass shot out like sparks, and Wesley turned the tractor.

"Yes," Margaret said. "Emma, there is one thing. There's something I would change." She threaded her needle. "When we were kids. Once we went to visit someone. The whole family went. She was called Jeannette, I remember, and when we got to her house, we walked to her neighbors' in the evening. Everything was dark and green and moist, the way it is on a summer evening near a stream. There was a stream there and wet stones."

The sound of the mower crossed the grass, and she counted the number of rows left.

"We sat outside, and the grown-ups talked, and I stood up behind the woman we were visiting and stroked her hair, brushed her hair with my fingers, and my mother said, 'Stop,' but the woman told me it was all right. Her hair was long and brown with gray hairs in it and later, when I asked my mother wasn't it pretty, she said no. But then she grew her own hair long and wore it long the rest of her life. You remember Mother's hair. Was long all down her back when she unrolled it."

"Oh," Emma said. "Your mother had wonderful hair. I always said she did." She looked at Margaret to see what it was she meant.

"I'm coming to the part I mean. I didn't come to it yet. On the walk home, well, back to Jeannette's house, we went past the stream again, but it was more like nightfall, and, down at the base of a tree there was a salamander. Jeannette saw it first—orange-coral colored, small, as if sticking to the wood, a brush stroke on the trunk of the tree—and I reached to touch it to see if it was real.

"Jeannette said, 'No, don't touch it,' but I already had. She said, 'His skin has to stay wet. If you touch him it will make it dry—just like burning him.'"

"Oh, I never heard that."

"Did you ever see a salamander?"

"No."

"That's why you never heard it. If you'd seen one, you'd know it would be true. And I wanted to not have touched it." Margaret looked up and thought it was a person coming up the lawn where the barbecue charcoal was in the chair, and then she saw it wasn't.

I WOULD PICK MORE DAISIES

Wesley made the last turn by the daylilies.

"So," Margaret said, "what I said about Wesley, about maybe it was a different mistake than the one I thought I'd made? Well, let's just leave it, shall we? As if I hadn't thought it?"

"What about the salamander?" Emma said. "What happened to it?"

"Oh, I don't know about that. It sped around the tree and by then I knew it was real."

Advice to Beginners
Ellen Kort

Begin. Keep on beginning. Nibble on everything.
Take a hike. Teach yourself to whistle. Lie.
The older you get the more they'll want your stories.
Make them up. Talk to stones. Short-out electric
fences. Swim with the sea turtle into the moon. Learn
how to die. Eat moonshine pie. Drink wild geranium
tea. Run naked in the rain. Everything that happens
will happen and none of us will be safe from it.
Pull up anchors. Sit close to the god of night.
Lie still in a stream and breathe water. Climb to the top
of the highest tree until you come to the branch
where the blue heron sleeps. Eat poems for breakfast.
Wear them on your forehead. Lick the mountain's
bare shoulder. Measure the color of days
around your mother's death. Put your hands
over your face and listen to what they tell you.

Contributors

DORI APPEL lives in Ashland, Oregon, where she is co-artistic director of Mixed Company theater and a clinical psychologist in private practice. She is the author of more than fifty published poems and stories, and seven produced plays, including "Girl Talk," co-authored with Carolyn Myers, which was published by Samuel French in 1992. §

KIRSTEN BACKSTROM teaches writing classes, makes sculptural baskets, works in bookstores, and does odd jobs to support herself, but writing is her primary commitment. She has written essays, reviews, stories, poetry, and four novels, often exploring lesbian themes. Most recently, her work has appeared in *Trivia* and *Hurricane Alice*. §

THERESE BECKER's poetry has appeared in numerous literary magazines and anthologies including *Contemporary Michigan Poetry: Poems From The Third Coast, The New York Quarterly, The Beloit Poetry Journal, Woman Poet—The Midwest,* and *Witness* magazine. She has an M.F.A. in creative writing from Warren Wilson College and conducts workshops on the creative process, throughout Michigan, with students in grades two through twelve. She is a member of the National Press Photographer's Association and her essays, photography, and journalism have appeared in all the major Detroit newspapers. §

CATHERINE BOYD, a resident of Santa Rosa, California, has had short stories published in *Ridge Review* and *The Stump*. Several of her feature articles have appeared in the Marin/Sonoma section of the *San Francisco Examiner*, one of the city's leading newspapers. §

DOROTHY HOWE BROOKS is a former data processing consultant who writes poetry and short fiction. Her work has appeared in *Slant, Dreams and Visions, RE Arts and Letters (REAL),* and *The Georgia Journal*. She lives in Atlanta with her husband and their two sons.

STEPHANY BROWN's work has appeared in *The Short Story Review* and in *Other Voices*. She lives in Flagstaff, Arizona, with her husband and three daughters.

LORI BURKHALTER-LACKEY was born and educated in Los Angeles, California, completing her photographic training at Otis/Parsons Art Institute. Her photography has been exhibited in many California galleries and has been featured in numerous Papier-Mache Press books, including *When I Am an Old Woman I Shall Wear Purple*. Lori lives in Los Angeles with her husband, David, and their three cats. §

GRACE BUTCHER has taught English for twenty-five years at the Geauga Campus of Kent State University in Burton, Ohio. She is a life-long runner, former U.S. half-mile champion and many times Masters age group champion. She is also a motorcyclist and former columnist for *Rider* magazine. Her newest book is *Child, House, World* (Hiram Poetry Review, 1991). §

ELEANOR BYERS lives in Coeur D'Alene, Idaho, where she is active in the local chapter of the Idaho Writers League. Her poetry has appeared in *Crab Creek Review, West/Word,* and *The Seattle Times/Post Intelligencer*. She has a B.S. degree from Washington State University and lived in northern Europe for fifteen years.

LIZABETH CARPENTER, raised at the confluence of the Iowa, South Dakota, and Nebraska river borders, received an M.F.A. in 1990 from the Iowa Writers Workshop. She has published work in *The Iowa Review* and in the 1992 Eve of Saint Agnes awards issue of *Negative Capability*.

ELLIN CARTER has retired from teaching and is free-lancing. Her poems have recently appeared in *Kalliope, The G. W. Review,* and *Earth's Daughters*; also in a chapbook, *What This Is And Why*, from Richmond Waters Press. §

JANET CARNCROSS CHANDLER, eighty-two, lives in a Sacramento retirement community. She is the mother of two, David and Dan, and the grandmother of two, William and Sasha. She holds an M.S.W. and was a social worker for thirty years. Now a poet for eighteen years, she has self-published three chapbooks and published *Flight of the Wild Goose* (Papier-Mache Press, 1989). Her newest book, *I Sing*, will be published by Papier-Mache Press in 1993. §

JOAN CONNOR has published more than forty stories in various anthologies and journals, including *Blueline, The Worcester Review, Re: Artes Liberales,* and *The Bridge*. She is currently working on her first novel begun on a fellowship at the MacDowell Colony.

MARIL CRABTREE lives in Kansas City, Missouri, where she weaves together a life as writer (of poetry, fiction, articles, and reviews), mediator (of domestic, interpersonal, and business conflicts), and happily married woman. Her work has appeared in *Daughters of Sarah, The Sun Magazine, Wildfire,* and other journals.

RUTH DAIGON is editor of *Poets On:*. Her latest book is *A Portable Past* (Realities Library Contemporary Poets Series, San Jose, 1987). Her poems appear in *Shenandoah, Poet Lore,* and *Kansas Quarterly*. She has published and performed her poetry in the U.S., Canada, England, and Israel and was a finalist in the Helicon Nine, Marianne Moore Poetry Contest. A professional singer, she was formerly a soprano with the New York Pro Musica, Columbia Recordings, CBS TV.

SUSAN EISENBERG is a Boston-based writer, union electrician, teacher, and activist, examining her choices. Author of the poetry book, *It's a Good Thing I'm Not Macho*, she directs the Tradeswomen Research and Education Project, gathering stories and wisdom from tradeswomen pioneers. §

SUE SANIEL ELKIND is a lifelong resident of Pittsburgh, Pennsylvania. She began writing at the age of 64 and has since published five collections—*No Longer Afraid* (Lintel, 1985), *Waiting for Order* (Naked Man Press, 1988), *Another Language* (Papier-Mache Press, 1988), *Dinosaurs and Grandparents* (MAF Press, 1988), and *Bare As the Trees* (Papier-Mache Press, 1992). She also founded and runs the Squirrel Hill Poetry Workshop in Pittsburgh. §

KAREN ETHELSDATTAR's poems and liturgies, including interfaith celebrations, affirm women and the feminine presence of God. She is co-founder of a women's ritual group, Eve's Well. Her poems have appeared in *Woman Spirit; Off Our Backs; New Women, New Church*; and in Starhawk's *The Spiral Dance*. Her name is taken to honor her mother.

MIDGE FARMER was raised in Denver and accidentally, through marriage, came "home" to Wyoming in 1959. She worked twenty-two years as a cattle rancher and now lives in Gillette where she is a house slave/writer. Her work has appeared in *Wordweavers, This Is Wyoming-Listen*, and the *Casper Arts Edition*.

RINA FERRARELLI is author of *Dreamsearch*, a chapbook of original poems (Malafemmina Press, 1992) and *Light Without Motion*, translations of poems by Giorgio Chiesura from the Italian (Owl Creek Press, 1989). She was awarded an NEA and the Italo Calvino Award. §

ALICE FRIMAN is a poet and a professor of English and creative writing at The University of Indianapolis. She has been published in journals such as *Poetry, Shenandoah, Prairie Schooner*, and *Poetry Northwest*. She is the author of five collections of poetry and the winner of the Consuelo Ford Award, 1988, and the Cecil Hemley Memorial Award, 1990, from The Poetry Society of America. Her new manuscript, *Inverted Fire*, is looking for a publisher.

MARIANNE GONTARZ is a social worker and a professional photographer, combining her work in such photography projects as the Boston Women's Health Collective *Ourselves Growing Older*. Her photographs illustrate a number of professional books and journals in the field of aging, including *A Consumer's Guide to Aging* (The Johns Hopkins University Press, 1992). She lives and works in Marin County, California. §

MAGGI ANN GRACE is a poet and fiction writer who holds an M.F.A. in Creative Writing from the University of North Carolina at Greensboro. She teaches writing to students of all ages, from public school children to women in domestic violence shelters. She lives in Durham, North Carolina, and is at work on her first novel.

NAN HUNT's explorations of dreams and other resources from the unconscious influence her poetry, essays, and fiction. She teaches in UCLA Extension's Writers' Program, lecturing widely on psychological approaches to creative processes. Her work appears in *Between Ourselves* (Houghton Mifflin), *Dreamworks, To Be A Woman* (Tarcher), and *Psychological Perspectives*.

RUTH HARRIET JACOBS, Ph.D., a sociologist and gerontologist at the Wellesley College Center for Research on Women, Wellesley, Massachusetts, authored *Be An Outrageous Older Woman* and *We Speak for Peach: An Anthology* (K.I.T. Press). Family Service America published her leaders' manual, *Older Women Surviving and Thriving*. §

TERRI L. JEWELL is a Black lesbian feminist poet/writer living in Lansing, Michigan. Her book *The Black Woman's GUMBO YA-YA: Quotations and Other Words* will be published by The Crossing Press in late 1993. Her work can be found in *African American Review, Sinister Wisdom, The Black Scholar*, and several other feminist anthologies. §

MARTHA B. JORDAN was born and raised in Mexico City. She is a founder of the multicultural Tramonane Poetry Group. Her translations and poetry have appeared in journals such as *Revista RyD* and *Manoa*. In 1987, she received the Henry M. Austin Award for Poetry from St. John's College (Annapolis/Santa Fe).

LINDA KEEGAN writes from McMurray, Pennsylvania. Originally from New Hampshire, she has worked as a journalist and paramedic. She is primarily a poet and her first chapbook, *Greedy for Sunlight*, will be published in the fall of 1992.

JUDE KEITH has been working in photography since 1978. She believes that you do not "take" pictures, but "make" them with the cooperation of light, the elements, and the subjects. Potentially the most literal art form, photography is inherently manipulation—casting a peephole for others into a world made of light, full of depth and shadows.

ALISON KOLODINSKY lives in Ormond Beach, Florida, and is a recipient of an Individual Artist Fellowship from the Florida Arts Council. She has a masters degree in clinical psychology but recently closed her private practice in order to write full time. Her work has appeared in *Poetry, Kansas Quarterly, Kalliope, JAMA*, and other publications.

ELLEN KORT, a free-lance writer, poet, and playwright from Appleton, Wisconsin, has garnered several awards for her work including Nimrod's Ruth G. Hardman/Pablo Neruda Prize For Poetry, co-sponsored by the Arts/Humanities Council of Tulsa, Oklahoma. Ellen has traveled the U.S., Australia, New Zealand, and the Bahamas to present poetry readings, Discovery Writing, Inner Awareness, and Mask-Making workshops.

LYNN KOZMA, a retired registered nurse, served in World War II. She is the author of one book of poetry, *Catching the Light* (Pocahontas Press, 1989). She has been published often by *Midwest Poetry Review, Bitterroot, Long Island Quarterly*, and *The Lyric*. She is an avid reader, gardener, and birder. A continuing student at Suffolk Community College, she is a member of Poets & Writers, Inc. §

JENNIFER LAGIER is a political activist working with the Regional Alliance for Progressive Policy. Her publication credits include *When I Am an Old Woman I Shall Wear Purple; The Dream Book: An Anthology of Writings by Italian-American Women; College English;* and *La Bella Figura*, among others. §

TRICIA LANDE is a native Californian, born in San Pedro and raised in Torrance. She has a masters degree in experimental psychology and a minor in Asian-American studies. Her short story, "Better Man," was just released in the anthology *A Loving Voice*. She is the 1992 recipient of the Marc A. Klein Playwright Award.

JANICE LEVY lives with her husband and two children in Merrick, New York. Her work has appeared in the anthologies, *Lovers* and *The Time of Our Lives*; literary magazines such as *The Sun*, *Prism International*, and *Buffalo Spree*; and several children's publications. She is the recipient of the *Painted Hills Review 1992* First Place Fiction Award.

BARBARA LUCAS is an associate professor of English at Nassau Community College, editor of *Xanadu*, and director of the Poetry Society of America on Long Island. Her work has appeared in *Beloit Poetry Journal*, *Kansas Quarterly*, *Birmingham Review*, *Slant*, and other journals.

DORIS VANDERLIPP MANLEY wrote "Good Intentions" during her years of being Superwoman. All the while, she could see the daisy field far off in the distance. Now retired, she lives happily in her little house—picking daisies as often as she wants to. §

JOANNE MCCARTHY's poetry appears in little magazines and anthologies, and in her collection *Shadowlight* (Broken Moon Press). She has published articles in *American Women Writers* and other reference works, and teaches English and creative writing at Tacoma Community College. In 1984 she spent a year in Germany on a Fulbright exchange.

SHIRLEY VOGLER MEISTER, an Indianapolis free-lance writer, has had columns, features, reviews, and poetry accepted by diverse U.S. and Canadian markets. She has earned awards for poetry, literary criticism, and journalism. Her poem, "The Coming of Winter," appeared in *When I Am an Old Woman I Shall Wear Purple*. §

ANN MENEBROKER was born in Washington, D.C., and has lived in Sacramento for forty years. She is an assistant at an art gallery and on the board of the Sacramento Poetry Center. Her most recently published collections include *Routines That Will Kill You* (BOGG Press, 1990) and *Mailbox Boogie, A Dialogue Through The Mails* (Zerx Press, 1991), with Kell Robertson.

BONNIE MICHAEL is a free-lance writer and poet living in Winston-Salem, North Carolina. She has published in major magazines, literary journals, and ten anthologies. She enjoys writing about women's and spiritual issues and travel, and reading for public radio. In her next life she plans to be a dancer. §

LILLIAN MORRISON is the author of seven collections of her own poems, most recently *Whistling the Morning In*; three anthologies of poems on sports and rhythm; and six collections of folk rhymes for children. Recent poems appear in *Aethlon, Light, Poets On*, and various anthologies. §

LESLÉA NEWMAN is the author of twelve books for adults and children including a novel, *In Every Laugh A Tear*; a poetry collection, *Sweet Dark Places*; and a book of short stories, *A Letter to Harvey Milk*. In 1989, she was awarded the prestigious Massachusetts Artists Fellowship in Poetry. §

LESLIE NYMAN, a resident of western Massachusetts, has been working as a registered nurse for fifteen years. She has been published in professional literature and is a member of her Health Maintenance Organization's ethics committee. She has been writing short fiction since obtaining a B.A. in English more than twenty years ago.

GAILMARIE PAHMEIER teaches creative writing and literature at the University of Nevada. She twice received a Nevada State Council on the Arts fellowship in literature, most recently for 1992-1993. She has published widely, and a collection of her work, *With Respect for Distance*, is forthcoming from Black Rock Press.

NITA PENFOLD struggles to write while filling her "empty nest" with deferred dreams. Her poetry has appeared in the anthologies *Cries of the Spirit* (Beacon Press), *Catholic Girls* (Penguin Books), and in over forty small press magazines including *Earth's Daughters* and the *Maryland Review*.

FRAN PORTLEY majored in English Honors at Duke University. She teaches poetry to children in the New Jersey JOY (joining old and young) program. Her poems have appeared in *When I Am an Old Woman I Shall Wear Purple, Parting Gifts, Heartland, Stone Country*, and many other publications. §

JACKLYN W. POTTER has published work in journals such as *Stone Country Journal* and *The Washington Review*, and will be in a forthcoming anthology of *Poets on the Air*, WPFW-FM radio. She directs the Miller Cabin Poetry Series and is president of The Poetry Committee of Greater Washington, D.C. Area. She teaches creative writing in College Park, Maryland. §

SANDRA REDDING, at fifty, received an M.F.A. in Creative Writing from the University of North Carolina-Greensboro. She now teaches creative writing courses at Guilford Technical Community College and at the Presbyterian Home in High Point, North Carolina. Short story publications in 1992 include *Crucible* and *The Nightshade Short Story Reader*. §

ELISAVIETTA RITCHIE's *Flying Time: Stories & Half-Stories* includes four PEN Syndicated Fiction Project winners. *Tightening The Circle Over Eel Country* won the 1975-76 Great Lakes Colleges Association's "New Writer's Prize for Best First Book of Poetry," and *Raking The Snow* won the 1981 Washington Writer's Publishing House competition. Editor of *The Dolphin's Arc: Poems on Endangered Creatures of the Sea* and other books, she has read at the Library of Congress and many other venues in the U.S., Brazil, the Far East, the Balkans, and Canada. She lives in Washington, D.C. and Toronto. §

ELAINE ROTHMAN moved to rural Connecticut after twenty years of teaching and counseling in urban and suburban schools. She learned about her new community through writing feature stories for local newspapers. Five years and two hundred articles later, she left journalism for a writers' course at the University of Iowa's Elderhostel program, and has written fiction ever since.

LORI RUSSELL is a free-lance writer and part-time home health nurse. Her short stories and poetry have appeared in *Milvia Street* and *Fire Folio*. A twenty-eight-year resident of the San Francisco Bay Area, Lori and her husband have recently relocated to The Dalles, Oregon.

PAT SCHNEIDER has published poetry, fiction, plays, and libretti. She is founder/director of Amherst Writers & Artists and AWA Press. *The Writer Alone & With Others* (working title) is forthcoming from Lowell House; *Tell Me Something I Can't Forget* is available from four-time Academy Award nominee Florentine Films.

DEIDRE SCHERER, a Williamsville, Vermont, artist, "paints" with fabric and thread, using unusual cutting, layering, and machine stitching techniques to achieve illusionistic effects. Her images of the elderly have traveled internationally and are featured on the covers of *If I Had My Life to Live Over I Would Pick More Daisies*, *Another Language*, and *Learning to Sit in the Silence: A Journal of Caretaking* (Papier-Mache Press). In 1993 she received a Vermont Council on the Arts Fellowship Award. §

CAROL SCHWALBERG is a hyphenate (author-journalist-critic-photographer-editor-university lecturer) whose short stories have appeared in *Ita* and *Fair Lady* and whose poems have run in *West* and *Black River Review*. She is neutral on the subject of cauliflower.

JAN EPTON SEALE is a native Texan. She is the author of two books of poetry and a new collection of short stories, *Airlift* (T.C.U. Press). Seven of her stories have appeared in the PEN Syndicated Fiction Project.

BETTIE M. SELLERS is a Goolsby Professor of English at Young Harris College, Georgia. She is the author of several collections of poems—*Spring Onions and Cornbread*, *Liza's Monday, Morning of the Red-Tailed Hawk*, and *Wild Ginger*—and has produced a documentary film, *The Bitter Berry: The Life and Works of Byron Herbert Reece* (1988 Georgia Emmy). In 1992 she wrote a resource manual, *The Bitter Berry*. §

JOANNE SELTZER has published hundreds of poems in literary magazines, newspapers, and anthologies, including *When I Am an Old Woman I Shall Wear Purple*, *The Tie That Binds*, and *If I Had a Hammer*. She has also published short fiction, non-fiction prose, translations of French poetry, and three poetry chapbooks. §

ENID SHOMER's award-winning stories and poems have appeared in *The New Yorker*, *The Paris Review*, and other journals. Her new books are *This Close to the Earth: Poems* (University of Arkansas Press, 1992) and *Imaginary Men*, a book of stories which won the Iowa Short Fiction Award and will appear in 1993. §

LINDA WASMER SMITH, a free-lance medical journalist, grew up on an Arkansas farm. She now lives in Albuquerque, New Mexico, with her husband and their two children. Her poetry has appeared recently in many literary magazines, including *Plains Poetry Journal* and *Light*. Her more than four hundred articles on health and medicine have been published in numerous national periodicals, including *American Health* and *Outdoor Life*.

NADINE STAIR is attributed with writing "If I Had My Life to Live Over I Would Pick More Daisies" at the age of eighty-five. She is believed to have been living in Kentucky at that time. Papier-Mache Press has been unable to contact a living relative to learn more about her poetry.

RANDEANE TETU has received several national awards for fiction. "Depth of Field" is listed in *The Best American Short Stories, 1989*. Her work has appeared in many magazines and anthologies, including the 1991 American Booksellers Association Honors Book, *When I Am an Old Woman I Shall Wear Purple* (Papier-Mache Press, 1987). §

BARBARA L. THOMAS began writing poetry after turning sixty. She has been published in *Raven's Chronicles*, *Upstream*, *Spindrift*, *Chrysanthemum*, and other journals. A long-distance swimmer in the cold, Pacific Northwest waters, she is a daughter of living parents born in the nineteenth century, a Shawnee granddaughter, a calligrapher, and a member of a small performance group, The Avalanche Poets. §

ANNA TOMCZAK has an M.F.A. in Fine Art Photography from the University of Florida. She has received numerous grants and awards, including an NEA/SECCA Southeast Seven Artist Fellowship and an Atlantic Center for the Arts Cultural Exchange Fellowship to La Napoule Art Foundation, France. Her work has been exhibited internationally in galleries and museums and is represented in several private, corporate, and museum collections.

CLAUDIA VAN GERVEN lives in Boulder, Colorado, where she has taught writing classes for the past fifteen years. She has been published in many magazines including *Prairie Schooner*, *Calyx*, and *Frontiers*. Her work will be appearing in three forthcoming anthologies.

SUSAN VREELAND received First Place in Short Fiction in the 1991 California Writers' Roundtable sponsored by the Women's National Book Association. Her short stories appeared in *Crosscurrents* and *Ambergris*, and her travel writing appeared in *Travel and Leisure* and *Los Angeles Times*. She is working on a novel about Canadian artist Emily Carr.

KENNETTE H. WILKES is an individual artist on the Alabama State Council on the Arts with an M.A. in creative studies. She has had reviews, interviews, and a novel excerpt published. Her poetry has been published in *Nimrod*, *Negative Capability*, *Green Fuse*, and the *Journal of Poetry Therapy*. First prize winner of the Oklahoma Collegiate Poet and Alabama State literary competitions in essay, one-act play, and contemporary poem. She currently has a trilogy of historical novels in progress.

§ Denotes contributors whose work has appeared in previous Papier-Mache Press anthologies.

Papier-Mache Press

At Papier-Mache Press, it is our goal to identify and successfully present important social issues through enduring works of beauty, grace, and strength. Through our work we hope to encourage empathy and respect among diverse communities, creating a bridge of understanding between the mainstream audience and those who might not otherwise be heard.

We appreciate you, our customer, and strive to earn your continued support. We also value the role of the bookseller in achieving our goals. We are especially grateful to the many independent booksellers whose presence ensures a continuing diversity of opinion, information, and literature in our communities. We encourage you to support these bookstores with your patronage.

We publish many fine books about women's experiences. We also produce lovely posters and T-shirts that complement our anthologies. Please ask your local bookstore which Papier-Mache items they carry. To receive our complete catalog, send your request to Papier-Mache Press, 135 Aviation Way, #14, Watsonville, CA 95076, or call our toll-free number, 800-927-5913.

"All of the stories and poems are accessible in the best sense of the word, and the photographs of individually aging women are powerful, and uncompromisingly beautiful in their austerity. There is no airbrushing here, no cosmetic layering like premature mortuary work; these faces are age itself, looking life full in the face."
—*Ms.*

"...wonderful inclusions, by unknown as well as better-known writers....I recommend this book because so little attention is given to work from, out of, and about women aging."
—*Belles-Lettres*

"...both touching and humorous and not to be missed."
—*Parentguide News*

"After reading it not once, but twice, before I put it away, I think that I shall go visit my mother and my grandmothers, *listen* to their wisdom and take them some flowers. And maybe, even now, I shall begin to wear purple."
—*The Daily Messenger* (TN)

"'Purple' mixes poems, anecdotes, sketches and pictures by older women that reveal their wisdom, humor, courage and reaction to personal losses. I reread portions...for the joyousness...and to understand the anguish and frustrations...No stereotypes here."
—*San Francisco Examiner*

"The writings and photographs that make up this delightful collection evoke the beauty, humor, and courage of women living in their later years and tell of the endearing moments of joy, and passion, to be found in the rich and varied world of midlife and beyond....wonderful."
—*Wetumpka Herald*

"The book is intense. It touched me, made me laugh and cry, and most of all, it made me think....The book is a gift and for sharing. I loved this book and recommend it to both young and old."
—*North Wind Network*

"Through prose and poetry, this poignant and sometimes humorous anthology speaks simply and profoundly to the problems that aging creates for women in a shallow, youth-obsessed culture. . . . Accompanied by dazzling and thought-provoking photographs of women of various ethnicities and social strata, this collection confronts the issues of aging and poverty for women in our society."
—*Whole Life Times*

"It is a touching, tender collection of writings about being old, and loving the old. The emotional impact in totality is tremendous. The quality of the writing has earned the collection, edited by Sandra Martz, the American Booksellers 1991 Honors Award."
—*Tri-City Herald*

"It is easy to see why this book has been taken to heart so eagerly by women all over America. . . . this book is a real gem."
—*The Bulletin* (WI)

". . .the book is a wonderful paean to old women, aging women and the women who care for them."
—*Indianapolis Star*

". . .a valuable anthology. It paints a rich picture of women as they age. . . It also shows that we're not alone, that women in a wide variety of circumstances have found unique ways of challenging the years' passing. . . . An especially thoughtful touch: the clear, large print, a relief for older readers."
—*Owl Observer*

"Poignant reflections, biting images and evocative black and white photos of aging women fill the pages in this unique anthology. In 60 quite different short stories and poems, the authors reaffirm the individuality of 'old women.'. . .these writings should teach readers old and young."
—*American Library Association Booklist*

When I Am an
Old Woman
I Shall Wear Purple

Edited by Sandra Haldeman Martz

Papier-Mache Press
Watsonville, CA

Copyright © 1987 Papier-Mache Press. Printed in the United States of America. All rights reserved including the right to reproduce this book or portions thereof in any form.

Foreword copyright © 1991 by Jenny Joseph
Afterword copyright © 1991 by Papier-Mache Press

04 03 02 01 00 99 98 97   47

Second edition
ISBN: 0-918949-15-7 Hardcover
ISBN: 0-918949-16-5 Paperback
Editor: Sandra Haldeman Martz
Cover Art: Deidre Scherer, "Laughing Rose," fabric and thread, copyright © 1985, from the collection of Mr. and Mrs. Stanley Feldberg.
Design: Lane Relyea
Typography: Deborah Karas
Editorial Assistance: Lee Rathbone and Roberta Shepherd
Copyediting: Bobbie Goodwin
Grateful acknowledgment for permission to reprint is made as follows: *Appalachian Heritage* for "Near Places, Far Places" by Sarah Barnhill; *Footwork* for "Aunt Marie at 99" by Tom Benediktsson; *Lion Tamer* (Waterford Press, © 1987 by Lillian Morrison) for "The Thugs" by Mura Dehn; *Kalliope, Dekalb Literary Journal,* and *Waiting for Order* for "Come to Me" by Sue Saniel Elkind; *Odessa Poetry Review* for "Late Autumn Woods" by Rina Ferrarelli; *New Mexico Quarterly* for "To an Old Woman" © 1986 by Rafael Jesús González; *Day Tonight Night Today #16* for "The Pianist" by Carolyn J. Fairweather Hughes; *Friendly Women* for "Becoming Sixty" by Ruth Harriet Jacobs and *Button, Button, Who Has the Button* for "Bag Ladies" © 1983 by Ruth Harriet Jacobs; *The Red Bluff, CA, Daily News* for "Investment of Worth" by Terri L. Jewell; *Rose in the Afternoon* (J.M. Dent and Sons) for "Warning" © 1974 by Jenny Joseph; *Fiction West* for "The Changes" © 1981 by Fionna Perkins; *The Problem with Eden* (Armstrong State College Press) for "Clearing the Path" © 1985 by Elisavietta Ritchie; *Artemis* for "Dear Paul Newman" by Marie Kennedy Robins; *Ellipsis* for "Sitty Victoria" by Vicki Salloum; *Morning of the Red-Tailed Hawk* (Green River Press) for "A Letter from Elvira" © 1981 by Bettie Sellers; *Full Moon* for "Last Visit to Grandmother" by Enid Shomer; *Ask the Dreamer Where Night Begins* for "Post Humus" by Patti Tana, © 1986 Kendall/Hunt Publishing Company; *Loonfeather* for "Oh, That Shoestore Used to Be Mine" © 1986 by Randeane Doolittle Tetu. Additional copyrights: "Like Mother, Like Daughter" © 1986 by Susan S. Jacobson and "Two Willow Chairs" © 1985 by Jess Wells.
Hardcover edition catalogued as follows:
Library of Congress Cataloging-in-Publication Data

    When I am an old woman I shall wear purple: an anthology of short stories and poetry / edited by Sandra Haldeman Martz. — 2nd ed.
       p. cm.
    ISBN 0-918949-15-7 : $16.00
    1. Women—Literary collections. 2. Aging—Literary collections. 3. Aged women—Literary collections. 4. Aged, Writings of the, American. 5. American literature—20th century. I. Haldeman Martz, Sandra.
PS509.W6W47   1991   91-13828
810.8 ′0352042—dc20   CIP

To my Grandmother, Mildred Anna Archer, who gave me hope, and to my Mother, Lula Jo Gregory, who gave me wisdom.

Sandra Haldeman Martz
Editor

Contents

1 Warning
Jenny Joseph

2 Sitty Victoria
Vicki Salloum

12 Grandma Sits Down
Rick Kempa

13 Aunt Marie at 99
Tom Benediktsson

14 Here, Take My Words
Karen Brodine

18 The Trouble Was Meals
Elizabeth Bennett

20 Like Mother, Like Daughter
Susan S. Jacobson

23 Near Places, Far Places
Sarah Barnhill

38 The Changes
Fionna Perkins

55 For My Mother
Michele Wolf

56 A Place for Mother
Joanne Seltzer

66 Birthday Portrait in Muted Tones
Dori Appel

67 Old Woman
Billie Lou Cantwell

68 A Woman at Forty
Enid Shomer

71 New Directions
Susan A. Katz

72	Late Autumn Woods	*Rina Ferrarelli*
73	Athlete Growing Old	*Grace Butcher*
74	Body	*Lillian Morrison*
75	I Know the Mirrors	*Janice Townley Moore*
76	Investment of Worth	*Terri L. Jewell*
79	Gracefully Afraid	*Mary Anne Ashley*
89	words never spoken	*Doris Vanderlipp Manley*
90	Clearing the Path	*Elisavietta Ritchie*
91	Dear Paul Newman	*Marie Kennedy Robins*
92	Reaching toward Beauty	*Hyacinthe Hill*
93	Love at Fifty	*Marcia Woodruff*
94	A Letter from Elvira	*Bettie Sellers*
95	Tin of Tube Rose	*Sandra Redding*
103	Survived by His Wife	*Margaret Flanagan Eicher*
104	Making the Wine	*Marisa Labozzetta*

113 Come to Me
Sue Saniel Elkind

114 Two Willow Chairs
Jess Wells

122 Planting
Cinda Thompson

123 Maybe at Eighty?
S. Minanel

124 Endurance
Fran Portley

125 Becoming Sixty
Ruth Harriet Jacobs

127 Social Security
Barbara Bolz

128 Litany for a Neighbor
Ellin Carter

129 The Wildcat
Catherine Boyd

132 Out of the Lion's Belly
Carole L. Glickfeld

147 Hurricane
Edna J. Guttag

148 Oh, That Shoe Store Used to Be Mine
Randeane Doolittle Tetu

151 Tending the Flock
Jennifer Lagier

153 Livvy Caldwell
Barbara Nector Davis

154 Translations
Margaret H. Carson

156   To an Old Woman
Rafael Jesús González

157   The Pianist
Carolyn J. Fairweather Hughes

158   Occupation
Bonnie Michael

159   All the Time
Michael Andrews

163   Bag Ladies in L.A.
Savina A. Roxas

164   glory
Charlotte Watson Sherman

166   Old Women
Barbara Lau

167   Bag Ladies
Ruth Harriet Jacobs

169   Endings
Lynn Kozma

170   Last Visit to Grandmother
Enid Shomer

172   Words for Alice after Her Death
Angela Peckenpaugh

176   The Thugs
Mura Dehn

177   The Coming of Winter
Shirley Vogler Meister

178   Post Humus
Patti Tana

181   Life's Rainbow
Sheila Banani

Foreword

The pleasure I get from reading or hearing poems is partly the gratifying of my appetite for stories. A writer, of poems, of fiction, of "nonfiction," is telling something, telling a tale, spinning a spiel. It may be an obvious narrative, the use of the first person suggesting a personal account through the immediacy of a human voice, a person there in the poem talking to you (Whitman's "I was the man. I suffered. I was there" in "Leaves of Grass"); or an "informative," "scientific" report on, say, snow (I write this deep in the snows of a Minnesota winter far away from the home of Papier-Mache Press in California where this beautifully produced volume is published).

We want to know how the world works; we want to hear what happens next, even if the happening is only the next step in a person's thinking. Because I acknowledge our insatiable appetite for stories, I have agreed to try and tell readers of this book the story behind the story of one of the poems in it. I am sure behind each of the varied writings here, there are other stories their authors could tell, but "Warning," the poem of mine whose first line affords this anthology its title, has been published in many formats around the world and there has been a lot of correspondence about it. I am often asked how I came to write it. Well, of course, as all written art must, it came from the raw life outside language: it came from years of idling, of walking round towns looking at the streets and people in them and wondering what they were really thinking; it came from sitting on benches in parks with nothing to do and noticing the inhabitants, listening to people talking to themselves or others on the tops of buses. It also came, I suppose, from two conflicting strands in my upbringing (the conflicting strands are the fruitful ones although uncomfortable at the time): the long attempt by elders to get the child to become a clean, competent, acceptable member of society—someone not a failure, someone not smelly, not a slut; and the inculcation of charitable attitudes that said you don't show distaste for the dirty, the shabby; you pretend not to notice the smell, you do not judge people by appearances, you do not mock the unfortunate. However (and the ball bounces back once again across the fence), you must make sure that you are not a laughingstock, too noticeable, a show-off, and above all, you mustn't be "silly" (never defined but instantly recognized).

It sometimes seems to me that the burden of keeping society going falls on the people in the middle, and that they get little thanks for it. "Warning" has a middle-aged woman, the sort who carries out these responsibilities, indulging in a fantasy of being a different person. I wrote the poem more than thirty years ago. I wasn't middle-aged and I had no children and of course when I wrote it none of the foregoing considerations were in my mind. All that was in my mind really were the words, like the tune on your brain you are trying to catch. Poems, including this one, as well as coming from the life beyond language, come from the life of language, so the rhythms of past poems, the forms of other writings contribute to the particular new rearrangement. "Warning" is one of many character-poems in a body of work written over thirty-five years where the person's story is told through his or her own voice. More than the others, though, it seems to have jumped off the page into people's affections and become for readers an active bit of their own real life again.

That gabby old woman, who is only the figment of imagination of a rather dull but reliable figment of the imagination, has also grabbed me, will-I, nil-I, by the hand and taken me with her into houses, minds, hearts I could not have found my way into on my own. I must admit to finding her a bit of a bore, going on so, after all these years so no one else can get a look in, and so I am very pleased that *The Inland Sea*, a selection of my poems, has also been published by Papier-Mache Press and is available in America, England, and Canada. We had to keep her out of that or none of the other voices would have been heard.

Plainly I am not going to be able to disown her now, for in her bold and generous way she has pushed me into some extraordinary adventures and chances, and for that I am duty-bound to be grateful to her. And how that happened is another, and really interesting, story.

January 1991, USA, Jenny Joseph

When I Am an
Old Woman
I Shall Wear Purple

Warning
Jenny Joseph

When I am an old woman I shall wear purple
With a red hat which doesn't go, and doesn't suit me.
And I shall spend my pension on brandy and summer gloves
And satin sandals, and say we've no money for butter.
I shall sit down on the pavement when I'm tired
And gobble up samples in shops and press alarm bells
And run my stick along the public railings
And make up for the sobriety of my youth.
I shall go out in my slippers in the rain
And pick the flowers in other people's gardens
And learn to spit.

You can wear terrible shirts and grow more fat
And eat three pounds of sausages at a go
Or only bread and pickle for a week
And hoard pens and pencils and beermats and things in boxes.

But now we must have clothes that keep us dry
And pay our rent and not swear in the street
And set a good example for the children.
We must have friends to dinner and read the papers.

But maybe I ought to practise a little now?
So people who know me are not too shocked and surprised
When suddenly I am old, and start to wear purple.

Photo by Lyn Cowan

Sitty Victoria
Vicki Salloum

"Aunt Alma," I asked yesterday, "why you sticking Sitty in the 'tomb'?"

She got angry. "It ain't the 'tomb.' It's The Asylum for the Aged."

"Then why you sticking Sitty in The Asylum for the Aged?"

"Victoria, I'm over eighty. I can't care for her no more. And what with you gone..."

I could see Aunt Alma crying and I really got scared because I knew then she was serious. "I'm not going!" I said. "I'm staying here with her! I can stay and care for her!"

"Young lady!" she said. "You got to get an education. That's what Mama always wanted, what Papa would have wanted. You just go and pack your things. You'll miss that plane tomorrow morning."

I put my hands down on my hips.

"Aunt Alma," I said, "the woman raised eleven kids, raised you and Uncle Youssef, raised me all those years after Mama and Daddy died, and now she has nobody else you want to stick her in the 'tomb'?

"Aunt Alma," I said, "what the hell's wrong with you?"

And then she slapped me in the face, and I didn't know what else to do so I went and sat with Sitty.

It's light. I sneak a peek from Sitty's bedroom door. She rises from the bed, bracing herself with blotched and shriveled arms. She sits in a giltwood armchair putting on her stockings, guiding an elastic garter up her swollen leg.

I walk through the back porch into the kitchen. Over the sink, through the open window, I see the morning come. A strange September morning. A loon in the air. The sky has taken on an eerie glow. I put on a pot of coffee, crack some eggs. Beyond the kitchen window an unusual morning wind turns suddenly wild, hurling leaves across the Summervilles' patio and against the side of their garage.

"*Sabah alkheir,* Sitty Victoria."

I bring her eggs to the porch. Sitty's sitting on the green sofa where she always sits. *"Ana bahibbik,* darlin'. *Inshallah nimti mnih."* She's always teaching me Arabic words, things like *Allah maik* and *Allah yakun*—"God be with you," "God go with you."

I catch the leg of a TV tray, slide it in front of her. I sit the breakfast tray down. Try to hand her an Arabic paper but she doesn't see me.

"Sitty," I'm on my knees, my face square in hers, "there's something I got to tell you, darlin'."

I touch her hand. It's cold. She's watching the wind bend the branches of a live oak next door. It's no use. I sit down, my arm touching hers, think about being stuck on that jet tomorrow. Think about a lot of things. How I've never been without her. How when I was a little girl, we'd pass the gardenia bushes by the Girl Scout hut at the Aurelia Street park where she'd take me swinging on clear April mornings and I could smell eternity. I swear I don't believe I'll ever see her again. She'll die in that place.

Uncle Youssef said her hair was raven black. Now it's white, streaked with yellow, pulled back in a bun at the nape of her neck. Aunt said she was tall, statuesque in her prime. We talked about it when I was pestering her once. We were chopping up parsley and tomatoes for *tabbouleh.*

"She left Beirut by herself, Victoria. Marry your Jiddy in the cathedral in New Orleans. They was peddlers over there half starving living over Mandot's Bakery on Chartres Street."

Aunt went to the cupboard, fetched a wooden bowl. "I was

sixteen when she told Papa we was moving here: 'Najeeb, we ain't gonna be peddling pans no more.'

"Sure 'nough, he loaded the wagon, put ten kids in it, with your Daddy, Victoria, still full in her stomach, and you'd a thought we was crossing a continent with how excited we all was at five in the morning heading for our new home on the Mississippi Coast."

Aunt slid the tomatoes in the bowl, started chopping more. Her hands never ceased. "I don't know how she done everything—got us the big house and that building on Pass Road that was our dry goods store. Papa tease her, call her a little immigrant girl with *kibbi nayyi* on her fingers and a brain bigger 'n his, bigger 'n most. After the jump, she built a town for him."

I look at her now, all hunched, shriveled, think how time always changes things. I raise my cup, sip lukewarm coffee, and try to think how old she is. Aunt said 104; Uncle Youssef, 108. Nobody alive knows. I glance outside, feel the ruckus in the air, hear the sky belting out angry screams. Strips of old newspaper and hot dog wrappers go flying over the Summervilles' fence and into our yard, but Sitty only sits, her hands in her lap, her brow furrowed, her head bowed. *Ya haram,* poor thing. She never does a thing but sit out here.

Once she tried to plant pecan trees way in the back near old lady Miller's but Aunt pitched a fit and brought her back inside. That's the next to last time she ever left this house. The last was when they caught her walking to the big house in that storm. She really missed the big house. Mayor Falk was cruising the beachfront highway when he saw her. He put her in his car and lectured her proper and deposited her safely at Aunt Alma's door. Now she won't do a thing but sit out here and think old thoughts, relive old memories. I wonder if she's thinking about what Jiddy did?

Aunt told me about it. She said, "Trouble has a way of sneaking up on you. It come for Mama at closing time." Sitty was closing out the register when the deputies came. Old Sheriff Elmo

Cobb's deputies. They took her up to the dingy roof of the Elnora Hotel. Took Daddy and Aunt Alma and Uncle Youssef up, too.

"But why, Aunt Alma? Why'd y'all all go up there?"

"Cuz," she said, "that's where Papa was. Victoria, I'm trying to tell you. Your Granddaddy—your Jiddy—he done killed himself."

Aunt Alma said she'd never forget that night—it was 1928 or '29 or something—or forget her Papa falling those fifteen stories from the dingy roof of the Elnora. Or forget her Mama standing there, her eyes all over him, as was the whole Pass Christian High basketball crowd that jammed Morey's Ice Cream Parlor across the street from the Elnora following the biggest game of the season, the game Pass Christian won against Biloxi High, whopped the socks off them in their first time playing each other since five years before when they had that big free-for-all in the Biloxi gym. And all eyes on her Papa, stunned and terrible, but none so terrible as her Mama's eyes.

"Why, Aunt Alma? Why'd Jiddy kill himself? Eleven kids, a dry goods store, a woman fine as Sitty. Why'd he want to die for?"

"Papa borrowed a lot of money to put in the stock market."

She said Sitty tried her best to talk Jiddy down, said she never gave up on him, never stopped talking to him in that voice of hers that makes you believe you can do anything, going on about how the children needed him, with all the need stuck in her eyes, and how important a man he was to her and how she'd always believed in him, after thirty-three years never would stop believing in him, how he wasn't to blame for what was done, he was only trying to help the family out. "We love you for that, my darling Najeeb, love you for what you tried to do for us; we're in God's hands now, Najeeb; God will see us through all this; God will take care of us, now, Najeeb; please come home with me now, Najeeb; oh please, dear God, come home with me. . ." And, afterward, Sheriff Cobb's deputies had to take them home.

I collect the breakfast tray, bring it to the kitchen. It's still early

morning but the sky is turning dark. I dump cold grits in the garbage pail, think about the thousand things I got to do before I leave. Through the open window, the wind's howling. Aunt's old teapot's in pieces in the sink. I go to the hall closet, take down the transistor radio. Early storm warnings are saying a hurricane's headed our way. I phone Aunt Alma, who's off visiting cousin Flora, then Uncle Youssef in case he doesn't know. He says he's come back from taking his lugger, The Jezebel, from the Gulf of Mexico harbor to the Back Bay of Biloxi. He says I should get moving, too, board the windows with plywood, fill the tub with water, help out around here.

But I go back to the porch and settle down beside Sitty, recall Aunt Alma's words on the only day she ever felt like talking about the subject. She said, "Mama never took the easy way out." She said after that terrible night, Sitty worked like a dog paying back Jiddy's creditors, though the menfolk advised her not to do that, to file for bankruptcy instead, because how could she expect to run that store and raise eleven kids and pay his debts all in a depression. But Aunt said Sitty never paid those men a mind. "Bankruptcy's a disgrace," she told those men, "and I'll never disgrace Najeeb's good name."

I look at her now, see how fragile she is, so worn and decrepit you'd think her flesh would dry up and crumble to the floor so there'd be nothing left but piles of flesh and bone to take a broom to. I take her hand; what does it matter anymore. Jiddy's gone. Mansour, her eldest, died right after him. Daddy, the one she loved so much, gone. Naome and Fayad, killed with their friends playing chicken with a freight train. And all the rest of them taken by sickness, except Aunt and Uncle Youssef.

I hold up my palm. Flit it past her face, feel the grief like a thousand needles.

"Sitty, darlin'," I can't stand it any longer. "I'm leaving for St. Mary's College on Monday."

I listen for a sound, some encouragement to go on, then steel myself against this onslaught of silence.

"And...darlin'...," I say, "Aunt can't keep you anymore. She's found a nice...home...for you..."

Her muzzy gaze settles on a spot somewhere in her lap.

"I'm going to write you every day. I promise I will..."

I need to say something more, reassure somebody, her or myself. I feel this panic coming on like I did before the accident, Mama and Daddy's accident, when I was so torn up inside and nobody even told me something irreversible would happen. "Oh, Sitty, I love you so, so much." But the words come out formal and ominous and sad.

We sit here together with nothing left. And then she looks at me. A sweetness fills her face. She cradles my cheeks in both her hands, kisses each twice in Arabic style. *"Ayni habibi,"* she says, "my eye and my love."

I am crying so hard and when I look at her again, she's staring at the kitchen. Her eyes are beautiful, a young woman's eyes. I know what's going on. She's back in the kitchen of the big house, fixing *sheik ik mihshee* and *hummus bi taheeni* with her girls in the days she ruled over that kitchen, making Sunday buffets and holiday feasts for when kin came to call.

That's where she belongs, in that high-ceilinged house. Not here. Now. There's no need of her now.

Only one thing I know: she can't rot in that tomb. Sitty and I, we'll move back to the big house. She and I lived there when Mama and Daddy were alive. And when they died—while turning in the front drive off the dark beach highway—she raised me alone there. Up till three years ago when Aunt Alma's husband, Uncle Abdou, dropped dead and we moved in with her.

This house is okay, but there'll never be another house for us like the big house with its grounds as huge as a football field and giant oaks all around and marigolds and hollyhocks growing near the slave house she used for a washhouse. Sitty bought that house and raised eleven children in it and raised me in it.

Still, it'd never work out. The old roof leaks and the balcony of the big house is about to cave in and the attic fan's broken and the paint's peeled and chipped. *Ya haram,* poor thing. She can't take the stairs anymore. Besides, there're no more kids for her to go back to. Not Daddy anymore. Not Mansour, Naome, Fayad, Jemille, Fedwah, Isabelle, Sadie, Shafee. Not Mama, either. Or Jiddy. It's no good living in a house with all those memories.

I look away. Look into the fading light. Bits of charcoal from the barbecue pit go flying across the terrace and slam into a lamppost. Those gale winds rage steady now. That screeching sends a chill up me, makes me know what God can do in a second. That's what Aunt said once, surveying the rubble after lightning struck the fence in front of the big house and sent it crashing down: she knew what God could do in a second. She knew His majesty. I can feel the wind's majesty as it slaps the branches of a live oak. Every bush, tree, and shrub in Aunt's backyard is doing a fast jitterbug; whirling, swirling, boogying to the beat. Sitty's eyes keep time. She sees the makings of anarchy out there.

"Let's go to the front parlor." I try to take her arm. She'll have none of it. She's luminous now, as though a blast of winter cold has sprayed her in the summer. This stormy song and dance is making her frisky. Her eyes are incandescent; she gives me such a look. Aunt locked herself out of the house one time on a visit to Sitty and me when we lived in the big house. She got that look, too, after the initial shock wore off and she wondered who she'd get to unlock the door for her, Uncle Abdou or Mama and Daddy, then remembered with horror there was no one left to unlock the door, not Abdou, anyway, Mama and Daddy, anyway, and the silliness crossed her mind about the time the horror did, that what was she getting so excited about when Uncle Abdou was dead, Mama and Daddy were dead, what was so important ever again for her to worry about, that same intoxicating feeling of having nothing left to lose is what's shining in Sitty's eyes, same as it was in Aunt's eyes.

I reach for her arm again. She's pliable this time, puts up no fuss as I help her from the couch. Once standing, she presses her fingers sternly against my cheek. Her eyes are stern, too, a worried mother's eyes. She needs no words for what she's saying: *Allah maik, Allah maik.* My heart nearly stops. There's a walker in the corner directly to her left. She makes her way with it to the back porch door. Five tortoise steps, she lifts the top latch. She turns the knob. Opens the door. Frowning, she glances at the steps below, braces for what's coming, and proceeds ahead.

The screeching, angry winds slam against her scalp, unraveling her hair from its place in her bun. Delicately, deliberately as a surgeon's hands move, she places both her hands on the wrought-iron rail and lowers her body sideways down the steps. I want to run after her, drape a shawl around her, warm the soft, fleshy mass of her cold, frail arms. Instead, I watch as her dress whips at her thighs and her hair swirls like a young girl's again. Even in good weather she couldn't take these steps alone. Even in good weather she wouldn't leave her walker behind. Even in good weather she could not get far. Still, she continues on, as doughty and durable as I have ever seen, treating each step like a sleek-edged cliff, unswerving, unerring, meticulous in her movements, till she departs the bottom step and is safely to the ground. Her feet planted firmly on the red flagstone, she loosens her hold on the rail, pauses to collect herself, and walks into the howling wind.

At one point she looks back. Her eyes are like a child's. When they meet mine, they recoil. The grief is in them for what they've seen. Don't worry about me, darlin'. I'll be fine, *Allah yukun,* Sitty. God go with you.

I run to catch up with her. Hand her the walker. She takes it from my hand and motions me away. With enormous composure, she walks across the terrace, past the wildly blowing azaleas in

Aunt's backyard, trampling the newly-planted begonias, till she reaches the driveway at the side of the house. She trudges up the driveway bound for the front of the house, her head jutting forward, her body forging on through the wind and rain.

In time, I cannot see her. I walk back to the house. Go to the front parlor. Wait beside a window. The fierce, raging winds sound like sledgehammers against the walls, but I can hardly hear for my own heart pounding. At the window, I see the fifteen-foot tides of the Mississippi Sound make a memory of the man-made beach on their journey over the seawall and across the lower highway. Soon the upper highway will be a memory, too. And her? I see her trekking up the front drive. It's not hard to imagine what madness she's planned: heave a left at the sidewalk that adjoins Highway 90, follow it three blocks till it takes her to the big house, one final scurry through those high-ceilinged rooms, rouse the long-time sleeping, hear the sound of their young voices, see a face or two. Never mind this scruffy storm. What's all the fuss about. It's surely worth the dying, so long they've all been gone.

The gale winds attack her as she tries to reach the sidewalk, beat her with a frenzy, and finally lay her down. I watch the walker go racing down the block past the Woodward home, hear the screams of the racing deathman after her. I long to go after her, hold her in my arms, keep her beside me always, love her forever. But I walk back to the porch like it's all a dream. Sit on the green sofa where she used to sit. Think how I'll be leaving this town.

Grandma Sits Down
Rick Kempa

Her knees lean against the front of the battered rocker,
getting their bearings, while she frowns out the window
at the garden, or squints into the poplars
to see if the sparrow hawks have returned. Slowly,
flat-footedly, like a fashion doll in the department store,

she rotates, knees locked, keeping contact
with the chair. Her hands grope for, find, grip the knobs
at the ends of the wooden arms. She's not looking
at anything now, it hurts, she's concentrating.
Holding her breath like an astronaut, knuckles white

around the knobs, she lets herself fall.
The chair shudders, reels backward, hangs
for a very long instant on the coasters' rims (her eyes
are shut, head pressed back) and then begins to oscillate.
She breathes out: Another successful maneuver, nothing

to be especially pleased about. She knows
not to take for granted she can get back up. Still,
the wind of her motion cools her cheeks. She continues
with the letter she's been writing: "The earth is beginning
to thaw. I am anxious to plant some seeds."

Aunt Marie at 99
Tom Benediktsson

You kept your hair bound tight all your life,
but now it falls over your fierce Apache nose.
"I just put in the time now," you say,

and your vague eyes lift serenely
past the roses I brought to where
cats lounge in the rest home window,

bring you an image of Mert Melugin
lounging in the dairy, talking to the cats,
fingers busy with a cigarette, August so hot

roses never had a chance, cats in the dairy
like melted butter—"But what's that worth?
Used to play pinochle but now I can't see to cheat!"

(and unspoken, "They all died, and bird-boned
old women are useless.") Smoke from August slash fires
blanks out the hills, and "Who's there?" you cry

with the startled anger that finally came
when you let your hair fall, too late
for anything but itself.

Here, Take My Words
Karen Brodine

I prefer to believe that the last time we saw each other, she rushed out of the house in a rage and hitchhiked home to her shack.

But this isn't fiction. So I have to say that the last time I say hello to that face, she looks past me to the wall and I'm not her granddaughter anymore, it can't matter to her anymore.

"Nabana," she says, "nabana!" and I peel one.

Her skin shines down the rest home hall like a beacon.

She is naked from the waist up and her body gleams as if it is a wet, white seal. Her breasts are longer and heavier than I remember and seeming to fade, the nipples soft and undefined from the whole breast. She leans forward from the straps that bind her to the chair, shifting her weight back and forth. She says hello to my mother but doesn't seem to see me.

"I'm hungry, don't you have a little something?"

"Didn't they give you breakfast, Mother?"

"I don't know, Mary. It isn't enough. Don't you have a little something?"

We have two bananas in the brown paper sack with two pairs of new socks—with blue stripes. The stripes make me mad, somehow, they are so cheerful.

"Get your clothes back on now, Mother. Here's your robe. Let's put your clothes back on. Karen, find her other slipper—it's lost." We talk of her in the third person, as if she isn't there.

"Lost who? Who's lost?"

"Mother, we've lost your slipper. I've got to get your clothes together."

"Get me together. Then we can all be together fine," she snorts sarcastically.

Here it is under the bed. We put the fuzzy slipper on her hard claw foot, clenched and curved from no use.

"Karen's here," my mother says.

"Where?"

"Right here," I say.

"You don't look like Karen."

"Maybe you're remembering me when I was little. And besides, I'm wearing a hat."

"I don't recognize you."

"I recognized you right away, Grandma."

"You did? That's good. How are you?"

"Oh, I'm fine."

"Well, I wish I was fine. Then we'd all be fine together."

She is picking at her buttons, trying to slip out of her robe. "Mother, don't take your clothes off again," says my mother.

"Why not?"

"Because you'll catch cold," I lie to her, feeling foolish. The room is very warm.

"Because they don't like it," my mother says, more honest.

We watch her hands roving like two determined animals over the robe. Her fingers light on a corner of it and she pulls it up. "Give me a look at this. What does it say?"

"Grandma, you can't read your robe and you can't eat your socks." She almost laughs at this. Then she looks hard at me, and points.

"Give me the little girl in there. Give me the little girl."

She changes the subject. "I'd like to get back to what I had."

"You had a lot."

"I did?" She brightens, thinking maybe of wished-for land, the ship to come in, the lucky break, the good job that leered around the corner.

"Yes. You had a lot. You're the strongest person I know."

"I'm glad to hear that," she says and her eyes focus on mine. We stare unsmiling at one another for a minute. I imagine that something goes between us, unspoken but solid, yet I'm not sure. Maybe it's just that I *want* some signal from her.

"Get me out of here," she says, pulling at the straps.

"Where would you go then, if you could leave?"

"Oh, I'd be going toward home. Get me a phone."

"Grandma, I can't, but who would you call?"

"I'd call for something useful."

"Well, they'll bring you your lunch soon," says my mom. "That's useful."

"I don't want lunch. Then I'll be like a lake."

I take her socks out and print on them with a marker. H. Pierce in red letters. She watches curiously.

"Can you sign my socks?"

A nurse comes in to say hello. "Gee, Harriet, you're not talking much." The nurse turns to us. "Usually she just chatters and chatters—gee, Harriet, you're not saying much. See you later."

There's a long silence. Then my grandmother looks at me and extends her hand, palm up. "Here," she says, "take my words."

I realize she has been hurt by the woman's words. My mother says, "Oh, don't pay attention to that woman, darlin'."

"Why?"

"Because, Mother, it doesn't matter. It's all right."

It is time for us to leave because we can't bear to stay any longer. An hour seems like a long time. "Good-bye," she says, politely, formally, to me, and as we leave, she is slowly shedding her clothes like soft, wilting leaves.

Photo by Lori Burkhalter-Lackey

The Trouble Was Meals
Elizabeth Bennett

Dad was the head of the family, for sure.
When he got us all together
it meant either a baby was on the way
or we were moving. So when the question was put,
How would it be if Grandma came to live with us?
I thought, no big deal.
I was glad we weren't moving.

I found a picture of Grandma,
a young dancer in a dress, sequins and feathers.
She had me tape it onto the mirror
over the dresser where she kept Grandpa's remains,
his gold cuff links, glass eye.

It was all right,
Grandma the dancer in residence,
all right for me, hard for Mother.
Dad would come home, pour a glass of Old Crow bourbon,
one for Mother, drink them both.

The trouble was meals.
Dad was used to holding forth
and the first night, halfway through chicken cacciatore
Grandma turned and said, "Rest your gums, dear."
She called everyone dear, all of us, the mailman,
even the exterminator.
She took to humming in a loud voice
and dropping her knife and fork on the floor.

One night she shouted, "Leftovers, leftovers,
where's the original?" and shoved her plate
on the floor. Baby threw his bottle
on top of the broken china. The plate crash
became a regular occurrence.

Fridays at school our teacher read us poetry,
"Poitry," she called it. One went,
"Old age is a flight of small cheeping birds..."*
I didn't like poetry. What I liked was shop.
I made a wooden bowl, sanded the rim smooth,
carved my initials on the bottom.
I brought it home to Grandma
and we served her dinner in it every night.
She still shoved it on the floor
but nothing broke.

When I was at the orthodontist's one afternoon,
Grandma took a nap and never woke up.
We cleaned out her room. I helped Mother.
She was in a mood to throw everything out,
flannel sheets that smelled of urine, everything.
She only kept the picture. That night after dinner
I found the bowl in the trash.
Dad said, we won't need *that* anymore,
but I washed and dried it
and put it on the shelf next to Old Crow
so I could find it when Mother got old.

---

*"To Waken an Old Lady" by William Carlos Williams from *Collected Earlier Poems of William Carlos Williams,* New Directions Publishing Company.

Like Mother, Like Daughter
Susan S. Jacobson

"When are you coming?"
"On Sunday, why?"
"Because I want to get
some things, make the bed..."
"Oh, Mom," she said.
I felt an echo in me:
I had made the beds
just the week before
on a visit to my mother's,
because of her back.
Always before she had,
but now I did, knowing
where everything was:
I had moved her there.

Looking for recipes
of dishes my daughter likes,
I found the ones for meals
I had made my mother,
in her new kitchen,
and put them away
like an echo in a drawer.
Reviewing their ways,
looking for similarities
in their rhythms
(there were none);
I weighed them against
my need to be alone.

I am related to neither now
(their blue eyes are so dissimilar)
and yet I am their link.
There are echoes back
and forth through me:
I live alone, as do
my mother and my daughter,
none of us in the house
where we were raised or
spent our marriages.
Each of us is careful
of the others, unyielding
in small significant ways.

I now mother my mother
when I can no longer
mother my daughter
who is older than I
have ever felt myself to be.

Near Places, Far Places
Sarah Barnhill

We are both widows, Momma and me, and we live together under the same roof. When my husband died it seemed the right thing to do for me to move back home, so my boy Cleeve and me did, did move in with Momma, since she didn't have nobody and I didn't have nobody. Then Cleeve went and got hisself in trouble and had to leave home and now there's just Momma and me. Two women in a big old white house on the Asheville highway. We got a good view, though, of the river and the valley and the mountains all around. And a good view is more than a lot of people got.

I was already living there with Momma when Mr. Van Fleet showed up. He came from Delray Beach, Florida, and drove up here every year to escape the heat. Sometimes his wife came with him, but she didn't like the mountains. She got carsick, and it rained too much to suit her. She was with him that year he stopped the first time though, and when she got out of the car, she stretched to get the kinks out and stood by the car door with her hands on her back. She had on dark glasses as big as beer mats, and she said nothing about the quilts.

Mr. Van Fleet had seen the quilts hanging on the clothesline, six of them stretched out in the sun to dry. We watched him stop in the middle of the highway, back his car up, and drive up to the house. He told us he was Mr. Van Fleet from Delray Beach, Florida, and offered to buy every last quilt.

Momma likes her quilts but Momma also likes making a dollar, so I wasn't too surprised when she agreed to sell all but one. She let him have Double Wedding Ring, Drunkard's Path, Goose in the Pond, Steps to the Altar, and Rob Peter, Pay Paul. But when it come to Widow's Mite she put on the brakes.

Photo by Rod Bradley

"It's got bullion stitching in it," she said. "And a piece from my momma's wedding dress."

"But you know there's pieces of Grannie's wedding dress in nearly every quilt you got," I told her.

"I know. But this one's different. Each of them gold coins stitched into every square's different. Just look at that work. And see here," she poked the quilt up at me, "this one's got Momma's initials stitched into it."

And there it was—ARC, for Addie Rae Case, stitched into the little yellow circle made out to look like a coin that was supposed to be part of the widow's mite.

"He'd give you a good price for it."

"I know. But this one's different."

"You are a stubborn soul, Momma."

"I know that too," she said.

Mr. Van Fleet came back the next summer and the summer after that and bought more quilts. French Bouquet and Burgoyne's Quilt and Noonday Lily. Others too, but I can't remember them all. And every summer he asked Momma would she part with Widow's Mite and every summer Momma said no.

Last August we were sitting on the porch shucking corn, working our way through half a dozen ears Moon had brought in early that morning before me or her was out of bed. Moon is my oldest boy and him and another man worked sixteen acres of bottom land near the International plant they'd been renting for the last seven years. This was the last summer for the corn though, and for everything—the tobacco and the beans and the tomatoes. International bought the land for a new extension and a parking lot, and as soon as Moon harvested the last ear of corn they started to break ground.

The phone rang. I had so much corn silk stuck all over me that Momma went to get it. She was gone a long time for her since she doesn't like talking on the phone, and when she came back she said it was Mr. Van Fleet and that he was heading back to Florida day after tomorrow.

"That's early," I said. "He usually stays till after the leaves turn."

"He says his wife wants him to get home."

"Something's not right here. When the man likes quilts and the wife tells him to get hisself home," I said. "But I reckon that's Florida for you."

"He's still going on about Widow's Mite. He offered me three hundred and fifty dollars for it this time."

"Take it," I said. "When Moon loses this land we're all going to need every little bit we can get."

"What's anybody need a quilt in Delray Beach, Florida, for anyway?"

"This corn is full of cut worms. Moon says rain early in the summer brings them on." This green worm stuck its head up at me and waved back and forth like someone's finger coaxing me on—to trouble, no doubt. I flicked it down onto the newspaper where all the shucks and silks was piled up.

"You reckon he's making something for hisself out of this?" Momma said.

"He's lucky to clear a dollar a bushel."

"Not Moon. Mr. Van Fleet."

I sat there looking down at the rows of pyramids we'd stacked the corn into. Most of the ears we froze just as they were. Some of it I made into creamed corn and filled enough quart bags for Moon and his family when they came for Sunday dinner. The rest I just put into little pint bags for me and Momma. I sat there looking down at those ears of corn wondering what to say about Mr. Van Fleet from Delray Beach, Florida.

Finally I said, "He doesn't need money, Momma. He's got two houses we know of, and you seen his car and his clothes."

I didn't tell Momma, but the thing I liked best—the only thing I reckon—about Mr. Van Fleet was looking at him. I don't mean he was handsome, because he weren't. He was bald on top and had a thin face and wore funny little glasses that pinched his nose. But he was about the cleanest man I have ever seen and his clothes always looked like he'd just got them out the dry cleaners. Sometimes he wore a gold chain around his neck, and once he had on a shiny blue, zip-up boiler suit. But he didn't look like a mechanic. He looked like an astronaut. Moon and Cleeve are the best boys in the world, even if Cleeve did get in trouble and get sent down to Raleigh, but I know that they'll never look like Mr. Van Fleet. It isn't in their nature.

"He collects them, Momma. Just like Moon and Cleeve collected all those license plates they tacked up inside the shed. He's retired and he's got money and he likes to collect things. And," I stopped and looked straight at Momma because I wanted her to take this last point in, "he wants Widow's Mite bad enough to give you three hundred and fifty dollars for it."

Momma set her jaw the way she does when something doesn't please her, and she looked out across the valley, past the sourwoods that were beginning to turn red and their feathery blossoms that hung down like peacock tails, past the smoke stacks of the International plant, past the old quarry cut at Bledsoe, and on to the mountains that circle the whole valley.

"Esther," she finally said to me, "you and me are both old women. A person would think you'd know by now that there's some things you don't never get back once you let them get away."

"Don't talk mopey, Momma."

"This ain't mopey. This is facts."

No use saying any more when Momma was like this, so we picked up the corn mess and went inside to start supper.

That evening we were setting on the porch when I saw his car between the gaps in the althea hedge that lines the driveway up to the house. It was creeping along, trying not to hit the ruts and potholes we hadn't gotten around to fixing since all the rain in July. Blue car, althea, blue car, althea, it went.

"You didn't tell me he was coming," I said to Momma.

"He said he might. I didn't say not to."

That gave me hope. Maybe she'd changed her mind about Widow's Mite.

Whenever Mr. Van Fleet came to visit he put me in a strange way. From everything he said I figured he was four or five years younger than me, but he always made me feel like I was younger, and not in the good sense that old women like to feel younger. It was more like him and Momma was the grown-ups and I was just the little kid who didn't know nothing. So when he came I usually just sat on my hands and didn't say much. They mostly talked about quilts anyway.

I watched him get out the car and thought he looked like something from TV. He had on white tennis shoes and white socks with a word stitched into the top that I couldn't see so clear. In fact, he had writing on everything, on his shirt and his short pants that had big deep pockets in them. I had never seen his bare legs before and I hadn't expected them to have such muscles in them. He was trim, I'll have to admit, no rolls on his waist like even Moon and Cleeve have. Brown, too, brown like all those folks from Florida. Like burnt biscuits, Momma said once.

"So how's tricks?" he said as he came up the porch steps. He was always saying things like that—"How's tricks?" and "Hang in there" and "Have a good one." I don't care for such talk, personally.

But Momma seemed to pay no attention, just got up from her chair and said, "Evening."

Momma told me to get some tomato juice I had just made and when everybody got all settled down, talk turned to what it always turned to: quilts.

"I tell you, Molly, this morning in that shop in Biltmore Forest I saw in their window a Widow's Mite for three hundred dollars.

I SHALL WEAR PURPLE 27

God's truth. That's why I upped my offer to three fifty."

"Whyn't you go ahead and buy that one?" Momma said.

"No antique value. And the filler was cheap. Probably just an old blanket." He drank some of his tomato juice but you could tell he paid no attention to what he was drinking. "And—this is the clincher—the blocks were quilted separately. The piecing gave it all away."

Momma said, "That's like plucking a chicken after it's baked."

They kept up such talk for a good thirty minutes while I just sat there and watched the dusk come in.

After a while, I began to think about all those quilts Mr. Van Fleet had bought. Wondering where Steps to the Altar and Drunkard's Path were, if they lay folded over a bed in a bright white bedroom that looked out over the blue ocean, or if Rob Peter, Pay Paul was draped over one of those rope hammocks you could lay down in and see palm trees and flowers that bloom the whole year long. It wasn't that I missed the quilts or put much more store by them. There was just too many of them squirreled away in Momma's old trunks or stacked up to the ceiling in closets for a dozen or so to make any difference. And I've never been much for sewing or darning. My hands are just too big and I feel all clumsy and fumble-fingered even if I have to wind a ball of yarn. What I realized sitting on the porch that night listening to Momma and Mr. Van Fleet go on and on was that those quilts would go places I'd never been and see sights I'd never seen, and probably never would. There I was, not able to admit to a soul that a bunch of patchwork quilts made by my grannie and great-aunts and women so long since dead I couldn't recall their names, that a bunch of old quilts had made me but one thing, and that was jealous.

Get rid of them all, that's what I wanted to do. Then maybe I'd forget about them and not be made such a fool of. Let them go with Mr. Van Fleet to Delray Beach, Florida, especially if his money is so hot it's burning a hole in his boiler-suit pocket.

"Sell," I suddenly said out loud.

Mr. Van Fleet slapped the arm of his rocker and said, "That's what I've been telling her myself."

Momma just kept on rocking like she hadn't heard a thing.

Mr. Van Fleet finally left when it was good and dark, and we had to loan him a flashlight so's he could see his way to get to his car.

When he was gone, I asked Momma, "You gonna sell him Widow's Mite?"

"I wish I had a nickel for every time you've asked me that. What makes you think I've changed my mind?"

"Because he leaves on Monday," I said. "And this is Saturday."

"That ain't answering my question. What makes you think I have changed my mind?"

She didn't wait for me to say something, because I reckon she knew I didn't have nothing to say. Momma always was the best at calling somebody's bluff. We stood there for awhile in the darkness at the top of the stairs, watching the evening stars come up over Hogback Mountain, not saying a thing.

Finally Momma says, "Night, Esther," and I say, "Night, Momma," and that is that.

The next day Moon and his family came for Sunday dinner like they always do. It was Moon and his wife Betty and my two grandbabies, Mandy and Melissa. They had just started school the week before—kindergarten and second grade—and before their Momma and Daddy could even get out of the car they came rushing in with presents they had made for me during craft time. Mandy, the oldest one, brought a turtle she had made out of modeling clay and poked thumbtacks into its back to look like a shell.

"His name is Bill," Mandy said.

"Where should I put him?"

"Up there." She pointed to the shelf on the window above the kitchen sink.

I had to shift pots of African violets and a bunch of old orange juice cans I had wandering jew and coleus rooting in to make room for Bill. I even turned him so he could have a view down toward the valley and the althea hedge.

"Melissa brung something too." Mandy reached for something in Melissa's hand but she jerked away.

"No!"

"Well show it, Melissa."

Melissa lifted those little hands of hers up toward me, and laying there was this funny looking dark, round thing that I thought at first might be a cookie cutter. I picked it up and held it to where the light shone on it. It was a little, hard clay paperweight with Melissa's hand print right in the middle of it. The tips of my fingers would barely fit into the little scoops in the clay her own fingers had made.

I stood there awhile looking at it.

"It doesn't do nothing," Melissa said.

"Yes it does. It sets up here on this windowsill next to Bill and looks pretty."

From the kitchen window I could see Moon in the backyard talking to Billy Walkingstick, the old Cherokee who's rented the cabin up above us for as long as I can remember. Moon and Billy had their hands in their back pockets, and every now and then they jabbed at the ground with their shoes. Betty leaned over a bed of petunias and marigolds and pinched off the dead blossoms.

It was times like these I found myself thinking about Cleeve. I should have seen it coming, should have known there was nothing to hold him here. He's not like Moon and Moon's not like Cleeve and I am not the first mother to birth out children who grow up so different you wonder if they can be brothers. Cleeve went and got mixed in with a bad bunch, and one night they went off and beat up an old man. Now Cleeve's down in Raleigh serving out a sentence for assault and battery. I lost something, with Cleeve. And

I didn't know how to keep from losing it. It seems like I turned around one day and he was no longer there, like he'd slipped from me, right out of my hands. And right then I felt like I didn't know Cleeve anymore, anymore than I could know that funny looking clay turtle setting in my windowsill. But the hurt was still there, I can tell you that.

I kept standing there looking out the kitchen window, leaning up against the cool enamel of the kitchen sink, and for a moment, I forgot where I was.

Then I heard Mandy and Melissa running through the house chasing Momma's six-toed tabby cat and Momma fussing at them. And then Moon and Betty came in the back door loaded down with pound cake and cobbler and okra. This was not time for standing at the sink moping about the way things chose not to turn out.

I gave up my place at the end of the table for Moon like I always did, and Momma sat at the other end. Melissa was still too little to sit in a regular chair, so we put her in the old high chair that her daddy and Cleeve and Mandy had all used. But she was almost too big for it and complained the whole time that it pinched her bottom.

If some stranger had walked in on our Sunday dinner he would have thought we just got through burying somebody. Moon should have felt like the cock o' the walk, what with being the only man there and setting at the head of the table, but I could tell his mind was on losing the sixteen acres and wondering what he could do to add to what he made at International. Betty was her usual quiet self, just chewing her food and looking at whoever happened to say anything.

And me of course. I was thinking about Cleeve, seeing him in some tiny grey room with no window in it.

But Momma was the one I couldn't figure out. What was her cause for setting there like she'd been smote dumb, barely looking at anybody and poking at her food like it might have been last week's oatmeal?

"Momma," I finally said to her when we were by ourselves in the kitchen, "something not suiting you? Why you setting there like death warmed over?"

"I got things on my mind."

"What things?"

"Esther, you act like folks get old and they stop thinking on things. Sometimes I believe I've waited till I got old before I *begun* to do my thinking."

"What's on your mind, Momma?"

"When I finish thinking on it I'll tell you."

And with that she walked back in the dining room carrying a dish of blackberry cobbler, and I knew it was no use trying to get it out of her until she was good and ready.

After dinner Moon and Betty took the girls for a walk along the river while Momma and me sat on the front porch in the cane bottom rockers and watched the cars that went down the old highway there in front of the house. Momma was fanning herself with the magazine from the Sunday newspaper, swishing the air around just enough to lift the hair up from the side of her face.

"What you looking at, Momma?" But I knew what she would say, and she did.

"Same thing I look at every time I set on this porch," she said and pointed with the magazine out toward the valley and the mountains. "I reckon I've set here for nearly sixty years. We were setting here that spring evening when the man from Fort Jackson come to tell us about Hollis." My brother Hollis got killed in Korea and the Army sent a man up here to tell us about it. Momma gave the man a piece of pie and a cup of coffee, then went in her bedroom and didn't come out again for two days. About the only time she talks of Hollis is when we set on the porch.

What she said next flummoxed me good.

"I have decided to let Mr. Van Fleet have Widow's Mite."

I stopped rocking.

"I've decided that," she said, like I might not have heard her. She kept looking straight out at the valley and the mountains.

Times like this are strange, I tell you. You expect to leap up and whoop and holler, shouting, 'Bout time, 'bout time! But that's never how it turns out with me. I just set there slack jawed and pop-eyed, holding my breath in case it won't last. I could hear my own heart beating, going Widow's Mite, Widow's Mite, Widow's Mite.

I took a few deep breaths and finally said, "What made you change your mind, Momma?"

She kept fanning away. "All of you did," she said. "Moon and the girls, and Cleeve. And you."

"They said something to you?"

"Not a word."

"What you mean they made you change your mind then?"

She finally stopped fanning and looked at me. "You don't learn everything through your ears, Esther. I just set there looking at everybody today, setting where they always do for Sunday dinner. I was missing Cleeve, and thinking about those who've gone. And I decided I was a foolish old woman to try to hold on to one faded old quilt if what money it could bring in could help people setting around the table. Moon's losing land, you've lost Cleeve, why shouldn't I part with Widow's Mite?"

Way out across the highway on the narrow path that runs between the field of corn and an unused pasture, I could see Moon and Betty walking with the two girls. Melissa was up on Moon's shoulders, cupping her hands under his chin like the straps of a helmet. She towered above everybody, even the tassels of the corn, and moved back and forth in a right stately sway. She made me think of a movie I seen once on the television with an elephant carrying an Indian princess who sat in a high-backed golden throne under a canopy of satin and silk the very color of the sunset.

"To be honest, Momma, the money won't matter all that much."

Momma rocked forward fast and brought her heels down on the floor with a clump.

"Just listen to you," she said.

She was right put out with me.

I couldn't sleep that night so I got up and went into the kitchen to make a cup of Sanka and a bread-and-butter sandwich. Standing at the kitchen window I could see the light on in Billy Walkingstick's cabin, and I knew he'd be asleep in his rocking chair with a copy of *National Geographic* spread out over his chest. Billy hardly reads anything else and the ladies in the bookmobile keep him stocked up. It's always struck me as funny to hear an Indian talking about places like Egypt and China and Timbuktu. But I reckon Billy knows more about strange places in the world than anybody else around. And I know for a fact that he's never been to Delray Beach, Florida, either.

So there I was standing in my and Momma's dark kitchen looking at the light from Billy Walkingstick's cabin and the light from the moon that shone on the backyard and the flower beds and seemed to creep its way up toward me standing at the kitchen window. And up onto the presents from my grandbabies setting there on the windowsill.

I picked them both up, in one hand even, they were so small and brought them up close where I could see them good. They felt cool and I rubbed them against my forehead like folks like to do with a cold drink bottle. They still smelled like children do, sweet and sour at the same time. And they made my heart take a funny leap like I could have knocked down dead anyone who came in and tried to take them away from me.

Momma was right: You do have to get old before you do some thinking about some things.

Momma and I didn't say nothing to each other but we both knew he would show up at his usual time, just after supper but before the sun went down. For a man from Florida he seemed to like to do all his visiting in the dark. But I reckon he needed most of his daytime to look at golf balls and tennis balls and to shop in antique stores.

Something else Momma and I did without saying nothing to each other was dress up. Momma had on her lavender and beige polyester she's worn for the last couple Easters, and Grannie's mourning brooch. I could even see the corner of one of her special Irish linen handkerchiefs sticking out from under her sleeve. I put on my one good summer suit and the beads Mandy and Melissa had given me the Christmas before. It was like we both knew something important was going to happen.

We sat down on the porch to wait, not saying anything about each other's dress-up clothes, not even looking at each other hardly. It kind of made me feel the way you do when you see a man with his zipper down.

About fifteen minutes before sundown we see the lights from the car turn into our driveway, and pick and creep its way up to our house.

"Top of the evening to you." Mr. Van Fleet stood at the bottom of the porch steps, waiting for someone to invite him up. He had on khaki pants and a matching khaki jacket like hunters wear, with big pockets and a belt and little flaps on the shoulders. If he'd had on one of those funny helmets he would a looked like somebody straight out of Africa.

"Evening," me and Momma said. We went on rocking.

"The last night in the mountains is always a sad time. This time tomorrow I'll be in the panhandle of Florida, sweltering in the heat and fighting off the bugs." He put one foot up on the first step. "You folks are lucky, do you know that?"

"We know that," Momma said.

"And I couldn't go without telling my favorite friends up here good-bye." He moved his foot up to another step. "That, and to come make one more offer to you for Widow's Mite, Molly. I'm even going to up it." And he reached into one of those big pockets in his jacket and brought out a long envelope. "Here's four hundred dollars. In cash—I thought you'd prefer cash. What do you say?"

Momma wasn't looking *at* him, but above him, toward the valley and the river. I was about to say something when she finally said, "I say all right."

Well, Mr. Van Fleet's face cracked into the biggest smile I'd ever seen on anybody and he let out a funny little sound like Hah, and came bounding up the stairs like he was going to grab Momma and the chair she was setting in.

I stood up real fast.

"My momma has given you the wrong impression," I said, putting myself between him and Momma. "We have decided not to sell Widow's Mite. In fact, we have decided not to sell anymore quilts at all."

He craned around me trying to see Momma and, "Molly, will you—Molly, wha—Molly?"

"You are welcome to come and visit us anytime you're in these parts, but don't be asking for more quilts."

Mr. Van Fleet kept on sputtering away, saying things about having come to a decision, about being reasonable, and such like. And Momma the whole time wasn't saying nothing. Finally I heard her stand up. She put her hand on my shoulder and sort of turned me around. She stood there staring at me in the twilight, her face poked up right next to mine.

"Molly, let's try to keep this between you and me," Mr. Van Fleet said. One thing's for sure, he wasn't too happy by this time. He even tugged at her sleeve a little, like a whiny little boy might do.

But Momma paid him no heed, just kept looking at me until at last she smiled like I hadn't seen her smile in a long time.

Mr. Van Fleet saw it too, and backed down the stairs a little bit. He stopped talking too.

"Mr. Van Fleet," Momma said, drawing herself up, "my daughter is right. I am sorry I misled you. Old women sometimes do foolish things." She set back down in her chair and stared out above his head again. "You drive safely tomorrow. You've got a long trip ahead of you."

He kept going But, but, but, but, sounding like a little motor boat, and flapping his hands around in the air. I felt sorry for him, I did. It seemed like he was more than just a long way from home.

He finally walked on down the stairs and out to his car. He slammed the door so hard it left a little echo in the air. I have to admire him for waiting to get good and angry.

Momma and me went on rocking. The evening star was up in the west, and the katydids were setting up their racket all around us. If Momma'd said anything she'd a had to shouted almost to have herself heard. So she set there not saying a word, because there's times, it seems to me, when it's best to just set. Billy Walkingstick would agree. He hisself says sometimes he sets and thinks, and sometimes he just sets.

And so we just set. A couple of old women looking out at the darkness and listening to the summer sounds, and grateful for a big old house with a good view.

The Changes
Fionna Perkins

In July I was back home. The border of poplars, the locust in Mother's flower garden, and the willow in front of the framing for the house we never had money to finish had leafed into shimmering greens. The bluebells were in bloom, and the scarlet and pink and purple petunias spilled over the rock terrace we'd built our first summer in Hillview Acres. Peas and new potatoes the size of marbles were ready to eat. But the cow had been sold, and the electricity was off.

At breakfast my first morning, Dad asked if I wanted to pick the raspberries again this year. "Good crop," he said. "Any you sell, the money's yours."

"Sure," I said, beaming, remembering that last summer I made enough for dress goods and new shoes for Mother.

This way I wouldn't have to take another job doing housework to buy clothes for school. Our last had been a real bad winter, worse than the ones before, Dad with no work and Mother seeming off somewhere, and at school in Latin and geometry my brain had stalled. I quit and took a job, but after sweeping and mopping all spring, I wanted to go back and finish high school so I could go on to college.

Dad went out to keep on with the irrigating. As I stood up to clear the table, Mother bounced over and gave me a hug, then held me at arm's length.

"Let me look at you," she said, all smiles and her black eyes sparkling. "I've missed my girl. You've grown, and you're thinner."

"I worked a lot, Mama, about all the time." We sat back down for a visit, and I said, "How's everything?"

"A little better now. Dad has work starting next week at the Olney ranch, and Brodie was hired to clerk at the feed store. First thing he did, he and Nancy ran off and got married, and they're living in town."

"Where's Wallace?"

"Logging on Black Mountain. Juana's with him."

"Heard from Laurel?"

At mention of my sister a shadow clouded Mother's eyes. Laurel, the oldest, had been gone from home a long time and seldom wrote but occasionally sent a box of clothes she was tired of.

For answer, Mother opened and closed her clasped hands and said, "Your cat, Feisty, sure missed you."

I was on my way out the next morning with a bucket dangling from my waist and a crate to dump the berries in when I remembered what I'd meant to ask her.

"Where did Hettie Temple go after she was in the hospital?"

"Back to her mother, I guess."

"Hettie's mother died. That's why she came to live with her father and stepmother."

"I don't know, Freda, only that she wasn't to be with Mrs. Temple again ever."

"But isn't Mrs. Temple in the insane asylum at Sweetdale?"

"She was the last I heard," said Mother.

Walking to the berry patch, I thought about Hettie, remembering the other kids at school making fun of her thick woolen socks and long skirts and the twang of her hill speech. If it was like everybody said, that insanity was inherited, Hettie was lucky one way; Mrs. Temple wasn't her real mother.

I didn't like to think of what had happened to Hettie and put my mind on berry picking. Dad had been right. We'd never had a crop like this. Every bush was a mass of white blossoms, green berries, pink berries, and ripe berries. It took me two days to pick halfway through the patch. By the time I was to the last bush,

enough more berries had ripened that I had to start over.

Before I could sell any, I had to pick our share, so every so often I took a filled crate in for Mother to can and make into jam and jelly. Near the end of the week, as I reached the stoop, I heard Dad's voice from inside, loud as though he was angry, saying, "...old enough to be on her own. Face it, Edith. We might have a chance if we sell out and go somewhere else."

I was fifteen. If he was talking about me, that meant back to mopping floors and no school in the fall. It's what we'd done for years, move from place to place, and I didn't think Mother wanted to go back to that. Where we lived was just a shack, but the land was ours, and we had the start of a nice house that was Mother's dream.

Not hearing anything more, I went on in. Dad looked up with a scowl, and Mother seemed pretty upset.

Sunday evening Dad tossed his knapsack into the pickup and drove off for the Olney ranch somewhere to the east about fifty miles. With him gone and the stillness and dusk settling around us, Mother and I, who only talked when we had something to say, didn't speak at all.

She was already at work when I got up in the morning, boiling sheets and washing our clothes by hand. While I picked, she canned. The shack with its one thickness of boards was sweltering. At our evening meal, Mother's place was bare of even a glass, and she looked tired and preoccupied.

"Don't you fell good, Mama?"

"I'm fasting."

"Raw eggs and beef scrapings?"

She just smiled. She'd tried that one on me the spring I whooped for weeks. It was from a book we had called *The Ralston Method*, which recommended fasting to rid the body of poisons. I suspected that Mother fasted as much to keep her weight down as to stay healthy because Dad didn't like her to be fat. Usually she didn't eat for a day or two and drank juice and lots of water.

In the morning she was out irrigating her flowers and again at the wood stove in the afternoon, making jam and ironing our clothes with the heated flatirons she used when we couldn't pay the light bill. Little rivers of sweat ran down her face.

Out in the berry patch, I wore a halter and shorts from Laurel's last box of castoffs. If I got too hot, I went to the well back of the shack and filled up on cold water and stood awhile in the shade. But mostly I just picked. Clouds of bees crawled and buzzed around my hands, and I was never stung. I liked bees, and I liked picking; it left my mind free to travel.

While moving from bush to bush, I zoomed off in my head in a movie-star wardrobe, driving my new Cord, which I'd only seen a picture of in a magazine; being a foreign correspondent in China and Paris; or autographing the books I intended to write, which everyone wanted to buy.

Then coming back to earth on our two acres in Hillview, I'd take more raspberries to Mother's long workbench. I was used to her being quiet in a warm, comfortable way, humming to herself and smiling when I appeared. This afternoon she didn't smile or look up, and I hadn't heard her sing once since Dad left.

"Sure hot," I grumbled and rubbed sweat off my face. "You drinking juice?"

"No."

"Water?"

Mother shook her head, and I felt a prickle of fear. She'd been a nurse and was hipped on the body's need for water by the quart. In summer around Middleton, the only things that didn't burn up and die without being watered were juniper, sagebrush, and jackrabbits.

"You'll get sick, Mama."

"It's the way I'm to do it this time."

I went back to the berry patch thinking that she'd never done a fast like this before and that something seemed to be pressing on her mind. A little black ball of worry bounced into my daydreams.

At noontime on Thursday, I dangled on the workbench eating a slice of bread and fresh jam and watched Mother living somewhere else. I spoke up so she'd hear me.

"Drinking water now, Mama?"

"I'm to abstain from all food and drink for three weeks." Suddenly she flung her arms wide. "I've had a wondrous vision, Freda."

I looked at her askance; our family was already overrun with visionaries. We imagined Christmases in a house that was only stud walls on a stone basement, trips we never went on, and noble deeds of Scottish ancestors centuries dead. Dad envisioned better governments and political systems, and all of us, even Mother, were haunted in the midst of the Depression with a vision of better days.

"What kind of a vision?"

"God is calling his people home."

With a look of rapture, Mother pointed to the tapestry sent us after Grandmother died, which hung over the studs on the back wall above her sewing machine.

"The lost tribes of Israel," she said in a hushed voice. "God showed me a vision in the tapestry. I saw all the vanished tribes gathering and moving together. I was among them. We were on our way to the Promised Land. I have to be ready, cleansed and purified."

Was this like the stories I'd read of Joan of Arc's *voices?* As I stared at the shadowed tapestry, the jousting knights began to move, and I quickly shifted my gaze, not wanting to see any of Mother's lost tribes emerging from the gold and black threads on their way to heaven or Palestine. One of us, I thought, better make sense, as Dad was always admonishing.

The next night I watched Mother at her cleansing, and my back hair lifted. She stood in the round tin washtub pouring streams of cold water over her body without a quiver. Her skin just seemed to sop it up. Her wild, fiery eyes burned holes in my head. I stared back, speechless.

A week of her fast was nearly over. By tomorrow evening Dad would be home, and I was sure he'd put a stop to whatever madness had taken Mother.

He brought a piece of beef for Sunday dinner, which Mother roasted. She made a cream sauce for the little potatoes and new peas, a canned milk and vinegar dressing for the leaf lettuce, and sponge cake to go under sweetened, crushed raspberries. I set a place for her, and she said grace but didn't eat. Dad told funny stories about the haying crew, and Mother and I laughed. In the afternoon he drove away in the old pickup.

Monday morning I awoke to heat pressing down; we were in for a scorcher. Mother was at the stove fixing poached eggs when I went to the tin basin to wash. At seeing only one plate, I lost my appetite.

"You've got to start eating, Mama," I pleaded.

She turned, not hearing me, and overnight her eyes had paled to a faded brown. She moved as if she had weights on her arms and legs, and her dress fit like a tent.

With an effort Mother straightened. "We have to get the place cleaned up, Freda. The Sunday school is coming for a picnic Friday."

"*Here?*"

"Yes, it's all planned."

"But, Mama, we can't have that whole bunch at a shack like this. Are we supposed to feed them?"

Her face had that unearthly look. "God will provide, Freda. There'll be a great feast and a miracle."

Now I was scared. This was something more than a fast. Mother had taught Sunday school at Calvary Baptist in Middleton for years, and at Easter made the kids a special breakfast in the church basement, but never were they invited to our place in Hillview. Cummings were too proud for that.

In a loud voice I said, "You've fasted long enough, Mother."
"No, it lasts till Friday."

She had said no water or food for three weeks. Had she been fasting before I noticed? I had counted on Dad to put an end to it, and now he wouldn't be home again for a whole week. She'd start a task and seem to forget what she was doing. At night I couldn't sleep for trying to decide what I should do. The Olneys might have a telephone, but this was Dad's first job since last fall. Wallace, the one I wanted, was as good as lost driving a Cat somewhere in the woods. My brother Brodie, in town, was closest.

At first sight of Mother in the morning, I was afraid to leave her for long enough to walk the five miles to Middleton to find Brodie.

"Why don't you stay in bed, Mama?" I urged.
"We've work to do for the picnic."

Her voice had a whistling sound, and her dimples and rounded cheeks had sunk to hollows; her bones stuck out. Her eyes shifted restlessly, bewildered, as if she was searching for something lost.

Picking would give me a chance to think. Three bushes down a row, my only thought was that Mother would die before Friday without water. If the picnic was tied in with her fast and I could stop it, she might start eating. I walked out of the berry patch, over under the willow in front of the stone basement and the unfinished wood framing sticking into the air, and out to the road up to the Gerstles. They had the only telephone around, and I didn't care that Dad said a Cumming should never be beholden.

My fingers shook finding Mrs. Baker's number. I was violating another rule, butting into grown-ups' arrangements, but she was the one in charge of the Sunday school.

Her sticky-sweet voice turned sharp when she heard who I was. "Why on earth are you calling me?"

"About the picnic, the picnic at our place Friday. We can't have it."

"Freda Cumming, did your mother tell you to call?"

"Not exactly." I wished I could lie and say a sentence without stuttering. "Mother's not feeling good."

"But this is only Tuesday. I'm sure she'll be all right by Friday."

I pictured Mother as I'd just seen her and screamed at the deaf woman, *"My mother's sick!"*

Mrs. Baker hung up.

Old Mr. and Mrs. Gerstle had been listening, and I explained that Mother had been fasting and with the heat and no food or water, she was in terrible shape. I hoped they would think of a way to help or come home with me and talk to her, but they only asked questions.

Scuffling down past the Cloud place, I clenched my jaws to keep from bawling and thought of Marie Cloud, Mrs. Gerstle's daughter, and the time her baby had convulsions. They had come in the night for Mother to go with Marie to the hospital. I began praying to God to make Mother's miracle happen early. But no one came all day.

She was swaying on her feet next morning.

"Please eat something, Mama," I begged. "Drink a little water."

"Not till the Father comes," were the only words she spoke.

By her eyes she didn't know me. As her aimless wanderings began, I followed. She dropped to her knees to pray, struggled up and outside, clinging to the chairs, the table, the walls for support, then back inside to flop a few moments on her bed. The old green smock she wore hung on her like an empty sack, and she had no clothes on underneath, which with Mother was unheard of. I was terrified that any minute she would drop dead at my feet. When I moved too near or reached for her, Mother's vacant mad eyes warned me away.

Hot as it was, she was bound to pass out, yet by afternoon was still on her feet, making her way to the well. She lay across the handle, pumping water to pour over herself, and I watched, numb. How could I make her go inside and lie down? I couldn't hit her; she was my mother.

At last Mother fell and lay gasping on the ground. I bent to help her up, but she pushed me away and got to her feet. Staggering back to the well, she drenched herself again and again. The sopping smock clung to her like wrinkled green skin, gaping open where she had torn at it in her agony. Stumbling, falling to her knees and pulling herself up, she reached the skeleton of the home she had dreamed of for so long. With an arm hooked around a two-by-four, she hung there swaying for the Gerstles on the hill and Marie Cloud across the fence to see. Not once had they been outside all afternoon.

Stepping closer, I peered into Mother's eyes. Whatever demon had been driving her had released its hold. Still, even helpless, she couldn't just collapse and let me carry or drag her inside. To see her brought to this and no one caring, I wished us both dead. Trembling, I held out my hand. She clutched it and let me help her across the dirt yard, up the steps, and around the cluttered table past the tapestry to her bed. She lay staring at the rafters, taking air in through her mouth. Her stringy wet hair on the pillow looked black again. In moments she was asleep.

By now it was nearly dusk, already night in the shack. I couldn't think what to do next or where to go for help. It was no use praying. How could I believe in a God that had told my mother to kill herself? Striking a match, I lit the coal oil lamp and started a fire to heat water to wash the dishes, then carried the surplus raspberries to the cooler.

Mother was sleeping, and I was still cleaning up when I heard an old rattletrap pull into the yard. In it were Wallace and Juana. How had he known we needed him?

"Where's Ma?" said Wallace.

"In bed. We have to do something or she'll die."

"I got the doc coming."

Before long a new coupe swung into the yard, the doctor's, and he and Wallace talked together in low tones. Juana stood in the shadows against the wall, silent.

I was still scared, but the worst was over. I went outside for air and was startled by the lights of a third car. Inside were two Baptists I saw only on Sunday, the summer preacher and Mrs. Baker. I wanted to tell her she was a day too late.

"How's your mother?" said the preacher.

"Everything's fine now. My brother's here and the doctor. It's been hot, and she wasn't eating much, that's all." To get rid of them quicker, I said, "I'll run see what the doctor says and come tell you."

Wallace had opened the cretonne curtains that hid our beds and moved the lamp to a chair by Mother's. She was awake and talking, and I hoped she wasn't telling them her vision. The doctor stood over her, his face flushed, and he looked angry. I hesitated a moment, then hurried out to persuade the Baptists to leave. Just as I reached their car the door of the shack slammed. It was the doctor.

I ran over to him to ask, "How is she?"

"The woman's crazy!" he shouted, and his voice could be heard around the world. "She belongs in Sweetdale."

"Don't say that. It's not true. She's my mother."

He shrugged and climbed into his coupe and roared off. The dust drifted back over my face and bare arms. I turned from the watching Baptists and looked up at the hogback that rose black in the night straight up behind Hillview like the clenched hand of God, as it had for a thousand years, a million. From inside I heard the sound of boots. Wallace stalked from the shack carrying Mother wrapped in a blanket. She hung over his arms like a bundle of rags.

The windows still showed black outside when voices roused me. I was in an auto court cabin in Middleton and couldn't even remember leaving home. Juana and Wallace sat at a table with Brodie drinking coffee.

"I no sooner hit Middleton than I heard about Ma on the radio," said Wallace. He sounded old and cold and tired. "Out in the yard naked and starving to death. A neighbor'd called the sheriff."

"Dad couldn't figure it," said Brodie. "When I went out to tell him, he said she was all right Sunday."

Wallace snorted. "Well, she wouldn't eat for the doctor, said she'd had a vision, and it was God's will. She didn't weigh nothin', seventy pounds, if that. If I hadn't got her to the hospital, Ma'd be dead."

Through the thin walls of the cabin from outside came a sound I'd never heard before, my father sobbing as if all his insides were tearing loose. But when Laurel arrived in the afternoon, hair frizzled and teetering on spike heels and giving me a cold stare, he seemed to have recovered.

"Your mother's in the change," he told her. "She hasn't been herself all winter."

"Wallace said the doctor told him she's insane."

"Happens to a lot of women, Laurel. A year or so ago, a woman out at Hillview went the same way and had to be committed."

Listening to them, I learned that Mother had been force-fed in the night and had started eating on her own once Dad had visited her in the morning. I wanted to say that Mother hadn't acted crazy till she'd gone I didn't know how long without water, but I was still too numb and scared, and they never paid any attention to me anyway.

More than once I heard Dad say, "She'll never live through it."

With all their talk of death and insanity, I didn't know what to expect by evening when they let me go to the hospital to see her, if she would be in worse shape than yesterday or maybe I'd be seeing her for the last time.

Mother was in bed but sitting forward with her hands clasped around her knees. Her hair had been washed and fell loose in silvery waves over her shoulders. At sight of her whole family trooping in, her gaunt face was radiant.

"Why, here's Freda," she said. "How's my girl?"

I searched Mother's eyes. Wherever she'd been, she was back; the madness was gone. I wanted to sink down beside her and put my head on her shoulder. But the Cummings wouldn't let me close, and in a few minutes Laurel edged me out the door.

"You might upset Mother if you stay too long."

Later, when we were all back at the cabin, Laurel talked a mile a minute. "We can't afford anything private. We can't even pay the hospital. What else can we do? She'll need care for a long time."

They were still talking and drinking coffee when I fell asleep with my clothes on. In the morning I asked to visit Mother again.

"Better for her if you don't," said Laurel.

"She coming home soon?"

"Not for awhile."

Juana fixed breakfast, and afterward Wallace and Laurel and Dad left for the hospital. I helped Juana with the dishes and made the beds. Then she put on another pot of coffee and told stories about her Indian grandmother. I watched the expressions change on her beautiful dark face, heard her hiccupy laugh, and didn't know a word she was saying. I listened for footsteps and remembered that it was Mother's day of *feast and a miracle*. She was the only miracle I could think of, that she was alive.

In late afternoon just Dad and Laurel came back.

"How's Mama?"

"Better," said Laurel. Neither she nor Dad would look at me.

"When's she coming home?"

My sister glanced at Juana and Dad, then at me, her eyes cold and her face like a piece of blank paper. "Mother's not coming home. She has to be taken care of."

"Where?"

"Now, Freda—" Laurel's voice sharpened—"don't be hysterical. We don't have money for her anywhere else. She's in the change. It's what happens to women then; they go insane. We just did what's best."

"Mama's gone? Where?"

"To Sweetdale."

Turning my back on them, I went over and stood at a window and stared out at the dreary street in the ugly town. Didn't they understand that Mother's vision wasn't real, that it was just something she'd imagined like my trips around the world being rich and famous? I couldn't believe the Cummings had heeded the unfeeling doctor and sent Mother away without even letting me say good-bye. After awhile I sat off by myself pretending to read a magazine and wished I had my cat for company.

A little later Dad said suddenly, "Do you remember Mrs. Temple, Freda?"

Oh, yes, I remembered Mrs. Temple, going berserk and taking after Hettie with a horsewhip, beating her unmercifully from room to room and out into the yard till Hettie to escape ran to the bathroom and swallowed all of a bottle of poison that burned her around the mouth and down her insides.

"Mrs. Temple came to the train to see your mother off."

I supposed that she, like Wallace and the Baptists, had heard about Mother on the radio. "How'd she get out of the nuthouse?" I muttered.

"She's over her change, been home a month. You'd never think to look at her she'd ever been insane."

But what about Hettie, I wondered. Barely saved and left scarred, would she ever find anyone to marry her or even give her a job?

Dad was on his feet, pacing. "What say we pack up and get on out home?"

Laurel and Juana were coming with us to stay the night. My brother still wasn't back. I'd heard Laurel tell Juana he was the one who signed the papers to send Mother to Sweetdale.

Wallace was probably somewhere getting drunk.

For My Mother
Michele Wolf

I sharpen more and more to your
likeness every year, your mirror
In height, autonomous
Flying cloud of hair,
In torso, curve of the leg,
In high-arched, prim, meticulous
Feet. I watch my aging face,
In a speeding time lapse,
Become yours. Notice the eyes,
Their heavy inherited sadness,
The inertia that sags the cheeks,
The sense of limits that sets
The grooves along the mouth.
Grip my hand.
Let me show you the way
To revolt against what
We are born to,
To bash through the walls,
To burn a warning torch
In the darkness,
To leave home.

A Place for Mother
Joanne Seltzer

PRELIMINARY ADVICE

Remember how you once went shopping
for the right nursery school
and when the teacher asked you
if your child was toilet trained
you lied and said she was.

Use the same strategy
in shopping for a nursing home.

Later—when you are told
of Mother's incontinence—
you will clench your fist and shout:
"What have you done to my mother?"

MORE ADVICE

Have a daughter-to-mother talk.
Ask her what she wants.
If she doesn't know
ask her if she's happy.
She will either say
she doesn't know
or she will be silent.
Tell her how much you love her.
Promise you won't forsake her.

A CHECKLIST

Place One has an eight-year waiting list.
Place Two has a nursing home odor.
Place Three is in a bad neighborhood.
Place Four is in another city.
Place Five won't take medicaid.
Place Six takes only terminal cases.
Place Seven doesn't offer therapy.
Place Eight puts three in a room.
Place Nine requires a hike to the dining room.
Place Ten demands Mother's money up front.
Place Eleven decides Mother won't fit in.

THE SEARCH

Though Mother says
she won't fit in anywhere
you keep on looking.

You learn about levels of care,
levels of caring.

The Jewish home offers
a night in the Rabbi's room
when the Rabbi isn't there

to newly matched couples
who hanker after
geriatric sex.

A SUDDEN ILLNESS

When Mother is discharged
from the hospital
you accompany her down
on the same elevator
with a young couple
bringing Baby home.

They call to mind
the Holy Family
until you realize
that every family is holy.

You feel holier-than-thou.

CONFUSION

While you ponder your choices
Mother continues to slip.

She thinks she will go to jail
for being a dope addict.

She thinks there's a conspiracy
against the family.

She worries about the poison
in the drinking water.

Though people call her *lady*
she isn't sure if she's a woman
or a man.

PLATITUDES

Mother is with God.
Mother is at rest.
Mother is with Dad.

Mother was ready to go.
Mother has paid her dues.
Mother is still with us.

Mother loved life.
Mother lived a full life.

Time heals all wounds.
You will mourn Mother
the rest of your life.

THE ORPHAN

There's no umbrella now
to separate you
from eternity.

Meanwhile an army
marches behind you
in the rain.

Your friends are dead
or dying.

You're a survivor
with all the loneliness
of survivorship.

LIFE MUST GO ON

Your hair has turned white.
Your skin is parchment.
You have a bulldog's jowls.

You ask yourself
what Mother's face is doing
in the mirror.

She sticks out her tongue.

You wonder where the years went
and with horror
realize you forgot to flush
the toilet.

IN CONCLUSION

Not wanting to be a burden
on your children
you sign yourself into
a nursing home.

You become active
in every group
and serve on every committee.

You are voted
resident-of-the-month,
a role model.

Mother would be proud of you.

Birthday Portrait in Muted Tones
Dori Appel

In this expanse of pale couches
and bone-colored carpet
the artifacts refuse to age. After
years of sun and heat, they still seem
like new arrivals popped from
cardboard cartons yesterday. The light
shining through the wide windows
makes me giddy. I want to press
bowls and baskets down harder
on their tables, pound chairs
into the rug, give things weight.
My brother sits in what was
once my father's place. His hair
is grey like mine. Here
where we were never children
we rekindle old resentments over
the three-tiered cake. We are
the bad fairies at this celebration,
avenging slights. Our mother,
if she notices, gives no sign.
She smiles as we push our presents
toward her, picks intently
at the wrappings with slow-motion
hands. Reaching from my nearer seat
to help, I see how white her hair is,
bent over the stiff, bright bows.

Old Woman
Billie Lou Cantwell

A time was
when I smiled sweetly
and coddled old women,
listened to their tales
of how it was
when times were
really bad.

Lately, I don't much
like old women
and try to ignore their
clutching tongues.
The times they rub today
chafe my own
recollections
of not so long ago.

A Woman at Forty
Enid Shomer

A woman at forty
stands long at her mirror
as though it were a pool
which could smooth
the distortions of her face.

On the street she walks
as if each step led her
to an altar, and any corner
might straighten out
her life.

She cultivates flowers,
drapes everything with polished chintz.
Among friends she speaks little
but her hands, moving from hair
to lips to lap

tell the same story
as the bit actress
who inadvertently points to herself
as she declaims the entrance
of the queen.

At night she listens for a knock
on the door, though everyone
she knows is asleep.
Through her window stars
which once granted wishes

are burning as they retreat.

New Directions
Susan A. Katz

Outside there is a thin
wind flirting with the trees
it has teased the curtains
into dancing; I keep time
in my head.

Memorizing the seasons, I touch
things as if my fingers
will learn them
again; weary of explanations,
at midlife I am more comfortable
with the truth.

Outside, the mountain ash hangs
heavy with orange berries,
like overripe breasts they weight
the branches down; I feel
the tug, my flesh molding
itself to gravity; closer now
to the soil than ever
to the sky.

Late Autumn Woods
Rina Ferrarelli

The press of green over
and the ritual of leaves

the wood has settled
into its prime dimensions
the lines etched in the light
pouring in from all sides.

Forts and nests abandoned,
the trash exposed.

Walking through
I can now see where the main path ends
and the others
branching off like veins on a leaf.

The palm of a hand
with a well-marked lifeline.
A wood thinned of possibilities.

Yet the sky, bluest in the north
and visible only in snatches before,
has opened up all around me,
as if a fog had lifted at last,
a heavy curtain.

Athlete Growing Old
Grace Butcher

The caution is creeping in:
the step is hesitant
    from years of pain;
a soft grunt bends the body over,
    and straightens it.
The skin loosens; everything moves
    nearer the ground.

To overcome the softening,
    the yearning toward warmth,
she exercises,
    makes her muscles hard,
    runs in the snow,
    asks herself when she is afraid,
"What would you do now if
    you were *not* afraid?"

She listens for the answer
    and tries to be
    like that person who speaks,
who lives just outside
    all her boundaries
    and constantly calls her
    to come over, come over.

Body
Lillian Morrison

I have lived with it for years,
this big cat, developed an
affection for it. Though it is
aging now, I cannot abandon it
nor do I want to. I would love
to throw it about in play but
must be careful. It cannot summon that agile grace of old. Yet
it's really pleasant to be with,
familiar, faithful, complaining
a little, continually going about
its business, loving to lie down.

I Know the Mirrors
Janice Townley Moore

I know the mirrors
that are friends,
the ones in semidarkness that hide
the hard crease of jowl,
or the ones with the correct distance
to fade the barbed wire fence
above the lips. But skin breaks
like dry riverbeds.
Rooms must become darker,
distance greater.
I grope for a solution,
knowing that no woman
ever looked better with a beard.

Investment of Worth
Terri L. Jewell

You value the earthen vase—
        each crack applauded
        for authenticity,
a slave's Freedom Quilt—
        hand-pulled stitchery
        a rare tale relinquished,
Victorian silver hairpins
        with filigreed flowers
        delicate as unconscious.
A collector of ancients
        quite proud of your tastes
        but scornful of
                curled brown leaves
                slight grey webs
                parched desert soil
        of a woman
        turned and tuned to her ripening,
                whose life is dear
                as a signed first edition,
                whose death as costly
                as a polished oak bed.

Photo by Michelle Noullet

Gracefully Afraid
Mary Anne Ashley

I have a friend who never does anything right. I don't mean morally. Socially. What I mean is, she won't be respectful when it could benefit her; she won't flirt; she won't color her hair; she won't lose any weight; she won't dress herself up; she won't wear makeup; she just won't try to get along. She wears the worst damned looking shoes you ever saw.

They're comfortable, she says.

Well, so what, is what I say. Who wants to be around anyone who wears shoes like that? No man wants to walk down the street with a woman who is fifty-two years old, whose hair is turning grey, who is twenty pounds overweight, whose idea of dressing up is a pink sweatshirt, and who wears shoes that look like that.

I personally know of a court case she lost because she refused to call the judge Sir or Your Honor during the *entire* proceeding. I was furious. I could have killed her. I went to a lot of trouble during that case. I drove her to the lawyer's office several times. I listened while she ranted and raved about justice and injustice and the class system. I sat with her through the whole mess. And she blew it. On purpose. I know that's why he decided against her. All that work. All that time. All that energy down the drain. She owed it to her lawyer, she owed it to me, and she certainly owed it to herself to sit up there and act right. She wasn't rude, don't get me wrong. She answered all the questions with a complete and intelligent response, but that's not what we're talking about. I tried to call him Sir and Your Honor a couple of times, she says. I couldn't get it out of my mouth, and that's the truth. Huh! The truth. It still burns me up to think about it. It's not as though she stood there and made a heroic political or social statement or anything like that.

If she made even the slightest effort with her looks she would be damned attractive. She is now. Almost. In a certain way. But she won't try. And she says that she will never again pay to have her hair cut. That she will never again sit still while someone cuts her hair. So she wears it in a long lank down her back or folded up on her head with two giant bobby pins holding it down. It looks like a big cow plop with straw sticking out.

Don't laugh at my hairdo, she says. I don't like that. Well, I'm not laughing on purpose, just to hurt your feelings, I say. You'd laugh too if you ever looked at it from the back. I don't mean to hurt your feelings, but if something is funny, it's funny.

Okay, she says, but I never laugh at your hair.

Well, of course she doesn't. Every hair of mine is in place. I don't set one foot out the door if my hair doesn't look just right. If your hair looks lousy, you look lousy all over. If you look lousy, you feel lousy. The first thing I do after my morning shower is to apply my makeup. Before I do my hair, I apply my makeup.

It's a work of art, she says.

I'll show you how to do it, I tell her. I've told her that a thousand times over the years. Never mind, she says, that's okay. During the time I've known her she must have spent a thousand dollars on nice cosmetics, but she just takes them home and puts them in a drawer. What a waste. She doesn't do that anymore. Thank God. I hate to see that kind of waste.

I love your sense of ritual and discipline, she tells me. It's true. I understand things like that. I wouldn't say that I'm rigid, but I do things in a certain way, and I benefit from that. You see the results of my work. She works, but you can't see the results. She isn't lazy. Far from it. It's just that she doesn't have a tight routine about anything, and so she does a little of this and a little of that. But nothing shows. No one room in her house is clean on the same day as any other. She is *not* dirty. No way. I couldn't be friends with someone who was dirty or lazy. But her place is always cluttered. Messy. I admit there is a certain charm to it. It gives the impression that she's hard at work on some emotional or intellectual task. Sometimes there is mystery and excitement around her place. I sit on her couch while she's in another room and feel as though she's going to haul out a canvas she's painted in secret. Or she's going to walk in carrying a manuscript she'll slam down on the table. Some literary masterpiece she's written while I wasn't looking. That's one of the things about her I like: she gives the impression that she's somewhere in the wings doing great, creative work. Or that she's behind the scenes developing a new school of philosophical thought. Of course, that's not the reality. The reality is that she's in her advancing middle age, with no good job, no steady job, with an almost-college degree which is worse than no degree at all because she has no money to go back to school. And besides, by the time she gets back to school, if she ever does, they'll have changed all the requirements so that she'll have to start all over again, and all her past work will have been for nothing. The reality is that she's headed for complete disaster. (She doesn't even own an iron. She says she did something with it, but can't remember what!) Sometimes she can't pay the rent; sometimes she can't feed her animals; and sometimes she doesn't have one thin dime in her pocket. I worry about her a lot. But it's her own damned fault.

Don't worry about me, she says, it's not helpful.

I can't help worrying about you.

Then it's your problem, not mine.

Well, that's gratitude for you. Thanks a lot, I tell her. Don't call me up the next time you need money for dog food, and don't turn to me when you need a ride job-hunting. Just don't call on me.

Okay, I won't, she says.

Don't, I say.

Now that that's settled, she says, let's talk about something else. Let's talk about you for a change. I know what. Let's go for a drive to Bodega Bay. I'll pay for the gas.

We'll charge it on her gas card, she means. Through the worst of times, she's held onto that. She was homeless once. Literally. Out in the streets, but she had that card. It's my ticket to ride, she says.

We love to go for drives. We see the same sorts of things. Along the Russian River, out to Jenner or up the coast to Fort Ross, or up the Napa Valley. When she had some money, we drove to Vacaville for dinner at the Nut Tree once a week. When we could stand the traffic, we drove to Berkeley to the Claremont Hotel, or to Normans to eat giant artichokes and walnut pie.

She was a sharp dresser. I felt good walking up the street with her. Not now. She is not one of those women who can throw on rags and look like a million. But one thing that makes me feel good about myself is that, embarrassed or not, I am the kind of person who does not abandon another person because of what she wears or doesn't wear. It's uphill work a lot of the time. Sometimes though, it's fun when we go someplace nice and I'm dressed up and she's not. It's bold and defiant. I feel like people envy my courage and loyalty. Other times, it's not fun at all. It's downright humiliating. I feel she's asking too much of our long friendship. More and more I feel that way.

We're getting older and we should try our best. But she says, No, I did that for forty years. That's half my life. She said that right after she had a dream that she was going to live to be eighty-one. We tell one another our dreams. We like our dreams. We feel friendly toward them, even when they are a little frightening. It's a bond between us. We're both relaxed about what our unconscious minds might cough up during the night. After she told me that dream, she said, Now that's it. The next forty years are mine. I said, Good for you! I had no idea she was talking about not wearing skirts anymore, about letting herself go.

She used to have a beautiful body. Now it's hidden under those twenty extra pounds. Mine is out there, highly visible. You've got a great body, she says. Well, I ought to, I reply.

I work darned hard to keep it that way. I work out in the gym every day. There's not an ounce of fat on me. I run every day. When she runs, she wets her pants. That's not her fault. I know that. She's had kidney infections since she was young. But she could do yoga. But she won't. She even likes yoga. She used to do it with her daughter-in-law. It's getting down on the floor and being out of this world that she says she doesn't like. So she's flabby and I'm not. I'm fifty-one years old and still look great. Like it or not, we get more high marks when we look good in bathing suits.

We both read the same books, and I understand feminist principles. But what is, is. We have to get along in the here and now. This is a man's world and until that changes, we have to do certain things. We have to say certain things; we have to look a certain way. Like it or not. When she kicks up a fuss, I tell her she's just kicking the slats of her cradle.

You know, it's funny. When we first met eighteen years ago, she didn't know beans about being angry or getting revenge or having a good toe-to-toe fight. That's one of the things she liked about me. You don't pretend to any of the virtues, she said. You get even when someone does you dirt, and you don't have fits of remorse about it. I like that about you. You know that anger doesn't kill. I know it too, but I still don't know how to use it. You said *that* to *them?* she'd ask, her eyes popping.

Sure I did, I'd say. So what?

I love the way you say, So what.

When we first met, she'd never given anyone the finger. Hardly swore at all. She couldn't get mad without saying, I'm sorry. Once, when she was sick, I gave her my favorite book on anger, how to express it. She read it, and came off the couch like she was shot from guns. She loved it. She loved it that I gave that book to her. You could say I had a big hand in the kind of person she is today.

She's a great one to have in your corner when there's a fight.

But as we get older, I get nervous about what she'll do next. I say, Please don't make a fuss. She says, Don't call sticking up for ourselves making a fuss. Besides, even if we make a fuss, what can they do to us? They've done just about all they can do. I'll never be a history professor and you'll never be a Hollywood screenwriter. We're just pokey people now, getting old, in our pokey places. For God's sake, let's not go to our graves without at least shooting our mouths off, she shouts.

And let's not go to our graves, I shout back, without you looking pretty for at least one day. I can hardly bear to look at you anymore.

She hung up. Who can blame her? I shouldn't have said that. It was mean. If I feel that way about her I shouldn't pal around with her any longer. It's not fair. It's not just a whim, the way she is. Not some stage she's going through. She's not going to change back. I see that. I'd drop her tomorrow. I think about it all the time. But she's fun to be with, like something funny or special or exciting is about to happen. Sometimes people envy me because she is my friend and not theirs. She's attractive in some elusive way. But it makes me furious.

We didn't talk for over three months after she hung up on me. I missed her. But it was a relief not to see her. Not to deal with her anger and insights. Just do my daily routine: relax, read novels, drift, and window-shop. Sightsee and be seen. Pick the daisies and smell the roses, as the old saying goes. But then I thought, Dammit, I want to see her, want to talk to her because there's something I have to say. So I called her. We got together, had a good time. But things were never going to be the same. We discovered that we could be content not seeing each other for long periods. What a relief.

What we differ about most is what is most important: our dignity. The important thing is respect. How do you get respect when you have that gut hanging down over your belt, and you wear those damned lace-up shoes? Your hair's a mess, and you obviously don't respect yourself. So how do you expect anyone to respect you? I ask her.

And how can you consider yourself dignified with cleavage like that? she says. How can you respect yourself when you dose your head with dangerous chemicals every six weeks? You're over fifty years old, for God's sake, and you bat your eyes like some silly fifteen year old. You spend half your life in front of the mirror. That's not my idea of dignity.

Maybe I do, I say, but I get the good jobs, don't I? I'm not the one who can't pay the rent. I'm not the one who's sick with money worries half her life. The *last* half of her life. Let's be clear about that. You don't even smile at anyone anymore. You still have to live in this world, you know. So what kind of respect are you getting for your trouble? Maybe every two years someone writes from Florida or Washington or God knows where and says he or she likes the story you wrote, but that's only one story. The only story you ever published, and I hate to throw that up to you because I think you're a wonderful writer. You know I do. But you aren't going to get published anymore. You haven't published a story in five years. And you are never going to get your degree, and we both know that because you have a crummy attitude. So where is all this respect that you work so hard to get? Go on, show me. Correct me if I'm wrong, but I don't see any of it lying around here. There isn't any manifested in your refrigerator. You don't even have margarine, for crying out loud. Sometimes you just have to kiss ass, for God's sake. You know that. Tap into reality for just ten lousy seconds!

I don't mean that. We end up yelling. It bothers me. She's very political, very realistic. I say it because I'm mad at her, and I worry about her. It's like having a friend who has a disease that is helped with medication, and then the friend won't take the medication, and you get mad. It's like that. The disease we both have is being born women into a man's world. It's not a nice disease, and it's a progressive disease, but you don't have to die from it. It doesn't have to be fatal. It's like she's turning a disease that's only chronic into a disease that's fatal. And that's scary.

Well, I've just about had it. I love her, and I know she loves me. I love all the fun we've had over the years, and I love the times we've helped each other out of jams and through bad times. But I *don't* want to write protest letters to wardens of women's prisons. I want to write shopping lists. Expensive shopping lists. I want a nice house and pool to sit by, reading or daydreaming, maybe in St. Helena. I've wanted that for all the years I can remember. I want a husband who is financially secure and generous, who is affectionate. One who won't invade my space. In return for what he gives, I'll give him good meals, good sex, and clean, pressed clothes. That's not such a terrible contract, is it? It would be comfortable and peaceful. But I could never trust her in that kind of environment. Not that she'd be rude. But she couldn't be trusted. Something bad would happen.

It shames her and makes her mad, she says, the way I hang around the golf course, the tennis courts. But I play golf, dammit, and I play tennis, and that's where I'm going to find a St. Helena man. Just because I haven't found one during the past twenty years proves nothing, no matter what she says. It only proves that I haven't found him yet, not that I won't. And when I do find him, she won't be an asset. I take that back. Men like her. She makes them laugh, so she'll seem an asset until they get to know her. After that, they'll think she's a communist. And I'll be tarred with the same brush, and I'll kiss that house and pool good-bye. Please don't recoil as though I'm some kind of monster, because I'm not. I'm a woman who will be in her sixties in just ten short years. A woman with practically no value anywhere in this world, so I don't intend to be in this world. I intend to be in the small world of the Napa Valley.

I intend to grow old gracefully, and you can't grow old gracefully if you've spent the last half of your life swimming against the current the way she has. I want to grow old surrounded by pretty things. And I can't do that if I'm worn out with worry because I have a friend who lands in fleabag flophouses, who lives in poverty, who might get hauled off to prison for associating with terrorists, who could die in a ditch beacuse she has no home. I can't look forward to that. I won't. Sometimes now, when she's talking, my attention fades, and I look at her and think, you're going to blow my old age, you old bat. And I hate that.

Last week we went to a powwow at the American Indian University near Davis. I feel lucky to have a friend who was invited to a powwow. I'm glad I went with her. Not that I had a good time. I didn't, but it was an experience that goes into my brain bank. And that enriches me. Next week, I'm taking her to Sebastopol to interview an old woman who was the first female member of the ILWU in Petaluma. That will be interesting. I'm looking forward to it. But it's scary too because I think this old woman's a communist. Don't worry about it, she says, everyone was a communist in those days. But I do. What if it came out ten years from now that I spent the afternoon at the home of a communist? What then? That would put me into the worst kind of light when I could least afford it. I don't intend to grow old with that kind of fear.

I don't intend growing old, living on the brink of disaster, frantic and anxious, the way she is most of the time. Don't kid yourself.

I'm a thin-ice skater, she laughs.

It's not funny, I say. That's not something to be proud of.

I don't want to be called from poolside one nice day to bail her out of some two-bit Central Valley jail. I don't want to explain to my future husband that he has to attend the Beaulieu Vineyard Concert-Under-the-Stars alone because I have to drive down to Oakland to attend to a batty old woman who was found raped and beaten in a downtown alley, and who managed to whisper my name and phone number before lapsing into a life-threatening coma. I just won't do it.

So I've made up my mind. After our get-together next week, I'm going to slip over to her place early in the morning. Before dawn. Leave all of her books I've borrowed on the front porch.

I don't want to do it that way. But I have to. She'll know what it means. I'm going to miss her like crazy. She'll miss me, too. But that's too bad—too bad to end it like that.

But my mind's made up. It comes under the heading: Old Age Security.

words never spoken
Doris Vanderlipp Manley

walking through the city I saw the young girls
with bodies all silk from underthings to eyebrows
legs shaven
heels pumiced
nails glossed
hair lacquered
thighs taut
eyes clear
glad-breasted tittering girls

and I wondered how even for an hour
you could love a woman who has no silk
no silk
only burlap
and that
well worn
tattered
and frayed
with the effort of making a soul

Clearing the Path
Elisavietta Ritchie

My husband gave up shoveling snow
at forty-five because, he claimed,
that's when heart attacks begin.

Since it snowed regardless, I,
mere forty, took the shovel, dug.
Now fifty, still it falls on me

to clean the walk. He's gone on
to warmer climes and younger loves
who will, I guess, keep shoveling for him.

In other seasons here, I sweep
plum petals or magnolia cones
to clear the way for heartier loves.

Dear Paul Newman
Marie Kennedy Robins

After all these years
it's over between you and me.
There's a younger man.
I get to see him five times a week
and he tries to bring me the world.
I worried a lot about your racing
in them fast cars, your beer drinking,
the fact that the color of your eyes
is fading a little with age.
Them eyes always reminded me of Ed Kozelka
who sat next to me in American history.
When you and Ed turned them blues on me,
it sure made my pilot light blaze up.
When reporters asked why you was
faithful to Joanne, you once said,
"Why should I go out for hamburger
when I can have steak at home?"
Now that Joanne is looking so plain,
I wonder if you are going to Wendy's.
Paul baby, it was fun, and
I'll never forget your spaghetti sauce.
I gotta move on.
I'm the same age as you, but in the dark
Peter Jennings will never notice.

Reaching toward Beauty
Hyacinthe Hill

Your love declines. You, thinking little lines
around my eyes are fallen lashes, try
to brush them off. I do exfoliate.
In this autumn of my being, parts of me
fly, like tossed and wintry-blasted leaves.
I don't regret their passing. I must work
to make a clean and crystal-perfect form.
I, alchemist, and I, philosopher's stone,
have sacrificed the fat, and froth, and fur
of youth, to walk through fire, leap in the dark,
swim inward rivers, pray at a wailing wall.
The wrinkles, sags, the greying hair are earned.
You mourn like a child over a broken doll.
Only the core of this crone was ever real.

Love at Fifty
Marcia Woodruff

We come together shy as virgins
with neither beauty nor innocence
to cover our nakedness, only
these bodies which have served us well
to offer each other.

At twenty we would have dressed each other
in fantasy, draping over the damp flesh,
or turned one another into mirrors
so we could make love to ourselves.

But there is no mistaking us now.
Our eyes are sadder and wiser
as I finger the scar on your shoulder
where the pin went in,
and you touch the silver marks on my belly,
loose from childbearing.

"We are real," you say, and so we are,
standing here in our simple flesh
whereon our complicated histories are written,
our bodies turning into gifts
at the touch of our hands.

A Letter from Elvira
Bettie Sellers

I saw your picture in the local news;
since you look like a nice lady,
I am writing you to find me

a princely widower, one who will appreciate
my three-college mind, the delicate lace
of my crochet, the gourmet taste of my cuisine.

He would need a house,
French provincial would be nice,
grey or maybe a forest green.

And a dog too, but not a boxer —
I don't like the way they look at me,
like these Methodists here in Baysville.

The preacher said I was reaching too high
and who would marry me anyhow. Some of them
are in drugs, the Mafia, you know,

and most of the Baptists are perverts.
The Board of Education is worse; they say
I'm too old to be teaching their children.

I enclose my picture, and my telephone number.
Have him call anytime; I'll be here.
I remain, yours very sincerely, Elvira Wade.

Tin of Tube Rose
Sandra Redding

I remember Mama sitting with the can of snuff clutched in her hand, just dipping and rocking, not a care in the world. Mosquitoes and flies would buzz right up in her face but, as long as she had a pinch of snuff in her mouth, she wouldn't even give them a swat. She'd just sit there, that glazed look in her eyes. Once I asked, "Mama, what in tarnation goes on in your mind when you're dipping?"

After spitting in that Kentucky Fried Chicken bucket she always kept close by, she answered. "Can't explain it, Lizzie. Maybe you ought to try it and find out for yourself."

Now I wasn't uppity, but I had no intention of trying snuff, but all that was before Ed died. A death can change a body's mind about a lot of things.

Ed was my husband. We'd been married going on forty years. The night he died, we were sitting in front of the TV arguing about those girls on *Charlie's Angels*. Ed said, "That blond's a real charmer, ain't she Lizzie?"

Well, I didn't agree with him, so I told him what I thought. Before you could say *peaturkey*, an empty can of Budweiser came rolling right over to my foot. At first, I thought Ed had thrown the fool thing at me for saying the blond he liked was skinny and conceited, but when I looked over at the recliner, he was slumped down just like all the air had been let out.

Doc Hollings said it was Ed's heart. "He couldn't have picked an easier way to go," Doc told me. Ed didn't feel much pain and it was over real quick.

That night, I got in touch with the children, all eight of them scattered over six states. "A family's no count," Ed used to say, "unless they stick together when the going gets rough." Well, I reckon we showed our worth 'cause every last one of them kids — even Eva Jane who lives way out in Oregon — managed to get there to see their daddy be put away.

The viewing was two days later at Thompson's Mortuary. By the time we got there, the place was already full of folks. Many of them I'd never seen before. Vergil Peters — he runs the flower shop down at the end of Main Street — must have had a special going on pink carnations 'cause they were stuck in every sort of wreath and basket. Why, they smelled so sickly sweet they could have suffocated King Kong. It's always seemed to me that death deserved a healthier smell than them hothouse flowers, but Ed was dead and people had shown their respect by sending pink carnations, and there wasn't one earthly thing I could do about it.

If the flowers weren't bad enough, people were staring at me. Now I'm not used to being stared at. I knew they were waiting to see me cry, but I'm not much of a crier. Fact is, the only time I ever shed more than a tear or two was when Rhett Butler told Scarlett O'Hara, "Frankly, my dear, I don't give a damn" in *Gone With the Wind*, which I managed to see all six times they showed it at the Rand Theater. Still, everybody expected it so to oblige them, I touched a Kleenex to my eyes, pretending. Then I bent over the casket and took one last look at Ed.

They'd put paint on his face. I could tell. And they'd dressed him in a dark blue suit that wasn't at all becoming. Why, I couldn't even remember the last time I'd seen Ed Chalmers in a suit. Oh, he had a plaid sports coat that he'd wear to Moose Lodge dances, but he'd have never worn anything as drab as that outfit they were putting him away in. I pinched one of the carnations from a wreath that had a plastic telephone fastened to it, the purple banner across the front proclaiming, "Hello, Jesus." Though I tucked the flower in Ed's buttonhole, it still didn't do much to brighten him up. I wanted the Ed I remembered, the Ed I'd bedded down with for most of my life. "Ed," I whispered so nobody else would hear, "why'd you up and die? I was just hitting my prime."

Now some folks might argue that fifty-eight is past prime for a woman, but I was forty-four before I had my last baby. To tell the truth, I was beginning to suspect there wasn't anything more to life than a dirty diaper. When most women I knew were going out to get jobs at the Kmart and Winn-Dixie, I still had runny-nosed younguns pulling at my skirttail. But don't think that ever stopped Ed Chalmers. He married me with one thing on his mind and for all I know, he died thinking about it as well.

Right after the fifth one was born, I had a serious talk with Doc Hollins. "Doc," I said, "how about writing me a prescription for saltpeter so I can put some in Ed's coffee?"

Doc almost laughed his grey mustache off. "That's a good one," he said.

"What do you mean, that's a good one?"

For just a second, he looked puzzled. "You do know, Lizzie," he finally said to me, "that there's no such thing as saltpeter."

Well, I didn't know. I'd heard about it all my life and I couldn't figure out why folks would talk so much about something that didn't exist. I wanted to ask Doc Hollins about something to prevent babies but I didn't. I was afraid he would start laughing again.

After the sixth baby, Mama started complaining. "Lordy, Lizzie," she said, trying to talk around the snuff in her mouth, "looks like you could keep your legs together."

I tried, but Ed pried them apart before that youngun was six weeks old. "Ain't no use yelling," he told me. "The sheriff won't arrest a man for raping his own wife."

Now I don't want you to think I had anything against sex. Fact is, I probably liked it just as much as that blond on *Charlie's Angels*, but I was tired—tired of having babies, tired of eating pinto beans.

I've heard it said that every dog has its day, and I reckon that's true. Mine came after I went through *the change*. That unopened box of Kotex sitting on the bathroom shelf became my flag of freedom. Some women complain that a hot flash is embarrassing, but, far as I'm concerned, it's not half as embarrassing as walking around all your life with a belly full of baby.

After *the change*, the children started growing up, one by one, and fending for themselves. For the first time in years, I had money for lipstick and dangling earrings. Why, I even bought myself a pair of fake eyelashes. Ed liked it. He liked it just fine. We joined the Moose Lodge and started going to dances on Friday nights. Saturday nights were extra special. While I bathed, Ed would look at pictures in his *Penthouse* magazine. Then we'd light the red heart-shaped candle that Sybil Ann, our eldest, gave us for Christmas.

Those were good years, and there could have been more of them if Ed hadn't up and died. Being a widow ain't easy, I'll tell you that. I missed Ed. I missed him terrible. Much as I'd criticized him, calling him a sex pervert back when he kept getting me pregnant, there was nothing that I wouldn't have done to have him back in that oak bed with me. Oh, I smiled and acted respectable in public, but inside I just churned for a man.

For a while, I didn't think about other men—only Ed. I remembered how he'd smelled of Aqua Velva and how black hairs, as well as a few grey ones, sprouted curly over his chest. But before long, I started noticing other men. Young men. Old men. It didn't matter none. I'm ashamed to admit it, but I lusted after all of them. Once I bought six rolls of paper towels just because they were wrapped up in the picture of a handsome mustached fellow. By then, I knew things had gone too far. "Lizzie, old girl," I told myself, "you better do something before you make a fool of yourself."

Before I'd even had a chance to figure out what I ought to do, I got a telephone call from Flora Mae Simmons. "You better get yourself to the revival meeting going on down at Shiloh Baptist Church." That's what Flora Mae said. I'll tell you, it gave me a real spooky feeling getting that call. It was just as if she knew all those wild thoughts were flying through my head. Now, I'm a believer. Always have been. But with all them kids to tend to, I'd gotten out of the church-going habit. After Flora Mae's call, I decided it was high time I got started back.

That night in the dimly lit church, I did my best to concentrate on what the preacher was saying as he stood there proclaiming the word of God with flashing white teeth, his voice all full of passion. When he shouted about sin and damnation, his pink, wet tongue flicked in and out of his mouth. I started wondering what he'd look like with his clothes off. I couldn't help myself. Wicked thoughts just flooded in. My imagination didn't stop with the preacher either. When we stood to sing "Blest Be the Tie That Binds," my addled brain stripped robes from every man in the choir, all the way from the chubby, bald one on the end to the redheaded tenor with a jiggling Adam's apple. But most shameful of all was what happened next. Looking for something to calm my wildness, I turned my eyes upward to the stained-glass window at the front of the church. There, all brightly-colored and thin as a sparrow, was Jesus stretched out on a cross. When I first looked, a piece of cloth covered his privates, but then my dirty mind started working again. Oh, sweet Jesus, he was nailed there just as naked as a jay bird. Lord, help my filthy soul, I said to myself. I had to do something, so when Preacher called for sinners to come forward, I was the first one in the aisle.

"Bless you, Sister Lizzie," Preacher said. I saw beads of sweat on his upper lip. I remember how Ed used to sweat like that when... "Preacher," I shouted out, "I've got sins to confess."

Preacher bent close and whispered, "God loves you, Sister Lizzie. Unburden your heart."

"When I was sitting back in the pew," I said, "I couldn't even listen to your sermon 'cause I kept imagining what you'd look like with your clothes off." Preacher's face turned red as a valentine. I kept talking. "Even worse," I said, trying to find suitable words.

"Yes, Sister Lizzie," he urged, his eyes filled with compassion.

I glanced back at the stained-glass window, the one with Jesus on it. Thank the Lord it was covered with the cloth once again. I knew then that I would never be able to confess to a preacher what I had imagined. It was just too sinful. So, right there in that house of God I lied. It just tumbled out naturally, almost as if it were meant to be said. "Preacher," I said, "I've been tempted to dip snuff."

Preacher looked puzzled. He stammered. Then he told me that he guessed there were worse sins. Finally, clearing his throat, he had the congregation bow for final prayer.

It was strange that at a time like that—the most shameful moment in all my life—I would think of snuff. Even after I got home that night I couldn't get it off my mind. I remembered how Mama had sat dipping, that contented cow look in her eyes. Fact is, I recollected, she didn't even start the habit until after Daddy had his accident down at the sawmill. I wondered.

The very next day, while shopping at the Winn-Dixie, I picked me up a tin of Tube Rose. Soon as I got home, I stuck a pinch in my mouth just the way Mama used to do. It didn't taste half as bad as I'd feared. The bitterness cleared my sinuses and kept my mind off other things.

Now I ain't claiming that Tube Rose can replace Ed. No snuff can do that. Plenty times, I sit here rocking, remembering how smooth Ed's skin felt against mine. No sir, there ain't no substitute for a man. But snuff—well, it's a comfort.

Photo by Lyn Cowan

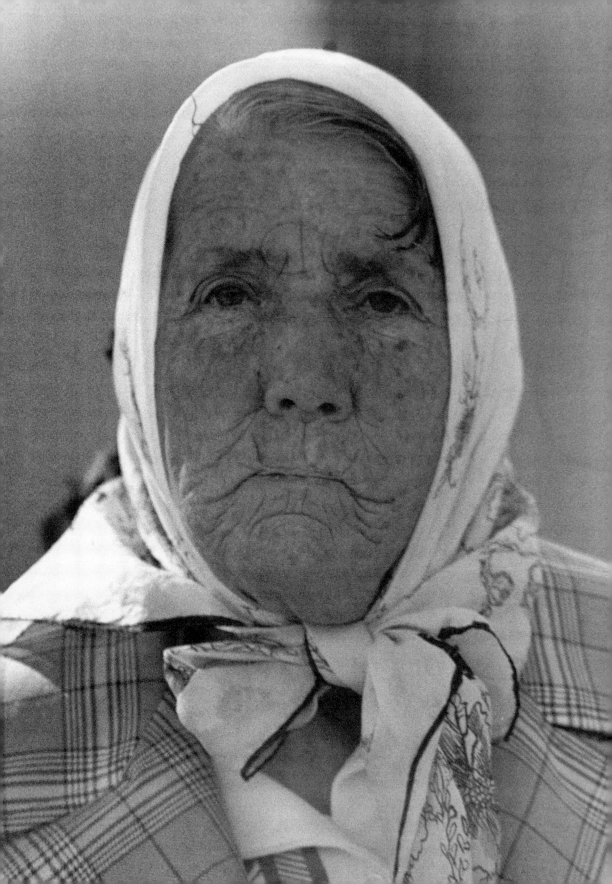

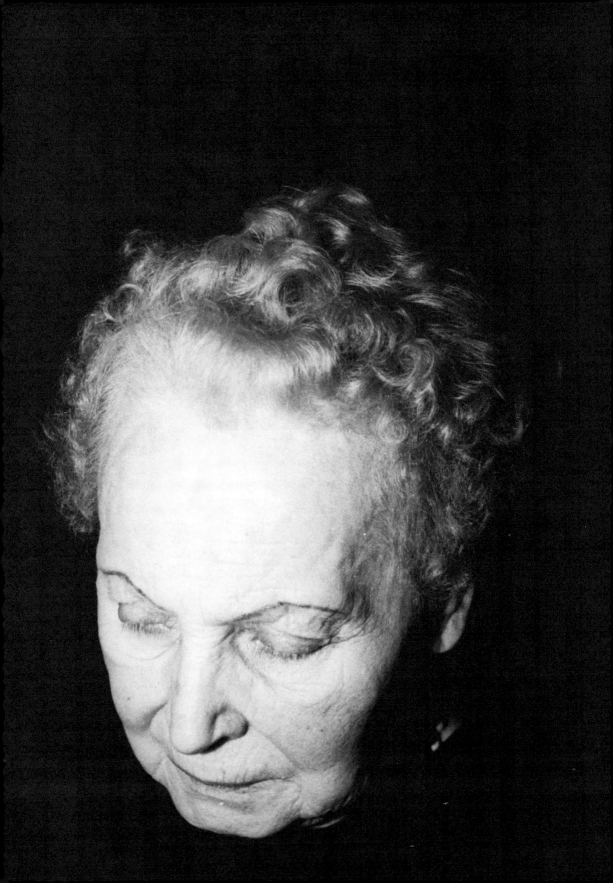

Survived by His Wife
Margaret Flanagan Eicher

Eyes swollen she lay in their bed—
head covered, legs drawn up,
cold though her forehead was damp—
who had warmed herself on his warm flesh.

Now his absence was a constant companion:
his hairbrushes, his keys,
his clothes still smelling of him
in his closet, covered, like museum artifacts.

She shuddered, remembering the shoes he wore
were still beneath the bed
exactly as he left them,
as if covered by a glass case.

All of the things he had handled,
used, inhabited, and finally left
were covered or lying about
like the frames of stolen paintings left behind.

Making the Wine
Marisa Labozzetta

Angelo is in the bathroom now, shaving. I can hear him singing "Gli Stornelli," belting out the same stanza over and over again in his deep, robust voice just the way he used to back in Italy. It is the only song he ever bothered to learn at all. Soon he will come into the kitchen for his orange and cup of black coffee. Peeling the rind in a circular fashion as though he were carving one of his fine pieces of wood, he'll say, "Caterina, take some; it's good for you," and hold out a slice with the same hand that is still gripping the sharp paring knife.

I try to steady my hand as I lift the cup of coffee to my lips. Steady. Steady. Ah! I have spilled some on the table and Sophie must help me put the cup down. She wipes the table—her clean table. Now Tom, Sophie's husband, has that look on his face as he sits across from me. He always looks like that when I spill something, or eat with my hands, or—almost all the time. I want to say to him, wait, you have no idea what it's like. You can't walk, you can't work, you can hardly think. But all I can manage are the same words each time, "I'm sorry." He gets up and walks out of the room.

Angelo is putting on his lumber jacket and going out to the garden. I tell him that I would go with him but my legs are very swollen. I have not been to the garden in years. Angelo goes religiously every day. He plants and weeds and keeps the rows of tomatoes, beans, eggplant, and squash neat like church pews. Then, at the end of the season, we can five hundred jars of tomatoes for Sunday gravy. Angelo has to have his pasta on Sunday. He loves to wake up to the aroma of his tomatoes seasoned with sweet *basilico* simmering for hours in the thick red sauce. When the children were young, they used to come home from church and dip chunks of thick-crusted bread in the bubbling hot gravy. "It's not done yet!" I warned them, but they loved it anyway. Then it was the grandchildren. They would walk over on Sunday mornings after church and do the same.

I never went to church. I wish I had. I made sure the children went, though. Children need religion, I used to think; but now I see it is old people who need it. Sophie won't take me. She says the Mass is too long and I will have to go to the bathroom. Once she brought the priest here to hear my confession. It was the third time I had gone to confession in my life. The first time was my First Holy Communion in Italy, all of us dressed like little brides. The second was fifty years later. I don't know what possessed me, but I wanted to go. Angelo laughed at me. He said I had nothing to confess. He said priests did not deserve to hear anyone's sins. When I came home, I told Angelo all about it, how I said it had been fifty years since my last confession. He called me a fool and, cursing, left the room.

Angelo taught me everything about life. I married him when I was almost sixteen; I didn't know anything. I didn't want to marry him but my parents made me. He was really very kind to me. With so much blond hair, blue eyes, and a Roman nose, my sisters thought he was wonderful. I thought he was too short. I didn't like any men; all I wanted to do was sit in a corner of the kitchen and read books. When Angelo came calling, I would pretend I was tired and go to bed. But he was so gentle, he took me to America and taught me everything. He told me there were diseases that people could get from making love. He knew because one of his *paisanos* had gotten sick from a town whore. She had wanted Angelo to make love with her but he wouldn't. He is so smart, Angelo.

Angelo is always hugging me and every night he wants to have a love affair with me. I don't like it so much. I'm tired at night and the heaviness of his body on my chest is suffocating. Sometimes I think he will crush my lungs. And it is messy; he soils my clean sheets. Angelo is disappointed, but I just don't like it. But there was one time. I don't like to think about it. Angelo was so angry. Father Cioffi had come to visit; Angelo was at the barber's. The baby was only six months old then, and Father Cioffi kept bouncing him onto our bed, then lifting him high into the air and down onto the bed again. When Angelo saw the rumpled bedspread and the priest's black shirt pulled partly out of his black pants, he was furious. He ordered him to leave without an explanation; then he called me *putana*, "whore," he said. I cried and explained that nothing had happened, but he left the apartment cursing. I was already in bed when he came back. He undressed quickly and began stroking my hair. When he climbed on top of me and pulled up my nightgown, I didn't mind; I was thinking of Father Cioffi, what it would be like, his tall strong body, his curly black hair.

I think I will wash the dishes for Sophie. I want to, but where is the soap? I know it's here on the sink. Is this it? No. That's Sophie's china ashtray. Now she's grabbing it out of my hands. "I only wanted to wash the dishes," I tell her. "Just sit down, Mamma," she says. "Just sit down."

Angelo will be coming in for lunch soon. He will want a plate of escarole, a piece of fresh Italian bread, and a large glass of red wine. I hope Sophie has remembered to fill the small bottle with wine from the basement. "How is the garden?" I ask him, as he comes in the door. "It will be a good garden this year, Boss." Boss. He has called me Boss forever. I do tell him what to do often. Maybe sometimes too much. But he needs it; he is too easygoing. There are always things to be done. You must work. Angelo likes to drink wine and laugh with people. His laugh is high pitched, almost hysterical. He does everything totally. I don't laugh too much. I have to work. Work is important. You can't have anything without working. Do you think we would have this land if I had not saved all our money? Oh, Angelo worked too, six, sometimes seven days a week in the lumberyard, but he never made much money. Every night, he came home with splinters, and he and Sophie would sit by the coal stove under the kitchen light. Sophie would take a sewing needle she had sterilized with the flame of a match and poke at his callused hand while he screamed. He is very strong, Angelo; but if he is hurt, he cries out a lot just like a baby. Like when he has attacks of the gout and screams when I walk into the room because vibrations make the sheet touch his foot. I stay awake all those nights. I want to sleep on the couch, to get some rest; I have to work the next day. But Angelo will not let me. He says I have to sleep with him in his bed every night. I am his wife.

I think I will put some coffee on for Angelo. Just turn on the gas. There. It will be done soon.

"Mamma, what are you doing!"

"What are *you* doing?" Damn you, Sophie! You are always taking things away from me. Damn you! I'll slap you! Again! Again!

"This is an electric coffeepot, Mamma. You've ruined it!"

But I never use an electric coffeepot. Angelo likes me to use the drip maker for his espresso. I keep it warm over the flame just before I pour it into his favorite demitasse. Then he puts in a few drops of *anisetta* and a twist of lemon rind. I never use an electric pot. And that man sitting across the kitchen table keeps staring at me with that look again.

"Sophie, who is that man?"

"It's Tom, Mamma."

"Why don't you let go of my hand? Sophie, you're hurting my hand!"

I must turn on the radio now. After lunch, Angelo likes to listen to the news and then the stock market report. We don't own many stocks, just a few of AT&T, but Angelo likes to know what's going on. I don't understand it very much. Still, if it weren't for me, Angelo would never have been able to buy those stocks. I work hard, day after day, in the machine shop sewing clothes. Even though Angelo is retired, I still work, and he drives me to the machine shop in town every morning and picks me up each evening. I look out of the fourth-story window of the factory and see him sitting in the old black Dodge. He is always there twenty minutes before quitting time. He is never late.

But Angelo spends too much money. Like the time he bought a sixty-dollar typewriter for Sophie during the Depression, and in cash! He could not turn away the young salesman standing in the doorway of our apartment. Or the time he bought me the diamond brooch for our fiftieth wedding anniversary. I was angry. He should not have ordered a custom-made brooch from Italy. I yelled at him for spending so much money. And I showed him. I never wore it until the day he died; since then, I have never taken it off.

Angelo is going outside now to work on the trellis he is building for my roses. He knows how much I love flowers. "Be careful," I tell him.

"Don't worry, Boss," he laughs.

"And the grape arbor, don't forget to fix the grape arbor!"

Every year Angelo and I make gallons and gallons of wine. The last time we made the wine it happened. I knew I shouldn't have made it; I felt the pressure mounting in my chest; it was getting hard to breathe. But we had to make the wine. If we didn't, the grapes would go bad. All that time and money would be wasted. We had to make the wine, and we did. And it happened. My heart. I remember the first time I opened my eyes after the attack. Angelo was standing over my hospital bed like a frightened schoolboy on his first day of class. Suddenly, he threw himself across my still body and wept even harder than when the baby died, harder than I had ever seen him before. I took his hand in mine and held it as tightly as I could. "Don't cry, Angelo," I said.

"I made it. Didn't I?" He nodded. "I made the wine, Angelo. I made it."

Angelo loves living here in the country. It reminds him of our *paese* in the mountains of Rome. Thanks to me, we were able to save the money to buy it. I used to cook cheap meals and sew the children's clothes so we could save. And little by little, we saved enough to buy a few acres, then a few more. And we never owed anybody—nobody. Angelo is different here with the grandchildren. In the city he was mean and strict with our children. He was afraid for them—this new country with all of its freedom. There were so many things to get in trouble with—gangsters, cars, subways. If the children were not home on time, he would go out looking for them; then, when he got them home, he would send them from one side of the kitchen to the other with a single slap. But here in the country he plays with the children, chasing them around the farm with his belt folded in half and snapping it, pretending he will catch their fingers in it if they dare to stick them in. But we are not in the country anymore, are we? And work? I can barely lift myself from this chair which has become a part of me, an extension of myself.

"I have to go to the bathroom again," I tell Sophie.
"It's too late, Mamma. Look what you've done!"
I don't remember doing it. One minute I had to go to the bathroom and the next minute I called Sophie. Maybe it wasn't the next minute. Maybe it was a long time after. Is that possible? I keep looking at Sophie, waiting for her to tell me if it was a long time after.

It is almost four o'clock. I have to turn on the television because Angelo will be in soon and he will want to watch our story. This and wrestling are the only programs he loves. When he watches wrestling, he screams and laughs as though he were right there in the audience. Oh, and *Gunsmoke*, he loves to watch *Gunsmoke*. But our story is his favorite. It's on every day and is about a nice girl named Nicole. Nicole has a lot of problems. Right now she is pregnant but can't find the father of the baby, who really loves her, but doesn't know she is pregnant. Every afternoon, we watch to see what Nicole will do. I hope Sophie is making stuffed peppers and sausage for dinner. Angelo likes to eat stuffed peppers and sausage on Monday nights. I think I smell sausage.

After dinner, Sophie gives me a bath. I wish I could bathe myself, but I can't seem to remember what to do. I get into the tub and I am fine. I go for the soap and I get confused. I get so confused. Then my head begins to hurt and I am dizzy. I'm afraid I will fall. But I'm sitting. My head hurts so much.

"Sophie, it hurts."

"What hurts, Mamma?"

"I don't know."

I always feel good after my bath, but I never want to take one. Sophie tells me it's good for me, but I'm afraid. Tom tells me I'm dirty and smell. I never know what will happen to me there in all that water. I don't care if I smell; I'm afraid.

Yesterday, or maybe it was last week, Sophie took me to a nursing home. It wasn't really a nursing home but something better. The floors were very shiny and it smelled like a hospital. There were groups of people sitting in wheelchairs singing old songs. They looked so young; I like to sing.

We sat in an office and a man behind a desk asked me a lot of questions. I knew I had five children, but I couldn't remember any of their names, just Sophie's. I couldn't remember one other name.

"She knows the words to old songs," Sophie said right away.

"Fine, then, let's hear one," the man said.

So I started singing "Ramona," but when I looked at Sophie, she was crying, without a sound, just tears streaming down her face.

Don't cry, Sophie, I can remember the words. Don't worry, I thought, I know the words.

Then a funny thing happened. The man said "No" to Sophie; he said I didn't qualify. And Sophie helped me out, and she was smiling.

Tomorrow is the anniversary of Angelo's death, and I want Sophie to take me to church to the Mass they will say for him. Angelo never went to church after the time with Father Cioffi, but they will say a Mass for him anyway. I didn't tell the priest he never went to church. He should have gone; we both should have gone.

I sleep with Angelo tonight as I have for all these years. He snores loudly and rhythmically to the noisy ticking of the alarm clock on the night table. I have never known any other man in this way except him. I want to have a love affair with you tonight, Angelo. What? No, I cannot promise I will like it, but I won't complain. Please, can we have a love affair tonight?

Come to Me
Sue Saniel Elkind

Come to me looking
as you did fifty years ago
arms outstretched
and I will be waiting
virgin again
in white that changes
to splashes of roses
as we lie together
Come to me smiling again
with your mortar and pestle
and vitamin pills
because I am given to colds
and coughs that wrack us both
Oh come to me again
and I will be there
waiting with withered hands
gnarled fingers
that will leave their marks
of passion on your back.

Two Willow Chairs
Jess Wells

This is a lesbian portrait, I tell my friends, pointing at the photo in a thick silver frame on my desk, but they don't understand. To them, it's just a snapshot of two empty chairs and they cock their heads at me, wondering why the photo has a place of honor and the chairs are the subject of such elaborate plans.

I took the picture when I was seventeen, which made the chairs brand new, my mother's sister, Ruth, and her lover, Florence, in their fifties, and their relationship in its fifteenth year. Flo's chair is made of boughs of willow, twisted into locking half moons, a rugged chair that somehow looks like filigree. Next to it on their lawn—a secluded, overgrown stretch of grass and overhanging vines—was Ruth's chair, a simpler one with a broad seat and armrests that gape like a hug. All around the chairs are flower beds usually gone to seed and grass that was never "properly cut," my stepfather would growl in the car on the way home from visits—grass thick like fur that Flo would wiggle her toes in, digging into the peat until her feet were black and she would hide them inside their slippers again.

The year of this snapshot, Aunt Florence was "struck with spring" as she used to say to me. We arrived on the Fourth of July to find blooming peonies and iris and marigold ("always marigolds against the snails" she would whisper to me, as if imparting the wisdom of womanhood). Florence and my mother wandered the garden, pointing at stalks and talking potting soil, promising cuttings to each other and examining the grapevines up the trellis, while Ruth and my stepfather faced each other silently, she slumped in the willow chair like a crestfallen rag doll and he sitting rigid, twisted sideways on the plastic webbing of a broken chrome chair. I wandered the yard alone with the garden hose. After ten minutes of listening to the women's voices but not hearing anything, Ruth got up and slouched into the house to start bringing out the beers, calling to the man in an overly loud voice, "So, Dick" (everyone else called him Richard), "how's business?"

Talking commerce was a great diversion for him, and my mother was already occupied with explaining her begonias, which left me to be the only one in the place grappling with the realization that this lesbian child was being deposited for the summer with the family's lesbian aunts because a new stepfather, two brothers, and a male cat were more than I could possibly stand. It was the first of many such summers, visits that after a few years turned into summers with autumns and then special Christmases and soon all important holidays and all important matters of any kind. That first summer, nervously pacing the backyard, I knew it would develop into this, and, when my parents finally left, Ruth and Florence and I stared at each other with wonderment. They'd never had a family before and all of a sudden they had a daughter, full-grown and up in their face feeling awkward. Since my mother was straight, there was something I could dismiss about her, but here were these two, with the weight of maturity *and* the righteousness of twenty years of lesbian lifestyle behind them. Now *that's* what I considered authority.

Aunt Ruth breathed a sigh of relief after the car had pulled out of the drive. Florence let some of her gaiety drop but turned to me, ready to fulfill her last social obligation of the day.

"Beetle," as she called me since I was a baby with big eyes. "Welcome." There was so much hesitancy in her voice, fear almost, as if this child, who did not really know about being a lesbian, were looking at a lesbian who did not really know about being in a family. I dropped the garden hose and wiped my hands on my pants, trying to smooth my carrot-red hair that was frizzy in six different directions, as Florence strode over and gathered me in her arms.

"I don't know about these chairs," Ruth said, getting up and yanking one out of the grass. "Let's take them back by the trellis," she said to me, "Florence's favorite spot." And we all grabbed chairs, me taking my mother's chrome one since it was known to all but Richard that his was the only broken chair in the place. We settled into the afternoon, our conversation picking up pace, while Florence shuttled lemonade and beers. That's when I got my first photo of the chairs.

Ruth was sitting sideways, her leg slung over the arm of the chair, head thrown back, her whole big body lit by a streak of afternoon sun. Florence was struck by spring only in selected places and the back of the yard was not one of them: the grapevines behind Ruth's head dangled low and free, the grass crept up around her chair even though it was early in the season.

We had become very quiet for a moment, and Ruth turned in her chair to talk privately to Florence. My camera caught her in midsentence, her mouth open, hand reaching for her lover's knee, her eyes still not aware that Aunt Flo was in the house and that she and I were alone, her face showing all the tenderness and history and trust in her femme as she turned to ask, "Wren, what was the name of that..."

Ruth looked back at me. "I wish you'd quit with that camera," she growled weakly as I laid the photo on the tops of the tall grass to develop, already sensing that I had exposed her. And in a way, she was right. Until then, I had used this camera as a form of self-defense, silently proving to my brothers how stupid they looked, threatening to catch them in the act, snapping photos of my mother as if trying to prove to myself that she wasn't just a phantom woman. But this day, this photo of Ruth and the empty willow chair was the first photo I had ever taken in an attempt to preserve something beautiful.

I handed the photo to Florence first, as she returned with two beers and a lemonade. She stared at it a long time, seeing the look on Ruth's face.

"Oh God, Wren, get rid of that! I look like a jerk," Ruth protested, but Florence held the photo to her.

"You look wonderful. Besides, I want a photo of my chairs. Here, Beetle, take a picture of the chairs for me. Rudy, get up. God, I wish the garden looked better."

Florence kept the two photos in her jewelry box for years. The two willow chairs stayed in their places in the back of the yard, and whenever I would visit (on leave from the army, or home from another city), we would first convene at the chairs, even during the winter, when we would huddle in big coats and share important news like a ritual before rushing inside for the evening.

Years later, when Florence gave the photos to me, there was one taken of myself and Flo sitting on a porch step, our pant legs rolled up from gathering mussels in the tidepools. Florence is gesturing to me, her arms in the shape of a bowl.

"Now look, honey," she said, "don't give up. Love is just a matter of the right recipe: a cup and a half of infatuation, a pinch of matching class status, two tablespoons of compatible politics, and three generous cups of good sex. Mix. Sprinkle liberally with the ability to communicate and fold into a well-greased and floured apartment. You bake it for at least six months without slamming the door and pray you have love in the morning. And it works—when you've got the right ingredients."

Of course their relationship was a serious one, so I have photos of times when the recipe wasn't quite right with the two of them, either. In the package with the other photos is a black and white from the '50s of Florence in a wool suit and a hat with a veil standing at the rail of an ocean liner. She and Ruth put all the money they had into a ticket for her to go to Europe, and even though it was the most incredible trip she'd ever taken, she looks miserable in the picture. The veil is down over her face, almost to her lips that are thick with lipstick, and she's wearing kidskin gloves but not waving. She looks very tight and cold to me in this picture, but they hung it in their house for years: Ruth liked how smart Flo looked, but Aunt Florence would stand in front of it, holding my hand (even though I was home on leave for the third and last year) and say, "Beetle, I keep it because it reminds me of when I was less frightened of running and being alone than of staying and loving." She turned to me, one hand on her hip. "Now isn't that incredible, to think that it's less scary to have a lousy relationship than a good one? That intimacy is more terrifying than loneliness? God, the world is so crazy, Beetle. It's like saying garbage is more delectable than food." Well, I stood in front of that photo with her, looking up at her glowing face, then back at the picture of that sunken young thing, and it seemed her face now wasn't wrinkled by age, just stretched from being so open. I thought about my latest crush in the barracks and how good Florence's choice seems to have been (after all, here was the home and the warmth and Ruth lounging on the sofa throwing cashews to the dog), but I looked back at that picture, those eyes big and scared, and I knew that's where I was, a veil over *my* face. I turned from my aunt and thought, *Oh Jesus, somebody send me a ticket and point me toward the ocean.*

Ruth kept the photo at her side of the bed, as if to remind herself of how far Florence had run and how close she now lived.

On Florence's side of the bed was a photo taken the summer after she returned. The two are in funny swimsuits with pointed bras, Ruth sleeping in Florence's arms. Flo is bending to kiss her on the neck and years later, she related to me that, lying in the sand with her lover in her arms, Florence could feel the years passing. She could feel Ruth getting older even though she was in her thirties, feel her getting heavier through middle age, belly growing across her hips, feel her shift in her sleep from an injury to her shoulder that she didn't have yet, saw the scars she would have in the future, Ruth getting smaller and more frail as she aged, wrinkling into buttery skin. And all the time, holding Ruth encircled in her arms, Florence knew that this would be the progress of her world, that this was her future and her life, that this woman between her arms was her home.

Of course Flo had pictures of her Mom and Dad, who have been dead for nearly two decades now, and the family at picnics, Ruth playing horseshoes on her sixtieth birthday, and pictures of me when I was a kid with teeth missing, though we won't go into that. There's another lesbian portrait in this stack from Flo—it's a picture of a dog.

Clarise was the spaniel that Florence had when she was lovers with the woman before Ruth (which is how she was always referred to, she never had a name), and Flo kept the photo on top of the television for years after she had left the woman and the dog. The little thing was sitting attentively on the beach, clumps of dirt hanging on its paws. It was the first dog Florence had ever learned to love, and every year, with a faraway look in her eyes, Flo would ramble on about how special and psychic and beautiful and protective it was. It was everything a dog should be. Just a few years ago, Ruth, sick and lying on the couch, threw off the afghan and snatched the photo off the TV.

"For godsake, Florence, it's over, and it's OK that it's over," she shouted, starting to cough. "The dog wasn't the only thing good, and the woman wasn't the only thing bad. Now com'on."

Florence went into the backyard and sat in her willow chair. It was her seventieth birthday and she should have a jacket, I thought.

"Stay here, Beetle," Ruth said.

"I don't see why you're jealous of a dog, Rudy. For chrissake, it was years ago."

"I'm not jealous. Florence doesn't know what to do with all those years spent with that woman, and so she puts them here," she said, tapping the glass frame. "When you're consumed with bitterness, where do you put all the good times? The dog. The only reason I'm even saying it is because she knows it herself. A couple of months ago, we went to Bolinas, remember...?"

"Where we used to gather mussels?"

"Right. Well, Wren thought the air would make me feel better or something, but who should come trotting up but the spitting image of that dog. Splatters mud all over Wren's newspaper, knocks the damn iced tea into the potato chips, and rolls over to stick up her tits. I mean it. Well, it finally dawns on Wrenny, Goddamn, maybe that Clarise was just a fucking dog, too."

Now I have the photo. I keep it with a bunch of others Florence gave me in a white, unmarked envelope. These are the painful pictures, the ones that bring floods of heat to your face, pictures you look at and smell perfume. There's a picture of Florence pointing at the flowerbeds with her cane, trying to get *me* to be struck with spring and do some planting while I waited for Ruth to get well. Then there's Ruth lying on the couch covered with the afghan, looking tiny and angry, and, after she died, a photo of Florence looking remarkably like her picture in the hat with the veil. Florence never went back to the chairs after Ruth died, never went into the back of the yard, only stared at it from the kitchen window, stricken now that Ruth, love, hope, and future were dead and decaying, confused by the sight of the grass and the flowers blooming, as if life were threatening to overtake her when she knew it was death that was the encroacher. The grapevines grew lower, entwining with the boughs of the willow chairs, as if threatening to scoop them into a cluster and throw them up to the sun to ripen, while the grass underneath fought to drown the chairs in green. I took a picture of the chairs last year in this condition, but I conveniently lost it. I do have a snap of me, fifteen pounds thinner from not sleeping while Florence lay dying, and one of my Mom at Flo's wake, crying like she couldn't at Ruth's. Maybe someday I could frame them and hang them and still be able to walk through the room, but I doubt it. Right now all I can manage is that first snap of the two empty chairs. My friends don't understand it. Nor do they understand why I'm borrowing a truck and calling around for a hacksaw.

"I have to save the chairs," I tell them, slamming down the phone on my mother and dashing for my jacket. The house has been sold, finally, my mother tells me, and the new owners are sure to throw Wren and Rudy's chairs into the dump—if there's anything left of them. They were nearly part of the grapevine forest last year when Florence died. First thing in the morning, I'll cut the chairs away from the underbrush and drive them to a field near Bolinas where they can sit together and watch the unruly grass grow up around them again, maybe this time forever.

Planting
Cinda Thompson

Two
Old people work
Side by side
She wears a hat
The old man boasts
No hair at all
She moves
And he kneels
He digs
And she nods while
He speaks
To the seed
She ardently covers
Row by row
They rise and bend
Over their garden
On earth
Sunflowers will bloom
Toward
Late summer

Maybe at Eighty?
S. Minanel

They say wisdom comes as you age
Now I'm in a real jam
at sixty I should be a sage
look what a fool I am!

Endurance
Fran Portley

We women who have lived
through many winters
are sisters to mountain flowers
found in rocky crevices
high in the Alps.

Hardened by wind and snow
we endure cold
absorb brief sun
reach long roots
to meager sustenance
lift bright blossoms to empty air.

Becoming Sixty
Ruth Harriet Jacobs

There were terror and anger
at coming into sixty.
Would I give birth
only to my old age?

Now near sixty-one
I count the gifts
that sixty gave.

A book flowed from my life
to those who needed it
and love flowed back to me.

In a yard that had seemed full
space for another garden appeared.
I took my aloneness to Quaker meeting
and my outstretched palms were filled.

I walked further along the beach
swam longer in more sacred places
danced the spiral dance
reclaimed daisies for women
in my ritual for a precious friend
and received poet's wine
from a new friend who came
in the evening of my need.

Social Security
Barbara Bolz

She knows a cashier who
blushes and lets her use
food stamps to buy tulip
bulbs and rose bushes.

We smile each morning as I
pass her—her hand always
married to some stick,
or hoe, or rake.

One morning I shout,
"I'm not skinny like
you so I've gotta run
two miles each day."

She begs me closer, whispers
to my flesh, "All you need,
honey, is to be on welfare
and love roses."

Litany for a Neighbor
Ellin Carter

Jubilate Dea

Because you wear a sunbonnet in your garden
    and wash doilies and dry them on
    newspapers on the carpet, and all
    your African violets bloom.

Because you live on the next street, not
    next door, and you do not even imply
    a comment on the state of my yard.

Because you took in my cat Mushroom when
    he left home, repelled by our new
    kitten, and succored him during
    a blizzard.

    (And even though he will never come
    home, for so long as you both may live,
    I still forgive you.)

Because, though they pass through an alley
    of Doberman pinschers, all the cats
    of the neighborhood congregate in
    your grape arbor, where they rise up
    and worship you.

The Wildcat
Catherine Boyd

The Schraders, who live up the street, saw it first. They heard their garbage can tip over, and when they turned on their floodlights it was tearing open green Hefty bags and devouring scraps. It lifted its small fierce head and screeched a warning to stay back — and in two bounds the wildcat was gone.

For a while, there were daily reports. The Keifer's trash can, lodged in a frame of four-by-four posts, had its rubber-clamped lid forced off; its booty was plundered. The Gabrielsons heard crying one night but aren't sure which direction the sounds came from. Todd Henny, coming home late from a planning commission meeting, passed the junipers on his long driveway and caught the reflection of the wildcat's steely eyes as it disappeared into the night.

Todd is a bachelor and a keeper of fish. He had left a window open that night, and he found its screen shredded. On his living room floor was a mess of broken glass, water, orange and turquoise gravel, and the remains of a half-eaten pacu.

After this a trap was set in Todd's backyard because he doesn't have any children who might step on it. The Stewarts and the Keifers put poison in their trash cans, and the Animal Control sent out a notice instructing us to call immediately if we ever saw it, no matter the time, day or night.

I often dream of the wildcat. Usually I dream I come upon it by accident in the yard, or while in the pantry, or going somewhere in the car. One time, in my dream, I was awakened by its calling. It was early morning, the light was soft, the air pure, the day clear and inviting in a way I had completely forgotten a day can be. I stumbled from bed and down the stairs. The wildcat was on the screened porch at the back of the house. It was not so small, and it gave me a quick look of recognition—and then it took off.

I swung open the screen door and followed as fast as I could. The wildcat scrambled over the fence, and it wasn't until I was halfway over that I remembered I am seventy-nine years old and can no longer scale six-foot walls. Still, I kept looking over the fence. I saw the wildcat dart playfully back and forth through a field of oats and dandelions, an endless field that wasn't there when I woke, feeling fit and happy, put my robe on, and went out to the backyard.

The presence of the wildcat in the neighborhood has brought a change to my routine. In the morning, after I've had breakfast, watched the *Today* show, and cleaned the kitchen, I turn everything off and lie on the couch in the living room with my eyes closed. I search my mind for dreams, or fragments of dreams, I may have had about the wildcat. If I find one, I re-create it a few times before going on with my day.

The mail comes at about ten-thity. It's mostly junk, solicitations for cruises or clubs or hearing aids, or publications that will tell you how best to care for your health and organize your finances. But there are often letters, too, and the magazines my late husband, David, and I read together at night for almost fifty years.

After lunch I check the local paper. I know if anything ever happened to the wildcat, it would be in the newspaper. There used to sometimes be an article, in the middle pages, a few lines describing the latest pilferage or fright the wildcat had caused, though for more than a month there has been nothing.

Every afternoon I drive a little farther to reach a pet shop I haven't used yet. I pretend to not be looking only for six pacu. I remember to not talk too much. I pay with cash, never a check or the Master Charge. When I get home, I put the fish in a bucket in the potting shed. I lock the shed door.

Sometimes I go to afternoon teas or dinner parties, and these times with friends are pleasant diversions from my routine. But I keep my nights to myself by claiming to retire at nine o'clock. I don't. As much as anything, I enjoy the late hours at my desk in the study, where I keep up a steady correspondence with my three children and their children.

When I'm sure the lights at the Worbys' house have been extinguished for the night, I put on my robe and walk out to the potting shed, get the bucket, and carry it to the flower bed near the back fence. I set it down. Then I go back inside, slide open a window to the living room, stretch out on the couch, and begin reading from whatever book I'll bring to bed that night.

When I hear the splashing sounds, I slip a marker in the book, look up to the ceiling, and sigh. I feel released. Content. Pleased. Although the splashing lasts but a few minutes, it's an integral part of my routine, a way of almost formally declaring an end to another day.

A sudden silence tells me it's finished. I go out to the back fence again. I pour the water out of the bucket, onto the flower bed. I whisper to my friend, "You'll always be safe with me."

Out of the Lion's Belly
Carole L. Glickfeld

She maintained that she'd had a marvelous sabbatical in Kenya, even in the face of those who were saying it had unhinged her and were calling for her dismissal from Lincoln Junior High School, where she taught art. These facts were undisputed: that before her year in Kenya, she had been a model teacher; she had been punctual, never arriving late to school nor failing to turn in her lesson plans in a timely fashion; she had graded her pupils' papers promptly and had been prompt for meetings with parents; she had promoted and achieved order, using only her softly modulated tones, never the shrill rage or the nasal sarcasm that were the modus operandi of the other teachers attempting to hold twelve-year-olds in check.

When the matter came to court, almost two years later, she again said, this time to the jury, looking past the shoulder of the interrogating attorney for the school district, that the sabbatical had been the highlight of her years, second only to the many hours she'd spent teaching Lincoln's junior high school pupils art, or, as she developed her notion, "those elements of art that would in some lingering way enhance and enlarge the vision of what in this life was important. Vision with a capital V."

"And did that year in Africa change your vision, Miss Inwood?" the attorney asked, pronouncing "Africa" as though it were a dark, vermin-infested cellar.

She blinked rapidly, and cocked her head. "But of course it did."

"In what way?"

"Why, in every way."

"Would you elaborate on that, Miss Inwood?"

She did or she didn't, according to your perspective. The paper had it that her lengthy anecdote was interrupted by the judge, who asked her to "get to the point."

Her anecdote centered on a fluffy lion cub, "a ball of the palest angora," rolling around on its back a few feet from its watchful mother, a few yards from a hotel veranda where Miss Inwood had sat drinking tea out of a fine china cup. "Imagine the moonlight, a platinum moon, a three-quarters moon, oblong, you know, and ever so slightly askew, a *trompe l'oeil*, of course. The lions were the color of the moon, almost without hue, luminescent, but later, when I attempted to paint them, I found—"

The key witnesses for the school district included two pupils, their mothers, and the school principal. The attorney referred to the Zweigs as "measuring sticks," because Miss Inwood had been Marilyn Zweig's art teacher both the year before the sabbatical and the year after. The testimony of Elliot Marcus and Mrs. Marcus was said to be "of value" because those witnesses represented pupils and parents "without preconceived expectations of what constituted Miss Inwood's usual behavior." The attorney went on to say, "I submit to you that we will fully detail the defendant's unfitness to teach, the intolerable situation that her behavior created, behavior which, and I state this advisedly, clearly demonstrates that she has gone off the deep end—"

"Objection!" said Miss Inwood's attorney, rising to his feet. "We are not presenting any psychiatric evidence here. Counsel has no expertise—"

"With all due respect," the plaintiff's attorney said, " 'off the deep end' refers to behavior at the most extreme end of the scale, the scale being the range of what we agree is normal, customary, acceptable. As I say, way, way off the scale's very end—"

Miss Inwood was my teacher. Not in a public school, but in her home. She had long since "retired," she told me, from public school teaching, giving private lessons "to a select few." I'd heard about her from a friend who used to take lessons from her, which she found "disturbing." The nature of the disturbance intrigued me, having less to do with the fine quality of the lessons than Miss Inwood's habits. "She's a trip," my friend said. "Practically buried in her art. It's her whole world, but then she goes off on these peculiar tangents, the same ones all the time."

Since neither single-mindedness nor eccentricity seemed to me faults, I called Miss Inwood. She said I would have to appear for an interview.

"How many samples should I bring?"

"Of your work? None, dear. Just bring yourself. Your best self."

Her house was a small colonial brick with a wrought-iron gate enclosing several giant oak trees. My satisfaction at having chosen an art teacher who had taste wavered, however, when she opened her door. Over her blouse and skirt she wore a pink organdy pinafore apron, trimmed with a two-inch white ruffle, red rickrack, and appliqued blue and yellow flowers.

"That's interesting!" she said, pointing to my hair. "Does it make you feel off balance?"

I had one of those fashionable asymmetrical cuts, above the ear on one side, below on the other. "Jazzy, rather," I said.

Her glance traveled down my clothes, a Shetland sweater over a buttoned-down shirt and jeans. She nodded and stepped aside to let me in.

"I've been baking. Excuse my apron. I mean, the raffishness of it. My sister-in-law has raffish taste. Isn't that a good word?"

My breathing resumed its normal rhythm.

"Go ahead, talk to me," she said, sitting me down at the kitchen table. "I have to punch this down and then you'll have my full attention." Her manner suggested a lady of a large country mansion, whose grace had a pleasant dottiness that signalled her safe remove from the real world.

"What are you making?" I asked, watching as she pummeled the ball of dough and then slapped it against the cutting board, picking it up and slapping it down again.

"Two whole wheat loaves," she said, looking up at me. Her blue eyes were small, crinkly, deeply set beneath her arched grey brows. She looked as though she were perennially asking a question. "So, you're the conservative type," she said, using her lower lip to direct her breath upward, blowing away a grey, curly wisp which had fallen onto her forehead. She shaped the dough into another ball, placed it in a bowl which she covered with a linen towel, and set it in the oven. "Away from drafts," she explained.

"Is your painting also conservative?" she asked, pouring me a cup of tea. She set down a platter of chocolate chip cookies and then poured herself some tea. "Is it?" she repeated.

"I don't think so. Although I haven't been what I'd call experimental."

"If we start our lessons soon, we'll have five months until I go to Hawaii. I always go to Hawaii in February." She paused, clearly expecting me to ask why.

"Not for a vacation?" I said.

"You think not?" Her eyes, beginning to dance, told me I was onto something. But what?

"To paint!" I guessed.

She slapped her hand on the table. "I could tell by the sound of your voice, dear, but I wanted to see you. Really *see* you, capital S, with my own eyes. If I may venture to say so, I think you are seeing me, capital S. So the matter of *whether* you will be my pupil is moot. Have a cookie."

I had been her pupil for a couple of months before she showed me any of her paintings, taking me into her attached garage, which she'd converted into a second studio with skylights. The paintings stood on the floor, leaning against the walls, and there

was one in progress, on an easel. "I won't let you guess which is which," she said, pointing out to me that her "riotous phase" was over and that she was in a more "subdued" period. Her riotous phase had solely to do with her sabbatical in Africa, it seemed, to which she referred more and more as our intimacy increased.

"Bougainvillea! You've never seen such bougainvillea: rich mauves and reds. And, my dear, the hibiscus, the yellow flowering acacia. The perfumes. Have you ever smelled freesia, fields of it which fairly *intoxicate* you? That was in the Central Province. My African students laughed. Oh, did they laugh! Why paint pictures of flowers when you could have them for the plucking? they asked."

"I thought you were there on sabbatical."

"And so I was. From my duties here. I taught in a little village, part of a Teachers' Exchange Program. I couldn't tell you who or what they exchanged for me. Hah! I was there to educate the natives. You can guess the end of that story. They educated me."

Her African paintings were almost magical, both eerie and lush. She painted them by moonlight or by the light of dawn. "My flora and fauna," she said, the way another grey-haired seventy-year-old woman might have said, "my grandchildren." She knelt by one of them. "Did you ever imagine acacia so verdant?" she asked. "Giraffe so peaceful?" Then rising, she pointed to another painting of hyena and jackals at sunrise. "Can you guess what they're up to?"

"Having their breakfast?"

"Bones, probably, left over from the catch of lions or cheetahs the night before. Scavengers of sorts. I too hate to think of bones going to waste. I always use them to make soup, don't you?" Then, pointing to a painting of fuschia and scarlet flowers lining a dirt road, she said, "Do you think the colors *outré*? They're actually understated from the real thing."

By contrast, her seascapes were muted, even the ones at sunset.

"Salable," she told me. "That's how I get to Hawaii, you see. I paint enough to finance my stay in the artists' colony. Don't you think that's a pretentious phrase? Artists' colony. The actuality is not, I assure you. A remote village in Kona. We live simply. What's expensive are the supplies I bring for everyone, boxes and boxes of chalk and charcoal, hundreds of tubes of paint, and a suitcase of canvases."

As she started out of the garage, I stopped, looking over some of the fauna and flora.

"I won't part with those," she said, possibly sensing that I wanted to acquire one from her riotous period.

"If you change you mind," I said.

After she returned from Hawaii (with many pastels of orchids and anthurium), she began to interject some of her former pupils from public school into her monologues—Marilyn Zweig and Elliot Marcus, in particular. But without so much as a hint that they had testified against her, had helped pound nails, so to speak, in her coffin.

One day, during our tea break, which came with clockwork regularity at two hours into the lesson (after which we would paint for another hour before calling it quits), she told me about the first time she'd laid eyes on Elliot.

"Now you have to imagine this leggy boy, almost thirteen you know, and tall, lanky. Like a flamingo, I thought, when he showed up in a peach-colored shirt on the first day of class. He was all arms and legs and folded himself into a chair sized for a normal boy, but too small for him. Folded himself like a bird would, into itself, and I knew that he was the one Mrs. Marcus had called me about.

"I always had mothers calling me, you know, just before the semester began, telling me what artistic geniuses their children were. In case I should fail to recognize them. But this one! Mrs. Marcus called to say her son had no talent for art. 'None whatsoever,' she insisted. Because he was a mathematical genius, a whiz at algebra and geometry and computers. He gets 'uniformly high grades,' she told me, not so subtly cautioning me against putting any dips in the records, you see. Dippety-do-dah, I wanted to tell her. Actually, I did. But that was later. She had her heart set on getting him into the best college, and didn't want art to stand in her way. In his way. No, I guess I got it right the first time. Oh, I nearly forgot the cookies."

She got up to get them, out of an oddly shaped ceramic cannister, which looked like some of the pottery seconds at the annual arts and crafts show. Possibly she'd fashioned it herself. She'd made the cookies, chocolate chip as always. Sitting down, she turned her limpid blue eyes on me and continued her story.

"She wasn't the most unreasonable mother, but her point of view, well, what can I say? She pretended that it was Elliot who thought art was irrelevant, and saying that to me, well, I might just as well have said to her, mothers are irrelevant. Between you and me, dear, they are. After they've given birth.

"So, she demanded to meet me in a coffee shop on the other side of town, in the freezing cold, the snow a foot high, and it was one of my two precious days off, a Saturday. Except, of course, I had a mountain of papers to grade, and a lesson plan to write. I said I didn't think the meeting was necessary. That Elliot's work would have to speak for itself. I gave her my best advice: 'Tell Elliot effort *is* relevant,' and I rung off.

"I remember that call distinctly, because I was working on a painting when the phone rang. You know how that goes, it rings and you try not to answer it, but you always do. I was trying to capture innocence, the purity of it, in a lion cub, not easy to accomplish. It's not just a cute little kitten after all. We never say, Oh, it's just a lion, when it grows up. So I was also trying to capture the inherent quality that commands our respect. I'd been working for months, dabbing at it and dabbing. I was afraid it would get away from me, the longer I was back. After the sabbatical." She smiled at me. "Shall we resume our lesson, dear?"

During the tea break the following week, she showed me the Lincoln Junior High Yearbook from twenty years ago, which contained the class picture where thirty students stood solemnly in four rows, wearing white shirts or blouses, their arms hanging down at their sides. Except for Elliot, whose elbows jutted out from his long thin body. Marilyn was in the front row, a petite little thing with dark eyes, reminding me of all the would-be poets in my own junior high graduating class.

When we returned to the kitchen table, Miss Inwood took right up again. "Well, where was I? Elliot Marcus. You wouldn't guess what he turned in for his first assignment. I asked them to use straight lines to divide a blank sheet of paper. In an *interesting* manner. He drew a checkerboard! I gave him a B, not because his checkerboard was interesting, but because his thinking of one was. Hah! And his mother called me to complain. She called the principal. He called me. I called her. *Nous avons fait la ronde!*" She made a circular motion with her fist, as though twirling a streamer.

"Did you change the B?" I asked.

"What do you think?" she said.

Her African paintings were reference points, sometimes used as object lessons. "When I tried to get the light filtering through the leaves of the acacia, I didn't merely dab splotches of zinc white," she said to me once, about a still life I was working on. At other times, they comprised her ode to a Grecian urn: "When I think of a time that was idyllic, this is what I think, you see," she'd say, pointing to a trail of elephants or a single reticulated giraffe. And sometimes she used them as a springboard for other subjects, punctuality, for one.

"So I kept dabbing at this painting, you know. And then came a day when I realized I'd never get it right. I slashed the canvas, jumped on it [she stood up and demonstrated the jump], beat it over a chair [she lifted her arms up and brought them down again and again] until it was bent and cracked in a dozen places. Imagine me, a sedate woman, fifty years old, sobbing and shrieking, rocking back and forth like she'd lost her child. Hah! So I started over. But the semester had begun by then, and I no longer had any daylight to speak of, so I'd set the alarm for sunrise and start in, wearing a robe over my nightie and wool kneesocks. Of course, the time would get away from me, and I'd have to run a few stoplights to make it to the schoolhouse on time, or almost on time. Not quite on time for Mr. Reynolds. You'd think the world was coming to an end when you were five minutes late. I offered to stay ten extra minutes after school. You must realize the first half hour merely consists of getting your keys and your mail and cleaning your erasers—all those exceedingly important tasks. But no, Mr. Reynolds preferred to make my time card a *cause célèbre*. I didn't come home in much of a mood to paint, but by next morning, hope dawned again, and there I was, creating more grief."

On my way out the door that day, she clutched my arm. "Noisome, palpable fear oozed out of the school district's administration like vile shades of acrylic, drying before they could be tempered. Don't ever let small-mindedness and pettifoggery cloud your vision. With a capital V." It was then I understood that her public career had come to an unhappy conclusion.

Stopping by the library, I made some inquiries and found the first of many newspaper clippings on the trial. I obtained a copy of the voluminous court record and read it through in two nights. In the court record, she admits to having thrown blackboard erasers across the room, along with chalk, and even a vase of flowers. A glass vase. "I never hurt anyone," she said, in her defense. "I obtained their attention. That's what I'm paid to do."

On a stifling summer day, she took me up to the attic after our lesson was over. She pointed out some miscellaneous objects, a leather desk blotter, a large rectangular desk clock, an atlas. I guess I had expected to see some African artifacts, but there were none. I almost choked on the dust she blew off a plastic bag containing photographs.

"This is me about your age," she said, handing me a picture of a thirtyish woman, wearing a high pompadour and a print dress with obvious shoulder pads. There were other pictures in the bag, but she didn't show them to me. Her glance fell on a set of small notebooks, then she seemed to change her mind about the wisdom of our being in the attic. Abruptly, she twirled the plastic bag closed, laid it down on a marble-topped end table, and descended the ladder. I followed dutifully, unable to see anything further because she held the flashlight.

"See you next week," she said cheerfully. "And if I don't, remind me." That was a reference to her use of "see," which was seldom casual. She often admonished me to "really see," "look," "absorb," "digest." The most scathing comment she could make about someone's work was that the artist didn't "see" what he or she was painting. Which usually wasn't my problem, thankfully. My problem was a matter of making others "see" what I saw. That is to say, technique.

I worked on my technique. Oh, God, how I worked on my technique! I never wanted to please anyone as much as her. She had a canny knack, though, of knowing when I was trying too hard. The lessons we had drove me to study books on composition.

"Is it Utrillo's *Rue Ravignan* you're trying to repaint? Well, don't waste your time, my dear," she might say gingerly, slicing me to the quick.

At such times I wanted to give up the lessons, because I knew I could never paint well enough. But I couldn't give *her* up. The two were inseparable. While I'd entertained thoughts of a friendship with her apart from our lessons, she put dampers on any effort I made to establish one. She would send me only a perfunctory postcard from Hawaii, never answering the letters I wrote her. When I asked her to my home one evening, she said, "I never go out nights." So I invited her to lunch, but her response was, "I'm not the lunching sort."

One afternoon we were painting a bowl of flowers she had arranged on a lace-clothed table. She put her brush down and came over to look, as she often did, to encourage me or to redirect my efforts, usually with light humor. This time, she seized my arm. "Marilyn Zweig!" she barked.

I looked up to see her blinking at me, as though I were Marilyn incarnate. She looked back at the painting. Then she took the brush from my hand and smeared some of the fine lines I'd drawn on the lace cloth and petals. If you've never had an art lesson and cannot imagine the visceral effect she had on me, imagine someone deliberately pouring grape juice on your favorite dress or tie.

"Take this out!" she demanded. "Marilyn Zweig was in my class for four semesters. I did everything I could to try to make her understand that most of her work was extraneous. I explained, I lectured, I took the entire class on a trip to the museum for her single benefit. I invited her to my home—a mistake, but we won't go into it now. I showed her the painting that had taken everything out of me.

"And just when I had given up hope, she turned in a term project that was stunning. Free of every superfluity. Later it won third prize in the Arts and Crafts Show, a simple line drawing of a black cat with a piece of colorful yarn." She crinkled her eyes, looking up at me, a signal for me to say something.

"That's wonderful!" I said. "You got through."

She smiled ironically, then walked over to a bookcase in the foyer, slipping a piece of paper out from a book. Handing it to me, she said, "What's that?"

It was an advertisement for a car, drawn against the New York skyline.

Without waiting for me to answer, she said, "It's Marilyn Zweig. And if it's not Marilyn, I'll eat this piece of paper. See what good being a public school teacher is?"

I looked at the drawing. No question but that it was cluttered: every window drawn in, every leaf on the trees. Photo-realism was a style I didn't care for, but because Marilyn chose it, did that make Miss Inwood a failure? Besides, the chance that the ad was actually Marilyn's work was one in a million. The style just wasn't that distinctive.

"But the term paper," I protested.

"I gave it an A plus. And then, when I was congratulating myself no end for my success, she said it was Elliot. He had explained it to her, told her I didn't like paintings that looked like photographs, so she should do something else. He suggested Japanese brushstroke. Do you think I should have learned something from the lesson?" She walked over to the other easel and took up her brush. "See what you can do, dear, with your petals. The less the better."

The trial had produced many exhibits: traffic tickets for speeding and running stop lights, time cards showing Miss Inwood's arrival and departure times, homework papers which contained fat red X's through them or abstruse comments, her appointments calendar (to indicate she'd been aware of meetings she missed or had attended late), and the expense voucher she'd turned in for the outing to the museum (a seventy-mile train trip each way for thirty students). They'd had to subpoena the painting of the lion cub.

She was declared "unfit to serve as a teacher," although she received back pay for the two months during which (before the trial) she was barred from entering the school. Thus, after twenty-seven years of teaching, she was retired, on a full pension, at the age of fifty-two.

One lovely spring afternoon after our lesson, she came out of the house with me and walked me to the front gate. "Did I ever tell you what Elliot did for his term project? He called it 'Chocolate Chip Cookie: Aerial View.' It was a gargantuan, misshapen thing. Lavender dough with purple chips. I could have given him another B, but from that he would learn nothing." She interrupted herself to ask what makes a chocolate chip cookie good.

"I don't know," I said; "I can only tell you what I like."

She smiled. "I ask that of all my pupils. Usually it's the chips or the nuts, sometimes the chewiness. Elliot's answer was, 'the baker.' I'd asked him the question once when he wanted to know what makes a painting good."

"Then what's your answer?"

"What makes anything good—or bad? The jury, of course. Trite but true. Anyway, I gave Elliot Marcus an A plus. He was a very logical young man, you see. I knew he would ponder it, that it would confound him. Because he had done nothing essentially different from the checkerboard, or the torus, or the Moebius strip he had been turning in all along, and certainly nothing to deserve the grade. His average, by the way, came out B plus, so it hardly signified. Except to Mrs. Marcus. But that's another story. I'll see you next week."

When I arrived at her house the next week, though, she didn't answer the door. I thought of calling the police, but on a hunch, I called the hospital. They asked if I was a relative. When I said yes, they said she had "expired."

She left me her diaries and the painting of the lion cub, the one she called, "Out of the Lion's Belly." One of her last entries explains the title: "They said Jomo Kenyatta wanted to bring his country out of the dark jungle and into the age of modern civilization. Indeed, on Kenya's Day of Independence, he said, 'I've snatched you out of the lion's belly.' To Mr. Kenyatta, and to anyone who may read this hence, I've performed some midwifery of my own, so to speak. I repent my arrogance."

Hurricane
Edna J. Guttag

Winifred, eighty years young
Five foot, two inches tall
Expert on ancient Persia and Egypt
Wanted expertise on hurricanes.
Hurried from the Village to the Jersey Shore
Preparing to interrogate
The Ocean's reaction
To jetting gusts and blasting rain,
Content to sit on the porch
Of the empty hotel
Ready to watch the view,
Arthritically fought the policeman, who
Finally able to evacuate her
Carried Winifred off along with possessions
That were not even hers
To the place where all the other evacuees were.
Afterward, regretfully, she noted aloud,
"But the Sea now is all quiet and calm."

Oh, That Shoe Store Used to Be Mine
Randeane Doolittle Tetu

"Oh, that shoe store used to be mine," Paynter pointed a cane at the green front between a flower store and a bakery. Mrs. Tuttle read the gold lettering, Geo. W. Crayton, Shoes. Paynter said, "Wear triple E myself's how I got started in shoes. Stores just don't carry out-of-the-ordinary sizes. I wouldn't be walking today 'cept for the fact that I decided to buy a shoe store and stock the right sizes."

"How many years?" Mrs. Tuttle asked.

"Ago or selling shoes?"

"Selling shoes."

"Well, eighteen or so I'd guess."

The feel of the weight of the shape of the shoe in her hand, the smell of the leather, the kneeling in front of a stockinged foot, then another, the carpeting, the slanted mirror which showed her up from a long way down, the metal-and-black foot measure with its sliding parts and smell of metal, the shoehorn in the belt did not breathe out of Paynter, and Mrs. Tuttle was surprised. Of all the lives they had sketched for Paynter back at the Manor, shoe store owner had not been one.

Angela said, "She never worked. She was supported. You'll see." And Mrs. Tuttle thought she was right.

"We don't know if she's a Miss or a former Mrs., and now we have three Amandas and will have to call her Paynter for short." They sent Mrs. Tuttle to be her buddy to walk into town. "You have a way about you, now, you know you do." Mrs. Tuttle knew she did. "You just come back and tell us all about her."

"Something nice about knowing there're people walking around in shoes you fit for them and feeling fine and doing all wonderful things because their feet don't hurt," Paynter said. At Woolworth's she bought perfumed talc and walked around the aisles.

"They have almond croissants here," she said at the bakery on the way back. "Wouldn't we like a coffee?" No one else was in the bakery, and Mrs. Tuttle sat so she could see the sidewalk. Paynter munched the almond croissant and sipped coffee to last a morning. When Mrs. Tuttle finished her Danish she said, "How long were you married?"

"Was married quite a while. Quite a while. Man by the name of Karl. Karl and I were married quite a while. I used to let him help in the store sometimes, mostly behind the counter. I really knew the customers best. He would get bored."

Mrs. Tuttle made her coffee last and said, "Never before stopped here."

"They make a good croissant. I never was much for baking." Mrs. Tuttle thought, Married to Karl eighteen years. Owned a shoe store. "Any children?"

"Children. My, yes. Now one's a musician. Plays in the orchestra, you know. And my son is an artist. He's in New York. Now wouldn't you think they could make up some grandchildren? But no. Neither of them married and no grandchildren."

Mrs. Tuttle added this and sat back. She was feeling grand. Some of the new ones guarded their privacy, tried to save their personalities, hold onto their former lives, not willing to recognize that they were no longer theirs to save once they entered the Manor. This one though was fine. This one was easy. Paynter would tell things fresh from the world with the blush still on.

When they left the bakery, Paynter said, "You go in and see what you can get for an out-of-the-ordinary shoe. You just see. I have eight more shoes like this in my closet you know, or I would never have given it up."

The flower store on the other side said PAYNTER'S in the stone block and MILDRED GRAYNOR in gold lettering on the door. Mrs. Tuttle stopped and looked at the shoe store window and at the flower shop under the striped awning. "It says Paynter's for the flowers, Amanda. You sure it was a shoe store you owned?"

"A shoe store? Why, no, my dear. I told Clayton flowers. And for eighteen years it was flowers."

"But I thought you just said that shoe store used to be yours."

Paynter looked off down the street to where the sidewalk petered out and turned into the path that would lead to the Manor. "Shoe store, flower store. I know it wasn't the bakery. I never was good at baking. Mildred Graynor," she added for good measure, "that's my grandson's wife."

Tending the Flock
Jennifer Lagier

They have been waiting nearly their entire lives for this time of day to be fed. As the elderly widow fights upstream through cobwebs and obsolete relics, her old chickens gather and rustle. Carefully, she unhooks the wire door leading from sunlight to the dusty floor of their coop. She lifts each foot like a fragile souffle, remembering last summer's spill and her black-and-blue hip.

The chickens recognize only her porcelain slop pan. For the first time since she has approached this place of quiet, they nervously croon and discover a common focus for their scattered attention. She begins flinging soggy corners of toast, flaccid carrot stumps, and the browning peels from this morning's potatoes. The chickens rush to peck the scattered scraps at her feet.

Varicolored feathers whirl and cackling hens gather around the old woman's ankles. Each has been officially named fifteen years earlier by her youngest son's daughter. Peter Pan, she called the banty. He was the most energetic of all of her roosters. But when his comb and tail feathers stayed undeveloped, the woman laughed at their mistake and renamed her Pandora. It doesn't matter now, she figures. The granddaughter has discovered boys and no longer visits.

This whole flock is too ancient and decrepit to lay. She knows they wouldn't even be good enough to stew. Besides, she feels rather attached. Pandora there is on her last leg and could go any hour.

Fifteen years. She leans against the gilded apex of a spidery shadow, waiting. Later, she'll edge to her sofa and nap until suppertime happens.

Livvy Caldwell
Barbara Nector Davis

Livvy Caldwell
 sits on all her years
  sometimes they rise on
   beanstalks to her eyes
    scramble to her fingers
     and her toes and then she
      weeps or taps her foot or
       curves her fingers on a melody.
      Livvy sits in a stiff-backed
     chair still as an abandoned
    plow terrified of memories
   forgetting to eat.

Translations
Margaret H. Carson

She sits there on the steps and listens
as the wind rustles the dry leaves
of the single maple standing between
the brick apartment building and the street;
but she is hearing wind moving through
pine trees and is once again back
at the lake, lazing an hour away
while children have their midday sleep.
Her foot, pressing against the cement step,
is pushing down upon the forest floor
to make the hammock rock where it is slung
between two trees down by the dock.

She does not see the old car with
the dented fender parked by the curb.
Her white-filmed eyes see only sunlight
glinting on water. The whish of hidden
traffic reaches her as sound of speedboats
racing up the channel.

She lies awake at night and listens to
the shuffling sounds that people in the hallway
make passing her door, and hears again
the scrabbling noises that the bats made
when they came to feed their young, hidden
within the outside double walls.
A wordless shout, down on the street
becomes the half-articulated cry

that sleeping children make, and when a car
sputters in starting out, she hears the snap of twigs
and knows that deer are passing on their way
down to the lake to drink.

Silence that settles both outside and in
is shattered as an ambulance sends out
its chilling cadence in crescendo and diminuendo.
But she is smiling as she falls asleep
hearing the loons' wild, eerie laughter.

To an Old Woman
Rafael Jesús González

Come mother—
    your rebozo trails a black web
    and your hem catches on your heels;
you lean the burden of your years
on shaky cane and palsied hand pushes
    sweat-grimed pennies on the counter.
Can you still see, old woman,
the darting color-trailed needle of your trade?
    The flowers you embroider
    with three-for-a-dime threads
cannot fade as quickly as the leaves of time.
    What things do you remember?
Your mouth seems to be forever tasting
the residue of nectar-hearted years.
    Where are the sons you bore?
Do they speak only English now
and say they're Spanish?
    One day I know you will not come
    and ask for me to pick
    the colors you can no longer see.
I know I'll wait in vain
    for your toothless benediction.
I'll look into the dusty street
made cool by pigeons' wings
until a dirty child will nudge me and say:
    "Señor how much ees thees?"

The Pianist
Carolyn J. Fairweather Hughes

Gnarled fingers of hands
that were once beautiful
fondle the yellowed keys.

When no one is listening,
she randomly strikes
a few dissonant notes.

Sometimes, I have to turn away
to keep from weeping
at her altered state.

But then, I see
the grey, wrinkled face smile
as chords, precise and graceful,

drop from her hands
like ripened plums.

Occupation
Bonnie Michael

Women who wait
   in dentists' offices
      while much-loved, freckle-faced children
      go sullenly in to be checked and x-rayed
      and lectured and given rubber toys
      and a new toothbrush to take home.

Women who wait
   in parked cars
      beside dance schools for emotional teenaged
      daughters with acne in scuffed pink ballet shoes
      and tights with runs and leotards
      that are already a size too small.

Women who wait
   in courtrooms
      with hostile lawyers and bored judges
      trying to get more money to pay baby-sitters
      so that they can go to work and get more money
      to pay attorneys' fees.

Women who wait
   in nursing homes
      to die of uselessness in ivory rooms
      with sterile walls and yellow curtains
      widowed by men who couldn't cry and couldn't touch
      and died of heart attacks.

All the Time
Michael Andrews

It was 93 degrees.
She wore 3 sweaters,
a sweatshirt,
some long pants,
a few dresses,
rolled down nylons,
sneakers,
a feather boa,
and a 47-year-old mink.
She bought the mink
for consolation
the day she outlived
her last husband.
One eyelid
was in a flutter
of perpetual motion.
Lipstick
ran all over her face
like a map of Chicago.
She was as crazy
as a 5 o'clock commuter.
Went to the Safeway
twice a week
with molding dollars,
social security checks,
and food stamps.
Stole Tootsie Rolls
and ate them before

she left the market.
Walked to the intersection.
Waited for the light
to turn red,
hunched low,
knees high,
lurched out in front
of oncoming traffic,
waved madly at
the skidding cars,
her wire basket
with coffee, doughnuts
and smoked oysters
bouncing right behind her,
chuckling and muttering
about insane drivers,
one eyeball rotating
in an orgasm of fear.

It was her little joke.

Once a policeman stopped her.
She kicked him in the shin,
scattered his citations
all over the street,
yelled rape
in her reed-piped voice
and scurried home
muttering about cops.
After that
the police left her alone,
but sometimes they
spoiled the fun
by stopping the traffic
at her favorite crosswalk.

Her house buzzed
with ticking clocks.
She didn't trust the electric ones.
Wound all 217 of them every day,
but never set the time.
She considered the random
firing of alarms
a form of music.
She kept the smoked oysters
for the dog in the freezer
with her third husband's appendix,
which the dog greatly desired.
But the old lady kept it
in memory of the surgeon
she married after he performed
the appendectomy in which
her third husband died
of cancer of everything.
Sometimes at night
she beat on the windows
across the airshaft
with a broom handle,
shouted obscenities and yelled
"You keep quiet in there.
You keep quiet."

After a while
they sealed up the windows.
It was getting harder
all the time
to get someone's
attention.

Bag Ladies in L.A.
Savina A. Roxas

Sunday on Santa Monica Boulevard
people stiffen and turn away
like Calder mobiles
when bag ladies kneel
to mark territorial
imperatives in vacant doorways
with the *L.A. Times*
from trash cans, brush
their teeth with water
from discarded Smucker's
jars, and defecate at the curb—
Rest Rooms Closed on Sunday—
bundle into a corner
with eyes that stalk those who
walk the palatial Boulevard
neither santa nor monica.

glory
Charlotte Watson Sherman

honey, i just sit here mindin my own business. i just act like i'm a part of this old stone building. i like to watch people try not to look at me. like they're scared they might end up here too. but you know, it ain't always that bad. specially in the summer. i likes to sit here and watch folks. the other day i saw a man with a miniskirt on. lord have mercy. he sure looked a mess. and he had purple hair. the color of the church robes over at macedonia blood on the cross a.m.e. oh, i know it ain't nothing like the old a.m.e. church that used to plot about colored folks' freedom. but i went anyway. well, people just too much into stylin and profilin for my taste. and i wasn't scared to stand up and tell the preacher that to his face. maybe i shouldn't have done it in the middle of his sermon. but he wasn't like no preacher we had back home, that's for sure. with his mouth all pinched up, trying to talk like some old white man. i sure did tell him. i said rev, why dontcha put some fire in your words & make us feel somethin. anything. i like to feel like i'm likkered up when i hear a good sermon. but this man wasn't even close to heatin up old sarah philips. and she can get happy over just about anything. and even she was sittin there lookin like a pew. but i don't go back there no more. and i guess they glad. i don't like nobody escortin a grown woman nowhere. especially out of no church in front of them old pretend-to-be-christian people. honey, i know them folks. i see plenty of em walkin down this very street. and they don't even turn they heads. now that's a christian for you. can't wait to get to church on sunday to moan about jesus and if he was right here on earth starin em in the face, they'd probably spit on him and keep on walking. just like they do me. now, i can get along pretty good with most of these winos down here. they don't mess with me too much. they know i ain't got no quarter to give em to buy a bottle and i cuss em out good and loud when they forget and try to panhandle me. now, i know they'll try to take advantage of some of the women down here that go around lookin like stray rabbits. and i done told a few of em to get em a piece of broken whiskey bottle and keep it right next to em so when some fool tries to get funny and starts rubbin up on em or grabbin on em they can either pull the piece out and give em a warning or they can do what i had to do one time and don't give no warning, just stick em. that'll teach em to leave you alone. see, they thinks i'm crazy. and ain't nothin a wino scared of more than a crazy woman down here. cept for not havin no more wine in life, of course. honey, sometimes i'll rise up like a tornado and just start spoutin scripture, right and left. and i'll walk up and down the street and maybe stand on the corner for a while and flag down cars. that's just to remind these folks that i'm still alive and not a stone wall. i just look this way. but i got a heap of sense. you know i never thought i'd be able to pack up all my life and put it in a paper bag. all my life in a paper bag. but it ain't so bad sometimes. i'm portable and i can go anywhere. i'm just tired of moving on. and i can wash up every day right here in the jailhouse bathroom. and i do keep myself clean. you know god takes care of fools and babies. i take care of myself. so it ain't so bad. really. i just sit and try to blend into the walls.

Old Women
Barbara Lau

Old women
wrap scarves around their necks
to hide their wrinkles,
and flatter their bosoms
with bold beads and brooches.
In dresses buttered with flowers,
in voices light as baby's breath,
how they bloom in the corner
of the cafeteria, billowing
over pictures of grandchildren
passed round and round like hors d'oeuvres
like jewels they plant on each hand
to occupy the spaces once held
and warmed by husbands.

Now twined around each other
arm in arm down the sidewalk,
defying the dark grave
with their colors and perfume,
old women
tending time more fragile than youth:
poinsettias in the snow.

Bag Ladies
Ruth Harriet Jacobs

We are all bag ladies
or becoming so.
Nothing lasts
not love
or the beloved
or hope.
Even mountains crumble
only the ocean waits
to catch our tears

Bags of memories
tell us who we were
before we were wise

The bags burden us.
Carrying about
our losses,
we stumble
clutching our unfreedom
against all threats
or promises
it being all we have
it being all we know
it being all we are.

Endings
Lynn Kozma

Frail as porcelain
she sits, unmoving
except for bone-thin hands
mending with care
forgotten clothes
which are not there—
threading unseen needles,
moistening fingertips
from parchment lips,
knotting the thread
carefully.

There—one more finished—
smoothing the wrinkles away,
softly laying it by,
slipping back
to the early May
of her life
as easily as breathing.

My planet—earth;
hers—a distant star.
Impossible to travel
that far.

Last Visit to Grandmother
Enid Shomer

I enter through a forest
of crystal stemware,
down a Persian runner path.
Bedridden, but still elegant,
her hair a bluish wisp of August sky,
she sits up to eat, seems
to watch TV, but cannot speak.

The objects she mothered
tend her now: gilt sconces,
cranberry lustres,
the japanned dresser
where hinged family photographs
cluster like butterflies.

She grabs my hand and pats it,
giggling like an infant
who has just discovered its toes.
Then she winces, covers her mouth,
points to her dentures,
brushes a crumb from the sheets.

Her nurse interrupts to take her
to the bathroom. The patient's
body, she points out, is spotless
as her Grand Baroque: all those
intricate folds of skin
and not one bedsore.

When I leave, the nurse
is helping her change for evening.
A small virtue to want to die
as she lived: in a good
silk dress, some detail
like bugle beads
at the collar and cuffs.

Words for Alice after Her Death
Angela Peckenpaugh

It came by surprise
like a blown fuse,
an old car you were used to
for a few errands, stolen.
We made room in our busy lives
to deal with your loss
as we had your illness.
You asked so little
I'm stumped with your elegy.
I'd rather rub your back
at your request,
or deal a hand of gin rummy.
At your own death you might
have let out one of your
high pitched sighs, your
reaction when landing on a chair,
shock of contact,
relief at getting there.

Now your old blue robe,
as familiar as the dark
green kitchen walls
will be in the last load
of laundry. The Fanny Farmer
box that held the savored
chocolate candy will
be emptied in the trash,
another act done

by one or two people
who kept looking in.

There won't be too much to move,
contents of closet, bureau, desk,
a bed and a few old chairs.
We already went through the pantry,
the spare room, eliminating
all but the nostalgic and necessary.

I find myself seeing your smile,
so welcome. It told of pain
for the time forgotten
in the pleasure of my brief company.
You were so grateful
for small acts of kindness
it was easy to feel blessed
for manicure, bed change,
buying a shower cap at the 5 & 10.
I see your white hair, eyes peeking
over the front door glass,
a blown kiss to assure me
you were safe inside,
but, frail package, how could
you be, really. That was
the old nurse's trick, to grin
and bear it, inquire about my health
first thing by phone call
in the morning. Yes,
you remembered my latest worry
and gave it an airing, before
we decided when I would see you.
I forgive you your resistances

to my consoling schemes—
for turning down good mystery books
because your eyes were failing,
for wearing the dress from India
only once, because the sleeves were tight,
and for picking at a Chinese dish
in a restaurant I had chosen.

Now I regret how little
your coin collection added up to
when I took it to the gold exchange.
The clerk said sometimes customers
salted the kitty for grandmothers
because they couldn't believe
how little their life savings
had come to. How little it all
comes to. But I used to remind you
at least you had interesting friends—
Buddhists and poets, an actor or two
and you agreed. And left alone
stains of fear and disease
on the sheets but didn't stain
our consciences with demands
we couldn't answer.
"What is the name of those beans?"
you wanted to know, embarrassed
to have forgotten.
I think I said every kind—pinto, string,
lima, green. But it was an avocado
that Jeff brought you,
on your mind. Hard to grasp,
like your bravery at the end,
trips down the old steps

to the washing machine,
outings in the car
to our affairs, picnic, rummage sale,
art show, when for you
a slow walk from bed to front room
must have seemed a trip to the moon.
It was no small feat
to heat up hamburger and add frozen
potatoes to the grease,
creating a little Yorkshire pudding,
that left you pleased.
Your presence now is like the backrub
you tried to give me—the touch is
weak but gentle, and full of apology.

The Thugs
Mura Dehn

The years don't serve their time,
they're runaways,
they bump each other off
sun up, sun down.

Time, master mugger,
snatched this century
out of my hands
and fled.

The Coming of Winter
Shirley Vogler Meister

The winter winds have chilled the warmth we knew
and whirl our unmet dreams like crumbling leaves
around the barren trees: a rendezvous
of weathered bones and somber dance which weaves
despair with sparks of hope that summon spring.
Beyond the wailing wind is sanguine sound—
the vigor-voice that wakes all slumbering—
the reassuring call of power more profound.

We acquiesce to freezing winds and test
our mettle 'gainst the spectral storms ahead,
for there are forces that we can't arrest
and states of nature that we need not dread.
Beyond the winds lie gentler joys and peace
that sanctify our fate and death's caprice.

Post Humus
Patti Tana

Scatter my ashes in my garden
so I can be near my loves.
Say a few honest words, sing a gentle song,
join hands in a circle of flesh.
Please tell some stories about me
making you laugh. I love to make you laugh.
When I've had time to settle, and green
gathers into buds, remember I love blossoms
bursting in spring. As the season ripens
remember my persistent passion.
And if you come in my garden
on an August afternoon
pluck a bright red globe,
let juice run down your chin and the seeds
stick to your cheek. When I'm dead
I want folks to smile and say   *That Patti,*
she sure is some tomato!

Life's Rainbow
Sheila Banani

Beginnings are lacquer red
    fired hard in the kiln
    of hot hope;

Middles, copper yellow
    in sunshine,
    sometimes oxidize green
    with tears; but

Endings are always indigo
    before we step
    on the other shore.

Photo by John Renner

Publisher's Afterword

Having originally intended to let the material speak for itself, it is difficult now to reach back five years and pull together the strands of circumstance that resulted in this collection. So much has changed. Based largely on the success of this book, Papier-Mache was able to transition from a part-time labor of love, operating evenings and weekends from the kitchen table, to a viable publishing house with more than a dozen titles in print, most focusing on work by, for, and about midlife and older women.

By its very existence, this book created a network of support and encouragement: the sixty-plus men and women whose work is included, the hundreds of readers who have taken the time to share how the book has touched their lives, the booksellers who have so graciously recommended it to buyers.

On a more personal level, the compilation of *When I Am an Old Woman* and the subsequent efforts to bring it to its audience have profoundly influenced my attitudes and feelings about growing older, especially as a woman, and especially in this society which has shown so little respect for old women.

In many ways the anthology sprang from this need to resolve anxieties about growing older. In early 1986, I was searching for a new anthology theme, one with the depth necessary to evoke passion in the writers, and enough breadth to provoke a range of perspectives. Fate intervened in the form of "Becoming Sixty," a gift-poem from Ruth Jacobs (see page 125), wherein she acknowledged the "terror and anger at coming into sixty," feelings that gave way to peace of mind once she began to count "the gifts that sixty gave." Immediately I knew there was something worth writing about here.

Over the following eighteen months I read more than six hundred poems and stories, selecting those that spoke to the heart, ones that brought tears and laughter, and ones that made me think—about letting go of youth, about support systems and adequate health care, about respect and consideration, septuagenarian sex, who defines the way we view reality...about letting go of life.

I came out the other side eighteen months older, a little wiser, more aware, less fearful.

As the collection neared completion, I kept thinking of a poem I had seen several times but could not place. It spoke of growing old, not gently, perhaps not even gracefully, but with a wonderfully outrageous sense of style. When a copy of the poem was finally found it was, of course, the beloved "Warning" by Jenny Joseph. Giving title to the book and presented as the lead poem, it became the "patron" saint of the book, eliciting instant recognition from the thousands of women who had loved and cherished the poem over the years.

In contrast, the exquisite cover art also came at the eleventh hour, but this time almost effortlessly. Deidre Scherer, a visual artist who works in fabric and thread to create stunning portraits of the elderly, responded to the call for submissions on women and aging, pulling from her collection "Laughing Rose," the colorful rendition of the old woman whose smiling face matched perfectly the spirit and spunk of Jenny's "old woman."

The continued success of the anthology is a bellwether of the growing importance of the issues of aging and the increasing interest in work about aging women. Such issues can only become more important as those of us in our midlife years move forward to old age, in larger numbers than ever before. It gives me great personal and professional satisfaction to be a part of this important and challenging era.

About the Contributors

MICHAEL ANDREWS is a southern California publisher, editor, and printer for Bombshelter Press. His books include *Poems for Amber, 3 Begats, Xmas Tree Massacre, 40 Turkeys So What, A Telegram Unsigned, Gnomes and the Xmas Kid,* and three fine print books/portfolios of poetry and photography: *Riverrun, Machu Picchu,* and *Riding South.*

DORI APPEL is coartistic director of Mixed Company Theater in Ashland, Oregon. Her award-winning poems and stories have appeared in many magazines and anthologies, and her story, "Double Feature," was cited in *The Best American Short Stories, 1989.* She is the author of seven produced plays, including "Girl Talk," coauthored with Carolyn Myers, which was published by Samuel French in 1992.

MARY ANNE ASHLEY lived in northern California, and studied poetry writing with Kate Rennie Archer at the Dominican Upper School in San Rafael. Her stories appeared in *Quindaro 15* and *Quindaro 16* and were read on public radio. She belonged to the Virginia Woolf Society and the International Geranium Society. Ms. Ashley died in 1994 at the age of sixty.

SHEILA BANANI from Santa Monica, California, earned her B.A. and M.A. from UCLA. A former sociology instructor and city planner, her poetry has been published in *World Order Baha'i Quarterly, Crosscurrent, ONTHEBUS,* and in *Abiding Silence, An Anthology.*

SARAH BARNHILL lives in the mountains of western North Carolina. Her fiction and nonfiction have appeared in numerous magazines, including *Appalachian Heritage, Cold Mountain Review,* and *Summit.*

THERESE BECKER is a member of the National Press Photographer's Association. Her journalism and photojournalism have appeared in numerous newspapers, literary journals, and anthologies. She recently received her M.F.A. in Creative Writing from Warren Wilson College in Swannanoa, North Carolina. Her poetry has also been widely published, and she teaches workshops on the creative process throughout Michigan. She has recently combined her poetry and photography in a chapbook, *The Fear of Cameras.*

TOM BENEDIKTSSON lives in northern New Jersey, where he teaches English at Montclair State. He is the author of a critical book on the San Francisco poet George Sterling and of a number of articles of literary criticism. His poems have appeared in numerous literary magazines around the country.

ELIZABETH BENNETT received her B.A. cum laude from Bryn Mawr College and has pursued graduate studies in Fine Arts at George Mason University. She won the 1987 Chrysler Museum's Irene Leach Memorial Award for free verse. Her poems and articles on poetry have appeared in the *New York Times, Poet Lore, Carousel, Phoebe,* the *Levia-*

thon, *The Creative Writers Handbook* (Prentice Hall), *Summer's Conversations,* and *Commonweal: Poems by Cancer Patients and Those Who Treat Them.* "The Trouble Was Meals" has been featured in a number of Ph.D. theses and was reprinted most recently in *Now I'm My Mother's Mother* by Ellen Erlich and in *A Phenomology of Women, Deriving Contextual Meaning* (National League for Women Press). She is presently living, writing, and aging in McLean, Virginia.

BARBARA BOLZ is a freelance writer who lives in Indiana with her partner, Kath Pennavaria, their son Adam, and two cats. She is currently finishing a new book, *I Got It! A Workbook About Menstruation for Girls and Teenage Women.*

CATHERINE BOYD, a resident of Santa Rosa, California, has had short stories published in the *Seattle Review, Crosscurrents, Summerfield Journal,* and *Ridge Review,* as well as in *If I Had My Life to Live Over I Would Pick More Daisies.* Several of her feature articles have appeared in the Marin/Sonoma section of the *San Francisco Examiner,* one of the city's leading newspapers.

ROD BRADLEY has published two novels, *TV Man* and *Gun Play* (as R.B. Phillips), and numerous poems in literary magazines. He lives in Los Angeles and works as a photographer and documentary filmmaker. He was a cowriter and still photographer for the Emmy-winning PBS series, *Smithsonian World.* His photographs are in a number of private collections and have been exhibited with Ansel Adams and William Eggleston.

KAREN BRODINE found poetic inspiration in her rigorous life of political activism and leadership in the Freedom Socialist Party and Radical Women. Her fourth book of poetry, *Woman Sitting at the Machine, Thinking,* was published by Red Letter Press. Ms. Brodine died of cancer in 1987 at the age of forty.

LORI BURKHALTER-LACKEY currently lives and works as a photographer in Los Angeles. She is a graduate of the Otis Parsons Art Institute. Her photography has been exhibited in many California galleries and has been featured in numerous Papier-Mache Press books, including *If I Had My Life to Live Over I Would Pick More Daisies.*

GRACE BUTCHER taught English for twenty-five years at the Geauga Campus of Kent State University in Burton, Ohio. She is a lifelong runner—a former U.S. half-mile champion and many times Masters age group champion. She is also a motorcyclist and former columnist for *Rider* magazine. Her newest book is *Child, House, World* (Hiram Poetry Review, 1991).

BILLIE LOU CANTWELL writes from her home near Trinity, Texas. She writes poetry, articles, short stories, and novels. Her work has appeared in many national, literary, and small press magazines and has been included in anthologies such as Paul B. Janeczko's *Perposterous* (Orchard Books).

MARGARET H. CARSON, a nurse until her retirement, began writing poetry in her late fifties. Since then a number of her poems have appeared in *Festival,* a publication sponsored by the Friends of the Steele Memorial Library in Elmira, New York, where she resides.

ELLIN CARTER's poems have appeared in many journals and anthologies—most recently in *Kalliope,* the *G.W. Review, Earth's Daughters,* and *Caprice*—as well as in a chapbook, *What This Is and Why* (Richmond Waters Press). Her newest collection is *Journey in Winter.*

LYN COWAN began photographing seriously ten years ago. She has had five exhibitions and has had numerous photographs published in magazines, journals, and local Minneapolis newspapers. Making pictures of older women began in 1985 with the "Whisper, Minnesota" project and continues as a personal interest. In her other life she is a Jungian analyst.

BARBARA NECTOR DAVIS is an editor, poet, playwright, and novelist whose work has been published in numerous journals and anthologies. *The Journey and Elders of the Tribe* is a collection of her poetry, illustrated by her husband, photographer Robert Martin Davis. In 1991 her play, *Amidst the Alien Corn,* was produced in New York at the Nat Horne Theater on West Forty-second Street's Theater Row and in San Diego. Ms. Davis has recently completed a collection of novellas.

ROBERT MARTIN DAVIS has been engaged in photography virtually all of his life. In 1984, after a successful one-man photography show, he retired from his position as Senior Administrative Law Judge to devote all his time to photography. He has won numerous awards and is a member of the Cobb Photographic Society, the Marietta Fine Arts Center, and the South Cobb Arts Alliance, which hosted his first one-man show in Georgia. More recently, Davis's work has been exhibited in a one-man show at the Marietta/Cobb Fine Arts Center Gallery.

MURA DEHN was a Russian-born dancer, choreographer, and filmmaker who became known as a specialist in American black dance. A pioneer in documenting the various styles of black social dance, she directed a company of black dancers until 1973. She started writing poetry when she was in her seventies. Ms. Dehn died unexpectedly in her home in New York City in 1987 at the age of eighty-four.

MARGARET FLANAGAN EICHER, a resident of upstate New York, has had poems published in various magazines and anthologies, including *The Haven, Alternative Fiction and Poetry, On the Line, Broomstick, Pacific Coast Journal, Slugfest, Gaslight, Ignis Fatuus Review, Chips off the Writer's Block,* and *Poetry Motel.* In its first issue, the *Caribbean Writer* published one of her earlier poems, written in 1984 when she was still in the Women's Army Corps in the Panama Canal Zone.

SUE SANIEL ELKIND was a lifelong resident of Pittsburgh, Pennsylvania. She began writing at the age of sixty-four and published five collections—*No Longer Afraid* (Lintel, 1985), *Waiting for Order* (Naked Man Press, 1988), *Another Language* (Papier-Mache Press, 1988), *Dinosaurs and Grandparents* (MAF Press, 1988), and *Bare As the Trees* (Papier-Mache Press, 1992)—and one poetry chapbook, *The Final Season* (Cottage Wordsmith, 1993). She also founded and ran the Squirrel Hill Poetry Workshop sponsored by the Carnegie Library in Pittsburgh. Ms. Elkind died in 1994 at the age of eighty.

RINA FERRARELLI is the author of *Dreamsearch,* a chapbook of original poems (Malafemmina Press, 1992) and *Light Without Motion,* translations of poems by Giorgio Chiesura from the Italian (Owl Creek Press, 1989). She was awarded an NEA and Italo Calvino Award.

CAROLE L. GLICKFELD's collection, *Useful Gifts* (University of Georgia Press), about a family with deaf parents and hearing children, won the Flannery O'Connor Award for Short Fiction. Her short stories have appeared in numerous publications, including *First for Women* and *American Fiction No. 3*. Senior-adult theater groups across the country have performed her play, *The Challenge.* Winner of an NEA Literary Fellowship, she is working on a novel, *The Salt of Riches.*

RAFAEL JESÚS GONZÁLEZ, a Berkeley, California, teacher and writer, received his education at the University of Texas at El Paso, Universidad Nacional Autónoma de México, and the University of Oregon. Widely published in reviews and anthologies in the U.S., Mexico, and abroad, his collection of verse, *El Hacedor de Huegos / The Maker of Games,* went into a second printing.

EDNA J. GUTTAG's poetry, short stories, and articles have appeared in such publications as the *New York Times, Newsworld, Bronx Historical Society Journal, Art News,* the *Villager,* the *Frozen Librarian, Westsider,* and the *New York City Tribune.* A resident of New York City, she received the Joyce Kilmer Award from NYU and a Poets & Writers Grant. Her poetry has been on exhibition at the Blomingdale Branch Library in New York. She was a former cochair of the West Side Arts Coalition Writers Group and a twenty-year board member of her Block Association. She is an ardent attendee of dance performances, theater, and the opera.

DAME HYACINTHE HILL was the author of *Shoots of a Vagrant Vine* (Avalon National Book Award), *Promethea, Squaw No More,* and *Poetry and the Stars,* receiving many awards and was internationally translated and published. She spent most of her life in New York, moving to California in 1988 where she died unexpectedly one year later at the age of sixty-eight.

CAROLYN J. FAIRWEATHER HUGHES works for the Allegheny County Court of Common Pleas, Family Division. Her poems have appeared in many literary magazines, including *Slant, Poets On,* the *Pittsburgh Quarterly, Wind, Northern Arizona Mandala,* and the anthology, *We Speak for Peace.*

RUTH HARRIET JACOBS, Ph.D., a sociologist and gerontologist at the Wellesley College Center for Research on Women, Wellesley, Massachusetts, authored seven books, including *Be an Outrageous Older Woman* and *We Speak for Peace: An Anthology* (K.I.T. Press). Family Service American published her leaders' manual, *Older Women Surviving and Thriving.*

SUSAN S. JACOBSON has served as a Poet in the Classroom for the Pittsburgh Public Schools for ten years, and was Poet in Residence for the Western Pennsylvania School for the Deaf for three years. She has given readings, residences, and taught writers' conferences in colleges, universities, and schools in Pennsylvania and Ohio. Widely anthologized, her poems appear in *Life on the Line,* the *Pittsburgh Quarterly,* and *On Nursing, A Literary Celebration.*

TERRI L. JEWELL, born October 4, 1954, is a black feminist living and writing in Lansing, Michigan. Her poetry, essays, and book reviews have been published widely, including in the *American Voice, African American Review, Calyx,* and *International Poetry Review.* She has also edited a volume of women's quotations, *The Black Woman's Gumbo Ya-Ya.*

JENNY JOSEPH, a poet and writer from Gloucestershire, England, has published four volumes of poetry and six children's books. *Persephone,* a book of prose and verse, won her the James Tait Black Memorial Prize for fiction in 1986, and her *Selected Poems* were published by Bloodaxe Books in 1993.

SUSAN A. KATZ is the author of a number of poetry collections, including *The Separate Sides of Need, Two Halves of the Same Silence, An Eye for Resemblances,* and *The Overflow.* She is currently editing *The Vacant Chair: Portrait of a Poet* and completing work on *Dreaming Missouri,* a poetry collection. She has coauthored a college-level text for teachers, *Teaching Creatively by Working the Word: Language, Music & Movement* (Prentice Hall, Inc.). Her work has appeared in dozens of journals and anthologies and has received critical acclaim. She is the recipient of a number of awards and served as Book Review Editor for *Bitterroot,* the international literary magazine, from 1985-1991.

RICK KEMPA is a tutor for the Writing Skills Improvement Program in Tucson, Arizona, and has an M.F.A. from the University of Arizona. "Grandma Sits Down" is set in the ranchlands of southern Idaho and honors Fern Callen, "one of the most special people in my world."

LYNN KOZMA, a retired registered nurse, served in World War II. She is the author of two books of poetry, *Catching the Light* (Pocahontas Press) and *Phases of the Moon* (Papier-Mache Press). She has been published often by *Midwest Poetry Review, Bitterroot, Long Island Quarterly,* and *The Lyric.* She is an avid reader, gardener, and birder. A continuing student at Suffolk Community College, she is a member of Poets & Writers, Inc.

MARISA LABOZZETTA is a graduate of Boston College and Georgetown University Graduate School of Languages and Linguistics. Her fiction has appeared in the *Florida Review,* the *American Voice,* the *Pegasus Review,* and the anthology, *Shells, Monuments to Life.* She is a winner of *Playboy's* Victoria Chen Haider Memorial Award for Literature and the Rio Grande Writers' Competition. She teaches a course on Italian-American literature at the University of Massachusetts.

JENNIFER LAGIER has published work in a variety of journals and anthologies, including *If I Had My Life to Live Over I Would Pick More Daisies, The Dream Book: An Anthology of Writings by Italian-American Women,* and *La Bella Figura: A Choice.* She earned master's degrees at both the University of California, Berkeley, and California State University, Stanislaus. Ms. Lagier currently works as a community organizer with the Regional Alliance for Progressive Policy and is a member of the National Writers Union, Local 7.

BARBARA LAU is a widely published feature writer, essayist, and poet, and the coauthor of *You Don't Have to Go Home from Work Exhausted.* She is currently pursuing an M.F.A. in Creative Writing and lives in Austin with her husband and daughter.

DORIS VANDERLIPP MANLEY lives alone in Cherry Valley, New York, in a small earth-sheltered house surrounded by woods and fields. Since high school days she has been creating poetry and visual art as a way of giving body to feelings too powerful to be lightly dismissed. Her poems have been included in a number of anthologies, and many of her drawings of beloved plants are in the New York Botanical Garden collection.

SHIRLEY VOGLER MEISTER, an Indianapolis freelance writer whose work appears in diverse U.S. and Canadian publications, has earned awards for poetry, literary criticism, and journalism. Her experiences as a nontraditional student (B.A., English, Indiana University, summa cum laude), as an advocate for the elderly, and as a poet have resulted in multimedia opportunities.

BONNIE MICHAEL is a freelance writer and poet living in Winston-Salem, North Carolina. Her poetry has appeared in many literary journals and has been included in ten anthologies. She is a regular commentator on public radio and regularly contributes articles to *Minorities and Women in Business,* a national magazine.

S. MINANEL, due to some right-brained activity, has had her graphics and doggerel published in periodicals such as *Redbook, Light, Personal Computer Age, AB Bookman's Weekly, Sky & Telescope, Sailing, Pacific Yachting, Ensign, Young American, Computeredge,* and *Beverly Hills, The Magazine.* She is still waiting to hear from her left brain.

JANICE TOWNLEY MOORE, a native of Atlanta, teaches English at Young Harris College in the mountains of north Georgia. Her poetry has appeared in over three dozen journals and anthologies, including *Southern Poetry Review, Kansas Quarterly. New Virginia Review, The Bedford Introduction to Literature,* and *Life on the Line* (Negative Capability Press). She is poetry editor of *Georgia Journal.*

LILLIAN MORRISON is the author of seven collections of her own poems, most recently *Whistling the Morning In* (Wordsong); three anthologies of poems on sports and rhythm, including *At the Crack of the Bat* (Hyperion); and six collections of folk rhymes for children. *Slam Dunk,* an anthology of basketball poems, is forthcoming.

MICHELLE NOULLET is a teacher and poet who has been working in the Southeast Asian refugee camps since 1980. She lives "in the last town on the road before you fall into the South China Sea."

ANGELA PECKENPAUGH, associate professor of English at the University of Wisconsin, Whitewater, is poetry editor of *Affilia* and has contributed reviews to *Calyx, Women's Review of Books,* and *Art Muscle.* Her poetry has been published in numerous magazines and anthologies, including *The Heartlands Today* and *Eating Our Hearts Out.* Her poetry books include *A Heathen Herbal* (Artists Book Works), *Courage and Color* (Mid-march Arts Press), and *Designs Like Branches or Arteries* (Morgan Press). Since 1991 she has performed a selection of river-related pieces accompanied by art and photographs.

FIONNA PERKINS is a poet and writer, Montana native, former San Francisco journalist, and longtime resident of California's north coast, whose poetry was first published in 1935. In the nineties her work has appeared in the *Haight Ashbury Literary Journal,* the *Gab,* and *Outlook.* Her stories of a winter with a wild bobcat, originally in *Cat Fancy,* were reprinted in Britain's *My Weekly.* She frequently reads her fiction and poetry in person and over the radio. In 1960 she started the first bookstore in Mendocino, and in 1989 she helped found the Coast Community Library in Point Arena.

FRAN PORTLEY majored in English Honors at Duke University. She teaches poetry to children in the New Jersey JOY (joining old and young) program. Her poems have appeared in *Western Journal of Medicine, Parting Gifts, Heartland, Potatoe Eyes, If I Had My Life to Live Over I Would Pick More Daisies,* and many other publications.

SANDRA REDDING is a grandmother and a student in the M.F.A. writing program at the University of North Carolina at Greensboro. Her work has appeared in several regional journals, including the *Crucible, Village Writer,* and *Share.* Five of her short stories have been published in anthologies including *If I Had My Life to Live Over I Would Pick More Daisies* (Papier-Mache Press).

JOHN RENNER is a high school principal. John's photographs often appear with Patti Tana's poetry. "Bubba" is a picture of their son, Jesse, and Jesse's grandmother Ada ("Bubba").

ELISAVIETTA RITCHIE's *Flying Time: Stories & Half-Stories* includes four PEN Syndicated Fiction winners. *The Arc of the Storm* and *A Wound-Up Cat and Other Bedtime Stories* are her newest poetry collections. *Tightening the Circle Over Eel Country* won the Great Lakes Colleges Association's 1975–76 "New Writer's Award," and *Raking the Snow* won the Washington Writer's Publishing House 1981–82 competition. Editor of *The Dolphin's Arc: Poems on Endangered Creatures of the Sea* and other books, she lives in Toronto and Washington, D.C.

MARIE KENNEDY ROBINS, transported from the South against her will at a tender age, returned after fifty years of urban gridlock. She began to write short stories and poems after she burned out as a teacher. A collection of her poems, *Quintessence,* was published by St. Andrews Press. She records for public radio with a group called Writers Ink in Fayetteville, North Carolina.

SAVINA A. ROXAS writes poetry and fiction. Her poetry chapbook, *Sacrificial Mix,* was published in 1992. *Teresa: A Life,* her turn-of-the-century novel, is with Evans Associates literary agency. Her work has appeared in the *Antigonish Review, Modern Haiku,* the *Black Fly Review,* and many other literary magazines as well as in anthologies. She won first prize in the 1989 Mississippi Valley Poetry Contest with "Vietnam Veterans Memorial."

VICKI SALLOUM earned a B.A. degree in Journalism from Loyola University in New Orleans, Louisiana, where she resides. In 1976 her feature writing for the *Palm Beach Daily News* in Palm Beach, Florida, won an award from the Florida Society of Newspaper Editors.

DEIDRE SCHERER, a Williamsville, Vermont, artist, "paints" with fabric and thread, using unusual cutting, layering, and machine stitching techniques to achieve illusionistic effects. Her images of the elderly have traveled internationally and are featured on the covers of *If I Had My Life to Live Over I Would Pick More Daisies, Another Language,* and *Learning to Sit in the Silence: A Jounal of Caretaking* (Papier-Mache Press). In 1993 she received a Vermont Council on the Arts Fellowship Award.

BETTIE SELLERS, Goolsby Professor of English at Young Harris College in northern Georgia, has published six poetry collections, the latest being *Wild Ginger.* Her documentary film, *The Bitter Berry: The Life and Works of Byron Herbert Reece,* received an Emmy and is accompanied by a critical book of the same name. Ms. Sellers received the 1987 Governor's Award in the Humanities for exemplary achievement in fostering an understanding and appreciation of the humanities in Georgia.

JOANNE SELTZER, an upstate New York writer and poet, has published hundreds of poems in literary magazines, newspapers, and anthologies, including *If I Had My Life to Live Over I Would Pick More Daisies, The Tie That Binds,* and *If I Had a Hammer: Women's Work* (Papier-Mache Press). She also published short fiction, nonfiction prose, translations of French poetry, and three poetry chapbooks.

CHARLOTTE WATSON SHERMAN, a resident of Seattle, is the author of a short story collection, *Killing Color* (Calyx Books) and a novel, *One Dark Body* (HarperCollins). She is currently editing an anthology of short fiction and poetry by African-American women, entitled *Sisterfire: A Black Womanist Anthology,* to be published by HarperCollins in 1994.

ENID SHOMER's stories and poems appear in the *New Yorker,* the *Atlantic, Poetry,* the *Paris Review,* and other magazines and anthologies. She is the author of two poetry books, *Stalking the Florida Panther* and *This Close to the Earth,* as well as of *Imaginary Men,* a collection of stories which won the Iowa Short Fiction Award. A recipient of fellowships from the NEA and the Florida Arts Council, she was recently awarded the Eunice Tietjens Prize from *Poetry* magazine and the Randall Jarrell Poetry Prize.

PATTI TANA is a professor of English at Nassau Community College, SUNY, and is associate editor of the *Long Island Quarterly.* Her third book of poems and stories, *Wetlands,* was published in 1993 (Papier-Mache Press).

RANDEANE TETU has received several national awards for fiction and is listed in *The Best American Short Stories.* Other stories appear in the anthology *If I Had My Life to Live Over I Would Pick More Daisies* (Papier-Mache Press) and in her collection of short fiction, *Merle's & Marilyn's Mink Ranch* (Papier-Mache Press).

CINDA THOMPSON believes that "the profound" should be simply put. A grandchild of coal miners and politicians, she is a native of southern Illinois, now living in Peoria. She has placed in several poetry and prose contests and is published in a number of other periodicals and anthologies, among them *The Tie That Binds* (Papier-Mache Press), *Looking for Home* (Milkweed Editions), *Cries of the Spirit* (Beacon Press), and *Filtered Images* (Vintage '45 Press). Currently working for a textbook publisher, she has also taught both literature and writing and very much enjoys public readings and appearances.

JESS WELLS is the author of a novel, *AfterShocks* (Third Side Press), which was reissued by The Women's Press for distribution in the U.K., Australia, and New Zealand. Her two volumes of short stories—*Two Willow Chairs* and *The Dress / The Sharda Stories* (Third Side Press)—have been anthologized in twelve locations and included in two university curricula. She is also the author of *A Herstory of Prostitution in Western Europe* (Shameless Hussy Press—the country's oldest feminist press at the time). An award-winning journalist, she resides in the San Francisco Bay Area.

MICHELE WOLF, a magazine writer from New York City, has had poems published in *Poetry,* the *Hudson Review, Southern Poetry Review,* the *Antioch Review,* and many other literary journals and anthologies. Her awards include a Literature Career Award from the National Society of Arts and Letters and residency fellowships from Yaddo, the Edward F. Albee Foundation, and the Virginia Center for the Creative Arts.

MARCIA WOODRUFF earned her B.A. in English from Smith College, her M.A.T. from Harvard University, and, after a twenty-five year interval, a Ph.D. from the University of Louisville. Her poetry and fiction have appeared in the *American Voice* and *Louisville Review.* In 1986 she was the recipient of a writing grant from the Kentucky Foundation for Women.

Papier-Mache Press

At Papier-Mache Press, it is our goal to identify and successfully present important social issues through enduring works of beauty, grace, and strength. Through our work we hope to encourage empathy and respect among diverse communities, creating a bridge of understanding between the mainstream audience and those who might not otherwise be heard.

We appreciate you, our customer, and strive to earn your continued support. We also value the role of the bookseller in achieving our goals. We are especially grateful to the many independent booksellers whose presence ensures a continuing diversity of opinion, information, and literature in our communities. We encourage you to support these bookstores with your patronage.

We publish many fine books about women's experiences. We also produce lovely posters and T-shirts that complement our anthologies. Please ask your local bookstore which Papier-Mache items they carry. To receive our complete catalog, please send your request to Papier-Mache Press, 135 Aviation Way, #14, Watsonville, CA 95076, or call our toll-free number, 800-927-5913.